Opium and
the Limits of Empire

Drug Prohibition in the Chinese

Interior, 1729–1850

Harvard East Asian Monographs 241

Opium and the Limits of Empire

Drug Prohibition in the Chinese Interior, 1729–1850

David Anthony Bello

Published by the Harvard University Asia Center
Distributed by Harvard University Press
Cambridge (Massachusetts) and London 2005

Printed in the United States of America

The Harvard University Asia Center publishes a monograph series and, in coordination with the Fairbank Center for East Asian Research, the Korea Institute, the Reischauer Institute of Japanese Studies, and other faculties and institutes, administers research projects designed to further scholarly understanding of China, Japan, Vietnam, Korea, and other Asian countries. The Center also sponsors projects addressing multidisciplinary and regional issues in Asia.

Library of Congress Cataloging-in-Publication Data
Bello, David Anthony, 1963–
    Opium and the limits of empire : drug prohibition in the Chinese interior, 1729–1850 / David Anthony Bello.
        p. cm. -- (Harvard East Asian monographs ; 241)
    Includes bibliographical references and index.
    ISBN 0-674-01649-1 (cloth : alk. paper)
        1. Opium trade--China--History. 2. Drug traffic--Government policy--China--History.
3. Drug abuse--China--History. 4. Narcotics, Control of--China--History.   I. Title. II. Series.
    HV5840.C6B45 2005
    363.45'0951'09033--dc22

                                                          2004027747

Index by the author

⊗ Printed on acid-free paper

Last figure below indicates year of this printing
14   13   12   11   10   09   08   07   06   05

"Provinces like Guangxi, Sichuan, Yunnan and Guizhou are places where barbarian ships cannot reach and foreign opium cannot penetrate. All these places come by opium from the locals' poppy-planting and paste-making."

—Guo Baiyin, 1839

To Jeanette

May our treaties always be equal ones.

Acknowledgments

Although the impossibility of thanking everyone involved in a project of this sort is conventionally recognized, few except copy editors, and those I inadvertently leave out, will blame me for trying. This book, like the doctoral dissertation that spawned it, has been a collective enterprise from start to finish, but it is only on an acknowledgments page that the sheer geographic scale of my gratitude begins to become apparent. On the right side of the Pacific, at the University of Southern California in Los Angeles, I must first thank my main advisor, John E. Wills, Jr., as well as Charlotte Furth and Bettine Birge for their prodigal support, encouragement, and toleration over the years. Across town, Benjamin A. Elman was unnecessarily generous with his time, and James Lee almost reckless with his.

A number of other scholars resident in North America have also read and commented on various incarnations of the manuscript, whole or in part, at one time or another. They include, in no particular order, Timothy Brook, Beatrice S. Bartlett, Peter C. Perdue, Matthew H. Sommer, John Richards, Paul Winther, and Ann Waltner. Kent Guy contributed in a less tangible but equally fundamental way, as did Alvin P. Cohen. Outside the continent, I must thank R. G. Tiedemann, Pierre-Arnaud Chouvy, and most especially Carl A. Trocki.

On the other side of the Pacific, I have become especially indebted to Angela K. C. Leung, Chuang Chi-fa, Lin En-hsien, Chu Yun-Peng, and Lin Man-houng in Taiwan as well as to the staffs of Academia Sinica's Sun Yat-Sen Institute for Social Sciences and Philosophy and the National Palace Museum. Across the strait, in Beijing I have received equally invaluable assistance from my advisors at the Institute of Qing History, Professors Dai Yi and Li Sheng. I am particularly beholden to Dr. Zhu Shuyuan for her guidance, which I sought on an almost daily basis, as I am to all her colleagues and staff at First Historical Archives of China. South of the Yangzi, I must pay tribute to Professor Gao Hua for his guidance and inspiration, along with many others at Nanjing University.

In addition to generous funding from the University of Southern California, grants from the following programs have helped make this book possible: Nanjing University–The Johns Hopkins University Center for Chinese and American Studies, the American Council of Learned Societies Graduate Program of the National Program for Advanced Study and Research in the People's Republic of China, the Institute of International Education Fulbright-Hays Scholarly Exchange Program, and a National Resource Fellowship. I also particularly thank Jean Oi and all the staff at the Center for East Asian Studies at Stanford University for my Post-Doctoral Fellowship in Chinese Studies.

Professors Lin Hsiu-ling and Wu Qing have been of considerable material assistance, providing me with food, shelter, and advice on how to avoid major diplomatic incidents while resident overseas. My former classmates Lynn Sacco and Rebecca Shea have fulfilled similar roles on the domestic front. Moreover, the contribution of students, colleagues, and staff at Southern Connecticut State University was not merely academic, and I would particularly thank Michele Thompson, Bruce Kalk, Steven Judd, Troy Paddock, Virginia Metaxas, and Polly Beals.

My time in the Beijing archives was served along with Grant Alger, Xia Hongtu, and Michael Chang, all of whom proved staunch companions, especially in bureaucracy's darkest moments. Hongtu also deserves special mention for her legible transcriptions of many (to me) illegible documents. Michael, along with Bruce Rusk and Hu Ming-hui, also suffered uncomplainingly as draft after draft of the manuscript's most rudimentary versions was inflicted on them. I am equally grateful to my classmate Paul Van Dyke and should provide hard-copy testimony to the virtual technical assistance on maps and tables uncomplainingly extended me by Tom Zakim, David "Jeep" Hauser, and Lei Guang. Although it is often difficult to discover every person involved in shepherding a manuscript through a press, this book would be far less coherent and much more belated without the input of the two anonymous readers for Harvard's East Asian Monographs series.

Unfortunately, I cannot list here all those whose ideas have influenced my own and must hope that the references in the manuscript can make what must remain a partial restitution. One convention I will not try to avoid is the traditional caution to the reader that I am solely responsible for the remaining errors and distortions in the book, despite the efforts of everyone else who has contributed to it. I must finally note that earlier versions of parts of Chapters 3, 5, and 6 have appeared elsewhere as articles.

I would have remained impervious to all the intellectual influences alluded to above without the long, hard civilizing efforts of my parents, Dorothy J. and Anthony E. Bello. Ayesha has also helped in this regard, but in the end history will record that Jeanette Barbieri has had the most radical effect upon me in all ways, times, and places.

D.A.B.

Contents

Figure, Tables, and Maps   xv

Weights and Measures   xvii

Abbreviations   xix

1 *Introduction*   1
   The Ethno-Geographic Limits of Qing Opium Prohibition 2/
   A Qing-Centered Contribution to the Historiography of the
   Opium Problem 8/   The Concept of Addictive Consumables 16

2 *The British Prohibition in India in Comparative Perspective*   22
   Addictive Consumables and Empire 22/   The British Roots
   of the Opium Problem 33/   Company Rule in India 45/
   Bengal Versus Bengal 49/   Bengal Versus Malwa 52

3 *Regional Administrative Structures*   64
   The Administration of the Han Core 67/   The Administration
   of Xinjiang 76/   The Administration of the Southwest 91/
   Ethno-Geographic Diversity and the Limits of Local
   Administration 111

4 *The Han Core and Policy Formation*   114
   The Local Roots of Central Prohibition Policy 115/   Opium
   as a Qing Addictive Consumable 142/   The Ideology of Qing
   Prohibition 154/   Qing Opium Dependency 166/   Prohibition
   and the Limits of State Power 173

5 *The Opium Problem in Xinjiang*   177
   Adapting Imperial Prohibition to Xinjiang 180/ The
   Ethno-Geography of *Qiangtu* 190/ The Multiethnic
   Diplomacy of Xinjiang Prohibition 205/ Opium in
   Qing Inner Asia 216

6 *The Opium Problem in Southwestern China*   222
   Opium Prohibition Comes to the Southwest 224/ The
   Geography of Southwestern Opium 248/ The Ethnography
   of Southwestern Opium 263/ The Economy of Southwestern
   Opium 271/ The Imperial Significance of the Southwestern
   Opium Market 282

7 *Opium and Qing Expansionism*   286

Appendixes

A *Dynastic Opium Policy Before the Daoguang Reign*   307

B *Translation of Shanxi Taiyu District Magistrate
   Chen Lihe's "Opium Prohibition Pledge" Stele*   313

Reference Matter

Character List   319

Works Cited   327

Index   349

Figure, Tables, and Maps

Figure

1   Britain-India-China triangular trade, 1827–40   37

Tables

1   Value of opium and tea in the Sino-British trade, 1816–38   39

2   Bengal and Malwa sales compared, 1817–36   54

3   Consumption case lists, 1843–49   140

4   Opium confiscations in Xinjiang, December 1839–January 1841   210

5   Opium offenses and amnesties in Guizhou, late 1838–February 1839   232

6   Opium confiscations in Yunnan, January 1839–April 1840   238

7   Opium offenses, confiscations, and amnesties in Guizhou, February 1839–September 1842   240

8   Trafficking and cultivation offenses in Guizhou, ca. February 1833   255

9   Opium offenses in Yunnan, March 1832–February 1836   258

10   Area of poppy cultivation in Guizhou, June 1839–October 1840   274

Maps

1   British India, ca. 1836   46
2   Qing China, provinces and territories, ca. 1820   66
3   Xinjiang, territorial subdivisions, ca. 1820   78
4   Yunnan, prefectures, ca. 1820   92
5   Guizhou, prefectures, ca. 1820   93
6   Sichuan, prefectures, ca. 1820   94
7   Xinjiang, main transportation routes   202

Weights and Measures

1 mace (*fen*) = 3.7 grams

1 tael = 37.3 grams

27 taels = 1 kilo

1 chest = 60 kilos

1 *shi* = 84 kilos

1,133 copper cash = 1 silver tael (pre-Daoguang average ratio)

$1 ("Spanish") = 5 shillings (0.25 of an English pound)

1 *mu* = 398.4 square meters

25 *mu* = 1 hectare

1 *li* = 0.5 kilometers

(SOURCES: *Hanyu da cidian*, pp. 7777–78; J. Y. Wong, *Deadly Dreams*, p. 406; Newman, "A Reconsideration," p. 771*n*; Lin Man-houng, "Yin yu yapian," pp. 123–25; Chuan and Kraus, *Mid-Ch'ing Rice Markets and Trade*, pp. 79–98.)

Abbreviations

Reign Periods

KX	Kangxi (1662–1722)
YZ	Yongzheng (1723–35)
QL	Qianlong (1736–95)
JQ	Jiaqing (1796–1820)
DG	Daoguang (1821–50)
XF	Xianfeng (1851–61)
TZ	Tongzhi (1862–74)
GX	Guangxu (1875–1908)

Books and Archives

Baxian dang'an   *Qingdai Qian-Jia-Dao Baxian dang'an xuanbian* 清代乾嘉道巴縣檔案選編 (Selections from the archives of Ba district during the Qianlong, Jiaqing, and Daoguang reign periods of the Qing dynasty). Edited by Sichuan daxue, Lishi xi and the Sichuan sheng dang'anguan. 2 vols. Chengdu: Sichuan daxue chubanshe, 1996.

China III   Irish University. *China III Miscellaneous Papers. 1809–1840* (Irish University Press Area Studies Series, British Parliamentary Papers: China. London: House of Commons, 1840. Reprinted—Irish University Press, 1977).

Gongzhong baojia   Gongzhong dang, Neizheng dalei, baojia 宮中檔內政大類保甲 (Palace Memorial archive, Interior Ministry category, *baojia*). Subject category of archival holdings in the First Historical Archives of China.

Gongzhong baojing   Gongzhong dang, Neizheng dalei, baojing 宮中檔內政大類保警 (Palace Memorial archive, Interior Ministry category, *baojing*). Subject category of archival holdings in the First Historical Archives of China.

Gongzhong DG   Gongzhong dang Daoguang chao zouzhe 宮中檔 道光朝奏折 (Palace memorials from the Daoguang reign). Comp. Gugong bowuyuan. Taibei: Gugong Bowuyuan, 1995.

Gongzhong jinyan   Gongzhong dang, falü dalei, jinyan 宮中檔 法律大類禁煙 (Palace Memorial archive, legal category, opium prohibition). Subject category of archival holdings in the First Historical Archives of China.

Gongzhong shenban   Gongzhong dang, falü dalei, shenban 宮中 檔法律大類審辦 (Palace Memorial archive, legal category, adjudication). Subject category of archival holdings in the First Historical Archives of China.

HDSL   Qing huidian shili 欽定大清會典事例 (Precedents for the collected statutes of the Qing dynasty). Guangxu ed., 1899. 12 vols. Reprinted—Beijing: Zhonghua shuju, 1991.

Junji   Junji chu 軍機處 (Grand Council copy archive). Subject category of archival holdings in the National Palace Museum, Taibei, Taiwan.

Junji chajin   Junji chu, lufu dang, chajin 軍機處錄副檔查禁 (Grand Council copy archive, investigations and prohibitions). Subject category of archival holdings in the First Historical Archives of China.

Junji diqin   Junji chu, lufu dang, diguozhuyi qinlue dalei, diyi yapien zhanzheng 軍機處錄副檔帝國主義侵略大類第一鴉片戰爭 (Grand Council copy archive, imperialist aggression category, First Opium War). Subject category of archival holdings in the First Historical Archives of China.

Junji jinyan   Junji chu, lufu dang, falü dalei, jinyan 軍機處錄副 檔法律大類禁煙 (Grand Council copy archive, legal category, opium prohibition). Subject category of archival holdings in the First Historical Archives of China.

Junji minzu   Junji chu lufu dang, minzu shiwu dalei, Weiwuer 軍機處錄副檔民族事物維吾爾 (Grand Council copy archive, minority affairs category, Uighurs). Subject category of archival holdings in the First Historical Archives of China.

Junji zashui   Junji chu, lufu dang, caizheng dalei, zashui 軍機處錄副檔財政大類雜稅 (Grand Council copy archive, government finance category, miscellaneous taxes). Subject category of archival holdings in the First Historical Archives of China.

Neige weijin   Neige, xingke tiben, weijin lei [tongben/buben] 內閣刑科題本違禁類 [通本部本] (Grand Secretariat archive, routine memorials for the Office of Scrutiny of the Board of Punishments, prohibitions violations category [provincial/board memorial]). Subject category of archival holdings in the First Historical Archives of China.

QSG   *Qingshi gao* 清史稿 (Draft official history of the Qing dynasty). 48 volumes. Beijing: Zhonghua shuju, 1977.

QSL   *Qing shilu* 清史錄 (Veritable records of the Qing dynasty). 60 volumes. Beijing: Zhonghua shuju, 1986–87.

SYD   Shangyu dang 上諭檔 (Record book of imperial edicts). Subject category of archival holdings in the First Historical Archives of China.

SYDD   Shangyu dang, dong 上諭檔冬 (Record book of imperial edicts, winter). Subject category of archival holdings in the National Palace Museum, Taibei, Taiwan.

WJD   Waiji dang 外紀檔 (Outer Court record). Subject category of archival holdings in the National Palace Museum, Taibei, Taiwan.

YPZZ   *Yapian zhanzheng dang'an shiliao* 鴉片戰爭檔案史料 (Historical materials from the Opium War archives). Edited by Zhongguo diyi lishi dang'anguan. 7 vols. Tianjin: Tianjin guji chubanshe, 1992.

ZZD   Zouzhe dang 奏折檔 (Palace memorial record). Subject category of archival holdings in the National Palace Museum, Taibei, Taiwan.

Opium and
the Limits of Empire

Drug Prohibition in the Chinese

Interior, 1729–1850

ONE

Introduction

The opium trade pursued by Britain along the eastern seacoast of China has become the symbol of China's century-long descent into political and social chaos. In the standard historical narratives of both China and Euro-America, opium is the primary medium through which the Qing dynasty (1644–1911) encountered the modern economic, social, and political institutions of the West. Consequently, opium and the Western powers' advent on the Chinese coast have become almost inextricably linked. Opium was not, however, simply a Sino-British problem geographically confined to southeastern China. It was, rather, an empirewide crisis that spread among an ethnically diverse populace and created regionally and culturally distinct problems of control for the Qing state.

This crisis should be examined from the perspective of Qing prohibition operations, which ultimately extended to every corner of the empire. Opium prohibition, and not opium war, was genuinely imperial in scale and is much more representative of the actual drug problem faced by Qing administrators. The expanded spatial view afforded by the perspective of prohibition also permits a much more comprehensive and accurate observation of the economics and criminology of opium. The Qing drug traffic involved not only distribution and consumption but also production, in the form of poppy cultivation, all of which occurred inside imperial territory. A more balanced examination of the three major categories of both the opium-marketing system and the state antidrug policy reveals the importance of the empire's landlocked western frontier regions, which were the domestic production centers, in what has heretofore been considered a coastal problem. In sum, an analysis of the Qing opium problem from the viewpoint of state prohibition reveals that the crisis was as diverse as the empire itself.

The Ethno-Geographic
Limits of Qing Opium Prohibition

The diverse nature of the opium problem was particularly acute on the empire's western frontier, specifically in the southwestern provinces of Yunnan, Guizhou, and Sichuan and the northwestern territory of Xinjiang. In the northwest, Central and South Asian smugglers, abetted by the neighboring Khanate of Kokand, colluded with the empire's own Han Chinese, Manchus, and East Turkestani traffickers to construct a transborder drug trade network distinct from that of the coast. In the southwest, Han Chinese merchants and bandit gangs linked up with indigenous minority peoples like the Dai and Yi to create similar networks almost entirely inside the empire. Moreover, both regions were sites of domestic poppy cultivation on a considerable scale in areas of mountainous wilderness or indigenous settlement effectively beyond the scrutiny of local Qing officials tied to towns inhabited mainly by Han Chinese.

The limitations imposed by geography and ethnicity on official administrative structures seriously undermined central government prohibition efforts on the empire's western frontier. No later than the early 1830s, smuggled foreign opium flowed inland from the coast even as cheaper domestic opium streamed eastward from the empire's western interior locales of Xinjiang and the southwest in response to the lucrative markets of China proper.

A shift in analytical perspective to prohibition also opens particularly illuminating comparative spaces, both within and beyond imperial territory. A study of prohibition permits interregional comparison between subimperial units like the northwest and southwest. Admittedly, these are not entirely comparable, especially in terms of the duration of prohibition, which lasted only several years in Xinjiang in contrast to around two decades in the southwest. The realization that this disparity, among others, even existed, however, is one of the many new insights produced by an "internal" comparative approach to Qing prohibition. Although this approach complicates analysis, particularly in terms of the amount of documentation generated and available, it also reveals the complexity, as well as the disparities, of regional administration faced by the dynasty in its attempt to implement opium prohibition uniformly and provides further evidence for the inhibiting effects of ethno-geographic diversity.

Other comparative spaces are also opened beyond the immediate boundaries of the Qing state. Limitations on the state's ability to pursue prohibition were hardly unique to the Qing, as even a cursory comparison of the experiences of the dynasty and its nemesis, Great Britain, reveal. The establishment of an effective opium monopoly to create a stable source of revenue by the East India Company in its Bengal domain in the latter half of the eighteenth century necessitated a suppression of competing sources throughout India, especially in areas beyond the Company's relatively small enclave. The Company's attempt to prohibit unauthorized production and distribution of opium for the China market in the late eighteenth and early nineteenth centuries failed primarily because of the weak or nonexistent Company administrative presence in strategic areas of central and western India. Even as the Company's own subjects cultivated illicit poppy and smuggled contraband opium, opium production for revenue purposes in Indian territories not yet under British control also undermined the Company's monopoly on the drug, which had been established for the same fiscal reasons.

The failure of even this limited form of prohibition becomes particularly significant for a re-evaluation of the Qing's notorious inability during the first half of the nineteenth century to impose an absolute ban on opium production, distribution, and consumption, a ban that was also pursued primarily to protect government revenues. Although this program was far more ambitious in scope and thus considerably different from that of the East India Company's, it failed for similar reasons of administrative weakness. The East India Company's experience with prohibition suggests that the Qing failure to stop the maritime Euro-American drug traffickers neither symbolizes nor explains the failure of "Chinese traditionalism" vis-à-vis "Western modernity," the classic formula of standard historical accounts of the origins of modern China.

The implications of this mutual failure can be fully explored only by shifting attention from the coastal trade to the traffic in the Chinese interior, partly because illicit production, which was relatively impervious to both British and Qing prohibition, was not a major dimension of the coastal problem. In the Chinese interior, particularly on the empire's western frontiers, however, cultivation was extensive, as was dynastic administrative weakness. Consequently, a comparative approach to Chinese and British experiences of prohibition grounded in a spatial reorientation of the problem to western China reveals important commonalities between the two imperial states. The futile prohibition programs of both Qing China and British India were motivated by revenue concerns and foundered because of weakness in local administration, facts that cannot be explained within the framework of a "tradition-modernity" binary. In short, neither Qing China's nor Great Britain's degree of modernization greatly determined the conceptualization of their respective prohibition policies.[1] Modernity, insofar as it has been constructed by the conventional analysis of the opium problem in the standard narratives of Chinese history, must be redefined.

Part of the imperative for this redefinition arises from the southwestern provinces' historical experience with opium. Although the drug trade in these vast areas initially lagged far behind that of the southeastern coast, the indigenous poppy producers of Yunnan and Sichuan would, by the end of the nineteenth century, wrest control of the Chinese traffic from British India to make the Chinese southwest the world's largest producer for the world's largest market. The origins of this economic triumph of Qing China over imperial Britain lie in the regional dynamics of the southwest and its interaction with the coastal trade. These dynam-

---

1. Assumptions about the inferior nature of the Qing imperial polity have generally precluded more balanced comparative approaches between the Qing empire, which is most often cited as a classic example of an outmoded state system, and its European contemporaries. Notable exceptions include Hevia, *Cherishing Men from Afar*; Goldstone, *Revolution and Rebellion*; and R. Bin Wong, *China Transformed*.

ics produced a southwestern opium-marketing system distinct from that of the coast. A spatial reorientation of the Qing opium problem, in the analytical context of transimperial prohibition, is the prerequisite for elucidating the origins of the southwestern system and its subsequent transimperial extension.

An examination of opium in Xinjiang is of equal, if not greater, significance for the initial revisionist chapter of China's modern history. First, there is evidence of a less developed, but distinct, northwestern opium-marketing system centered on Xinjiang, extending through Gansu, and possibly reaching all the way into Shanxi. Second, and of even greater significance, the history of prohibition in Xinjiang reveals that the opium traffic, heretofore considered an exclusive relationship between Chinese and Euro-Americans, extensively involved Central and South Asian merchant smugglers, including the Central Asian Muslim Khanate of Kokand. Consequently, consideration of the Xinjiang traffic alters the paradigm of the coastal trade between the Chinese and the British, which led to the Opium War.

This sense of inevitability, as conveyed by the standard histories of both China and Euro-America, is undermined by the historical record of Qing-Kokandi relations and of the dynasty's prohibition operations in Xinjiang. This territory's local administrators experienced problems in controlling foreign commerce similar to those encountered by their colleagues on the southeast coast but did not end up in a shooting war with foreign traffickers and their sovereigns. Thus, a spatial reorientation of the Qing opium problem to Xinjiang shows that the Sino-British conflict on the coast was not a unique problem of interstate foreign relations inevitably and fatally engendered by a narrow-minded Chinese dynasty's inability to deal with a radically different culture. Qing opium-prohibition diplomacy in Xinjiang belies the conventional narrative's juxtaposition of the parochialism of China with the cosmopolitan modernity of the West, and instead reveals a degree of sophistication and flexibility more readily associated with "rational" approaches to foreign relations.

Obviously, in light of Qing-Kokandi relations, a focus on the opium problem in western China constitutes not only a geo-

graphic reorientation of the standard narrative but an ethnic one as
well. Indeed, the drug traffic in both the northwest and the southwest involved people who were neither Han Chinese nor Euro-
Americans. In the southwest a number of indigenous peoples, including the Yi, Dai, and Miao, were crucially involved in many
aspects of the opium trade, particularly in local cultivation and distribution. In the northwest, merchants from Kashmir, Badakshan
(present-day Afghanistan), India, Bokhara, Russian Central Asia,
and Kokand were involved in the transborder smuggling traffic
that often relayed the drug to local East Turkestani merchants.
Most of these northwestern participants, as well as an undeter-
mined number of southwestern ones, were Muslims, who, as a
group, played a fundamental part in the distribution of opium
throughout western China and eastward into China proper.

These facts effect a fundamental ethnic reorientation of the
opium problem in the sense that Euro-American traffickers were
completely absent from these western regions, where opium could
be produced, distributed, and consumed with no direct participation by those involved in the coastal trade. This reorientation
should not be interpreted, however, as evidence that Euro-
American participation in the opium traffic was negligible or irrelevant. The Euro-Americans began the coastal traffic on their
own initiative and, as such, were unquestionably the deliberate instigators of the mass consumption of the drug in China proper.
Euro-American coastal trafficking was the prerequisite for the
spread of opium throughout the Qing interior.

The coastal traffic, however, was neither the only dimension of
the opium problem with which the dynasty had to contend nor
the ultimate source of every regional opium problem within the
empire. Moreover, even when the origins of the drug could be
traced to the coast, agency did not always lie in the illicit machinations of traffickers or the ravenous appetite of consumers; sometimes it lay in the regular functions of the state's penal apparatus,
as records from Xinjiang concerning coastal exiles will show. In
sum, the Qing opium problem could not be confined to its original
ethnic and geographic relations among the Han Chinese and Euro-
Americans on the southeast coast because of the imbrication of so-

cial, political, and economic organizational structures intended to unify the empire's diverse regions.

Ethno-geographic diversity and its ability to limit state power is one of the most notable aspects of the history of the Qing empire, itself a product of an intricate interaction of Manchu, Han, and Mongol, to list only the main actors.[2] Diversity was a consequence of the dynasty's origins in Manchuria and the extension of its rule into China proper, which ultimately necessitated the northwestern projection of Qing power into Central Asia and a commensurate consolidation of control on the empire's southwestern borders. The dynasty's westward expansion became a major project in terms of both military and administrative incorporation. Administrative innovation was a particularly notable result. Both the beg system of the northwestern territory of Xinjiang and the native chieftain (*tusi*) system of the southwest were indigenous administrative structures modified by the dynasty into instruments of Qing indirect rule.

In terms of the opium problem in western China, the effect of these structures, so different from those of the *junxian* system of provinces, prefectures, departments, and districts characteristic of the Han-dominated core of China proper, was to complicate prohibition operations by the central government. The implementation and enforcement of the central government's comprehensive opium ban through provincial and subprovincial administrations substantially limited prohibition to areas of China proper, especially its urban zones, where the imperial administration was concentrated.

Prohibition was much less efficacious when conducted via frontier structures of indirect rule like the beg and native chieftain systems, and it was nonexistent in those western regions, notably southwestern Yunnan, completely lacking in administrative structures, indirect or otherwise. These limits on administrative control, themselves a result of territorial expansion, decisively determined the course of central government prohibition policy. This policy

---

2. For an extensive introduction and bibliography concerning the ethnic dimensions of the Qing imperial achievement, see Rawski, "Presidential Address: Reenvisioning the Qing."

became increasingly directed at Han urban traffickers and consumers of the drug because these two groups were more accessible to local officialdom than either foreign traffickers or indigenous rural cultivators. The general confinement of the Qing administrative apparatus to urban Han China reduced pressure on the Central Asian traffickers and multiethnic cultivators of Xinjiang as well as the indigenous rural poppy growers of the southwestern provinces. This urban confinement ensured the continuation of distinct regional opium problems in both areas.

A Qing-Centered Contribution to the Historiography of the Opium Problem

The vast scholarly literature on the imperial social and political order's great crisis and near-collapse in the mid-nineteenth century has focused on conflicts between Chinese and Westerners along the empire's eastern coast and in its capital, Beijing.[3] In terms of the opium problem, this reduction of the complex relations among people to binary reifications of Britain versus China, West versus East, and Modernity versus Tradition has led Euro-American historians to treat the problem primarily as one of foreign relations between the dynamic nation-state of imperial Britain and the stagnant feudal state of imperial China. Opium's production, distribution, consumption, and criminalization are seen, when seen at all, as of secondary interest at best. The domestic dimensions of the opium problem are also ignored in important Japanese scholarship. Inoue Hiromasa, for example, in his studies of the debates over opium policy among Qing elites, dismisses the domestic dimensions of Qing prohibition as "confused" and far less important than the dynasty's efforts to contain maritime traffickers.[4]

---

3. Standard works in English on the Opium War and related issues include Chang, *Commissioner Lin*; Fairbank, *Trade and Diplomacy*; Greenberg, *British Trade*; Morse, *International Relations*; Spence, "Opium Smoking"; and Wakeman, "Canton Trade." Important revisionist works in English include Tan, *China and the Brave New World*; and J. Y. Wong, *Deadly Dreams*. This list is by no means exhaustive, but if one work can be considered a template for the literature of the opium problem, it is probably Edkins, *Historical Note*.

4. Inoue, "Shindai Kakei Dōkō ki no ahen mondai," p. 59.

Actually, it is impossible to provide an adequate account even of political conditions at the Qing court without serious consideration of opium and the relations it engendered well beyond both the capital and Guangzhou. Notable among several relevant works on court politics is James Polachek's study, which employs a factionalist model from political science to argue that the hard-line prohibition policies of the Daoguang era were little more than an excuse for one clique of moralizing dissident literati, known as the Spring Purification circle, to best another clique of legalizing "realists" centered in Guangzhou. Polachek has certainly exposed the partisanship and ulterior motives of the prohibitionists, but factionalism did not exclusively determine prohibition policy. The selection of Guangzhou, as opposed to Suzhou in Jiangsu, as the main target of prohibition operations, for example, was not, as Polachek suggests, a result of the machinations of the Spring Purification circle. All sides involved in the 1836 debate were quite familiar with nearly a century of documentation pointing to Guangdong and the provincial capital of Guangzhou as the centers of both the opium trade and the silver drain. Suzhou's drug problem, in contrast, was hardly comparable, even though the number of resident addicts was estimated at 40 percent of the city's population, a figure based on a single anecdote by a metropolitan censor.[5] In light of this historical record, which long predated court factionalism during the 1830s, it would have been "irrational" to focus prohibition efforts anywhere but Guangzhou.

I am not arguing that Qing opium policy was free of politics; rather, I am saying that it cannot be reduced to politics. That officials, censors included, distorted the dimensions of the opium problem for political purposes is undeniable. Prominent officials doubtlessly saw the drug crisis as an opportunity, but it was a crisis, in the literal Chinese sense of the word as "dangerous opportunity," precisely because it was not entirely amenable to political manipulations of imperial Chinese or British officialdom. The main empirical and theoretical approaches in the Western litera-

---

5. Polachek, *Inner Opium War*, pp. 9-13, 102, 127-28. Suzhou undeniably had a serious drug problem, sustained by what Bao Shichen guessed in 1820 to be "no less than 100,000" smokers (*Yapian zhanzheng*, 1:537).

ture on the opium problem have almost exclusively been influenced by elite politics in one version or another. Opium was, however, produced, consumed, distributed, promoted, and prohibited by a network of social relations far beyond those of a tiny elite in Beijing, Guangzhou, Calcutta, and London. A more comprehensive analytical scope that integrates but does not privilege elite politics is required to accommodate the complexity of social relations created by the drug's use.

These relations have been minor considerations even in revisionist works genuinely concerned with giving opium a more significant place in the narrative, such as Hsin-pao Chang's *Commissioner Lin and the Opium War*, the standard work on Sino-British relations leading up to the first Opium War (1839–42). Chang, whose book was intended to place "special emphasis on the opium traffic as an immediate cause of the war because it has not received adequate attention," still found the Opium War to be at bottom an inevitable clash between an "agricultural, Confucian [and] stagnant" culture and an "industrial capitalistic [and] progressive" one. Opium itself was ultimately irrelevant to this relationship since Chang opined that "had there been an effective alternative to opium, say molasses or rice, the conflict might have been called the Molasses War or the Rice War."[6]

Scholars in the People's Republic of China, in contrast, see the opium problem as the primary cause of a war started by imperialist powers to force the trade on China.[7] Consequently, there has been far more work done on the Qing state's attempts to control opium; much of this work concerns the "strict prohibitionist clique" (*yanjin pai*) and "lax prohibitionist clique" (*chijin pai*) at court.[8] Con-

---

6. Chang, *Commissioner Lin*, pp. x, 15.

7. For a representative statement of this thesis, based mainly on Western sources and reprinted as recently as 1992, see Ding, *Diguozhuyi qin Hua shi*, chap. 1. For a more recent and nuanced version, see Lin Dunkai and Kong Xiangji, "Yapian zhanzheng qianqi."

8. One of the most important articles in the considerable scholarship devoted to issues of prohibition is Wu Yixiong, "Jinyan zhenglun." The Chinese scholarship on the opium problem in particular and on the war in general is enormous. An indispensable handbook to the field of Opium War studies in Chinese both in- and outside the People's Republic of China is Xiao, *Yapian zhanzheng yu Lin Zexu*

siderably less work has been done on regional issues or on the ways center and locality interacted to condition prohibition policy and its implementation.[9] Despite its much more active engagement with the opium problem itself, PRC scholarship shares many of the assumptions of its Euro-American counterparts in that the primary focus remains Sino-Western diplomatic relations and materials related to opium are generally employed to elucidate the nature of these relations for the ultimate purpose of charting China's path to political and economic modernity. Consequently, conclusions regarding the nature of the Qing state are remarkably similar to those reached in the West and have tended to portray the regime as corrupt, incompetent, and backward as opposed to the historically advanced, if morally depraved, British. Recently, in the wake of successful economic reform in the People's Republic, this narrative has taken on a particular nationalistic tone: while continuing to decry the drug trade, it seeks to rehabilitate many Qing officials as attempting conscientiously, if futilely, to stop it.[10]

Despite the general emphasis on elite politics to the neglect of virtually all other aspects of the opium problem in the scholarly literature, a small but critical body of revisionist work has begun to focus on the political and social import of the drug itself. Yangwen Zheng's "The Social Life of Opium in China" (2003), for example, is concerned with the cultural significance of opium consumption. By contextualizing opium smoking as part of a southeast coastal fad for foreign wares dating from the eighteenth century, Zheng explains

---

yanjiu beilan. Important Chinese works include Mou, *Yapian zhanzheng*; Yao, *Yapian zhanzheng shishi kao*; Xiao and Yang, *Yapian zhanzheng qian Zhong Xi guanxi jishi*; and Mao, *Tianchao de bengkui*.

9. There are some notable exceptions to the general neglect of regional studies in the scholarly literature. One article outstanding for its attempt to integrate local sites of prohibition operations with central policy decisions is Xiao, "Fan yapian douzheng." There are also a few regional studies, most of which do not generally explore the opium problem prior to 1839 and are based on only part of the documentary record currently available. Some of the more significant among them are Zou, "Jindai Xinjiang"; Yang Xingmao, "Yapian ru Gan"; Wang Gesheng, "Dongbei zhong yingsu"; and Qin Heping, *Yunnan yapian wenti*. Qin's book is particularly valuable for its insight as well as for the sources it employs.

10. See, e.g., Ma Weiping, "Jinyan yuanyin bianxi"; or watch director Xie Jin's *Yapian zhanzheng*.

how the drug became an aphrodisiac endemic to urban culture.[11] This certainly adds a dimension to standard narratives on the drug traffic and augments explanations of widespread opium consumption as simple addiction and criminality.

Other revisionist contributions, like Tan Chung's *China and the Brave New World* (1978), emphasize the intimate connections between opium and imperialism. Tan argues that the Sino-British conflict arose not from a cultural or commercial conflict but from the opium traffic. Tan set out to reinvigorate this somewhat neglected nineteenth-century Western explanation, which he recognized had been generally undertheorized.[12] Although Tan's work provided an alternative to contemporary Western theoretical frameworks to explain the role of opium in Sino-British relations, its effect on scholarship in the field was negligible.[13] This obscurity was almost undoubtedly because of the strong anti-imperialist tone of his works and the main target of his criticism, the "Fairbankian School," whose theories regarding sinocentrism, the tribute system, the Canton system, and the treaty-port system amounted in Tan's view "to flogging the Chinese tradition as a whipping boy to chastise the crimes committed by the prince of Western imperialism [i.e., Britain]."[14]

Despite the controversial aspects of his work, Tan made a major contribution to the scholarship on the opium problem, which can be summed up in his assertion that the triangular trade between Britain, India, and China provided "Indian opium for the Chinese, Chinese tea for the Britons and [the] British Raj for the Indians!"[15] In effect, he provided considerable statistical and theoretical refinement to the earlier work of Alexander Michie, David Edward Owen, and Michael Greenberg, all of whom noted the existence

---

11. Zheng, "Social Life of Opium."

12. Tan, *China and the Brave New World*, pp. 1–12.

13. None of Tan's work, the foundation of which was published in 1974, found its way into the bibliography of the 1978 *Cambridge History of China* volumes on the late Qing, nor was it cited by Polachek in his 1992 book, *The Inner Opium War*, the next major study in English of the subject following the Cambridge volumes.

14. Tan, *Triton and Dragon*, pp. xii–xiii.

15. Tan, "Trade Triangle," p. 44. Tan's "British Raj" is meant to refer to the rule of the East India Company rather than that of the British government.

and significance of a triangular trade involving opium and British imperialism connecting South and East Asia.[16]

Recently, J. Y. Wong in *Deadly Dreams: Opium, Imperialism and the Arrow War* (1998), building on the work of all these predecessors, has provided the most sophisticated statistical analysis of the significance of the opium traffic for British imperialism to date. His findings confirm that opium sales to China were indispensable for the maintenance of British paramountcy in India and for that of the foundations of British imperialism in general. He also presents convincing evidence that the opium trade was the main cause of the conflicts of both the 1839–42 Opium War and the 1856–60 *Arrow* War.[17]

The works of Tan and Wong represent a considerable advance in the field of Opium War studies because they provide a coherent narrative, backed by statistical evidence, for the fundamental role of the drug traffic in the development of imperialism in South and East Asia. Nevertheless, all these studies are concerned with establishing a teleology of the modern Chinese nation; neither Chinese nor Euro-American narratives, whatever their specific differences, are much concerned with what the larger record of the empire's historical experience with opium prohibition reveals about the Qing state itself. The questions driving both the Chinese and the Euro-American narratives are more characteristic of modernization theory as well as traditional explanations like dynastic decline. This common theoretical impetus accounts for the similarities between these two narratives and for a persistent gap in the literature both in- and outside China on the opium problem itself. Put another way, such narratives are the results of a general absence of questions generated from what Mark Elliott, in a variation on Paul Cohen's influential "China-centered" approach, has called "history from a 'Qing' perspective."[18]

---

16. Michie, *An Englishman in China*; Owen, *British Opium Policy*; Greenberg, *British Trade*.

17. J. Y. Wong, *Deadly Dreams*, pp. 331–454.

18. Elliott, "Bannerman and Townsman." James Millward (*Beyond the Pass*, pp. 13–15) has also called attention to a trend toward "Qing-centered history," which takes into account the dynasty's concern with ethnic distinction and its consequent effect on dynastic institutions and the territories over which it presided.

A Qing perspective on the opium problem must expand beyond the coast to include the empire's western territories. The Manchu rulers of the last "Chinese" dynasty were deeply concerned about threats to their authority in the western provinces of Yunnan, Sichuan, Guizhou, and what would later become the territory of Xinjiang. The ethno-geographic reorientation of the opium problem away from the traditional narrative of a Sino-British diplomatic and military conflict on China's eastern seacoast produces a more "Qing-centered" account. At the same time, this approach expands the study of the opium problem within the empire by focusing on the central government's attempts to implement prohibition over its vast territory through a series of local administrative structures designed to control specific segments of the extremely variegated population of the empire's landlocked western zones. In other words, any account of the Qing opium problem cannot ignore dynastic expansionism.

Two important works have laid the foundation for this approach by exploring the spatial extent of the opium problem beyond the Chinese coast. The first is W. S. K. Waung's pioneering "Introduction of Opium Cultivation to China" (1979). Based mainly on British sources, the article called attention to the significance of domestically produced opium in the Qing empire, primarily after the first Opium War. Waung was able to show that "by 1879 at the latest, production of native opium," particularly in China's top three provincial producers of Sichuan, Yunnan, and Guizhou, "had definitely surpassed the total foreign import."[19]

Waung's article is considerably expanded and augmented in Lin Man-houng's unpublished Ph.D. dissertation, "A Study of the Spread of Opium Smoking in Late Qing Society: A Supply-side Analysis (1773–1906)" (National Taiwan University, 1985; in Chinese), which employs a greater number of both Chinese and English sources. This work, which constitutes the most serious and sustained book-length engagement in the literature with the opium problem itself, is concerned primarily with the economics of the opium trade as it existed throughout the empire. Lin particularly emphasizes the two provinces of Yunnan and Sichuan, each of

19. Waung, "Opium Cultivation," p. 217.

which would successively become the center of Chinese opium production during the latter half of the nineteenth century. Perhaps the most significant impact of Lin's work on the general narrative is her demonstration of the sheer expanse of the opium problem throughout the empire. In effect, she built on Waung's work to achieve a fundamental reorientation of the opium problem, one that must form the basis for all subsequent studies. The extent of the domestic opium traffic traced by Lin makes it impossible to continue to treat the opium problem as purely one of Sino-Western relations.[20]

Lin's study, although it certainly improved on Waung's contribution, maintained a similar approach in that it was more an overview of the imperial traffic and its economic dynamics in relation to British Indian opium. She gathered materials on regional aspects of the opium problem from across the empire, but these were intended more to demonstrate the transimperial nature of the trade in an international context than to trace a history of the opium problem as it manifested itself in one or more regions. Consequently the dynamic relationship between central policy formation and its regional implementation through a variety of local administrative control structures did not occupy an important place in her dissertation. Lack of attention to local administration also precluded an inquiry into the effects of ethnic diversity on the traffic. Finally, source limitations that now no longer obtain affected her study, as well as Waung's; with the availability of many crucial documents held in the First Historical Archives in Beijing, we can now achieve a much fuller picture of the Jiaqing-era prohibition, antidrug operations in Xinjiang, the number of court cases, and the amounts of opium confiscated.[21] These archival materials substantially augment, and in some cases alter, Lin's initial analysis of the opium problem as it existed throughout the empire during the Jiaqing and Daoguang periods.

A more intense examination of the opium problem in key western regions therefore becomes both crucial and possible, particu-

---

20. Lin Man-houng, "Qingmo shehui liuxing xishi yapian yanjiu."
21. These source limitations have persisted in Lin's subsequent publications. See, e.g., Lin Man-houng, "Yin yu yapian."

larly when transimperial policies like prohibition are employed as themes to order and compare imperial diversity in ways previously unexplored in the historiography. The resulting construction of imperial space as a realm of offenders and enforcers, however, remains incomplete without a more sophisticated analytical concept of opium itself, which functions as mere contraband when considered in its purely legal aspect. Imperial space could not even be considered a zone of prohibition enforcement if opium had not already been a commodity in high demand. In this sense, imperial space as constructed by commodified opium must be considered a market system; this in turn necessitates the refinement of the terms "drug" in general and "opium" in particular as concepts. In the process, and in contrast to the bulk of the existing literature on the Qing opium problem, opium becomes a much more historically significant factor.

The Concept of Addictive Consumables

The significance of an altered and expanded perspective on the opium problem is not limited to issues of Qing history; it also has implications for understanding the role of the opium trade in the wider realm of world history. Until quite recently little progress had made beyond the fundamental contribution of David Edward Owen's *British Opium Policy in China and India* (1934) to historical understanding of the China traffic in a broader context encompassing both Britain and India. Although Owen contended that Europeans were instrumental in organizing the drug industry that brought so much harm to China, he sometimes portrayed this commerce as an aberration of individual traders rather than a deliberate policy of empire.[22] In a long overdue re-examination of the basic issues concerning the relationship between opium in Britain, India, and China, Carl A. Trocki has identified drug trades in general, and the opium trade in particular, as the "crucial component" of British imperialism rather than as an "aberration."[23] This argument merits closer examination because it connects regional opium

---

22. Owen, *British Opium Policy*, pp. 18, 214.
23. Trocki, *Opium, Empire and the Global Political Economy*, p. 7.

problems in a manner that not only helps explain the persistence of the trade and its world-historical significance but also provides a framework for a fruitful comparative analysis of how opium was handled by both British India and Qing China.[24]

Unlike virtually all other Western authors on the subject, Trocki argues that opium itself was of decisive significance and uniquely qualified to effect the transformation of the socioeconomies of its producers and consumers. The drug's distinct historical effects arose directly from the nature of the opium trade itself. The ability of opium to provide consistent, large amounts of revenue for the imperial enterprise, coupled with its engendering of a critical mass of capitalists who profited from the trade and who provided vital support for the imperial lobby throughout the nineteenth century, was one important factor.[25] Both these functions laid the foundation for the global capitalist structure through the development both of European imperial capital and its attendant international merchant class and of indigenous capitalist groups in South and Southeast Asia as well as China. In sum, the drug traffic obliterated traditionalist obstacles to the market while simultaneously creating a class of consumers for the newly commodified drug (10–11).

Citing the work of Sidney Mintz on sugar, Trocki observes that the trade in "drug foods" (Mintz's term) such as coffee, sugar, tea, and tobacco "drastically transformed European society" by becoming the "first true commodities." I prefer the term "addictive consumables" mainly because both tobacco and opium as articles of mass consumption were smoked rather than eaten. Linking all

---

24. Opium was legal in Britain itself during the Daoguang-era prohibition in China, and no significant control over its popular and extensive use in patent medicines, candy, and even suppositories was exerted until 1868 when authority to dispense it was technically restricted to licensed professionals. It was, however, never strictly outlawed during the nineteenth century. It is interesting to note that the British attached the greatest stigma to opium smoking, which does not seem to have been particularly extensive despite popular contemporary lurid tales of Victorian opium dens. For detailed accounts, see Berridge and Edwards, *Opium and the People*; and Barry Milligan, *Pleasures and Pains*.

25. Trocki, *Opium, Empire and the Global Political Economy*, p. 10. Hereinafter page references to this work are cited in the text.

these consumables, however, was the sustained and increasing mass demand for them arising from their addictive qualities, which Trocki argues were the true prerequisites of capitalist market development in its formative stages (27–28).

The fact that addictive consumables came from beyond Europe provided the impetus for imperialist expansion, which in turn could be financed only through the development of markets for mass consumption. Soon, the basic elements of capitalist growth—economies of scale, comparative advantage, and the division of labor—came together to construct free traders who sought to remove "protectionist" barriers to their drug products, over which they sought their own monopolies (27–29).

The addictive properties of these consumables were also crucial in that they "made workers work," in the sense both of enhancing endurance and of providing a physical stimulus for continuing consumption (31). The structure of mass consumption that arose in consequence necessitated a correspondingly immense structure of mass production and a commensurate political structure to tap the resultant wealth.[26] In Trocki's view, sugar became a true commodity in Britain through the West Indian sugar plantations, tobacco through the North American tobacco plantations, and tea through the tea trade of the East India Company in China. The Chinese, however, were not yet incorporated into the British system of transoceanic production and consumption as the slaves of the New World or the laborers of the Old were; nor could they be drawn into it by either sugar or tea, both of which were produced within China's economic autarky. To the contrary, the Chinese enjoyed a monopoly on one of the most important British addictive consumables, tea. A new commodity attractive to China was required in order to gain full control of tea and shift its monopoly profits to Britain (31–32).

It is important to add that botanical evidence for the importance of addictive consumables for human society, as well as for their distinctiveness, long predates the modern period. No truly wild vari-

---

26. Sidney W. Mintz (*Sweetness and Power*, pp. 151–86) provides a classic analysis of the linkages among the structures of mass production, mass consumption, and the state regarding addictive consumables in general and sugar in particular.

ety of the opium poppy, *Papaver somniferum*, has yet been found in nature. In other words, all known forms of the poppy are products of human cultivation, which can be traced back to antiquity. This is true even of "feral" poppies, which exist briefly at the margins of organized cultivation. Human intervention is a prerequisite for the plant's long-term survival. *Nicotiana tabacum* and *Erythroylon coca*, which produce tobacco and coca, respectively, have similar histories of exclusive cultivation.[27] The "artificial" nature of these addictive consumables suggests that they are substantially human constructs that have persisted across history regardless of social or economic variation. Human agency and addictive consumables like opium are inextricably linked at the transhistorical level.

It is, consequently, not necessary to subscribe fully to Trocki's theory regarding the connections between addictive consumables, imperialism, and capitalism, which have only been adumbrated here, in order to explore the theory's ramifications for select aspects of the Qing opium problem as it relates most directly to Britain and India. For my purposes, what links the three together at the conceptual level is the idea of the addictive consumable as a true commodity. This concept helps explain why opium, as opposed to cotton or molasses or rice, became an ideal, indeed the only, solution for the British in China and in India.

The concept also explains why the production, distribution, and consumption of addictive consumables were of such enormous interest to the state, which was in constant search of substantial, regular revenues to fund consolidation and expansion. Some consumables, such as tea and opium, were of such significance that they evolved into strategic commodities controlled by government monopoly, an infallible sign of considerable and abiding state interest. Certainly, addictive consumables were also capable of generating immense profits for private individuals as well as substantial state revenues, and the inevitable results of these dual and often antagonistic capacities were varying degrees of state prohibition, which in turn engendered smuggling networks.[28]

---

27. Merlin, *On the Trail of the Ancient Opium Poppy*, pp. 53–54.
28. Tea smuggling, for example, was a serious problem in both the British and the Qing empires caused directly by state attempts to control the distribution and

State motives for the prohibition of addictive consumables were hardly uniform and could range from a desire to shield subjects from the harmful effects of consumption to an attempt to preserve the state's exclusive control over the product. Indeed, the state has not even been consistently in favor of prohibition; the colonial Spanish government in Peru, for example, successfully fought Catholic clerical prohibitionists throughout the sixteenth century to protect the coca production on which the colony's indigenous labor force in the silver mines depended for financial incentive and stamina.[29] Even in this unusual example, as in those of both British India and Qing China, the state's revenue concerns were the ultimate determinant of its prohibition policy in particular and its relationship to the production, distribution, and consumption of addictive consumables in general.

At the level of historical events, the most important aspect of the specifics of the relations between Britain, India, and China, again for my purposes, is Britain's abortive attempt to control the "native" production of opium by actors in regions outside the reach of British Indian administration. Ironically, the issue of local control was decisive for both the British and the Qing empires, neither of which was able to satisfactorily control the drug trade through prohibition. The ability of the British to profit from this mutual failure owed more to the nature of opium as both a true and a strategic commodity than to the dynamic modernity of the British nation-state and its rational, inevitable triumph over the muddled traditionalism of the Qing regime.

---

sale of this addictive consumable. For the British problem, see Mui and Mui, *The Management of a Monopoly*, pp. 13–14. For the statutes on Chinese tea smuggling, which were quite similar to those of the salt monopoly, see *HDSL*, 9:410a–11b.

29. Gagliano, *Coca Prohibition in Peru*, pp. 13–91. The Spanish soon discovered that indigenous peoples in Peru valued coca more than gold or silver and could be induced to mine these metals for the colonial government in exchange for coca (ibid., pp. 22–23). Catholic priests objected to coca consumption in part because of inhumane conditions on the coca plantations, but primarily because consumption was connected with indigenous belief systems that were retarding their conversion efforts (pp. 47–49). While some moderate labor reforms were enacted, prohibition failed because the Spanish Crown recognized coca's vital role in sustaining silver mine production (pp. 57–59).

From a Qing historical perspective, an analytical approach to the empire focused on the effects of ethno-geographic diversity can profitably be conducted through a comparative history of its different regions, as discrete units both with their own unique experiences and in dynamic relation with one another as well as with the imperial center.[30] A somewhat more conventional comparative approach between Qing China and British India is employed in Chapter 2; my intent is to demonstrate that revenue was the primary motive for the Company's prohibition efforts in India and that prohibition failed because of weaknesses in the Company's local administration. The subsequent chapters explore these same points in more detail for Qing China. The study proceeds on the basis of a division of the empire into spheres of operations linked by central government policy, but differentiated by the organization of their respective local administrations, whose salient characteristics are summarized in Chapter 3. Among the three major spheres examined in this study, that of the southeast coast has been taken as the paradigmatic ground of prohibition operations as formulated by the central government. Both the central government's formation of prohibition policy and relevant aspects of that policy's "classic" implementation on the southeast coast primarily through the *junxian* administrative structure of the Han core are examined in Chapter 4. Chapters 5 and 6 present contrasting experiences with prohibition, framed by the administrative apparatuses of Xinjiang's beg system and the native chieftain system of the southwestern provinces, respectively. The regions covered in Chapters 4, 5, and 6 are also characterized, distinguished, and linked in terms of the opium-marketing system that arose in each. Chapter 7 presents conclusions drawn from the prohibition experiences of Qing China, select Chinese provinces, and British India in terms of their relationship to Qing imperial expansionism and the nature of empire itself.

---

30. One of the most notable recent works employing this approach is Will and Wong, *Nourish the People.*

TWO

The British Prohibition in
India in Comparative Perspective

Addictive Consumables and Empire

The revenue-generating power of addictive consumables such as tea
and opium that so attracted the attention of the British state was
rooted in the capacity of these consumables to create and sustain a
structure of mass consumption from which considerable revenue
could consistently and easily be extracted. This capacity arose in
large measure because of their psychophysical effects on consumers.
Scholars of early modern Europe have increasingly drawn attention to a "consumer revolution" as significant in its historical consequences as that of the industrial revolution's radical expansion of
production.[1] As an integral part of the historical development of
the early modern world, extra-European commodities made a fundamental contribution to this revolution. The demand for "tropical" (i.e., non-European) commodities was instrumental in the establishment, maintenance, and spread of European empires. Indeed,
European imperial expansion up through the eighteenth century
was "more than anything else . . . the product of the escalating demand for a group of non-European commodities by the Atlantic
community."[2]

---

1. For a comprehensive survey of recent scholarship on the consumer revolution and the "empire of goods" it engendered, see Brewer and Porter, *Consumption and the World of Goods*.

2. Shammas, "Revolutionary Impact," p. 168.

Tobacco, sugar, and tea were the most significant commodities in the British consumer revolution and, consequently, for the maintenance and expansion of the British empire.[3] Of the three, tobacco and sugar were products of the New World and were, consequently, of greatest import for the British imperial enterprise in the Americas. Tea, in contrast, was a product of East Asia, namely China, which remained the exclusive source until around 1840, when the first Assamese tea gardens began to produce enough for commercial export.[4] The concerns of the tea trade and much of the activity of empire connected with its development as an addictive consumable was thus centered in the China commerce conducted by the British East India Company from its Indian headquarters in Bengal.

Tea was also a strategic commodity for the British empire, and this fact was duly reflected in the East India Company's management of the tea trade with China. Perhaps the most obvious manifestation of state concern for the stability of the tea trade was the British government's formal requirement that the Company maintain a year's supply of the commodity in its warehouses in England as a precaution against an interruption in the supply from China.[5] It was the extra-commercial significance of tea, rather than purely economic issues of monopoly control per se, that determined Company operations and distinguished them from those of private commercial enterprises involved in trade with the East.[6]

As "the largest and most valuable component of mid-Qing international commerce," tea was also esteemed by the Manchus, who presided over the coastal trade with the British as well as the interior traffic with the Russians.[7] The coastal trade, which began

---

3. Shammas, "English and Anglo-American Consumption," pp. 178–85. For specific studies, see Mintz, *Sweetness and Power*, on sugar; Goodman, *Tobacco in History*, on tobacco; and Burnett, *Liquid Pleasures*, for tea and other caffeinated drinks.

4. Burnett, *Liquid Pleasures*, p. 61. An indigenous tea shrub had been discovered in Kathmandu in 1816, but a major Indian tea industry did not fully develop until the late 1800s.

5. Mui and Mui, *The Management of a Monopoly*, pp. 50–51.

6. Ibid., pp. 56–57.

7. Gardella, *Harvesting Mountains*, p. 33. For an account of the trade with the tsarist empire, see Khokhlov, "The Kyakhta Trade."

no later than the seventeenth century, was a relatively recent development in comparison to the tea and horse trade with Inner Asian peoples on the empire's northern and western frontiers, the origins of which date to the Tang dynasty.[8] Both the coastal and frontier trades were under a considerable degree of state management, in part because the dynasty viewed tea as a means not only to acquire steppe horses for the Qing military but also to keep peace on the frontier. These concerns, however, were applicable mainly to the Inner Asian horse and tea trade, which had been in decline since 1735 and ceased altogether after 1840.[9]

Another reason for sustained attention of the Qing state to the tea trade was revenue, and the steady growth of the coastal trade since the eighteenth century only encouraged the Qing to continue and expand the management of the coastal trade in tea as a strategic commodity. Dynastic control of tea added income to local officials' pockets as well as to the privy purse.[10] In contrast to the declining Inner Asian trade, the coastal trade underwent an enormous expansion during the nineteenth century, rising from an annual volume of 10,000 tons at the beginning of the nineteenth century to a peak of 125,000 tons in the 1880s.[11]

The coastal tea trade would not have developed on such a scale without the emergence of an enormous demand for the beverage in Britain. It remains unclear why tea became such a popular article of mass consumption during the eighteenth century.[12] Tea is a com-

---

8. Lin Yongkuang and Wang, *Qingdai xibei minzu maoyi shi*, pp. 29–81.

9. Ibid., p. 41.

10. For the importance of tea to Song revenues, see Paul J. Smith, *Taxing Heaven's Storehouse*. For the benefits of the tea revenue to local and central coffers, see Cranmer-Byng and Wills, "Trade and Diplomacy Under the Qing," p. 67.

11. Hao, *Commercial Revolution*, p. 162.

12. It is certainly possible, as Kenneth Pomeranz does in his *The Great Divergence* (p. 117), to date the start of British mass consumption of tea to the mid-nineteenth century. Such distinctions, however, rely in part on how mass consumption is defined. The mass consumption that made tea into a strategic commodity began long before the 1840 drop in prices cited as a benchmark year by Pomeranz. The more important date is actually 1784, the year the Commutation Act was passed. The act reduced the British import duty on tea from 119 percent to 12.5 percent. This reduction undermined the tea smuggling trade that had flourished during the eighteenth century and laid the foundation for the massive in-

paratively mild stimulant that is sometimes classified as a psycho-active drug mainly because of its caffeine content, which stimulates the central nervous system and the cerebral cortex. When taken in moderate amounts, tea can increase mental and muscular activity as well as relieve fatigue.[13] These psychophysical effects were the basis of tea's attraction for British consumers, most of whom were poor laborers in search of cheap, nutritious calories, which tea, particularly in combination with sugar, was well suited to provide.[14]

Tea was also distinctive in another way: it was the only major addictive consumable used by the British masses that was not produced in one of Britain's colonies. In other words, the British empire did not control the production and distribution of tea to the same degree that it did those of sugar and tobacco. Britain's minimal control over tea was a major determining factor in its relationship with the Qing empire. The two states were linked primarily by a commerce in a number of important articles, including cotton and indigo. Nevertheless, as Sir George Staunton, a former chairman of the Select Committee, the East India Company's supreme executive body in the Chinese port of Guangzhou, frankly explained to the House of Commons in 1840, tea was the most important article of trade between Britain and China:

The British intercourse with China is the source from whence this Country is supplied with tea, an article in such universal use as to be nearly equivalent to a necessary of life, and through consumption of which a greater Revenue of between Three and Four Millions sterling is annually

---

creases in tea consumption in the following century. Tea sales in Britain had already jumped from 6.8 million pounds per year in the 1770s to 19.7 million pounds by the 1790s (Bowen "British India," pp. 534–35). I consider this adequate evidence of mass consumption prior to 1840. Moreover, the fact that tea was a contraband article throughout most of the eighteenth century, in large measure because of the commodity's excessive taxation, makes full comparisons of per capita consumption statistics impossible.

13. Burnett, *Liquid Pleasures*, p. 49.

14. Ibid., pp. 54–55, 187. There were, of course, social motives for tea consumption in particular and the consumption of all caffeinated beverages in general, all of which had started out as articles of elite consumption and were often valued as alternatives to alcohol, the indigenous European addictive beverage (ibid., pp. 1–4). For the effect of sugar on the consumption of caffeinated beverages in general and tea in particular, see Mintz, *Sweetness and Power*, pp. 108–17.

raised with greater facility and certainty and with less pressure on the people than in the case of any other tax. . . . This trade moreover employs . . . British Shipping, is the medium of the Export of Manufactures and Production of Great Britain and the British Possessions in India . . . [and affords] a certain convenient channel for remittance to Europe.[15]

A pamphleteer of the early nineteenth century, in terms remarkably similar to those of Staunton concerning tea, explained the importance of the commodification of opium, whose significance transcended its contribution to the tea trade:

The opium trade has enabled India to increase ten-fold her consumption of British manufacture; contributed directly to support the vast fabric of British dominion in the East, to defray the expenses of His Majesty's establishment in India, and by the operation of exchanges and remittances in teas, to pour an abundant revenue into the British Exchequer and benefit the nation to an extent of six million pounds sterling yearly without impoverishing India.[16]

Like tea, opium is an addictive consumable, albeit of far greater psychophysical power. Morphine and codeine are the two opium alkaloids primarily responsible for the drug's widespread consumption.[17] The powerful analgesic properties of both alkaloids have made opium a primary pain reliever since antiquity.[18] Morphine, however, is most addictive and, consequently, the chemical most responsible for the euphoric effects of opium smoking.

The overwhelming majority of those charged with opium consumption during the Qing prohibition campaign cited pain relief as their motive for smoking.[19] This suspiciously uniform official rec-

---

15. "Resolutions by Sir George Staunton," in *China III*, p. 1.

16. Greenberg, *British Trade*, pp. 106–7.

17. Alkaloids are "a group of nitrogenous plant products having a marked physiological action" (Maher, *Opium and Its Derivatives*, pp. 25–26).

18. For studies of the role of opium in antiquity, see Scarborough, "Opium Poppy"; and Merlin, *On the Trail of the Ancient Opium Poppy*. Opium, or *afyun* in Arabic, is believed to have been brought by Arab traders to China during the Sui-Tang period (Yule and Burnell, *Hobson-Jobson*, pp. 640–41; Li Gui, *Yapian shilüe*, p. 5517).

19. Late nineteenth-century medical experts agreed on virtually none of opium's chemical or medical properties except its ability to relieve pain (Winther, *Anglo-European Science*, pp. 161–62). A large group of representative, and often moving, examples of consumption for purposes of pain relief can be found in the

ord contrasts with many private writings by urban elites on recreational smoking as an aphrodisiac, pursued as part of the wider fad for foreign luxury items sweeping southeastern coastal cities over the eighteenth and nineteenth centuries.[20] Certainly the two motives are not mutually exclusive, but it is curious that the connection between opium smoking and sex does not appear in the official record. A regional urban craze for things foreign may have enabled opium smoking to gain a bridgehead in China among elite decadents, but it cannot fully explain the drug's wider geographic and social appeal over time or even the marked consumer preference for Indian opium.

The attempt to explain mass consumption trends is further complicated by opium's considerable chemical variability, which can arise from an extremely wide range of natural conditions as well as from the production process. In addition to environmental factors such as climate and soil as well as plant genetics, the chemical composition of a given batch of poppy sap, or latex, can be radically affected by human intervention. As detailed by anthropologist Paul Winther, the number of incisions made in the poppy capsule to collect the latex, the season and time of day during which these incisions are made, and even the nature of the latex storage container affect the chemical content of opium as an end product. The effects of containers, for example, were discovered in the 1960s when researchers found that the clay in the earthenware

---

"prohibitions violations" (*Neige weijin*) category of the routine memorial holdings of the First Historical Archives of China. These are investigative reports from the provinces submitted through the regular bureaucracy, in contrast to the secret transmission route of the palace memorials. These records are particularly valuable for their wealth of detail, often lacking or abbreviated in other types of documents, and for the vital statistics on offenders, which include their ages and familial relations, as well as transcripts of their confessions. The confessions of offenders arrested for consumption almost inevitably contained an explanation for their use of the drug. Typical cases, which begin to appear almost annually in relatively large numbers after consumption was declared a capital offense in mid-1839, include Neige weijin, DG 20.11.14, #10117 (buben); DG 21.11.16, #10119 (tongben); DG 22.10.14, #10121 (buben); DG 23.7.24, #10124 (buben); DG 25.10.17, #10128 (tongben); DG 27.5.2, #10130 (buben); DG 28.7.13, #10132 (buben); DG 29.intercalary 4.22, #10133 (buben); DG 30.7.7, #10134 (buben).

20. Zheng, "Social Life of Opium," pp. 9–23.

jars used by nineteenth-century Indian cultivators to store the latex could leach significant amounts of morphine, thus reducing the amount of crude opium's most active alkaloid.[21]

The practical economic effects of such human and environmental factors in Qing China manifested themselves primarily as a preference for Indian opium above all other imported types. The multiple incisions typical of Indian harvesting practices, for example, reduced the morphine content of both Bengal and Malwa opium in comparison with their Turkish competitor, which was derived from capsules subjected to only a single incision. This difference in morphine content may also have been enhanced by the stage at which the latex was harvested, since codeine is a precursor of morphine in the poppy's life cycle. The morphine content of modern forms of Indian opium averages 8.5–12 percent, compared with 12 percent for Turkish opium; the difference was even more pronounced during the nineteenth century. Other differences between poppy products are unaffected by processing and arise from the plants' genetic diversity. The codeine content of Indian latex, for example, is 3.5 percent, versus less than 1 percent for Turkish latex, and this ratio remains unaltered after these latexes are processed into opium.[22]

Certain types of processing, as well as particular methods of consumption, may have enhanced the analgesic effects of codeine or other less powerful alkaloids by suppressing the effects of morphine, thus making Indian opium more compelling to ailing Chi-

---

21. Paul Winther, personal communication, April 16, 2004. I am very grateful to Professor Winther for sharing his research findings, which constitute the main source for the discussion of the significance of processing on opium's alkaloid content that follows.

22. Ibid.; Maher, *Opium and Its Derivatives*, p. 13. Maher also gives figures for Iranian opium, which has a morphine content of 11 percent and a codeine content of 2.5 percent. These figures are based on modern methods of processing. Nevertheless, production methods still employed today in Southeast Asia to produce smokable paste are basically no different from those employed in the nineteenth century and require only a large boiling container and a fire (Justice Department, *Opium Poppy Cultivation and Heroin Processing*, p. 12). Very little sophistication is needed to extract a morphine base of 50–70 percent purity from this paste, which is then further processed to produce heroin, the modern end-product of poppy cultivation (ibid., pp. 13, 27).

nese smokers than Turkish opium. "Chinese" opium smoking, as opposed to "South Asian" ingestion in liquid or solid form, might be critical in this regard. The South Asian method would certainly result in the user's indiscriminate absorption of around 40–44 alkaloids, including morphine, whereas the Chinese method of smoking a much more refined paste could not only reduce the number of alkaloids absorbed considerably but also alter their effects through volatization. The precise effects of volatization on the most active group of alkaloids, known as the morphinane or pyridinphenethrane group, is unclear, but it is apparent that morphine is only the primary alkaloid among a larger number capable of producing a range of analgesic, euphoric, and other physiological effects in the smoker. Indeed, these alkaloids can depress, stimulate, or do both depending on variations in their combination or dosage as well as individual physiology.[23]

In sum, an opium user's experience depends on both the type of opium and the consumption method employed. Indeed, given all the variables, different "vintages" of latex from the same plant variety or even the same plot of poppies could also affect an individual consumer differently. This variation in opium as a consumer product helps account for the marked preferences of consumers. Generally speaking, the much higher morphine content of the Turkish opium that reached Chinese smokers resulted in a much harsher and potentially more toxic smoking experience than did the mellower Indian opium, which yielded a "quality smoke . . . not too bitter and not too tepid."[24] These variations also constitute a challenge to mass production, a challenge met initially and consistently only by the producers of Bengal opium. The high level of quality control exerted by these producers was crucial for constructing a Chinese mass market for opium because this control ensured a commodity that consistently blended analgesic and euphoric alkaloids into a pleasant smoking experience.[25] In this sense, the Bengal producers

---

23. Winther, *Anglo-European Science*, pp. 23–24; Winther, personal communication, April 16, 2004; Merlin, *On the Trail of the Ancient Opium Poppy*, pp. 92–93.

24. Winther, personal communication, April 16, 2004.

25. Paul Winther (ibid.) has called particular attention to quality control in the production of British Indian opium.

successfully imposed a uniform control over opium's diverse, variable chemical content, and this success was almost certainly instrumental in the popularity of the drug in China.

Product uniformity also increased the probability of a more uniform consumption experience, including physical dependency. Whatever the initial reason for taking opium, pain relief was certainly the final motive in many cases. Smokers run a considerable risk of becoming addicted to morphine and, in effect, winding up dependent on the drug to relieve the pain of withdrawal symptoms. In practical terms, ever larger doses of opium are needed to achieve the same physiological effects, as a user's central nervous system builds up a tolerance for the drug. There is, however, considerable individual variation within this general pattern, and every consumer eventually finds a threshold dose, often a moderate amount, which need not be exceeded. Nevertheless, reaching this threshold indicates the formation of a physical dependency that must be fed in order to avoid the onset of withdrawal symptoms, which can range from the mild irritations of watery eyes or a runny nose to the more severe manifestations of abdominal cramps, diarrhea, vomiting, and anxiety attacks. Despite the often extreme conditions it produces, withdrawal is generally not life threatening and can be greatly influenced by mental attitudes and other medical conditions.[26]

The results of the process of consumption, toleration, physical dependency, and withdrawal can produce an addict, whose subjective experience of this process is "not [necessarily] the positive euphoria produced by the drug but rather the relief of the pain that invariably appears when a physically dependent person stops using the drug."[27] Questions regarding the exact nature of addiction remain contentious.[28] There is, however, no question that the

---

26. My description of addiction is primarily based on the discussion in Berridge and Edwards, *Opium and the People*, pp. 278–79.

27. Lindesmith, *Addiction and Opiates*, p. 8.

28. The concept of addiction remains unclear and contentious in part because it involves both physiological and sociological factors, in addition to psychological elements that are themselves increasingly seen as indistinguishable from the physiological. The World Health Organization's 1964 definitions have become current for an understanding of some of the key concepts of addiction, particularly that of physical dependence, defined simply as the emergence of withdrawal

agent primarily responsible for creating a physical dependency on opium is morphine, and it is the psychophysical effects of this opium alkaloid that are decisive for the construction and enhancement of a "'learnt drive' [that] is the repeated experience of withdrawal and the concomitant experience of repeated and wonderfully reassuring relief which is afforded by the next drug dose. The addict is conditioned to crave the next dose."[29]

This conceptualization of addiction is an almost purely medical one that, despite its qualifications, tends to portray all opium consumers as addicts suffering from serious psychophysical impairment. The characterization of all Chinese opium consumers as full-blown addicts has recently been challenged by R. K. Newman, who maintains that late nineteenth-century missionaries and other virulent opponents of the drug greatly exaggerated the physiological dangers of opium consumption. Citing modern, and therefore as Winther has shown somewhat anachronistic, studies of the physiological effects of opiates that have found no direct correlation between chronic consumption and physical or mental deterioration, Newman argues that our understanding of the Chinese opium problem must be refined by more precise distinctions between those who suffered from opium addiction and "the many millions of light and moderate consumers who were not addicted at all." Making these distinctions would shift attention away from "foreign opium and the problems of addiction" to "the native variety of the drug, the conditions of production and the social controls over consumption."[30]

A more sustained and serious engagement with the domestic dimensions of the opium problem is clearly essential for a more precise evaluation of the significance of the drug's production, distribution, and consumption for both Chinese and world history. A greater focus on these domestic dimensions, however, does not preclude consideration or even downplay issues of foreign traffic and addiction, because both were fundamental factors in the gene-

---

symptoms when drug use stops. For a particularly lucid technical discussion, see Nutt, "Neuropharmacological Basis for Tolerance and Dependence."

29. Berridge and Edwards, *Opium and the People*, p. 279.

30. Newman, "A Reconsideration," pp. 766–68, 793.

sis of China's domestic problem. This is not simply an issue of preserving an anti-imperialist nationalist historiography for China, although such a historiography has raised many legitimate objections to the putatively more rational narratives proffered in most standard Western accounts.[31] It is, rather, that opium's capacity to engender dependency or addiction in a critical number of users was the primary source of the socioeconomic and political power instrumental to the maintenance and spread of British imperialism.

The formation of the addict subject from the intersection of the power of opium and Chinese bodies was also of enormous significance for Qing authorities, whose prohibition sentiments and policies were clearly fueled by their conviction that all opium users were serious, even dangerous, addicts.[32] Indeed, as noted by twentieth-century research, criminalization of drug consumption can transform users from relatively innocuous, moderate consumers into desperate, criminal "drug fiends" and generate an illicit subculture based on contraband drugs.[33]

There is much to suggest that such a transformation was effected by the intensification of Qing prohibition efforts during the 1830s. This intensification resulted in a concept of opium consumers as serious addicts that was, if anything, more extreme than that decried by Newman. It greatly influenced the development of Qing "social controls over consumption" and ultimately led to the implementation of capital punishment for opium consumers in 1841. Underlying these subjective perceptions, however, was the fact that the cycle of consumption, toleration, physical dependency, and withdrawal had produced a burgeoning in aggregate demand from Chinese consumers, whatever their degrees of addiction, and it was this demand that increased the revenues of British India and decreased those of Qing China.

As will be shown below, it was concern over state revenues, rather than genuine concern over the plight of addicts, that ulti-

---

31. Tan's *China and the Brave New World* is a representative example.

32. The preamble to the famous 39 statutes of the New Regulations on opium prohibition of 1839 decries opium consumers as rebels and degenerates (*Yapian zhanzheng*, DG 19.5.15, 1:558).

33. Lindesmith, *Addiction and Opiates*, pp. 220–23.

mately drove the opium policies of both imperial states. Nevertheless, although "addicts" were not the immediate cause of the Sino-British confrontation over opium, they were the motive force underlying the British imperial structure of opium production and distribution as well as the Chinese silver drain. In other words, opium consumers had profound and fundamental effects on the revenues of both imperial states.

The British Roots of the Opium Problem

A brief review of the mechanics of the East India Company's China trade is a prerequisite for an understanding of how opium came to play such a major role in the histories of the British and Qing empires. The drug's initial import was directly connected to the commerce in tea, itself the major preoccupation of the Company's China trade. During the first quarter of the nineteenth century, opium would supplant tea as the primary article of commerce because of its superior capacity for generating private and public wealth. It was the common pursuit of this wealth that united Company servants, the minions of the British empire, and free-trading merchant smugglers, despite the many issues that divided them.

The general conditions of the East India Company's China trade are well known and have been described in detail many times.[34] The East India Company was founded in 1600 and controlled India for almost 260 years, until it was terminated in the wake of the 1857 Indian Mutiny. Until 1833 the Company enjoyed a monopoly on British trade with China, primarily to ensure a stable source of tea revenues for both the British government and the Company Raj. This emphasis on stability, rather than profitability, accounts in large measure for the relatively harmonious relations between the Company and its Chinese counterparts. This group of Chinese traders known as the "foreign emporiums" (*yanghang*) or "hong"

---

34. For an overview of the literature, see Marshall, *British Bridgehead*, pp. 183–88. The classic account of the Company's East Asian commerce remains Morse, *Trading to China, 1635–1834*. For works specifically concerned with the East India Company's China trade with particular emphasis on its opium operations, see Greenberg, *British Trade*; and Owen, *British Opium Policy*. The standard work on the East India Company itself is Philips, *The East India Company*.

(i.e., *hang*) merchants were exclusively licensed by the Qing government to trade with and control foreign traders, whose activities were restricted to a sand flat along the Guangzhou waterfront.[35] The "Guangzhou (Canton) system," which operated in its fully developed, and much more restrictive, form from 1760 to 1834, regulated relations between maritime Euro-American traders and the local Qing bureaucracy not only in the commercial sphere but also in the social and judicial fields to control smuggling and generally restrain the excesses of the local foreign community.[36]

Asian trade structures like the Guangzhou system necessitated considerable adaptation on the part of the Company, whose standard factory system required the control of large localities.[37] This type of totalizing organization was an important element in the development of a commodity, which is a product intended for mass production and consumption for purposes of capital development. Britain's and the "Hon'able Company's" mutual addiction to tea and empire initially ensured compliance with Chinese regulations and provided the stimulus for adaptation.

It is significant, however, that the free-trading opium traffickers, whose lobbying efforts in conjunction with those of similarly minded groups in Britain itself would help end the Company's trade monopoly in 1833, considered both the Guangzhou system and the East India Company to be obstacles to "free trade."[38] Traders seem to have meant by this term control of a mass market of a particular commodity by a few individuals for their private benefit who simultaneously sought to socialize as many of their operating costs as pos-

---

35. These emporiums were also known as the "thirteen emporiums" (*shisan hang*) and as the "state emporium" (*gonghang*), the latter term generally being confined to the period 1760–71 and intended to unite various competing emporiums into a single unit holding similar powers of monopoly trade rights; see Cranmer-Byng and Wills, "Trade and Diplomacy Under the Qing," pp. 59–60.

36. Fairbank, *Trade and Diplomacy*, pp. 48–53; Cranmer-Byng and Wills, "Trade and Diplomacy Under the Qing," pp. 59–60.

37. Chaudhuri, *English East India Company*, pp. 53–54; Prakash, *European Commercial Enterprise*, pp. 4–5.

38. Contrary to contemporary conventional commercial wisdom, the East India Company's monopoly was apparently no less economically efficient, more stable, and cheaper than free-trade control of tea (Mui and Mui, *The Management of a Monopoly*, pp. 46, 51–52, 90).

sible. In 1831, for example, a "Petition of British Subjects in China" was sent to Parliament. The petitioners, all of whom were British merchants, stated that neither the East India Company nor they as "individuals pursuing their separate interests" could place British trade in China on "a firm and equitable footing." Consequently, they proposed the appointment of an official British representative in Guangzhou to "remove the impression among Chinese authorities that foreigners in China have forfeited the protection of their own sovereign."[39] Thus the free traders sought to resolve the internal contradictions of their own ideology by shifting the costs of doing business in China to the public purse for the enrichment of their own private ones. In this sense, as in many others, their goals were incompatible with those of the British government, as pointed out by Britain's first superintendent of trade in Guangzhou, John Francis Davis, appointed after the reduction of Company authority in 1833: "It is more difficult to deal with our own countrymen at Canton than with the Chinese government."[40]

The motivation for British subjects to endure the restrictions of the Guangzhou system was the private profits and public revenues to be derived from the tea and, to a lesser extent, silk and porcelain trades with China. These mutual benefits between somewhat antagonistic economic interests were realized through an elaborate structure of commercial relations linking Britain, India, and China known as the "country trade," which was a private carrying trade between India and China. The country traders, who were independent English and Indian subjects generally of a free-trade bent, were instrumental in the transport and sale of Company products, initially mainly cotton and later opium, in exchange for Chinese goods, mainly tea and silk. The primary issue dividing private British and Chinese merchants, the East India Company, and the British and Qing empires was the control of the profit in silver realized from these various exchanges. Generally speaking, the shift from Indian cotton to Indian opium, which began to occur in the late eighteenth century, caused a corresponding shift in the flow of silver profits from China to Britain.

---

39. *China III*, p. 4.
40. Ibid., p. 240.

This triangular trade linking Britain, India, and China involved not only the exchange of goods but also the remittance of profits realized from these exchanges. Quite early in the East India Company's China trade, it became more cost-effective to entrust the shipment of high-value Indian cotton to China to the country traders, who exchanged it for goods of relatively low value, such as sugar, for the return trip to India.[41] Consequently, country traders, on the conclusion of their transactions in Guangzhou, realized a profit in specie of between one and two million pounds per year, which they then handed over to the Company bank in Guangzhou for bills that could be cashed at the Company's Court of Directors in London or in Calcutta.[42] These exchanges gave the country traders a convenient, stable, and reliable way of remitting their profits back home while providing the Company with the cash necessary to make its tea purchases in China after transfers of specie from the Company's main base of operations in Bengal were suspended entirely in 1768.[43] In turn, whatever the Chinese had paid out to purchase cotton was more than made up for by the Company's purchase of tea, whose sale in London provided 10 percent of the government's annual revenue, an amount one scholar has calculated as nearly equivalent to the contemporary annual cost of the Royal Navy.[44]

The triangular trade between Britain, India and China was quite detailed; its main commercial outlines are represented in Fig. 1. The lines corresponding to various favorable trade balances represent a net inflow of silver from one state to another, and the arrows represent the direction in which goods flowed. It may appear that silver was flowing into India from both Britain and China, but the figure is only a simplified illustration of the trade relations of the three states and does not include the British state's revenues both in Britain and in India from various taxes on tea and opium. It also does

---

41. Greenberg, *British Trade*, p. 11.

42. This estimate is based on figures given in ibid., p. 11; and J. Y. Wong, *Deadly Dreams*, tables 15.8 and 15.9, pp. 377, 379.

43. Prakash, *European Commercial Enterprise*, p. 294.

44. J. Y. Wong, *Deadly Dreams*, pp. 350–52.

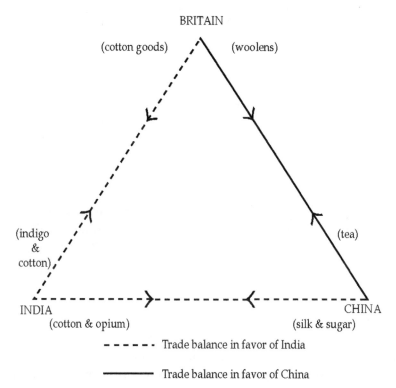

Fig. 1 Britain-India-China triangular trade, 1827–40 (based on statistical tables 15.8 and 15.9 in J. Y. Wong, *Deadly Dreams*, pp. 377, 379).

not fully reflect the private fortunes amassed, especially by country traders like William Jardine and the Parsees, from opium smuggling. Finally, it should be noted that whatever profits India was able to derive from this triangular trade were consumed by the East India Company's costly Indian Raj, the maintenance of which, as will be seen below, put India further into debt year by year.

The figure also does not clearly reflect the fact that some goods were far more important than others in the balance of trade. The trade in British woolens, for example, was rather negligible and quite coercive as the *hong* merchants, who increasingly found themselves in need of Company financing, were often obliged to accept large consignments of unwanted woolens to secure loans.[45]

---

45. Wakeman, "Canton Trade," p. 166; J. Y. Wong, *Deadly Dreams*, p. 447.

By no later than 1823, however, Bengal opium had overtaken Guangzhou's former trade staples of tea and cotton as the most lucrative Indian article of commerce.[46]

Had the British trade remained confined to tea, there would have been little incentive to disrupt a system of commercial relations long stabilized by the early nineteenth century. During the 1828 trading season in Guangzhou, for example, the total sales by the Company and private traders amounted to $20,364,600, of which $9,123,131 was in cotton and other goods. This income almost completely balanced the Company's $8,479,285 in tea purchases for the season. In 1828 the legitimate trade was more than sufficient to pay for all tea purchases even after nine years of declining cotton sales in China. In other words, neither Britain nor China was experiencing an intolerably unfavorable balance of trade in terms of cotton for tea. The imbalance appeared only when opium entered the picture: the remaining $11,241,469 came from Chinese drug purchases.[47]

Statistical tables on the Sino-British trade provided by H. B. Morse for the years 1818 to 1833 confirm the trend noted above. They show quite clearly that the British empire's $195,942,151 worth of cotton and other product sales to China over this period easily covered the entirety of Great Britain's $124,182,160 in tea purchases. When British purchases of other Chinese goods totaling $84,988,952 are added in, however, Britain did end up with a considerable deficit of $13,228,961. This shortfall was more than made good, however, by India's $104,302,948 worth of opium exports to China, leaving the British empire with a $91,073,987 trade surplus, a figure fairly close to the value of the aggregate Indian opium trade during this period.[48] Moreover, as Morse's statistics also show, this gap would only continue to widen (see Table 1).

Although the figures concerning opium sales in China are extremely problematic, not the least because the Indian carrying trade in opium from Bombay and Calcutta converted itself into a

---

46. Greenberg, *British Trade*, p. 81.
47. Ibid., p. 13.
48. My calculations are based on Morse, *International Relations*, 1:90–91.

Table 1

Value of Opium and Tea in the Sino-British Trade, 1816–38

Year	Chests of opium consumed	Total opium value (dollars)	Total tea value (dollars)
1816–17	3,698	$4,084,000	-
1817–18	4,128	4,178,500	-
1818–19	5,387	4,745,000	$5,483,600
1819–20	4,780	5,795,000	5,537,168
1820–21	4,770	8,400,800	6,997,225
1821–22	5,011	8,822,000	7,593,184
1822–23	5,822	7,989,000	8,337,218
1823–24	7,222	8,644,603	8,661,321
1824–25	9,066	7,927,500	7,735,437
1825–26	9,621	7,608,200	7,511,377
1826–27	10,025	9,662,800	7,358,814
1827–28	9,525	10,425,190	9,585,106
1828–29	14,388	13,749,000	8,578,778
1829–30	14,715	12,673,500	8,755,547
1830–31	20,188	13,744,000	8,554,196
1831–32	16,225	13,150,000	7,925,405
1832–33	21,659	14,222,300	7,792,274
1833–34	19,362	12,878,200	7,775,510
1834–35	-	-	-
1835–36	-	-	-
1836–37	-	-	-
1837–38	28,307	19,814,800	-

SOURCE: Adapted from Morse, *International Relations*, pp. 90–91, 209–10.

smuggling trade upon arrival at Macao and Guangzhou, there are enough reliable data to discern the main trends of the traffic in relation to the legitimate commerce in tea. Table 1 clearly shows the triumph of a British Indian addictive consumable over a Chinese one, a victory with grave implications for the people of all the states involved.

The shift in the Sino-British balance of trade in favor of the British, visible from 1819 on, is indicative of the economic difference between an addictive consumable such as opium and a conventional commodity like cotton. The country trade, as a nascent capitalist enterprise, was inevitably drawn to opium's greater mass market potential. Unlike states, private merchants were initially more concerned with the quantity rather than the stability of profit, and by 1830 the opium trade at Guangzhou had probably become the single most valuable item of commerce in the nineteenth century.[49]

This shift in the flow of silver from the Qing empire to the British empire exacerbated an extant silver shortage within China, which was causing a serious devaluation in the copper coinage, the medium of wages and retail exchange throughout the empire's bimetallic economy. The complex relations between silver and copper in this economy tended to drive both metals out of legal circulation whenever the market value of their ore content exceeded their denominated value. Hoarding and counterfeiting also disrupted the supply of both metals and seriously affected state revenues, especially when copper's steady depreciation during the first half of the nineteenth century caused a commensurate rise in the value of silver.[50]

Silver itself was used primarily for wholesale transactions involving large sums, as well as for tax payments. The metal circulated in the form of lumps, small ingots, and even foreign coins until a standardized Qing coinage appeared late in the nineteenth century. Adding to the monetary confusion was the fact that since there was no standardized silver coinage, the services of a professional money-changer were required to determine its value relative to copper; the transaction costs made silver even more expensive. In slightly less chaotic contrast, copper coins circulated in officially authorized, counterfeit, and foreign forms. The result was a plethora of exchange rates heavily dependent on an adequate supply of both metals, over which the government exerted no effective control.[51]

Monetary problems in China were also created by global trends, most notably the decline in world silver production in conjunction with an economic depression in Europe. These conditions made it

---

49. Greenberg, *British Trade*, p. 104; Wakeman, "Canton Trade," p. 172.

50. Dermigny, *Le Commerce Canton*, 3:1352–55; Lin Man-houng, "Yin yu yapian," pp. 123–25, 128–29.

51. Yeh-chien Wang, "Chinese Monetary System," pp. 426, 433; idem, *Land Taxation*, pp. 59–60.

unprofitable to export silver from the Americas to China as the metal's value relative to gold on world markets rose beyond its already considerable value in China itself. Consequently, the rising overseas demand for silver, a commodity like any other, caused considerable amounts of undervalued silver, already being hoarded in response to the low value of copper, to move out of China in response.[52]

Nevertheless, of all the variables affecting the silver supply, "foreign trade was the single most significant one," since domestic supply sources were insignificant.[53] Consequently, China's silver supply was extremely sensitive to shifts in trade balances with its maritime trading partners. In the eighteenth century, this balance was favorable to China, ensuring, along with expanded output from Yunnan copper mines, an adequate money supply. The situation changed for the worse in the nineteenth century, in part because of the declining output of the Yunnan copper mines and a decrease in imports from Japan.[54]

The decline in the Yunnan copper output probably occurred not because the mines themselves petered out, but because rising production costs made the ore too expensive to extract. Rising copper production costs also contributed to the inflated price of silver in relation to copper, which began during the last decade of the eighteenth century. The value of silver rose to more than double the standard of 1,000 copper cash per silver tael by the mid-nineteenth century. According to one censor, a tael of silver was worth 1,100 to 1,200 copper cash in the early years of the Daoguang reign, a price he compared favorably with the 2,500–3,000 cash needed to purchase a tael at the time he was writing in 1855.[55] State

---

52. Dermigny, *Le Commerce Canton*, 3:1343–45, summarized in von Glahn, *Fountain of Fortune*, p. 256.

53. Yeh-chien Wang, "Chinese Monetary System," pp. 430, 431.

54. Ibid., p. 442.

55. Lee, *Political Economy of a Frontier*, pp. 219–21. There are no production figures for Yunnan copper mines during the nineteenth century, but extant production quotas show a clear decline from the previous century (ibid., p. 226). Silver-to-copper ratios for the Daoguang reign can be found in Yan, *Jindai jingji shi tongji*, p. 37. These ratios differ considerably from the generally higher ones cited in Dermigny, *Le Commerce Canton*, 3:1353. For various provincial ratios between

attempts to discourage the illegal melting of cash by reducing its copper content also contributed to the inflation of silver.[56] All these problems were instrumental in draining silver from imperial circulation, but by the 1830s most Qing officials blamed the opium traffic, which did result in a net outflow of silver from China, for the consequent devaluation of copper.[57]

Although virtually all Chinese scholars accept that the opium traffic was the most significant factor in undermining the Qing monetary system, many Western scholars have challenged this explanation, citing, among other causes, the decline of Yunnanese copper production and silver hoarding.[58] Nevertheless, all sides generally agree that imported silver was important to the Chinese economy and that China began to experience an unfavorable balance of maritime trade around the time Indian opium imports started expanding. Of at least equal importance for my argument is contemporary Chinese officialdom's belief that the traffic was the primary source of the country's silver drain and, thus, a major danger to state revenues. This conviction, which is neither unchallengeable nor entirely fallacious, was decisive for the intensification of Qing prohibition policy.

Defense of revenue was also the motive for prohibition in British India, an impetus no scholar has questioned. Stability of income was of such fundamental importance that even the free traders eventually, if belatedly, came to appreciate it. Major opium traffickers like William Jardine and James Matheson began to recognize the value of a stable market only after their machinations resulted in a "ruinous competition" between themselves and a horde of free-trading traffickers who infested Guangzhou in the

---

1644 and 1848, see Lin Man-houng, "Yin yu yapian," pp. 128–29; and Chang, *Commissioner Lin*, pp. 39–40. For the observations made in 1855, see *Daoguang Xianfeng liangchao chouban*, XF 5.7.3, p. 365.

56. Dermigny, *Le Commerce Canton*, 3:1354–55.

57. For representative examples, see *YPZZ*, DG 11.5.24, 1:84–86; DG 13.4.6, 1:138–39; DG 14.9.10, 1:157–59.

58. Owen, Greenberg, Yeh-chien Wang, Lin Man-houng, Hao, J. Y. Wong, and Chang, for example, accept that the traffic was largely responsible for the empire's monetary problems. Morse, Dermigny, Fairbank, Wakeman, and Polachek cite other factors as more decisive.

wake of the demise of the Company's monopoly. In yet another moment of conflict between free-trade ideology and external conditions, Matheson wrote soon after 1833 that "we are sighing almost for a return of the Company's monopoly in preference to the trouble and endless turmoil of free trade."[59] The "ruinous competition" engendered by the elimination of the Company's exclusive rights soon led to calls for "fair trade" that sounded little different from the system during the heyday of the East India Company's monopoly.[60]

The Company Raj itself had good reason to desire fiscal stability over uncertain profit; its extensive opium monopoly in its Indian territories alone is estimated to have supplied about 15 percent of the state's revenues for the entire nineteenth century.[61] A recent study has shown the monopoly provided an average of 10.6 percent of state revenue from 1821 to 1858.[62] It has been estimated that the pre–Opium War British profits from the China trade were no less than 10 million pounds, an amount that represented about half the total revenue from British India without entailing any commensurate military or administrative expenditures.[63] Such lucre was as attractive to British merchants and officials as opium was to addicts.

The system of indirect drug-dealing wherein country traders sold Company opium in China permitted the Company to operate in ostensible compliance with the laws of China, which had banned opium in 1729 and forbade the hong merchants to deal in it. The Company, with the stability and regularity of the tea trade always uppermost in its considerations, feared any public connection with opium smuggling would disrupt its vital commercial activities. In effect, anonymity was the Company's motive for employing the country traders to transport its opium to China for sale.[64] Thus, the Company's hypocritical desire to obtain legitimate tea with the earnings from contraband opium engendered the

---

59. Beeching, *Chinese Opium Wars*, p. 42.
60. Greenberg, *British Trade*, p. 188.
61. Owen, *British Opium Policy*, p. vii; Fairbank, "Legalization," pp. 220–21.
62. J. Y. Wong, *Deadly Dreams*, p. 398.
63. Tan, *China and the Brave New World*, p. 94.
64. Greenberg, *British Trade*, p. 11; Wakeman, "Canton Trade," p. 172.

coastal smuggling trade run by private merchants who would ultimately overthrow both the Guangzhou system and the Company
monopoly and foment a war between Great Britain and the Great
Qing, all in order to secure and expand their markets.[65]

British merchants were the immediate driving force behind the
nineteenth-century opium trade. Nevertheless, their governments
in Britain and India, despite much breast-beating over the "perni-
cious article of luxury," were ultimately responsible for the establishment and maintenance of the drug trade. This trade continued
well into the twentieth century, long after the British traffickers
had been replaced by "native" ones.[66]

The nativization of the opium traffic was of immense significance for everyone involved. The most important dimension of
this process for the present analysis occurred relatively early on in
India itself, where competition between Company-produced "Bengal" (comprising both Patna and Benares varieties) opium and the
cheaper Malwa variety, grown in western India outside the Company's Bengal enclave, ensued as a result of the successful commodification of opium by the country traders. During this competition, it became clear that the Company Raj itself did not possess
the degree of local control sufficient to dictate the terms of opium
production and sale, and the government was forced to compromise with the native producers in the western subcontinent. The

---

65. The political history of Sino-British relations that led to the war has been
told many times and in considerable detail. The standard work in English remains
Chang, *Commissioner Lin.* Jardine, whose Chinese nickname was "Iron-headed
Old Rat," almost literally planned the war for British Prime Minister Palmerston
as well as framed the terms of peace (ibid., pp. 193–95).

66. The quote is from Edmund Burke's account of the trial of Warren Hastings, India's first governor-general and father of its opium monopoly. The quote
continued to the effect that opium "ought not to be permitted but for the purposes of foreign commerce" (cited in Owen, *British Opium Policy,* p. 48). This
neatly sums up the actual practice of the British government until it "voluntarily"
gave up the opium trade for good during Japan's occupation of much of its East
Asian colonial possessions during World War II. Both Owen (ibid., pp. 281–82)
and Trocki (*Opium, Empire and the Global Political Economy,* p. 161) provide ample evidence of the British government's addiction to the power generated by
opium; its only dilemma was whether to draw a higher percentage of profit from
a smaller provision of opium or a lower per unit profit from larger shipments.

ultimate result of this compromise was an enormous increase in the production of both varieties of opium, a radical reduction in its asking price, and a commensurate increase in Chinese consumption by the 1830s that forced the Chinese government to enact the harshest set of prohibition regulations in its history.

Company Rule in India

The establishment and consolidation of East India Company rule in Bengal along the northeastern coast was a prerequisite for the expansion of both British power in Asia and opium in China. The development of Sino-European commerce and

the spread of the opium trade via them in Southeast Asia and on to the China coast, were given new impetus by the growth of English power in Bengal. It was this new empire, restless, rapacious, optimistic, intolerant of settled forms of commercial relations, ultimately bringing state power in its wake, that was setting maritime Europe on a collision course with the Qing empire.[67]

Momentous as it was, Company rule did not really begin to extend beyond the three presidencies of Calcutta, Madras, and Bombay until the last years of the eighteenth century, and its hold was particularly weak in western India (see Map 1).[68] Even in the Company's core territories in Bengal, there were periodic revolts as well as continuous conflicts on its frontiers.[69] Although the Company's initial interests in India were purely commercial, it soon became embroiled in political and especially military affairs as it began to compete for power with other Indian states.[70]

The residency system developed, if erratically, as a British response to this competition. Throughout most of the latter half of the eighteenth century, the Company posted individual residents as its commercial representatives in various independent Indian states. Toward the end of this period, they began to be trans-

---

67. Cranmer-Byng and Wills, "Trade and Diplomacy Under the Qing," p. 87.
68. For a discussion of the weakness of British presence in western India in the context of the Malwa opium problem, see Farooqui, *Smuggling as Subversion*, p. 15.
69. Marshall, *British Bridgehead*, pp. 95–97.
70. Bayly, *Indian Society*, chap. 3.

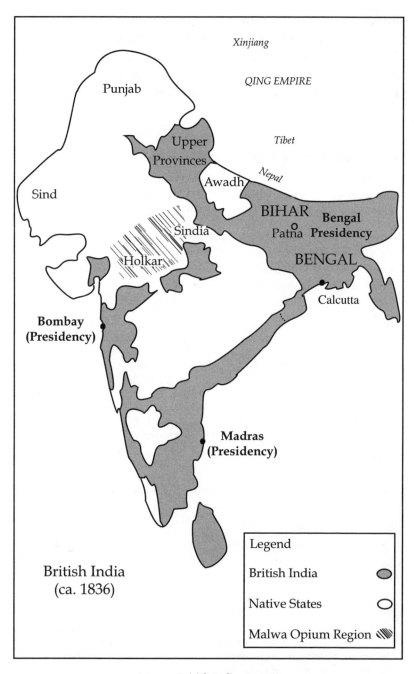

Map 1   British India, ca. 1836

formed into ambassadors from the three presidencies, Bengal foremost among them, to Indian courts. By the early nineteenth century, the governors-general of India were asserting direct control over the residencies in order to forge them into a structure of indirect rule. This development, however, was unsystematic, and between 1840 and 1857 direct annexation of native states was increasingly substituted for indirect rule through residencies. The 1857 Indian Mutiny revealed the dangerously provocative nature of annexation and forced a restoration of indirect rule in a more organized form.[71]

The geographic and economic foundation of Company rule in India was Bengal, which was expected to finance the trade of all other Company settlements throughout Asia as well as its own political and military operations on the subcontinent. This dual burden ensured that the finances of British Bengal were in a state of almost continuous crisis throughout most of the era of Company rule. This situation produced an obsession with the stabilization and protection of revenue, a "priority inescapable at any period in the Company's rule," both to pay the troops and to maintain trade.[72]

By the early nineteenth century, the answer to the revenue problem appeared to be the opium monopoly, which had been established in 1772–73 by Bengal Governor-General Warren Hastings. The monopoly, however, was not a British innovation, but "a hereditary gift to the British successors of the great Mogul [Mughal] Emperors," who had taxed poppy cultivation since the beginning of their reign in the early sixteenth century.[73] The Company initially sold opium primarily to individual employee-entrepreneurs, who then resold their purchases at much higher prices as export, or "provision," opium. The ensuing corruption prompted Hastings to treat opium revenues as excise funds rather than as Company profits on its private commercial account. His act was one of the first steps in a series of shifts away from the contract system to the agency system. By 1797, the agency system had become a full-

71. Fisher, *Indirect Rule in India*, pp. 32, 77, 436.
72. Marshall, *British Bridgehead*, pp. 84, 116.
73. Watt, *Dictionary of the Economic Products of India*, 6:34–35.

blown official monopoly presided over by British residents at the main opium production centers of Patna and Benares.[74] Individual "initiative" was further curtailed when private cultivation was outlawed in 1799. By this time the Company's opium monopoly was fundamentally in place, and it functioned as expected for the next 25 years.[75] Declines in the Madras textile market, the crash of the indigo market in the Delhi-Agra region, and the suspension of raw cotton purchases by the Company in central India in the wake of the abolition of its China trade monopoly in 1834 contributed to an increasing dependence on opium sales to China as a major and reliable source of state revenue.[76] As in Qing China, British opium policy in India came to be driven largely by revenue concerns; by 1842 the Company may have derived as much as 20 percent of its income from opium.[77]

These concerns were central to the Company's active defense of its opium monopoly and its efforts to restrict poppy cultivation to circumscribed regions within Bengal. The Company's sustained attempts to prevent the production and sale of Bengal opium by the native state of Awadh (Oudh) and of Malwa opium by Sindia demonstrate the importance of opium to the Company regime. The difficulties encountered by the Company reveal, however, that indirect rule through the residency system was not yet an effective instrument for the exercise of British power into the semi-independent native states, a number of which were also heavily dependent on the drug trade for their revenues.[78]

The Company's prohibition objectives and operations were, however, quite limited in comparison to those of the Qing, and this difference is significant. The Company never attempted, for example, to ban the production, distribution, and consumption of opium entirely. Instead, it focused on preventing drug production and dis-

---

74. Owen, *British Opium Policy*, pp. 18–44.

75. For a concise chronological overview of the British opium monopoly, see Richards, "Peasant Production of Opium."

76. For regional economic decline, see Bayly, *Indian Society*, p. 124.

77. Tan Chung ("Trade Triangle," p. 35) charts the rising significance of revenue derived from the opium monopoly in Bengal: 5.2 percent of the total Bengali revenues in 1792; 7 percent in 1812; 10 percent in 1822; and 20 percent in 1842.

78. Chowdhury, *Commercial Agriculture in Bengal*, pp. 14–15.

tribution by unauthorized individuals, as well as states, to protect the Company's opium monopoly from internal and external competition. Moreover, the Company apparently never confronted widespread Chinese-style consumption, since opium smoking spread to India from China only relatively late in the nineteenth century.[79] Yet, even limited prohibition proved unenforceable in British India for some of the same reasons its more absolute form could not be enforced in Qing China. The following analysis focuses primarily on these more subtle similarities between the two imperial approaches to prohibition, rather than their more obvious, and admittedly important, differences.

Bengal Versus Bengal

Even before the emergence of the Malwa opium problem in areas outside its sovereign territory, British India itself had experienced an opium-smuggling problem in Bengal during the late eighteenth century. The trajectory and resolution of the problem were remarkably similar to those encountered later in Malwa and are worth a closer examination in terms of their significance for the Qing experience.

The establishment of the Company's monopoly in its eastern Indian territories of Bengal and Bihar was instrumental in removing the Dutch as competitors during the 1770s.[80] This market consolidation also created a domestic demand in India, to which external producers soon responded. In addition to illicit cultivation and smuggling within the Company territory of Bihar, the Company's legitimate domestic rivals in the opium industry, which included both Indian and British individuals, contracted with peasants or their landlords under the protection of various native states beyond Company authority.[81] Indeed, illicit cultivators in Bengal and Bihar were believed to conceal the provenance of their contraband

---

79. For a typical statement declaring opium smoking in India to be of recent and Chinese origin, as well as quite socially disreputable, see Watt, *Dictionary of the Economic Products of India*, 6:41.

80. Prakash, "Opium Monopoly," pp. 76–77.

81. Chowdhury, *Commercial Agriculture in Bengal*, pp. 8–10; Prakash, "Opium Monopoly," pp. 71–72.

opium by labeling it as legal, if equally unwelcome, imports from bordering native states, especially Awadh to the northwest.[82] The effect of both types of opium production was, however, the same: the Company's opium monopoly was being undermined.[83]

From early on, the monopoly was characterized by an abhorrence of competition from any source and for good reason. The experience with Awadh opium showed that the monopoly on overseas exports could not coexist with a domestic policy of free-market opium produced by Indian native states operating through their European and Indian minions. It also shows that the most economically advanced European state was still hostile, near the beginning of the nineteenth century, to many of the practices now upheld as putatively constitutive of a free market.

In the last decade of the eighteenth century, exports to both China and Malaya from the Gorakhpur district in Awadh expanded. The increase in both the quantity and the quality of Gorakhpur opium stimulated further anxiety. Fears peaked around 1794 when the Bengal Board of Trade's inspector of opium expressed concern over any further decline for Bengal opium in the Chinese and Malay markets:

One of these two things must happen, either these people will be weaned from the habit of using this drug, or, which is most likely, the high price offered by them for good opium will encourage some of the other countries of Hindoostan to cultivate the poppy for the purpose of supplying them with it. . . . Should it take place, the monopoly of this valuable article would be totally and irrecoverably lost to these provinces.[84]

Further inquiry revealed that the stimulus for the Gorakhpur competition ultimately lay with the "speculations of Europeans" having "no support or countenance" from the Indian government, in Awadh's case one James Augustus Grant, an entrepreneur who

---

82. Wright, "Gorakhpur Opium," p. 6. Illicit cultivation was identified within a few miles of the Company's main production center of Patna.

83. Wright (ibid., p. 7) notes the official objection to even the legitimate Awadh opium imports as "diminishing the exchangeable value of the Company's opium" by "enlarging the sphere of competition both in the home and foreign markets."

84. Quoted in ibid., p. 8.

held the contract for the native state's monopoly.[85] Thus, at the end of the eighteenth century, the Company itself faced a challenge from a native state employing both Indian and European opium managers and smugglers, a number of whom were its own ungovernable subjects.

The problem and the range of options considered by the Company were remarkably similar to those confronted by the Qing government in the 1830s. Prohibition of Awadh opium was discussed in 1791, but this was prevented by the terms of the existing Company-Awadh commercial treaty. The Board of Trade subsequently refined this proposal into a two-pronged scheme: either convince the ruler of Awadh to conduct his own prohibition campaign or impose a prohibitively expensive tax on opium imports from Awadh. By 1796 it was imperative for the survival of the Company's monopoly that "some form of restriction be put upon the increase in manufacture of opium in Awadh."[86]

Another proposed option was a new trade agreement with the nawab of Awadh to purchase his state's output for the Company.[87] Here the difference between the position of the Qing and that of the Company Raj is decisive. The British opium problem was primarily economic and exportable, and hence more susceptible to this type of resolution. Once the Qing rejected legalization in 1838, such negotiations were no longer open to it. Of at least equal importance is the fact that the dynasty could not redirect the energy of its entrepreneurial class of opium producers and traffickers to points outside its borders and beyond its immediate political responsibilities.

In the end, the nawab agreed to implement a prohibition program against his poppy-growing subjects, although his exact motives remain unclear, as does the success of this ban. The Company's threat to levy a prohibitively expensive tax on Awadh opium was one incentive. The wish to avoid antagonizing a powerful neighbor was also probably a factor in the nawab's final decision. Grant, who had been instrumental in the establishment of

---

85. Ibid., p. 9.
86. Ibid., pp. 7, 10, 11.
87. Ibid., p. 9.

Awadh's opium monopoly, was less easily handled, but he was finally driven from the trade.[88]

It is an indication of the persistence of alternative sources of Bengal opium that the Company's region of monopoly opium production stabilized only "after the annexation of Oudh [Awadh] in 1856."[89] Annexation occurred only a year before the outbreak of the Indian Mutiny that would end Company rule in India. The Company appears to have been unable to keep Bengal opium production within its own bounds during virtually the whole of its tenure, and prohibition in Awadh was no more successful than it had been in British India.

Military power was another option for the British when prohibition either failed or could not be fobbed off on another regime. The nawab's perception of a British military threat was quite justified, as the 1843 annexation of the northwestern native state of Sind would demonstrate.[90] Annexation was the final act in the drama of a more serious challenge to the dominance of the Company's Bengal opium, the Malwa opium production of western India.

Bengal Versus Malwa

The development of the competition between Bengal and Malwa opium and its effects on both the drug traffic and Sino-British relations have been told in a number of works, including Amar Farooqui's recent book on Malwa opium production.[91] As in the case of Awadh opium, however, there have been no comparative treatments of the Company's response to Malwa opium. Although the Company, unlike the Qing, did not perceive consumption and

---

88. Ibid., pp. 11–16.

89. Richards, "Peasant Production of Opium," p. 69.

90. Owen (*British Opium Policy*, p. 102) notes the effect of the annexation of Sind but considers it fortuitous. J. Y. Wong (*Deadly Dreams*, pp. 419–25) convincingly demonstrates that the increase in Malwa transit revenues from Bombay, the only other alternative to Sind ports for the overseas opium traffic from western India, was the decisive consideration for annexation.

91. Owen, *British Opium Policy*, chap. 4; Greenberg, *British Trade*, pp. 124–36; Trocki, *Opium, Empire and the Global Political Economy*, pp. 77–87; Farooqui, *Smuggling as Subversion*.

trafficking per se as problems to be eradicated, it did try to discourage opium cultivation by this group of indigenous producers in Malwa outside the strictures of the Company's monopoly and the imperial state's authority.

In this sense the problem was similar to that the Company faced with Awadh opium, with a significant exception. Indigenous merchants of native states were directly interested in the much more lucrative Malwa traffic, and their presence precluded a repetition of the tactics used against Awadh. Contrary to the orientalist assumptions of Company authorities regarding the crucial contribution of European entrepreneurs to commercial success, the absence of European participants proved to be one of the most decisive factors in the expansion of Malwa opium.

These assumptions had been expressed with notable candor by the British resident at Lucknow in regard to Awadh opium:

Prior to the exertions of Mr. Grant the quantity of opium manufactured in Awadh was small, because there was no export for it owing to a want of enterprise in the breast of the Nabob's native subjects, and for the same reason I believe that it would diminish immediately that European industry ceased to give encouragement to the manufacture. That industry, protected against competitions of equal enterprise, is sufficient to pay the duties which this government receives and to operate on the Company's monopoly.[92]

This equivocal, self-serving attitude toward "enterprise," which was simultaneously a mark of European racial superiority and a threat to the distinctive European industry for which it constituted a prerequisite, is characteristic of the fundamental contradiction within the ideology of the Company and the British Raj, both of which sought to exploit the fruits of enterprise without paying the price in authority demanded by entrepreneurs. In the end, the "native" enterprise of both China and India proved its superiority by driving European merchants out of the trade, but by this time a shift in imperialist ideology stigmatized the opium traffic as the provenance of "racially inferior" Asians and Jews.[93]

---

92. Wright, "Gorakhpur Opium," pp. 10–11.
93. Trocki, *Opium, Empire and the Global Political Economy*, chap. 6.

Table 2
Bengal and Malwa Sales Compared, 1817–36

Season	Chests consumed		Avg. price/chest (dollars)		Total proceeds[a] (dollars)	
	Bengal	Malwa	Bengal	Malwa	Bengal	Malwa
1817–18	-	-	1,300	-	-	-
1818–19	-	-	840	680	-	-
1819–20	2,400	1,200	1,260	1200	-	-
1820–21	3,615	2,291	-	-	-	-
1821–22[b]	2,910	1,718	-	-	6,038,250	2,276,350
1822–23	1,822	4,000	2,300	1,350	2,828,930	5,160,000
1823–24	2,910	4,172	1,640	1,112	4,656,000	3,559,100
1824–25	2,655	6,000	1,175	760	3,119,625	4,500,000
1825–26	3,442	6,179	900	735	3,141,755	4,466,450
1826–27	3,661	6,308	1,025	960	3,667,565	5,941,520
1827–28	5,114	4,361	1,010	1,185	5,105,081	5,277,000
1828–29	5,960	7,171	940	1,040	5,604,235	6,928,880
1829–30	7,143	6,857	865	885	6,149,577	5,907,580
1830–31	6,660	12,100	920	580	5,789,794	7,110,237
1831–32	5,960	8,265	972	722	5,683,010	5,818,574
1832–33	8,290	15,407	782	605	6,551,059	8,781,700
1833–34	9,535	11,715	655	682	6,089,634	7,916,971
1834–35	10,207	11,678	-	-	-	-
1835–36[c]	10,051	-	1,773	-	18,000,000	-

SOURCES: Unless otherwise noted, data are compiled from seasonal "Opium Statements" in Morse, *Trading to China*, 3:339, 365, 384; 4:21, 69, 85, 101, 120, 141, 160, 183, 197, 251, 273, 341, 372.
[a] All figures obtained from Greenberg, *British Trade*, p. 220.
[b] Consumption statistics for 1821–22 to 1825–26 are from Greenberg, *British Trade*, p. 220.
[c] All statistics for this season obtained from J. Y. Wong, *Deadly Dreams*, p. 406.

Almost as soon as Awadh had agreed to prohibit opium production, competition arose among the western Indian states, centered in the Malwa region (in present-day Madhya Pradesh). Table 2 demonstrates the serious effects of this competition on the consumption (i.e., chests sold on the China market rather than simply transported there) of Company Bengal opium in China.[94]

---

94. The figures in Table 2, like all figures concerning the opium traffic during its illegal phase, are compiled from a number of sources that are neither complete nor entirely reconcilable. This is especially true concerning the number of opium

It is clear from Table 2 that by the 1822–23 trading season the threat of Malwa, in terms of sheer numbers of chests, had materialized. The full implications of Malwa's arrival in China appear between 1827 and 1829 when price per chest for Bengal opium dipped below that of Malwa. By the end of the period covered in Table 2, Malwa opium consistently outstripped its Bengal competitor in terms of both quantity and profit. The quality of Malwa extract was superior as well, at least until 1843 when adulteration of Malwa became rampant.[95] The general drop in price per chest experienced by both types of opium was also due to Malwa production for a mass market, which triggered a flood of Indian opium into China.

Malwa may have been produced as far back as the 1770s and seems to have arisen in order to meet the demand of Dutch and Portuguese merchants discontented with the drug quotas assigned them under the Company's monopoly system.[96] This dissatisfaction is visible in Table 2, especially after the 1821–22 trading season. Most shipments of Malwa opium prior to this season had been sent to China by the East India Company, which had attempted to control Malwa by direct purchase from native-state producers in western India. Nevertheless, approximately 25 percent of the opium sold in China in 1822 was native-state Malwa transported through the Portuguese ports of Daman and Goa in direct competition with the Company. As a result, by 1823, Company records were terming all Malwa "smuggled."[97]

Despite the fragmentary nature of the available statistics, it is clear that the East India Company did not suddenly discover a threat from Malwa in the early 1820s. As early as 1803, the Company Raj had become aware of Malwa's threat to its Bengal mo-

---

chests sold, or consumed, in China in contrast to the number simply shipped there and lying around as stock. Consequently, there is a considerable discrepancy between the figures in Table 2 and those of other sources. Figures for Malwa are particularly problematic owing to the fact that it was smuggled both out of India and into China.

95. Paul Winther (personal communication, April 16, 2004) draws attention to the significance of Malwa adulteration. For Malwa's greater purity, see Farooqui, *Smuggling and Subversion*, p. 72.

96. Farooqui, *Smuggling and Subversion*, p. 14.

97. Morse, *Trading to China*, 4:69, 85.

nopoly, and it was later estimated by the British that during this period around 700 chests of Malwa per year were finding their way into China via Macao. As in the case of Awadh, prohibition was the government's preferred response. In 1805 the Company prohibited cultivation in its territories in the Bombay presidency and the export of opium through the port of Bombay to China. As Qing rulers would seek to do within their own domains, Governor-General Lord Richard Wellesley's goal in implementing the Bombay policy was the "ultimate annihilation" of Malwa. Again, as in Qing China, the state's estimation of its power to assert local control exceeded its grasp. The Malwa-producing areas of western India lay well beyond the Company's sphere of control and "from the moment of the inception of its Malwa opium policy, the Company was confronted with the dilemma of not being a major territorial power in western and central India."[98]

The Company's opium problem was directly related to an absence of territorial control. This connection would also emerge in the Qing case. The dismal results of both these attempts reveal that British India and Qing China lacked local control structures sufficient to enforce their respective prohibition policies, which admittedly differed considerably in degree. Another difference of particular significance lay in each empire's response to this limitation. The British compromised with the renegades; the Qing confronted them.

By the time the Company became paramount in western India around 1817 in the wake of the Napoleonic Wars, Malwa cultivation was well developed. It was at this time that observers noted that the competition between Malwa and Bengal opium had become "critical." With the consolidation of British power in western India after the successful conclusion of the Third Anglo-Maratha War in 1818, the Bombay presidency intensified its prohibition operations in an attempt to intercept Malwa opium as it was transported through various small native states in Gujarat to the sea. The prohibitions included any Company opium intended for sale through the ports of western India as well. Agreements were duly concluded with a number of these states to prevent the transit

98. Farooqui, *Smuggling and Subversion*, pp. 14–15.

of opium through their territories. In a chain of reasoning not dissimilar to the Qing rationale for focusing prohibition efforts on distribution rather than on consumption or production, the British hoped that cultivation would stop if exports could be prevented. Nevertheless, strategically situated states, such as Sind, remained outside the agreements, and the flow of Malwa opium continued even as the British enhanced their regional influence after 1818.[99]

When it became clear that prohibition had failed, the Company exercised an option that the Qing would briefly consider but ultimately reject. The Company decided to enter the Malwa opium market and buy up the competition. This policy soon failed as well, in part because of the Company's inexperience in dealing with the commodity on the free market. This attempt by the Company to corner the market and maintain the monopolistic environment to which it was accustomed was refined in 1821 when the Company sought to contract directly and exclusively with the native states for their opium crops. This effort to duplicate the monopoly conditions obtaining in the eastern territories of British India was ultimately undermined by indigenous business interests who would have been shut out by a Company monopoly.[100]

Significantly for this comparative analysis, the main areas of this indigenous resistance were those parts of Malwa, especially the region controlled by the Sindia family, under a form of indirect British rule not entirely unlike the beg or native chieftain systems employed by the Qing empire. Sindia, and its neighbor state of Holkar, were the major regional powers in Malwa and were concerned with stabilizing their rule by regularizing revenues. Opium was a crucial dimension of their programs, since it functioned as a form of remittance in the regionally important tobacco trade with Gujarat on the coast. The Company's entry into the regional economy and its attempt to establish an opium monopoly were directly opposed to the interests of these native states.[101] Sindia, unlike many local native states with minor opium interests, remained unwilling to sign a prohibition agreement with the Com-

99. Ibid., pp. 16–18.
100. Ibid., pp. 18–20.
101. Ibid., pp. 38, 42.

pany. This resistance, combined with problems of enforcing prohibition in signatory states, effectively terminated the largely ineffective British prohibition efforts by 1827.[102]

The Company could defend its opium revenues only by expanding its own production. Indeed, the success of Malwa revealed that
the Chinese market was larger than the Company had thought,
and this realization helped to encourage its new policy of expansion.[103] The stimulus of Malwa opium competition, for both Chinese consumption and Bengal production, was the most important
factor in the tripling of Chinese opium imports from 10,000 chests
per year in the 1820s to 30,000 per year by 1835.[104] This massive increase accelerated the outflow of silver that provoked the Qing
government to the sterner prohibition measures that ultimately resulted in the Opium War.

The stimulating effect of Malwa opium, however, would not
have occurred had the Company been able to extend its opium monopoly to the Malwa fields of western India. The Company failed to
do so mainly because of its relatively recent arrival on the scene:

The British were, comparatively speaking, late-comers to western and
central India—as builders of an extensive formal empire. The lack of an
administrative machinery which would exclusively serve the East India
Company's interests in the crucial period of expansion of the trade in
Malwa opium, made the opium restrictions inoperative for all practical
purposes. What is more, colonialism does not function in a geographical
vacuum: 'Princely rule was suffered to exist by the British in areas where
difficult topography . . . and remoteness from the heartland of imperial
power made the setting up of a direct administration hazardous and
costly.' Given the contradictions between British colonial rule and indigenous enterprise backed to some extent by Indian rulers, contradictions which were played out during the 1820s and 1830s against the back-
drop of the trade in Malwa opium, the lack of, or delay in, setting up a
proper administrative machinery meant that opium regulations could not
always be translated into action. The acquiescence of Indian rulers was essential, but had not been forthcoming.[105]

---

102. Ibid., pp. 94–103.
103. Owen, *British Opium Policy*, pp. 105–6.
104. Ibid., p. 110.
105. Farooqui, *Smuggling and Subversion*, p. 144.

As the following chapters show, the indirect nature of the Qing administrative structure, especially in Xinjiang and southwest China, undermined prohibition for similar if not for precisely the same reasons as in India. The main administrative problem in the Qing domains was not related to imperialism in its nineteenth-century European manifestation. It was, however, connected with the underdevelopment of central government administrative structures in regions that had only begun to be incorporated into the Qing empire relatively recently in terms of the extraordinary scope and continuity of Chinese history. The employment of structures of indirect rule like the beg and native chieftain systems were the Qing equivalent of the British system of residents in Indian native states. From this perspective what is most significant for a study of the opium problem is the similarity of the British and the Qing empires' problems of territorial control rather than the overt differences in culture, technology, or ideology.

Prohibition failed in both British India and Qing China for reasons that have little to do with China's being less modern or "Western" than Britain. As noted above, the Malwa problem was alleviated in a very traditional way. The British military conquest of the Sind, which possessed the last port on India's western coast through which Malwa could move to China, undermined the Company's main competitor by 1843.[106] Within British India itself, however, Malwa remained a necessary evil, since it was so "essential and indispensable in many districts" that British authorities were purchasing it for resale among their own subjects no later than 1848. This Malwa was subject to such exorbitant taxation, however, that it began to be smuggled into British territory from neighboring native states.[107]

Conquest was hardly a characteristically modern solution and was clearly less than absolutely successful as a prohibition strategy. Even as late as 1890, the impossibility of enforcing prohibition in a much more orderly British India was affirmed by Raj financial official George Watt:

---

106. J. Y. Wong, *Deadly Dreams*, pp. 419–25.
107. Impey, *Malwa Opium*, pp. 19–21.

Should occasion arise for the Government of India to abandon its opium supervision and to discontinue the Bengal traffic, the difficulty in prohibiting the cultivation of opium in the Native States of Central and Western India would be almost unsurmountable. If cultivated it would find its way all over India and even to China, in spite of every regulation that might be passed against the traffic. Such illicit traffic is at present checked powerfully by the natural effects of competition in trade, but were Malwa opium to enjoy a monopoly no such restrictions would then exist.

Watt specifically noted the "immense importance" of the Indian native state of Indore's exports of Malwa opium, which constituted about 44 percent of the total traffic in Malwa and Bengal opium for the Chinese market.[108] In effect, British India was forced to come to terms with its own renegade competitors rather than suppress them outright.

The real success of the Raj was to position itself to profit from the failure of its own prohibition operations and thereby avoid what would otherwise have been serious consequences. Like its free-trader compatriots, the Company shifted the costs of its muddled ambitions onto China in the form of a grossly expanded opium production. Consequently, China found itself to be a consumer (supplicant) rather than a producer (suzerain), with no means to shift the human and economic costs of its dependency beyond its own territory.

It would be an error to claim that the motives, methods, and goals of the British and Qing prohibition efforts were entirely the same. It is the contention of this chapter, however, that the prohibition policies pursued by these two different imperial states shared significant commonalities that have been ignored because previous narratives have dwelt almost exclusively on their often insignificant differences.

As noted above, the most important difference is that British prohibition policy attempted to control and restrict certain forms of production and trafficking while effectively ignoring consumption. Yet even with these limited objectives, the prohibition policy of the nineteenth century's pre-eminent modernizing state was essentially as ineffective as the more ambitious plans of one of that

---

108. Watt, *Dictionary of the Economic Products of India*, 6:102–3.

century's more egregious examples of state dysfunction, Qing China. This common failure points toward deeper similarities between these two ends of the development continuum.

One significant commonality was the hostility of powerful political interests in both empires to market or free-trade ideology, which was seen as incompatible in practice with the strategic interests of the state. Specifically, neither Great Britain nor Qing China wished to expose its revenues to the vicissitudes of the market. On the British side, this reluctance meant not only the creation of entities like the East India Company to preside over the generation of large portions of state revenues but also the deliberate erection of state monopolies, such as that created in India for opium in 1773, to avoid the destabilizing effects of unregulated production. [109] In short, the administrations of both Great Britain and Qing China eschewed free-market principles, part of the foundation of economic modernity, in managing their own revenues.

One of the fundamental characteristics of political modernity, state-to-state diplomacy, was also about as effective in the pursuit of successful prohibition policy in British India as it was in Qing China, which has traditionally been supposed incapable of comprehending the idea of interstate equality. The Indian prohibition record often shows the general impotence of diplomatic relations for purposes of drug control. Company negotiations with Sindia and Holkar failed to reach an agreement on Malwa opium acceptable to all sides. It was only the military annexation of Sind, not reliance on abstract principles of interstate equality, that finally allowed the British to gain a measure of control. As Watt recognized, however, this fell far short of an absolute prohibition.

In the case of Awadh, negotiations of a sort were pursued for more than five years. The results of this process, a kind of nominal compliance that also permitted offenses to persist, seem comparable to those of similar negotiations between the Qing and the khanate of Kokand (discussed in Chapter 5). In sum, the Company did not handle prohibition diplomacy any better than the Qing.

---

109. Owen (*British Opium Policy*, p. 23) provides ample evidence of the opposition of senior Bengal administrators to free trade in opium.

Administrative "rationality," another conventional prerequisite of political modernity, was also lacking on both sides. As is shown in subsequent chapters, the Qing response to the opium traffic exposed fundamental weaknesses in the dynastic structure of local control, but administrative weakness in the face of the mass production, distribution, and consumption of an addictive consumable was not unique to the Qing, as demonstrated by the British prohibition record in India. One common source of administrative weakness was the various apparatuses of indirect rule employed by both Britain and the Qing.

These were, however, by no means the only causes nor were they problematic in precisely the same way—witness the ethno-geographic diversity that necessitated the imposition of an array of structures of indirect rule in the first place. Nevertheless, it is clear that corruption plagued both the Qing and East India Company administrations. Indeed, the Company was almost constantly engaged during the late eighteenth century in defending itself against charges of corruption and administrative incompetence.[110]

Moreover, one primary motive behind the reforms pursued by Parliament near the end of the eighteenth century was the regularization of the foreign trade in addictive consumables and the revenue derived from this commerce:

A rationalization of Company government was also required by the vast growth of Indian country and international shipping and by the slow change in India's commercial relations with the rest of the world. For instance, the Company's stake in western India had to be reorganized and put on a firmer footing after 1784 when the cotton (and later opium) trades to China from Gujarat through Bombay dramatically increased, bringing new profits to private British traders and welcome relief for the Company's own battered finances.[111]

Revenue was a decisive issue for both the British and the Qing empires, and the immediate impetus for prohibition arose from this shared concern to defend the financial fount of state power.

---

110. Marshall, *Problems of Empire*, pp. 21–51; Ray, "Establishment of British Supremacy."

111. Bayly, *Indian Society*, p. 77.

State defensive capabilities on both sides would be degraded by corrosive elements that ultimately drew their power from the mass consumption of opium. Herein lies the truly modern dimension of the opium problem common to both imperial states. The scale of both mass production and mass consumption overwhelmed the administrative supervisory apparatuses of British India and Qing China.

In order to understand this process in the Chinese context, it is necessary to examine the administrative structures through which prohibition was implemented. Consequently, before examining the specifics of the regional opium problems of both Xinjiang and the southwestern provinces of Yunnan, Guizhou, and Sichuan, it is necessary to understand the nature of their unique administrative structures and how these structures contributed to the rise of regionally distinct opium problems that hindered and ultimately swamped the intensified prohibition efforts of the 1830s.

THREE

Regional Administrative

Structures

The empire's diverse administrative structures were the products of Chinese historical development in general and Qing historical development in particular. The organization of territory into "prefectures" (originally "commanderies," or *jun*) and "districts" (*xian*) essentially began with the establishment of the dynastic system itself and was the basis for the administration of the eighteen provinces of the Han core during the Qing dynasty. Imperial expansion in the Yuan, to a lesser extent in the Ming, and especially in the Qing, however, caused a number of additions to the standard *junxian* system, most notably the cooptation of indigenous administrative systems, including the native chieftain (*tusi*) system in the southwest, the *beg* (Ch. *bo-ke*) system in Xinjiang, and the *jasak* (Ch. *zha-sa-ke*; banner prince) system in Mongolia.[1] All these institutions were intended to act as intermediaries between the imperial center and the indigenous peoples of newly conquered territories, who could not, without great cost, be brought under the *junxian* system.[2]

---

1. For overviews of the *beg* system, see Miao, *Boke zhidu*; and Fletcher, "Ch'ing Inner Asia," pp. 78–79. For overviews of the *jasak*, also termed the "banner league" system, see Ma Ruheng and Ma, *Qingdai de bianjiang zhengce*, pp. 258–75; Di Cosmo, "Qing Colonial Administration," pp. 300–302; Legrand, *L'Administration dans la domination sino-mandchoue en Mongolie Qalq-a*, 2:111–21; and Lin Enhsien, *Qingchao zai Xinjiang*, pp. 57–67.

2. The experience of Taiwan is most instructive in this respect. Ostensibly a prefecture of Fujian when first occupied by the Qing in 1683, most of this strategi-

An additional administrative layer, composed of Qing civil and military residencies, whose senior officials were generally termed *amban* (Ch. *dachen*), existed in many frontier areas of the empire's Inner Asian territories.[3] Because these residencies were frequently located in isolated border regions, they were often closely linked with military structures, such as the Manchu banner garrisons and the Han Army of the Green Standard, both of which were found throughout the empire. Within the jurisdictions of the residencies, military personnel often undertook administrative duties performed by the civil personnel of the magistrate's yamen in areas of the Han core under *junxian* authority. This situation arose primarily as a result of Qing expansion into Inner Asia and a shortage of both Han residents and qualified civil administrators.

Because of the Manchu conquests both of China proper and of adjacent territories in Inner Asia, the Qing imperial center cannot be characterized as a purely Han construct. It comprised such major Manchu institutional innovations as the Court of Territorial Affairs (Lifan yuan), which was the key link between the regular central bureaucracy supervising the Han core and the intermediary administrations of various Inner Asian border territories.[4] The resulting system of administration often split subprovincial units into a number of differing systems; this hybrid can only be

---

cally important island remained a frontier zone inhabited only by "wild" indigenous peoples. High administrative costs, which could not be funded locally, limited the island's incorporation to a relatively small area centered on the prefectural capital of Tainan. The island's unique geographic and ethnic conditions, which created much unrest, severely limited the dynasty's ability to incorporate the island into the *junxian* system (Shepherd, *Taiwan Frontier*, chap. 7). The imposition of alternative administrative systems was apparently even more problematic. The throne rejected a suggestion by a Fujian official to organize the troublesome indigenes into native chieftainships on the grounds that there was no pre-existing body of hereditary chieftains from which to organize such a structure (ibid., p. 272).

3. For a recent overview, see Di Cosmo, "Qing Colonial Administration."

4. For recent studies of the Lifan yuan, see Zhao Yuntian, *Lifan yuan*; and Chia, "The Lifanyuan and the Inner Asian Rituals." I use the term "territory" to designate those parts of the Qing empire outside the eighteen provinces of China proper, where non-Han peoples predominated. The central government, with varying degrees of success, generally sought to close these territories to large-scale Han colonial settlement.

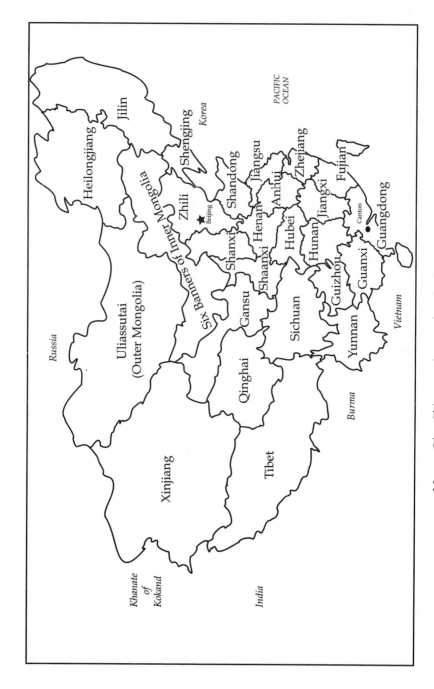

Map 2   Qing China, provinces and territories, ca. 1820

described as "Qing" in style, an amalgamation of Manchu, Mongol, and Han institutional practices.

Since the underlying intent of all imperial administrative structures was to maintain central control in a regionally and ethnically appropriate fashion, they inevitably had an impact on the enforcement of imperial law, including prohibition. Moreover, the empire's ethno-geographic diversity also influenced the local manifestations of the opium problem as it spread to different regions of the empire. The court, in its attempt to enforce prohibition, encountered a number of obstacles because of this diversity, which it attempted to overcome through its local administrative apparatuses, each of which was presumed able to implement the prohibitions after modifying them to local conditions. The importance of the empire's ethno-geographic diversity and the administrative structures that arose because of this diversity makes an examination of the provincial and territorial administration of select areas essential for an understanding both of the regional development of the opium problem and of its overall development throughout the Qing domains.

The following account examines the regional administrative contexts for three geographical divisions: the territory of Xinjiang, the southwestern provinces, and the Han core. Local administration is analyzed primarily in terms of the *baojia* system, which was the Han core's quasi-official security arm, Xinjiang's *beg* system, and the southwestern native chieftain system. As the empire's administrative template, the *junxian* apparatus penetrated every region to a greater or lesser degree, and its effects on the other systems are duly noted. These regional administrative contexts form the general background for more specific evaluations in Chapters 4–6 of the opium problem in each of the three regions.

The Administration of the Han Core

The *junxian* jurisdictions were divided into an ascending hierarchy of districts, prefectures, and provinces, administered by imperial bureaucrats, the vast majority of whom were Han Chinese.[5] These

---

5. Wen, *Baojia zhidu*, p. 204.

officials had a wide array of duties, including tax collection, public works, security, and the administration of justice. Technically, there was no need for a system of indirect imperial rule in *junxian* areas comparable to the *beg* system of Xinjiang or the native-chieftain system of southwestern China. In practice, however, in those provinces where large populations of Han and non-Han peoples lived in close proximity, several administrative systems often overlapped. Regardless of the necessity for this kind of administrative overlap, the *junxian* system was the center's preferred form of territorial incorporation, even in frontier areas of the southwest, northern Xinjiang, and Taiwan, where the court perceived particularly acute administrative vacuums.

Despite the elaborate organization and considerable extent of the *junxian* system, direct official surveillance of the populace remained an impossible goal for Qing rulers. One authority has estimated that in the early nineteenth century each of the approximately 1,500 district magistrates was responsible, on average, for 250,000 people.[6] These low-level officials might be assisted by as many as several hundred auxiliary personnel, mainly clerks and runners. Yet magistrates were generally skeptical of these unsalaried men, who were stereotypically portrayed as incorrigible extortionists of the populace.[7] This state of affairs at the lowest level of the bureaucracy was the consequence of a dynastic tendency to understaff and underpay its local administration, ostensibly in the name of lightening the tax burden on the peasantry. This neglect only exacerbated the already considerable obstacles to local control presented by the empire's extent and its limited communications infrastructure.

The *baojia* system of public registration was a primary method for coping with the problem of local control without recruiting large numbers of expensive and/or venal personnel to maintain surveillance of the populace. This subadministrative structure was intended to induce the population to monitor itself by keeping reg-

---

6. Hsiao, *Rural China*, p. 5.

7. Bradley Reed's *Talons and Teeth* provides the most recent and detailed analysis of local government at the district level in the late Qing and challenges the official view of auxiliary personnel as inevitably corrupt.

isters that could be scrutinized by officials, mainly for purposes of tax collection and law enforcement.

Generally speaking, registration units were based on households, every ten of which constituted a *pai* and was headed by a member responsible for keeping the registers up to date and reporting any suspicious activities to official authorities. As a general rule, ten *pai* constituted a *jia* of 100 households and ten *jia* a *bao* of 1,000 households, each with a leader. Although the heads of these three sections had particular responsibilities to maintain their registers and make periodic reports regarding their status, all registered members were supposed to report criminal activity to the head of their *pai*, who would then relay the information through the quasi-official *baojia* hierarchy to the regular officials. These officials conducted the actual investigations, seizures, and arrests.[8] Two copies of the register for each *jia* were maintained; one for the *jia* section head and one for the district magistrate. The section head periodically submitted a revised copy to the magistrate, who would update his copy. Innkeepers were expected to maintain similar registers of their guests.[9]

All *baojia* submitted reports certifying the absence of illegal activity within their jurisdictions to their respective districts. The district magistrates, in turn, sent similar certifications concerning their jurisdictions to prefectural-level authorities. They in turn presented prefectural certifications to the governor or governor-general, who then produced a provincial-level certification as part of the year-end report to the throne.

---

8. See Hsiao, *Rural China*, pp. 43–83, for a comprehensive overview of the *baojia* system. Hsiao notes that there was considerable regional variation in terminology and content in the *baojia* system, which also evolved and declined over time. At some point before the nineteenth century, at least some *baojia* personnel in some places also became responsible for rural tax collection, which has added to the confusion over the exact nature of their duties at a given time and place. In documents concerning opium prohibition, *baojia* personnel were clearly intended to function as police informers, although they were occasionally themselves implicated in opium offenses.

9. The specifics of the selection of *baojia* personnel and their duties, which could also cover such functions as fire protection and dispute resolution, are explained in detail by Huang Liuhung, who served as a district magistrate in Shandong and Zhili during the 1670s (see Huang, *Fuhui quanshu*, pp. 465–74, 498, 501–3).

Restoration of the *baojia* by the Qing began almost as soon as the dynasty was established in Beijing in 1644, and its development can be divided into three historical stages.[10] In the initial period, running from the beginning of the dynasty to around 1707, two different systems of surveillance were in place: the *baojia* system in the south and the *baoshe* system in the north. During the middle period, lasting to about 1757, the *baoshe* was abandoned for the more systematized *baojia*, which both the Yongzheng and the Qianlong emperors sought to refine and expand.[11] Despite sporadic attempts to impose the *baojia* on a number of non-Han groups, the *baojia* remained primarily a form of administrative control restricted to *junxian* regions with large Han populations.[12]

During the Jiaqing and Daoguang reigns, the system went into decline despite frequent attempts, especially by the Jiaqing emperor, to reinvigorate it. There was, however, considerable organizational variation over time in different regions of the empire.[13] In many coastal provinces, for example, the expanding population of "shed people" (*pengmin*) of the mountains, first registered in 1739, were re-registered into *jia* consisting of ten households in 1824.[14]

---

10. This periodization is based primarily on Wen, *Baojia zhidu*, pp. 216–22, and supplemented by Hsiao, *Rural China*, pp. 47–56.

11. Authorities assert that the throne also attempted to impose *baojia* on non-Han peoples throughout the empire; see Wen, *Baojia zhidu*, p. 220; and Hsiao, *Rural China*, pp. 47–48. The impression of ubiquity, however, is false. Wen provides evidence for *baojia* extension only throughout the "prefectures and districts" of "each province." Hsiao gives the impression that Miao and Muslims were generally organized into *baojia*, but the sources he cites make it quite clear that only Miao living in close proximity to Han settlements are meant. "Wild Miao" are specifically excluded. Moreover, it does not appear that any new form of organization is to be imposed on the Miao who already are said to be organized in their own *hezhuang* units, which were similar to *baojia*. The "Muslims" referred to are the Hui of Gansu exclusively; see *Qingchao wenxian tongkao*, 23:5055b, 5056c. These exaggerations are symptomatic of both authors' approach to the *baojia* system as an almost totalitarian form of surveillance.

12. Wen, *Baojia zhidu*, p. 204; *Baojia shu*, 1:6b–7b.

13. *HDSL*, 2:993b–98b; Hsiao, *Rural China*, p. 44. This situation has created disagreement among scholars on a number of issues, such as the degree of gentry participation in the *baojia* system; see Hsiao, *Rural China*, pp. 48, 67–72; and Ch'ü, *Local Government*, p. 153.

14. *QSL*, DG 4.5.16, 34:83a–b. Technically, as previously mentioned, units of ten households were termed "*pai*" under the *baojia* system, but were known as

Most opium documents cite *baojia* regulations from late 1814 as the precedent for the routine examination of provincial registers.[15] The 1814 statutes were simply part of the sporadic but ongoing effort by the dynasty to reinvigorate the *baojia* system, which often fell into neglect.[16] The perennial nature of this problem was probably connected less to any particular historical event than, as one official noted, to the simple fact that those *baojia* personnel who discharged their duties faithfully were vulnerable to reprisals from offenders and their relatives.[17]

The impetus to revive the system between the mid-eighteenth century and the first quarter of the nineteenth century owed much to the large-scale upheavals, particularly the White Lotus rebellions, of this period. Decrees to expand the scope of the *baojia* system to many frontier enclaves of Han settlement, for example in Mongolia, were issued.[18] From the fourth year of his reign in 1799, the Jiaqing emperor, who was convinced of the efficacy of the *baojia* when properly supervised by regular officials, issued a number of edicts mandating improvement of the system. Perhaps the most significant of these was the 1814 edict relieving *baojia* personnel of their dangerous duty of arresting offenders. Henceforth, *baojia* heads were be responsible only for reporting offenses to the regular authorities.[19] This shift increased the burden on local administrations for law enforcement in general and, subsequently, the opium-prohibition campaign in particular. This expansion of responsibility was probably an important reason why officials were reluctant or unable to suppress opium in their jurisdictions.

The Jiaqing emperor's ostensible reason for this and the other 1814 revisions was the conventional justification of the system as ef-

---

"*jia*" under the *zongjia* system. Both systems had existed in the early Qing, but the *zongjia*, which had been administered by the Board of War, disappeared by the eighteenth century. The *baojia* system, administered by the Board of Revenue, remained, but in an altered form that probably reflected an amalgamation of both systems; Hsiao, *Rural China*, p. 44.

15. See, e.g., *YPZZ*, DG 15.12.20, 1:195–96; Gongzhong jinyan, DG 14.12.24.

16. For an example of similar legislation from 1746 during the Qianlong reign, see *HDSL*, 2:993b.

17. *Baojia shu*, 2:25.

18. Hsiao, *Rural China*, pp. 48–49.

19. Ibid., pp. 49–51; *Qingchao xu wenxian tongkao*, 25:7759b–60a.

ficacious in bandit suppression. The emperor also cited the ebb and flow of population throughout the empire as necessitating constant updates of the registers, a task that officials had neglected. In another edict of the same year, he decreed that in the fall *bao* section heads in rural villages and hamlets were to compile and submit registers to district and department magistrates, who were to personally verify the registers. Officials would issue mutual responsibility certificates (*hubao ganjie*) to households, which would then revise the lists of their respective residents inscribed on the door plaque of every residence. Officials from the circuit and prefectural administrations were ordered to make supervisory inspections of their jurisdictions to ensure compliance and submit reports to provincial authorities, who were to include this information in their year-end reports to the throne.[20]

The 1814 revisions were, in effect, a reform program intended to relieve *baojia* personnel of all duties except those essential to police surveillance, which was to focus both on the compilation and annual examination of *baojia* registers and on a subsequent issuance of mutual responsibility certificates. The certificates committed these personnel to the declaration that no criminal activities existed within their jurisdictions. The accuracy of the registers compiled by section heads was to be verified by regular district officials, who were to go to the villages and personally inspect the door plaques. In addition, prefectural and circuit officials were to make spot checks to ensure compliance by the districts and to submit reports to the provincial governors and governors-general for relay to the court at the end of the year.[21]

The aspect of this system that found especial favor with the Jiaqing emperor was the concept of mutual responsibility between the section heads and those under their charge. If criminal activities went unreported and were subsequently discovered, both the offenders and their *baojia* supervisors were punished, as were the rest of the households in the *jia* section to which the offenders belonged.[22] The immediate impetus for the emperor's interest in the

---

20. Hsiao, *Rural China*, pp. 52–53; *Qingchao xu wenxian tongkao*, 25:7760a.

21. Hsiao, *Rural China*, p. 53.

22. Ibid., pp. 53–54; *Qingchao xu wenxian tongkao*, 25:7760a.

baojia system and its mutual responsibility procedures seems to have been the infamous Eight Trigrams Uprising of 1813 under Lin Qing, which penetrated the outer precincts of the Forbidden City itself. *Baojia* personnel in some areas had detected the rebels just prior to the uprising, but official response was slowed by both bureaucratic inertia and the fact that many *baojia* personnel were also members of the Eight Trigrams sect. The emperor was determined to prevent the harboring of seditionists and felt the mutual responsibility system to be integral to an early warning system that would have stopped the Eight Trigrams rebels long before they broke into the palace grounds.[23]

In terms of opium-prohibition enforcement, however, mutual responsibility was limited to the offender and the immediate *baojia* section head, usually the "rural agent" (*dibao*), a general term for the head of a *baojia* section, or the "community liaison officer" (*xiangyue*), who performed functions similar to those of the section head.[24] Consequently, there was considerable variation in the extent and application of mutual responsibility within the *baojia* system; this has not been extensively examined in the standard accounts of the subject, which ignore the local records documenting how dynastic law was executed in the provinces and territories of the empire at different times and under different

---

23. Hsiao, *Rural China*, pp. 53–54; Naquin, *Millenarian Rebellion*, pp. 156–66.

24. Other scholars provide an entirely different definition of the *xiangyue* post as encompassing the responsibility for periodic public lectures on morality as defined by the Sacred Edicts; see Hsiao, *Rural China*, p. 185; and Hua Li, "Qingdai baojia," pp. 107–8. The lecture system itself was known by the same term. Opium-prohibition documents from Xinjiang, however, provide an explicit, alternative definition of the post as being responsible for "reporting the comings and goings of merchants and passing along their petitions for trading licenses and matters concerning litigation" (Gongzhong jinyan, DG 20.2.19). See Chapter 5 for details on a trafficking case involving the community liaison official Rong Jixiang. The importance of the *xiangyue*'s function in the *baojia* system is also affirmed by the essayist Lu Shiyi, who set out to clarify the confusion surrounding the term. The *xiangyue* is one who literally "binds" (*yue*) the people of a "village" (*xiang*) together in order to accomplish three main tasks: community sustenance through the community granary, community education through the community school, and community defense through the *baojia* system. He was, in other words, the head of the village (*Baojia shu*, 3:1a). Regional variation may account for discrepancies in the use of the term.

ries of the empire at different times and under different conditions.[25]

There is considerable scholarly consensus that the *baojia* system was generally ineffective throughout the dynasty, particularly after the inception of the Daoguang reign in 1821.[26] The views of many Qing officials during the Jiaqing and Daoguang periods were more complex, however. One contemporary private secretary, Peng Songyu, who had served in Yunnan, described the annual department and district *baojia* reports on poppy cultivation as instruments "used to deceive provincial authorities, who in turn use them to deceive the throne."[27] It was generally contended that the *baojia* system could function effectively if suitably adapted to local conditions and conscientiously administered by local magistrates. A simplification of procedures was seen as the prerequisite for the success of both these proposals. Technically, the semi-literate section heads, who were often forced to accept these positions and feared reprisals, were supposed to record the perambulations of large numbers of male and female residents as well as their ages, occupations, and other detailed biographical data. The two main aspects of the simplification process were the elimination of yamen runners, who were always assumed to practice extortion, from the administration of the system and radical reductions in the scope of information compiled in the registers.[28]

---

25. The standard view of the *baojia* requires revision in light of newly accessible documents from the provinces and territories of the empire. Hua Li's 1988 article, "Qingdai baojia," only begins to take up this task on a small scale. Kungch'üan Hsiao's unsurpassed study of the structures of rural control, while recognizing the difficulties involved in generalization, portrays the *baojia* system of mutual responsibility in somewhat contradictory terms as both grossly inefficient and sinisterly ubiquitous (see, e.g., Hsiao, *Rural China*, p. 46). Indeed, this is characteristic of Hsiao's overall view of Qing local institutions, which seems deeply influenced by anachronistic concepts of totalitarianism.

26. Hsiao, *Rural China*, p. 46; Wen, *Baojia zhidu*, pp. 223–24; Ch'ü, *Local Government*, pp. 151–52. In contrast, the more recent study by Hua Li ("Qingdai baojia," p. 119) provides a more balanced assessment, but also holds, without providing supporting evidence, that the system went into decline during the Jiaqing and Daoguang reigns.

27. Peng, *Yu chou ji tan*, pp. 68–69.

28. *Baojia shu*, 2:21a, 24a, 32b, 34a, 41b. For several essays on the *baojia*, see chapters 74 and 75 of the *Qing jingshi wenbian*. Wen, *Baojia zhidu*, pp. 273–363,

Geography and ethnicity, however, continued to cause problems. Regions of sparse settlement or isolated locations were considered unsuitable for comprehensive implementation of the *baojia*.[29] Some officials were far less pessimistic and held that although the system required diligence from local magistrates, it could successfully be imposed even on non-Han peoples.[30] Nevertheless, even the more sanguine admitted that the system all too often existed in name only.[31]

In effect, most Qing officials who wrote on the subject were arguing that the *baojia* system needed reform, but its success ultimately rested on the shoulders of local officials. This assertion meant, as one writer suggested, that surveillance and enforcement tended to be limited in practice to urban areas.[32] Statistical evidence from the opium-prohibition operations of the 1830s and 1840s shows that enforcement in some provinces, particularly Guizhou, was quite uneven, and the overwhelming majority of cases came from the provincial seat.[33] This uneven coverage was endemic to the *baojia* administrative system, which required oversight by urban-based regular officials and so experienced commensurate difficulty in penetrating rural areas.

Whatever the *baojia* system's faults, and they were clearly considerable, it did provide dynastic officials with more direct access to the populations they ruled and enabled the central government to intervene in a manner unthinkable within structures of indirect rule. In 1840, for example, imperial investigators could be dispatched from Beijing to Taizhou prefecture in Zhejiang to evaluate the results of poppy-eradication operations, but no such missions

---

also provides extended excerpts from essayists on the *baojia*. Despite the overlap between the essays in the *Baojia shu* and those in the *Qing jingshi wenbian*, neither collection is comprehensive. A cursory examination indicates that Wen obtained his material, which he supplements with his own commentary, entirely from the *Qing jingshi wenbian*.

29. *Baojia shu*, 3:32b–33a.
30. Ibid., 2:22b, 3:25b.
31. Ibid., 2:21b. This particular observation was made in 1826.
32. *Baojia shu*, 3:32b–33a.
33. See Chapter 6 for details.

ever appeared in native chieftainships or Muslim settlements.[34] Of course, direct intervention was also possible for local officials in China proper as well, and this fact precluded them from disclaiming responsibility for prohibition because of a complete lack of enforcement infrastructure or fear of provoking interethnic incidents, excuses repeatedly made by officials in frontier zones.

Indirect administrative structures were used by the dynasty precisely in order to avoid such incidents and were the consequences of the territorial incorporation of both Xinjiang and the southwest into an imperial structure. Unfortunately, incorporation was only partial under indirect rule, and large parts of Xinjiang and the southwest were concealed from official surveillance.

The Administration of Xinjiang

The search for opium in Xinjiang was to be conducted over an enormous region diverse in climate, terrain, and inhabitants. After decades of military campaigns, the Qing finally took control of the entire region from the Zunghar Mongols in 1759, dubbed it Xinjiang (the "new[ly opened] frontier"), and divided the immense expanse into three "marches" (*lu*): the Eastern March (Donglu); the Northern March (Beilu), also known as Zungharia; and the Southern March (Nanlu), also known as Kashgaria or Altishahr (Turki for "six cities"). This division corresponded roughly to geographical and social conditions at the time of the Qing conquest. The Tian Mountains (Tianshan), Xinjiang's basic geographic dividing line, bisected the region into northern and southern halves.

The Eastern March, northeast of the Tian Mountains along Xinjiang's eastern border with Gansu, included *jasak* as well as Han civil administrative structures. The Eastern March encompassed two Muslim *jasak* regimes, Turfan and Hami. Between 1696 and 1732, both realms formally submitted to the Qing and became the foundation of the dynasty's structure of indirect rule in what would become Xinjiang. The rulers of both Hami and Turfan became members of the Qing aristocracy on par with semiautonomous Mongol *jasak*s, who were confirmed by the Qing

---

34. See Chapter 4 for details on the Taizhou inspections.

throne and whose nomad subjects lived in territorial divisions determined by the dynasty and scattered throughout Xinjiang and
Qinghai as well as present-day Inner and Outer Mongolia.[35]

During the latter half of the eighteenth century, the Eastern
March experienced an extensive influx of Han colonists and exiles
organized under the civil *junxian* administration of the Shaan(xi)-
Gan(su) governor-general. As early as 1761, there were already an
estimated 3,200 convicts and 6,670 settler families working in agricultural colonies around Urumqi, which became the *junxian* department of Dihua in 1773.[36] Around 1820, one official source put
the Han population of the department at 103,052 people grouped
into 12,028 households. In contrast, the largest concentration of
East Turkestani population was listed in the same source as 66,413
people in 14,056 households at Kashgar in the Southern March (this
figure is undoubtedly too low, since these same numbers for
Kashgar are given in a source dated 1762). An 1818 census put
Kashgar's East Turkestani population at 15,700 households, which,
if the 1762 proportion of 4.7 people per household is maintained,
represents approximately 74,180 people.[37]

The Northern March, also to the north of the Tian Mountains,
consisted mainly of steppe. Before the conquest, it had been sparsely
populated by Mongol and Kazakh nomads; following the Qing
takeover, it was almost immediately settled by Han and East Turkestani agricultural colonists as well as by an enormous military garrison with its own agricultural colonies. Between 1760 and 1763, there
were some 3,000 convicts, 538 Han settler households, and 11,900
Muslim households tilling the fields of the civil agricultural colonies
around Xinjiang's main military administrative center of Ili. Some
twenty years later, an observer estimated that nearly 10,000 Han

---

35. Fletcher, "Ch'ing Inner Asia," p. 75; Huang Jianhua, "Xinjiang Weiwuerzu
zhasake zhi," 149–52.

36. Fang, *Xinjiang tunken shi*, 2:564; Niu, *Qingdai zhengqu*, p. 503.

37. The source of the 1820 statistics is *Jiaqing chongxiu yitong zhi*, 16:13650 for
Dihua and 33:26230 for Kashgar. The 1818 household figure for Kashgar is cited in
Millward, *Beyond the Pass*, p. 33n. See Miao Pusheng, "Weiwuerhzuu renkou
kaoshu," for a comparative analysis of some of the most important sources for
East Turkistani population figures during the Qing, including those from the
Jiaqing chongxiu yitong zhi.

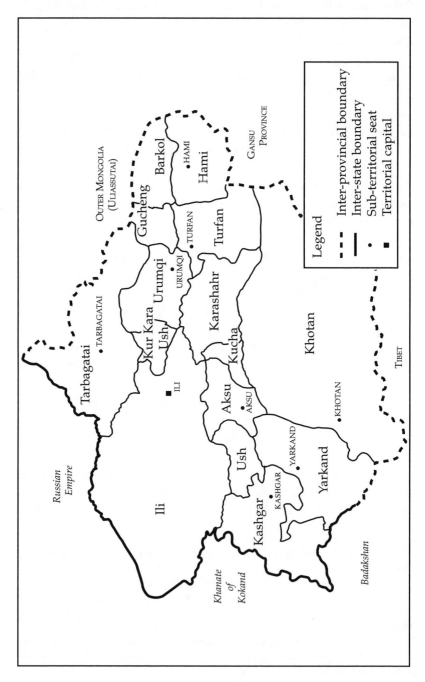

Map 3 Xinjiang, territorial subdivisions, ca. 1820

merchants were operating in the town. This was in addition to the approximately 163,000 banner and 3,000 Green Standard military agricultural personnel, who commenced operations in the area in 1764 and 1757, respectively.[38] These immediate post-conquest troop levels, however, were later reduced to around 20,000, over half of whom were elite banner troops.[39] Around 1820, there were in Ili 14,787 Manchu and Mongol banner troops and 3,098 Green Standard troops, in addition to a civilian population of 20,356 East Turkestanis and 823 Han.[40]

The administrative situation in the Northern March was similar to that of the Eastern March; it also contained *junxian* administrations in the few Manchu-Han-dominated urban areas and *jasak* administrations among the Mongols of the steppe. The Northern and Eastern Marches were also linked through the mutual subordination of their *junxian* units to the civil administration of Gansu.[41] The high concentrations of Manchu-Han populations in urban areas of both marches was instrumental in attracting opium from beyond the Qing frontier for shipment east into China proper.

In contrast to the large Manchu-Han populations of the Northern and Eastern Marches, most of the inhabitants of the Southern March, south of the Tian Mountains, were East Turkestani Mus-

---

38. Fang, *Xinjiang tunken shi*, 2:564; Zhao Juntong, *Xi xing riji*, 2:28a.

39. Lin En-hsien, "Qingdai Xinjiang," pp. 168–69.

40. *Jiaqing chongxiu yitong zhi*, 33:25980.

41. There is some confusion in the sources as to the precise extent of the Zhenxi independent subprefecture, which seems to have been intended for unified civil control of all of Xinjiang's *junxian* units across both the Northern and the Eastern Marches. During the first fourteen years after the Qing conquest of 1759, *junxian* administrative units in both marches, including Barkul (Zhenxi), Hami, Turfan (Pizhan), Urumqi, and Ili, were subordinated to the civil jurisdiction of Gansu as independent subprefectures. By 1773, Barkul had been elevated to Zhenxi prefecture, to which the other subprefectures were then subordinated. That same year, however, Urumqi, or the department of Dihua, was detached and made an independent unit. There were apparently no other significant changes until the 1850s (Niu, *Qingdai zhengqu*, pp. 503, 505). Nailene Josephine Chou ("Changing Frontier Administration," pp. 23–24) restricts Zhenxi prefecture's jurisdiction to "northern Xinjiang, excluding the Ili and Tarbagatai region." Ili, however, remained part of Zhenxi as a civil administration, but it also maintained an independent military administration as Northern March headquarters, which encompassed Tarbagatai.

lims living in oasis towns. They were organized into over 60,000 households in 1818,[42] and the total population may have been as many as 650,000 by 1831.[43] The Southern March also contained a rotating garrison of about 6,000 Qing soldiers, mainly Green Standard troops.

Military government residencies united the three marches and made Xinjiang a zone of military territorial administration. Military residents, subordinated to the military governor at Ili (*Ili jiangjun*) in the Northern March, presided over all major towns in Xinjiang. The northern region also had a councilor (*canzan dachen*), stationed in the far north at Tarbagatai. In the Eastern March, the Urumqi banner commander-in-chief (*dutong*) was in overall command; in the south, another councilor, stationed in Yarkand, was in charge. All the main administrative divisions of the Southern March outside Yarkand, as well as a few in the Eastern March, were run by superintendents (*banshi dachen*). The tasks of all these officials were almost exclusively military. Those in the more urbanized Southern March had to rely on indigenous structures, namely, the *beg* system, to carry out the bulk of the civil administration required by the large number of East Turkestani inhabitants.[44]

Xinjiang's hybrid administration was also reflected in the organization of its borders. In effect, the territory had two borders, an imprecise demarcation of political and cultural influence almost literally embodied in the peoples of the region who nominally accepted Qing suzerainty and a more precisely delineated perimeter of military guard posts or checkpoints maintained well inside Xinjiang's more nebulous boundaries.[45]

---

42. Millward, *Beyond the Pass*, p. 33*n*.

43. Miao, "Weiwuerzu renkou kaoshu," p. 74.

44. Millward, *Beyond the Pass*, pp. 32–33, 12–13; Lin En-hsien, "Qingdai Xinjiang," pp. 168–69. For administrative overviews of the marches, see also Fletcher, "Ch'ing Inner Asia," pp. 58–60; Lin En-hsien, *Qingchao zai Xinjiang*, pp. 3–12.

45. For example, according to the *Jiaqing chongxiu yitong zhi* (530:26326–27), Kokand was part of the Qing empire and a map of the khanate was duly provided showing its relation to other proximate vassal "tribes" (*bu*). Such works made clear, if not precise, distinctions between the boundaries of the empire proper and its vassals. Thongchai Winichakul notes the importance of cultural context for the modern interpretation of older maps produced from a non-Western tradition: "The classification of a local geography and the whole globe as separate categories

The locations of the checkpoints could shift with regional transhumance. Checkpoints could be manned by banner or Green Standard troops as well as by units under the control of Mongol allies or *begs*; their tasks were primarily surveillance and other duties associated with border control. The interstate boundaries of the Qing were thus not garrisoned, and it was often possible to travel for hundreds of kilometers into Qing territory before coming to a checkpoint. It is hardly surprising that checkpoint lines forming the outer perimeter of Qing settlement in Xinjiang were often considered interstate boundaries by foreign neighbors with designs on Qing territory such as the Russians.[46]

By the latter half of the seventeenth century, Xinjiang, once part of the fourteenth-century Chaghadai Khanate of the Mongol empire, had come under the rule of indigenous Naqshbandi Sufi holy men, known as Khojas (*Hezhuo*), Sufi saints whose elite families derived their immense prestige from claims of descent from the Prophet Muhammad. At this time, the *beg* system reached its full development as an indigenous institution of administration. Sufism, especially the Naqshbandiyya and Kubrawiyya orders, was a powerful regional social force in part because its religious leaders could count on considerable political and social support from their masses of disciples. "Attempts to curb their power or restrict their influence were always dangerous, even on occasions when there was undeniably some justification for them."[47]

The two most important sects of Sufism in Xinjiang, known before the Qing conquest as eastern Turkestan (or Moghulistan), were the White Mountain and the Black Mountain (Aqtaghlik and Qarataghlik, respectively). These two rival groups, whose dis-

---

in the indigenous knowledge about space is comparable to the separate classification in modern science today of geography and astronomy or astrophysics" (*Siam Mapped*, p. 31). In the *Jiaqing chongxiu yitong zhi*, the category of space is intended to depict a relation between the Qing suzerain and his foreign tributary. In such a context, precise geographical demarcation may be secondary or even irrelevant, whereas in a different context, the Qing military checkpoint line for example, such demarcation might be paramount. For a similar distinction in the Thai context, see Thongchai, *Siam Mapped*, p. 33.

46. Wei Yunzhi, "Xinjiang kalun."

47. Lapidus, *History of Islamic Societies*, p. 428; Spuler, "Central Asia," p. 477.

agreements were more political than religious, struggled continuously for supremacy.[48] This factionalism, which permeated society at every level, was exploited by all subsequent conquerors of the region. At the same time, Islam proved to be the most important force for the maintenance of East Turkestani identity and the continuing resistance against all would-be conquerors.[49]

Eastern Turkestan's first external conquerors were the Zunghar Mongols, who began their conquest of the southern region of Altishahr in 1678 from their home territory of Zungharia in present-day northern Xinjiang.[50] In the aftermath of this conquest, the Zunghars, pressed by military commitments in Outer Mongolia, did not occupy Altishahr directly. Instead they relied on the indigenous *beg* system in southern Xinjiang, headed by Khoja religious authorities whose families were held hostage in Zungharia, to institute a system of indirect rule in the south.[51]

Immediately after the defeat of the Zunghars in 1755, the Qing initially attempted to perpetuate this system in southern Xinjiang while largely preserving the *jasak* system in the northern steppe. Yet although the Zunghar inhabitants of the Northern March, having been wiped out or deported, were no longer an administrative problem, the Khojas were not willing merely to exchange one set of overlords for another, however indebted they were to the

---

48. Jin, *Yisilanjiao shi*, p. 455. The two sects were also known as the "White Hats" and the "Black Hats."

49. The capacity for Islam to both unite and divide the East Turkestanis is particularly evident in the Jahangir Jihad of 1820–28 (Chen Wangcheng, "Zhanggeer shijian").

50. The Zunghars were one of the four western Mongol, also known as Oirat or Confederate, tribes, who were called the Kalmucks in Turkish. All these terms contrasted the four tribes, who lived in "Outer Mongolia," with the eastern Mongols of "Inner Mongolia." The four tribes were the Torghut, Khoshuut, Choros, and Dorbot. The most powerful tribe of the four, the Choros, later became known as Zunghars, which was originally another designation for all four tribes and means "people of the left hand." There is considerable variation throughout the sources in designations of these tribes. The Oirats, for example, are also known as the Eleuths, and both terms were also used to designate the Choros tribe alone. See Grousset, *Empire of the Steppes*, pp. 519–20; and Millward, *Beyond the Pass*, p. 27.

51. Ma Dazheng and Cai, "Zhungaer guizu," p. 292.

Qing.[52] The Revolt of the Big and Little Khojas, which lasted from 1756 to 1759, ended the political role of the Khojas in the Southern March of Xinjiang, as Altishahr came to be known under the Qing. The revolt convinced the dynasty that it needed a direct military presence in the territory and that it could no longer rely on the Khojas to head the civil administration. Xinjiang's dual system of Qing military residents presiding over a civilian administration staffed exclusively by East Turkestani *begs* was the dynasty's response to the Khojas' revolt.[53]

The Khoja revolt forced the dynasty to modify the Zunghar system of indirect rule, primarily in order to eliminate the Khojas as political authorities and gain more direct control over the local *beg* administrators. This modification was effected mainly by putting Altishahr's civil officials in the *beg* system under the immediate authority of the Qing military officials of the three marches and the ultimate authority of the court in Beijing.[54] In essence, the Qing governed the local East Turkestanis through the *begs*, who ran the day-to-day civil administration of the Southern March. In consequence, among their responsibilities was acting as the region's frontline investigators during the implementation of the opium prohibitions.[55] A 1761 proposal to impose the *baojia* system on the

---

52. Guo, "Tongyi Xinjiang," p. 318. Qing rule, in Chinese sources past and present, is always characterized as a vast improvement over the heavy exactions and hostage system of the Zunghars, who did, however, prohibit the slave trade endemic to the region. The overall impression left by such observations is that Uighur indigenous rule was the least socioeconomically progressive form of organization for the region, a situation that was only improved by Zunghar and Qing rule. For a standard account of this type, see Ma Dazheng and Cai, "Zhungaer guizu," pp. 292–95.

53. *(Qinding) Pingding Zhungaer fanglüe*, 3:2073b, 2077b–78a.

54. Miao, *Boke zhidu*, pp. 24–45; some of these modifications had to be performed more than once. For example, the Qianlong emperor's 1760 attempt to separate church and state by barring *akhunds*, who were official religious functionaries, from participation in civil administrative affairs had to be reinstituted in the wake of the suppression of the Jahangir Jihad in 1828 (*QSL*, DG 9.2.4, 35:313a).

55. Lin En-hsien, *Qingchao zai Xinjiang*, pp. 68–109. Ranks among *begs* were numerous. The *hakim begs* are the ones most frequently encountered in documents relating to opium suppression. They were the general supervisors of all affairs great and small in a particular town and the environs under its jurisdiction. See

Southern March, as had already been done in the Eastern March, was rejected because of the confusion it would create and because of the problem of finding reliable locals to fill the posts.[56]

Han merchants, however, were another matter, and the Qing attempted to impose the *baojia* system on them wherever they appeared in sufficient numbers. In Yarkand, home to approximately 200–400 Chinese merchants in the 1830s, a *baojia* system was used to keep an eye on Han activity.[57] This system could on occasion be projected to cover Muslim settlements after a fashion. A community liaison official was punished in 1840 for failure to detect opium trafficking between Han merchants and the Muslim settlement of Karghalik, one of ten such areas subordinate to the Yarkand regional administration. This official was explicitly labeled Karghalik's community liaison officer, but there is no evidence that the Muslim villagers were themselves organized into *bao* and *jia*.[58]

The hybrid administration of Xinjiang was particularly unstable during the Daoguang period. It combined some of the worst elements of both regional autonomy and military government. On the one hand, the dynastic policy of indirect rule, which was ostensibly intended to avoid the exploitation of East Turkestanis by ethnically alien Qing officials, tended to leave local *begs* largely unsupervised. In some cases, the practice of indirect rule precluded even the most cursory inspections by senior territorial administrators of major Muslim enclaves such as Khotan for fear that members of the official entourages would take this opportunity to practice extortion on the local residents.[59] These problems became particularly clear in the aftermath of one of the most serious local uprisings, the Jahangir Jihad of 1820–28. According to the Imperial Commissioner Na-yan-cheng, the famous Manchu official sent to re-establish stable dynastic rule in Xinjiang after the rebellion,

---

also *Huijiang zeli*, 2:1a. Information on the various gradations of *beg* officialdom can be found in *juan* 2 of this work, as well as in QSG 12:3402–6 and *Huijiang zhi*, 137–200.

56. QSL, QL 26.6.9, 17:126a-b, quoted in Lai, "Qian, Jia, Dao san chao," p. 136.

57. These population estimates are cited in Millward, *Beyond the Pass*, pp. 148–49.

58. Gongzhong jinyan, DG 20.2.19.

59. Lai, "Qian, Jia, Dao san chao," pp. 145–46.

hakim begs (the Muslim equivalent of the Southern March's Qing superintendents) were purchasing their posts from regular Qing officials and recouping their expenses through random exactions once in office.[60]

This venality exemplifies the corrupt connections between *begs* and regular Qing officials, both of whom the throne blamed at various times for regional instability. In general the imposition and maintenance of military rule in Xinjiang, with the consequent downgrading of civil institutions, has been held ultimately responsible for this instability, since the Qing state considered its management of garrison strength more important than its administration of civilian populations.[61] Of equal significance was the deliberate dynastic policy of cutting up Xinjiang into a number of spheres of overlapping authority in order to prevent any one official from gaining control of the territory's enormous garrison. An extreme fragmentation of authority was the result. The watershed events of 1826–30, which culminated in a direct invasion of the Southern March by the Khanate of Kokand (1710–1876), exposed the weakness of Qing control in the region and fundamentally altered its character.

Opium prohibition in Xinjiang occurred within a larger struggle for regional dominance between the Qing dynasty and Kokand, an expansionist Muslim Uzbek state whose foundations had been laid in the mid-eighteenth century in the neighboring Ferghana Valley. The territory of the khanate was a fragment of the previous Uzbek Shaybanid Khanate (1500–1599), which was itself a fragment of the old Chaghadai Khanate.[62] Kokand's periodic attempts to conquer Altishahr, which manifested themselves mainly as internal revolts sparked by the offspring of deposed Khojas living in exile in the khanate, were the main reasons that the region constituted "the weakest appendage of the Ch'ing empire" throughout the tenure of the dynasty.[63]

---

60. Chen Wangcheng, "Zhanggaer shijian," pp. 170–76.

61. Lai, "Qian, Jia, Dao san chao," pp. 272–73.

62. For a concise narrative of the permutations that resulted in the Khanate of Kokand, see Grousset, *Empire of the Steppes*, chap. 8.

63. Fletcher, "The Heyday," p. 395.

The khanate's challenge to Qing rule in Xinjiang was by no means exclusively military. Indeed, long after the Qing had eradicated large-scale military resistance to its rule in Turkestan, problems of local control created or exacerbated by Kokandi trade activities, as well as by religious and cultural affinities with the East Turkestanis of Altishahr, remained endemic. The Kokandis took advantage of these connections even as they sent submissive emissaries to the Qing. They were able to gain local influence because as Uzbeks, they "had racial and religious relation[s] with the Uighur people in Eastern Turkestan, particularly in Kashgaria, as Turkic Muslims. They [thus] had a common antipathy against the Manchurians [Qing] who were pagans to them." This aversion manifested itself in an unending series of plots involving the Kokandis, descendants of Khojas, and various local *begs* to resist the Qing presence in the region.[64]

Before 1820, Kokand and the Qing empire conducted formalized trade relations, and Kokand's penetration into Altishahr had been commercial and cultural rather than military. Kokandi merchants frequented the major towns of Eastern Turkestan and gradually became influential. Their major trade center in the region was at Kashgar, through which they carried on trade with China and the Pamir region in such goods as tea, silk textiles, and rhubarb. They soon came to monopolize this trade and settled down permanently in the region. However, they continued to maintain close ties with their native land, which often used them as its agents and as sources of wealth from which to increase its strength.[65]

Thus, behind a facade of tribute relations, the Kokandis were making preparations to replace Qing regional hegemony with their own. Aside from various military operations designed to occupy areas where the Qing forces were not, the Kokandis worked to exploit various weaknesses of the Qing in Eastern Turkestan. One of the most serious of these was the prevalence of a subculture of smuggling, which made a mockery of Qing efforts at local control and smoothed the way for subsequent Kokandi military operations.

---

64. Saguchi, "Eastern Trade," part III.
65. Ibid., p. 89.

This smuggling traffic in wares of all sorts probably predated the arrival of either the Qing empire or the Khanate of Kokand in Eastern Turkestan. However, Kokand used smuggling not merely for profit but also for power. The infrastructure of smuggling that ran throughout Eastern Turkestan was an interethnic construct composed of various Central Asian traders, many of whom had become permanent residents through marriage with local Uighur women, Chinese traders, border guards, and minor officials.[66] Through this nexus, Chinese officials indirectly colluded with Kokand. Qing documents reveal official fears that Chinese merchants were actively assisting their Kokandi counterparts in evading Chinese government trade regulations and that frontier guards were allowing merchants from the Kokandi trade center of Andijan to bribe them into "inspecting only a part of their merchandise."[67]

These activities were identified by Chinese officials as one cause of the numerous, large-scale upheavals in Eastern Turkestan in and after 1820: "Since the collusion between Khoqandian and Chinese merchants has never come to light, Andijan merchants took full advantage of their bribery tactics to increase their profits in each of the Eastern Turkestan towns. . . . [The Kokandis thus] freely passed the border and lived in [the] thousands in many towns west of Aqsu."[68] There was, thus, an elaborate infrastructure for smuggling goods into Xinjiang that predated the opium traffic and probably the Khanate of Kokand, but served the khanate's regional ambitions. In the early 1830s, transborder opium smuggling in Xinjiang from points west arose in the context of Kokand's continuing attempts to control the commerce of the Southern March by extramilitary means.

From 1759 until approximately 1820, the relations between Kokand and the Qing empire were between nominal vassal and nominal suzerain. However, from the beginning of the nineteenth century, the cracks that began to appear in this relationship foreshadowed Kokand's rise to regional domination and its transition to a new status as an openly independent state. During the 1820s, a

---

66. Ibid., pp. 81, 82, 85–86.
67. Ibid., pp. 53, 81.
68. Slightly modified from translation in ibid., p. 82.

qualitative change in the heretofore relatively peaceful Qing-Kokandi relationship culminated in Kokand's large-scale military incursion into the Southern March in 1830. These forces plundered the western regions of the Southern March and persuaded 20,000 indigenous East Turkestani residents to emigrate when military threats to the khanate by its eastern neighbor Bokhara forced these troops to withdraw.[69] Nevertheless, despite this withdrawal, "Kokand had made her point. Altishahr was remote, difficult to defend and dependent on foreign trade. Kokand, independent, adjacent and protected by a huge mountain range, had achieved a special position in Altishahr and could make endless trouble unless the Ch'ing came to terms. In the invasion of 1830, the empire had lost its bargaining position."[70]

In the negotiations that followed, the Qing made a number of concessions to Kokand that would lead in 1835 to what Joseph Fletcher called "China's first 'unequal treaty' settlement."[71] Initially the dynasty acceded to Kokandi demands in 1833 that it be permitted to establish political and commercial agents in major Southern March trade centers, but it refused to grant the khanate the power to levy customs duties on all foreign merchants operating in the region. Kokandi incursions continued into the nominally Qing territory of Sarikol, itself technically part of Yarkand's administrative region, which stretched west beyond the Xinjiang checkpoint line for over 200 kilometers. Kokand was able to extend its right to tax both the Kazakh and the Kirghiz nomads resident in this region and in the Pamirs with the acquiescence of the court, which now designated the checkpoint line as a kind of quasi

---

69. I have largely followed the periodization and analysis provided by Pan, *Zhongya Haohanguo yu Qingdai Xinjiang*, p. 24. Accounts of the 1830 incursion can be found in Fletcher, "The Heyday," pp. 360–85; and Pan, *Zhongya Haohanguo yu Qingdai Xinjiang*, pp. 119–53. In the various official postmortems both of the numerous and violent upheavals that preceded the 1830 incursion and of the incursion itself, collusion between Kokandi and Qing merchants was seen as an important contributing factor because these connections enabled thousands of Kokandis to pass the border freely and live in the towns west of Aksu (Saguchi, "Eastern Trade," 82).

70. Fletcher, "The Heyday," p. 371.

71. The treaty is discussed in detail in ibid., pp. 375–85.

border. Beyond this, it renounced all responsibility for the protection of nomadic peoples, a policy that continued even after the re-establishment of nominal Qing sovereignty in the region in 1836.[72]

The system was also weakened by the suspension in 1832, in deference to Kokandi demands, of duties paid by foreign merchants at the checkpoints. This simultaneously terminated inspections of foreign wares by Qing officials. This Qing concession would have particular significance for the opium traffic in the territory, as subsequently noted by local officials, because it enabled all merchants entering Xinjiang to smuggle in unharassed a variety of goods, including opium.[73]

The settlement in the 1835 treaty in effect added yet another administrative layer to the Southern March by granting Kokand consular jurisdiction over foreign merchants in the Southern March as well as the power to levy taxes on them. The Daoguang emperor had conceded extraterritorial rights to the Kokandis, who also profited from the duties they levied on goods entering the Southern March. This abdication of local control to the khanate would prove instrumental for the expansion of the Central and South Asian opium traffic into Xinjiang.

Although Qing control of limited urban space was facilitated by the presence of comparatively large numbers of Han residents in the Northern and Eastern Marches, the complex society of the oasis towns of the Southern March proved particularly resistant to incorporation into the Qing empire through the traditional *junxian* bureaucratic structure employed in most towns of the north and east. Furthermore, Xinjiang, because of both its frontier character and its large Inner Asian populations, generally lacked the "unofficial" structures of social control usually associated with Han gentry society that would otherwise have helped to relieve the official administrative burden.[74] In essence, the social effects of the

---

72. Ibid., pp. 375–76, 381.

73. *YPZZ*, DG 19.12.22, 1:785–89.

74. Lin Zexu relied heavily on local gentry in his initial prohibition operations against Han consumers and traffickers in 1839 precisely in order to circumvent the corrupt Guangzhou administration (Wakeman, "Canton Trade," pp. 184–85).

geography of Xinjiang precluded the development of gentry social structures and necessitated rule through the *beg*s in the Southern March.[75]

An extremely complex and variegated administrative apparatus, partly dependent on quasi officials such as *beg*s and local *baojia* personnel and largely unable to penetrate distant and sparsely inhabited rural locales, was the overall result of Xinjiang's historical experience before the implementation of the opium prohibitions. This situation was exacerbated by the ambitions of the Khanate of Kokand, which successfully superimposed its own administrative structure on the Southern March. It was this final administrative layer that proved of decisive importance to opium trafficking in the territory, in that it created a kind of extraterritoriality that sustained and augmented a well-developed system of smuggling, which in turn shielded opium traffickers, among others, from frontier inspections. None of these obstacles to Qing local control would have existed without the Khanate of Kokand, which broke the dynastic monopoly on force so essential to the maintenance of administrative order.

In sum, the administrative heterogeneity of Xinjiang meant continuous regional instability, which made strict enforcement of the prohibitions impossible, especially since the dynasty had suspended its border-control system for foreign merchants after 1832. A similar problem existed in southwestern China, particularly in the province of Yunnan. In contrast, however, there was no well-organized alien state whose machinations acted as a mainstay of the local opium traffic. Instead, administrative blind spots entirely within the provincial boundaries of the empire itself proved fatal to prohibition efforts.

---

75. By 1842 in Hami, for example, there had been a total of only thirty successful candidates for the official exams throughout the dynasty. Moreover, all these men held either the lowest or no official position. Hami, which had had the longest exposure to Han political and cultural influence of any place in Xinjiang, had still not produced a gentry that could mediate between officialdom and the local masses for purposes of tax collection, security, and the like (*Hami zhi*, 46:1a-2a).

The Administration of the Southwest

Like the *beg* system in Xinjiang, the native chieftain system of the southwest was a means of administering the numerous indigenous minority peoples. The existence of this separate administrative jurisdiction provided a relatively inviolate space free of routine central government surveillance. Qing administrative absence was total, however, in the "wild" (*ye*) zones, especially in southwestern Yunnan, inhabited by indigenous peoples under no recognized system of administrative organization connected, however indirectly, to the dynasty. In effect the administrative space of the southwest was divided into three levels that ran the gamut of local control: the *junxian* jurisdictions, the native chieftainships, and the wild zones.

The Ming dynasty witnessed the general administrative consolidation of the southwest into the *junxian* system. Shifts in territorial jurisdiction among administrative regions constituting the borders of the three provinces of Yunnan, Guizhou, and Sichuan continued through the Qing. Moreover, intraprovincial administrative transformations also occurred during this period, most notably that of the administrative conversion of many regions populated by ethnic minorities from indigenous to central government rule (*gaitu guiliu*), which had been pursued since the Ming in one form or another.

Although the overall effect of these changes was to enhance the control of the center throughout the region, this control was neither absolute nor undisputed. Shifts of prefectures from the control of one province to another, often arising from conversion operations, caused disputes not only between Qing forces and those of the expropriated native chieftains but also between groups of provincial officials.[76] Even when successful, conversion operations

---

76. One of the most notable of these conflicts occurred between the provincial administration of Sichuan and Ortai, the imperial official who implemented one of the largest conversion operations of the Qing. Ortai wanted to shift Sichuanese territory to the control of Yunnan to form Wumeng prefecture (later known as Zhaotong prefecture) as an integral part of his strategy for the conversion of Yi ("Lolo") native chieftainships in northeastern Yunnan / southeastern Sichuan between 1726 and 1732 (Kent Clarke Smith, "Development of Southwest China," pp. 138–39).

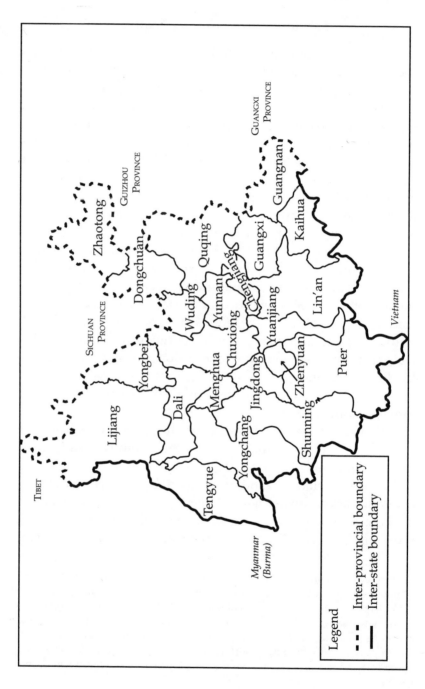

Map 4 Yunnan, prefectures, ca. 1820

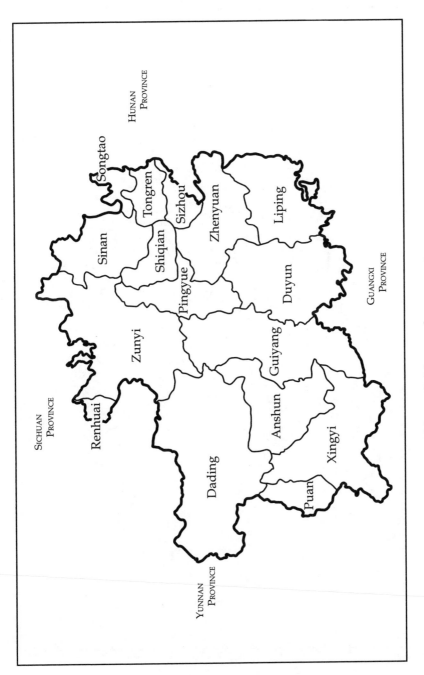

Map 5 Guizhou, prefectures, ca. 1820

SHAANXI
PROVINCE

HUBEI
PROVINCE

HUNAN
PROVINCE

Taiping

Kuizhou

Suiding

Zhong-
zhou Shizhu

Youyang

Baoning

Shunqing

Chongqing

GUIZHOU
PROVINCE

GANSU
PROVINCE

Long'an

Mianzhou

Tongchuan

Xuyong

Maozhou

Chengdu

Zizhou

Xuzhou Luzhou

Maogong Zayu

Qiongzhou

Jiading

Songpan

Meizhou

PROVINCE

QINGHAI

Ningyuan

Yazhou

YUNNAN

TIBET

Map 6. Sichuan prefectures, 1898

were often intended to replace only those at the highest levels of native administration and left the lower administrative levels in the hands of indigenous leaders.[77] Thus, a number of regions underwent a largely nominal conversion, and the native chieftain system persisted at the grassroots level. Moreover, in many areas of indigenous settlement, local, non-Han legal systems, which might be embodied in their own separate written codes, persisted even after conversion operations had been completed.[78] The western and southwestern regions of Yunnan remained particularly impervious to incorporation by the central government.

The native chieftain system of the Qing dynasty was, broadly speaking, a holdover from the Ming dynasty, which had initiated a more systematized and formalized structure of indirect imperial rule in the southwest than had previously existed.[79] The official ranks of this system, filled by indigenous elites of radically varying degrees of assimilation, were formally intended to mirror that of their *junxian* counterparts. They included, for example, a primary division between military and civilian branches of responsibility.[80]

---

77. Even so drastic a conversion policy as Ortai's, however, had quite limited objectives in terms of degree and spatial extent. Ortai, for example, opposed radical assimilationist policies and wished to preserve the lower levels of the native-chieftainship infrastructure, and to transform titles in name only (ibid., pp. 141–42). For further evidence of the continuity of native power at the lowest administrative levels, see You, *Yunnan minzu shi*, pp. 525–26. For an overview of the Chinese scholarship on the complex nature of conversion operations, see Ma Ruheng and Ma, *Qingdai de bianjiang zhengce*, pp. 33–36.

78. Lee, "Law and Ethnicity." I am grateful to the author for his permission to cite this paper.

79. The following overview of the native chieftain system is based on You, *Zhongguo xinan minzu shi*, pp. 362–68; Herman, "Empire in the Southwest," pp. 50–52; Gong, *Tusi zhidu*, pp. 110–12; and Ma Ruheng and Ma, *Qingdai de bianjiang zhengce*, pp. 34–36, 382–406. For a detailed treatment of the Qing reforms of the *tusi* system, which were centered mainly on issues related to inheritance and education, see Herman, "Empire in the Southwest," pp. 52–68.

80. The native chieftain system employed a wide range of terminology that was differentiated not only by administrative category but also by historical era and region. The Yuan formally initiated the system, known as the "native military and civil chieftain system" (*tuguan tusi zhidu*). The ranks and organization generally persisted through the Qing. The civil/military distinction, however, became fully articulated only after the Ming (Gong, *Tusi zhidu*, p. 23n). Herman ("Empire in the Southwest," p. 50) notes that civil native chieftains came under

The native chieftain system did not remain static during the Qing but many of the problems that arose during this period were legacies of the Ming system. Chief among these was that posts in the system, unlike those of the central government, were hereditary, with the higher-level posts occupied by a contumacious indigenous elite.[81] All successions to these offices, whether by son, brother, or widow, had to be approved by the central government. Such nominal central control over the succession to native chieftainships proved insufficient to restrain local elites, who became local tyrants, or, at least, so the Chinese sources inform us.[82]

Worse still, from the court's point of view, were incidents of collusion between native chieftains and Han opponents of Qing rule, such as that between the last Ming claimant to the throne, the Yongli emperor, and a native chieftain in Hunan.[83] The disruptions

---

the supervision of the Board of Personnel, military ones under the Board of War. In contrast, other works classify civil ranks as *tusi* and military ranks as *tubian* (see Li Pengnian et al., *Liubu chengyu cidian*, pp. 152 and 243, respectively). Even this distinction, however, is rather too neat, as demonstrated by Luo Raodian's *Qiannan zhifang jilüe*, p. 339: one group of officials listed as *tusi* are subdivided into those who obtain their patents of rank from the Board of Personnel and those who obtain their patents from the Board of War; a second group, the *tubian*, obtained their commissions from the provincial governor-general rather than from the central government. This group is composed almost exclusively of supernumerary military ranks. Luo's explanation seems to hold good for Guizhou at least, and I am inclined to accept it. If it is correct, supernumerary military ranks were "locally" appointed officials. Nevertheless, the sources are clearly in conflict over the precise nature of the terminology, and Gong persuasively observes that the civil/military distinction was used by imperial courts (seemingly throughout the imperial period) as dictated by time and place but was not really descriptive of the specific functions of the native chieftain officialdom. They were nominal distinctions only and probably mainly significant for purposes of prestige and pay (see Gong, *Tusi zhidu*, p. 23n).

81. Native chieftains generally enjoyed considerable autonomy; see Lombard-Salmon, *La Province du Gui Zhou*, pp. 212–13.

82. Qing officials in turn often tyrannized over native officials and their subjects, with disastrous results for all concerned. Official abuse appears to have been the immediate cause of the 1735 Miao uprising that effectively ended Ortai's activist conversion policies in the southwest (Zhongguo diyi lishi dang'an guan, *Miaomin qiyi*, QL 1.12.15, 1:228–30).

83. Liu Fengyun, *Sanfan*, p. 119n. The effects of interethnic collusion continued to plague the dynasty and constituted one of its most important security concerns in the southwest. Confessions exacted in the wake of the massive and costly

that arose from the incompetence, malice, or resistance of native chieftains often provided Qing forces with pretexts to implement conversion operations in the southwest, the high point of which was the series of operations executed by Ortai, the famous Qing official and imperial confidant, throughout the Yongzheng reign.

Two conflicting themes pervaded Qing relations with the indigenous peoples of the southwest.[84] The first stressed the fundamental alienation of these peoples from the mainstream of imperial institutions and culture, as expressed in the Kangxi emperor's vermilion rescript of 1709 to Guizhou Governor Chen Shen. The emperor cogently summarized this minimalist approach to local control by conveying his sense of the limits of Qing power to transform the region as well as the fundamental contradiction faced by the empire in its relations with the "Miao" (*Miaozu*), a term probably used in this context as a general reference to the indigenous peoples of the southwest.

The native chieftains are of myriad types, and their customs vary. From antiquity the royal regulations were unable to bind them. It is completely impossible to control them as We do the subjects of the interior, and this has been so from the beginning. We must make the best of it and attempt only a general type of control. An excessively stringent application of the law will be a source of endless trouble, but if words and laws are too lenient, this will certainly lead to an extraordinary number of criminal acts. Preventing incidents from occurring must be our main policy, for an excess of incidents will be too costly for Our state to bear.[85]

Qian(long) Jia(qing) Miao Uprising of 1794–96, for example, revealed the participation of *tuman* (i.e., the national minority known today as the *tujia zu*), Han, and Hui, all of whom sought to regain lands taken from them by Han and Miao landlords (Hu, "Qian Jia Miaomin qiyi," pp. 196–97).

84. Scholars have noted the terminological difficulties concerning the precise definition of southwestern indigenous peoples during the imperial period; see, e.g., Lombard-Salmon, *La Province du Gui Zhou*, pp. 110–17. This ambiguity is especially true of the term "Miao," which could stand for a single ethnic group or as a general term for the indigenous people of the southwest as a whole. Despite the inevitable anachronisms, unless otherwise indicated, designations such as "Dai," "Yi" and "Miao" in this book correspond to those used in the contemporary People's Republic of China.

85. *Kangxi chao hanwen zhupi zouzhe*, KX 16.2.1, 1:601.

A typical formulation of the alternative, more activist viewpoint was expressed by one of its most vigorous proponents, Ortai, in a late 1726 memorial advocating intensification of conversion operations. Ortai singled out the native chieftain system as a source of regional strife that could no longer be tolerated and, in the process, noted the effect of regional geographic conditions on conventional bureaucratic institutions.

I think that the Ming's former division of the area into native- and central government–controlled zones originally arose from the new frontier's malarial climate, to which Chinese officials were not accustomed. So, they relied on native chieftains for control, and this led to repression. Now, after many centuries, the policy of "using barbarians to control barbarians" has become "using thieves to control thieves." Miao and Yi [bandits] worry neither about pursuit nor execution, and the native chieftains [being outside the ranks of conventional officialdom] cannot be punished by dismissal or land confiscation. Reports of misconduct regarding bribes used to halt inquiries have been received, but higher officials do not inquire too deeply into these matters . . . so the inhabitants of the border are without appeal. If we do not uproot the sources of these abuses and rectify military, penal, financial, and tax affairs, we will not be able to deal with the fundamental problem of unrest.[86]

For Ortai, the aboriginal officers' position outside the control structure of regular Qing bureaucratic channels was a fundamental cause of regional instability. He believed that "all reports of rogues by Miao (*Miaozu*) and Lo (*Yizu*; i.e., Yi) involve aboriginal officers, who make great depredations without restraint. Under cover of their aboriginal offices and chieftains' authority, they carry out their murderous and thieving plans. Both Han and barbarian are harmed by this, the border's great scourge."[87] Ortai's solution was an intensification of conversion operations.

Regional instability, however significant an issue for the center, was only part of the incentive for conversion. The major structural imperative was regional socioeconomic development, particularly that of the copper-mining industry, which began almost immedi-

86. *QSG*, 34:10231.
87. *Qing jingshi wenbian*, 86:5a.

ately after the defeat of the Three Feudatories in 1681.[88] Although
the Qing initially did not wish to restore the previous system of
official landowning, which had abetted the Ming loyalist Wu San-
gui's regime, the need to raise provincial tax revenues soon forced
the dynasty to permit the sale of land to private cultivators. The
ensuing large-scale Han colonization of the minority areas of
southern Yunnan increased contact between Han immigrants and
the region's indigenous peoples, and stimulated various commercial contacts between them, including traffic in opium. [89]

It has been estimated that this commercial and industrial expansion quadrupled the population of the southwest from five million
in 1700 to twenty million by 1850.[90] The six main southwestern
commercial routes, one connecting the region to Myanmar, one
connecting it to Vietnam, and four connecting it to the rest of
China, experienced a commensurate development. One of the most
important of these routes was the Yangzi River, or Chongqing,
route, which linked southern and eastern Sichuan with the major
eastern trade centers of Hankou and Shanghai. Yunnan's provincial
capital of Kunming was also connected to this southeastern Sichuan
network through the northeastern Yunnanese prefectures of Dongchuan and Zhaotong. Dongchuan, which possessed the largest
number of copper mines in Yunnan, was an important economic
center in its own right. An alternative branch of the Yangzi route
went overland from Kunming via the northwestern Guizhou town
of Bijie in Dading prefecture. Another, more easterly route went
from Kunming to Hankou via the Guizhou provincial capital of
Guiyang. Another route along the West River linked Yunnan to the
Lingnan provinces of Guangxi and Guangdong. Southwestern merchants, as well as those from Hunan, Hubei, Jiangxi, and Guangdong, flocked to the Sichuan-Yunnan-Guizhou border region to

---

88. For an overview of the mines of the southwest, see Lee, *Political Economy
of a Frontier*, chap. 9.

89. You, *Yunnan minzu shi*, pp. 502–3. This wave of Han immigration, which
began around 1700, was the second major influx of people into the southwest during the late imperial period. The first, which was much more ethnically diverse,
occurred over the duration of the Yuan and Ming dynasties (Lee, *Political Economy of a Frontier*, pp. 62, 63, 70).

90. Lee, "Food Supply," p. 712.

trade in all manner of goods, including copper, cotton, salt, and cloth. Opium flowed along all these routes from western Yunnan northward into Sichuan and eastward through Guizhou into Lingnan as well as from Lingnan into the southwest.[91]

Large-scale immigration and its related commercial development were both beneficial and disruptive to dynastic control of the southwest. By the Daoguang reign, Han settlers had penetrated into some of the farthest reaches of the region but could not as yet provide an adequate revenue basis for the central government to effect a thorough socioeconomic conversion to a *junxian* administrative structure.[92] Luo Raodian's 1847 administrative work on Guizhou succinctly summarized the relations between officialdom and the general populace: "Officials must be appointed to open up Guizhou; for officials to be appointed, people must come from all directions [to support them]. The two are without question mutually related." Unfortunately, provincial revenue was insufficient to pay for administrative costs, and Guizhou's administration had to be subsidized, not only for the province's own development but also for continuing control of Yunnan.[93]

An early 1831 land dispute from Tengyue subprefecture, on Yunnan's western border with Myanmar, reveals how Han settlers could serve both to disrupt and to facilitate Qing attempts to maintain administrative order in frontier areas.[94] The case concerned an encroachment by eighty Yi families from the native chieftainship of Nandian on land that lay on the border between it and the district of Zhanxi. The land had been illicitly pawned by a previous native chieftain to Han settlers, who had no title to it but had been

---

91. For a historical overview of Yunnan routes, see Lu, *Yunnan duiwai jiaotong shi.* Ming-Qing studies include Liu Xiusheng, "Guonei shangye jiaotong," pp. 10–11; Chen Hua, *Quyu shehui jingji,* p. 337; and Lee, *Political Economy of a Frontier,* chap. 3. For the flow of opium along these routes, see Benedict, *Bubonic Plague,* pp. 51–53.

92. Lee, *Political Economy of a Frontier,* pp. 29–30.

93. Luo, *Qiannan zhifang jilüe,* pp. 273–74. Actually, neither Yunnan nor Guizhou generated enough revenue to pay for its administrative costs, which often included expensive military operations. The Qing solution was to transfer revenue from more prosperous provinces into the southwest (Zhang Pengyuan, "Luohou diqu de ziben xingcheng," pp. 50–55).

94. This account can be found in Chuxiong Yizu wenhua yanjiusuo, *Wuding Yizu,* DG 11.3.21, #4, pp. 26–30.

working the land for a few generations. The memorialist, Tengyue Subprefectural Magistrate Zhou Shu (served 1829–32), noted that this type of land acquisition was common in places lying adjacent to "tribal areas" (*yifang*), where such "old practices," illegal since 1770, had not been completely eradicated.

The Nandian native chieftain argued that his dispatch of landless Yi families was intended to secure the land from bandits, who were just being brought under control after years of depredations. Prefectural authorities, however, noted that each mountain peak of the region was originally the home of several different groups, some of whom had resisted past attempts by the Nandian native chieftain to subordinate them. These attempts included the installation of a subregional native chieftain by Nandian to coordinate settlement of the area by more compliant peoples. The introduction of the Yi families was part of this strategy, but it met a united resistance by local Han and other "wild tribals" (*yeyi*). A number of Han residents brought the case to prefectural authorities, who were anxious to prevent this localized dispute from expanding into a major border conflict.

Magistrate Zhou Shu was reluctant to enforce the letter of the law, which would have returned the illicitly pawned land to the Nandian native chieftainship, since that would have deprived Han settlers of a livelihood they had come to depend on for generations. Zhou also did not wish to force the Yi families from their newly acquired land for similar reasons. He noted that whatever the law technically required, its spirit was to prevent incidents, and these would surely continue if either side was driven to desperation. In the end, both sides kept their land, but their titles to it were formalized and restricted. Further settlement by Nandian was prohibited, but the native chieftain was to be paid rent by the Han settlers. Zhou Shu was satisfied because he felt that it was advantageous for Han settlers to be present, for they would provide surveillance of the majority tribal populace, which tended to collude with "wild [tribal] bandits." The decision was thus also intended to legitimate the Han presence, which would "firm up our frontier pickets," since the nature of tribals was as undependable as that of "dogs and sheep." Zhou's attitude was consistent with that of many local officials, who had a marked preference for Han colonists. Han settlement of recently pacified areas was thought to stabilize them and was promoted by some local officials, even though it was generally acknowledged that such influxes were a major cause of conflict between Han settlers and indigenous peoples.[95]

The Tengyue case is representative of the tensions that accompanied dynastic expansion into the southwest. The conflict between Han settlers and indigenous peoples, who often lost their land through economic transactions, is a typical tension. It is, however, impossible to distinguish between competing groups on the basis of ethnicity alone, for, as this case also shows, some indigenous groups could side with Han settlers against neighboring tribals. Indeed, in this particular case, the main source of conflict was the Nandian native chieftainship's attempt to consolidate its jurisdiction, via a subregional native chieftainship, over indigenous peoples resident in part of Nandian.

There were also conflicts between the prefectural authorities of the *junxian* system and the Han settlers as well as between the authorities and native chieftains. These are particularly interesting because they illustrate the larger dilemma faced by the dynasty in its attempt to consolidate its rule over the southwest. For provincial officialdom, Han settlers were a mixed blessing: they were the most reliable sources of frontier stability and revenue, but they were also a major cause of costly frontier incidents involving the indigenous peoples. Native chieftainships were viewed in a similar fashion: they were often the only way to keep order among the bewildering diversity of the indigenous populace, but their largely unsupervised activities could prove just as disruptive to local order. Aside from alliances based on ethnic affinities, provincial officials were also troubled by the rich possibilities for interethnic collusion for economic benefit among their multiethnic charges.[96]

Attempts to control the southwest's diverse and mobile populations, most directly through the *baojia* system, often followed the Han immigrants, who often could not be controlled by native

---

95. Lombard-Salmon, *La Province du Gui Zhou*, p. 242.

96. For many of the same patterns in Qing frontier policy in Taiwan, see Shepherd, *Taiwan Frontier*, chap. 1.

chieftains. Ethnic tensions, exacerbated by mobility, no doubt in part reflected the preferences of local officials like Magistrate Zhou Shu.[97] Population registration is an important indicator of the degree of administrative control exerted by provincial authorities over an area, since it is a prerequisite for revenue extraction and other regular administrative activities, including enforcement of the opium prohibitions. To judge from registration figures, administrative control in the southwest was not high throughout most of the Qing period. During initial registration efforts in the 1740s, for example, "at least half the southwestern population did not register." No formal registration of non-Han ethnicities was even attempted before 1756. Furthermore, these statements are only generally applicable to the region as a whole. Many prefectural and subprefectural localities reported no population figures at all, perhaps because they had yet to organize *baojia* units. Finally, "all residents in the areas under native rule continued to be excluded from registration . . . [although] non-Han in areas under control of the central government were included in the reported population. . . . Han who lived within native jurisdictions were almost always excluded from the regularly reported population."[98]

It should be emphasized that the presence of either the *baojia* or the native chieftain system in a region was not a decisive determinant of the ethnicity of the local inhabitants, whose precise ethnic composition remains unclear.[99] The immediate cause of the large-scale uprising in the Miao Territory (Miaojiang) of southeastern Guizhou in 1873, for example, was the local Han subprefectural magistrate's attempt to use the existing *baojia* system to extort

---

97. As Han immigrants entered southeastern Guizhou, for example, local officials requested that the resulting mixed population of Han and Miao be registered under the *baojia* because of the native chieftainships' inability to control the immigrants (*QSL*, DG 6.6.29, 34:624b–25a).

98. Lee, "Food Supply," pp. 721–24.

99. It has been estimated, for example, that the non-Han populace comprised over 56 percent of Guizhou's total inhabitants in the eighteenth century and that the Han did not constitute the majority until the second half of the nineteenth century (Lombard-Salmon, *La Province du Gui Zhou*, p. 170). James Z. Lee (*Political Economy of a Frontier*, pp. 101–5), however, has stated that exact figures are lacking and that it is only certain that non-Han outnumbered the Han.

money from its Miao members. The intimate relationship between territory and ethnicity is exemplified by the existence of the ethno-geographic term "Miao Territory," which was inhabited primarily by "uncivilized" Miao (*sheng Miao*).

Xu Jiagan's 1878 account of this region demonstrates the complexities facing any attempt to determine precisely the ethnic composition of a southwestern locale amid the contemporary socioeconomic transformation. Xu observed that the local Miao stockades were so wild and remote that "civilization" (*zhengjiao*) could not penetrate them. There also were "Han who have been assimilated into Miao" (*Hanmin bian Miao*) as a result of settler interaction with the locals. Finally, there were relatively permeable enclaves of "civilized" Miao (*shu Miao*), "over half" of whom were Han and their offspring who had gone native. To add further ethno-geographic complexity, Han surnames were not reliable indicators of ethnic identity, since many Miao had adopted them.[100]

One method by which Qing administrators sought to maintain control over this diversity was to group various conglomerations of Miao, as well as other southwestern indigenous peoples, into "tribes."[101] In some sense these methods were an administrative acknowledgment of the existence of what C. Pat Giersch, borrowing

---

100. Xu Jiagan, *Miaojiang*, pp. 162–63, 199. Aibida's 1749 work, *Qiannan shilüe*, which contains unattributed interpolations from the later Jiaqing and Daoguang reigns, lists a number of Han surnames adopted by the Miao of Songtao subprefecture in northeastern Guizhou and notes that assimilated Han were known as "assimilated [into] Miao" (*bian Miao*) (p. 171; quoted in You, *Yunnan minzu shi*, p. 689). Han inhabitants of Anshun prefecture, who, according to local accounts, had arrived in the early Ming, were also said to have become indistinguishable from the indigenous Miao (Luo, *Qiannan zhifang jilue*, p. 282). For an example of administrative confusion over the precise ethnic identity of regional transfrontiersmen, see Giersch, "A Motley Throng," 85–87.

101. As Norma Diamond ("Defining the Miao," pp. 92–100) has shown, the Miao, even today, are spatially, linguistically, economically, and culturally diverse; in essence, the Miao identity was an externally imposed Han construct, which arose initially from late Ming Yunnan-Guizhou gazetteers' distinctions between wild and civilized types. The court was extremely sensitive to ethnic identification to facilitate its largely futile attempts to keep the diverse residents of the southwest separate and peaceful while weeding out disruptive elements from among all of them.

from Richard White's work on Algonquin-European relations, has termed the "middle ground" of Yunnan. This is a dynamic and not always physical space in which indigenous peoples, Han settlers, the Qing state, and its Southeast Asian neighbors interacted to form relations beyond the exclusive control of any one of these groups.[102] Southwestern administrative discourse, however, went beyond a simple binary of controlled or uncontrolled space to construct the region in a more complex fashion; state perceptions of "ground control" were more nuanced than assumed within the middle-ground approach.

Whatever the ethnic components of their resident populations, distinct ethno-geographic spheres of influence within the southwestern provinces were acknowledged in the terminology of official communications. Local officials sometimes distinguished, for example, between shared boundaries of Qing native chieftainships (*jing*) and those of centrally administered Qing prefectures (*bian*). In this terminology, "Yunnan" chieftainships like Gengma could be characterized as "beyond the border" (*bianwai*).[103]

These discursive distinctions were intended to describe the limits of dynastic local administration in both spatial and ethnic terms. They were predicated on a fundamental intraprovincial bisection commonly expressed as *neidi* and *waidi*. *Neidi* is translatable as "Yunnan proper" and refers to that part of the province under direct *junxian* administration. *Waidi* is used to describe territory outside this kind of administration, although it does not inevitably refer to areas entirely outside nominal Qing sovereignty. An essay written by Liu Bin, who served as a private secretary to Yongbei prefecture regional military commander Wang Yigui during the 1710s, exemplifies the practical significance of this ethno-geographic terminology for local administration. "On the Native Chieftainships of Yongchang [Prefecture]," which also covers those in Shunning prefecture, is in part devoted to clarifying the distinction between the "tribals of Yunnan proper" (*neidi zhi yi*), "the tribals

---

102. Giersch, "A Motley Throng," pp. 72–73.
103. *Xu Yunnan tongzhi gao*, 5:3977–81; *Yongchang fu zhi*, 437b; *Yongchang fu wencheng*, vol. 20, 13:3a.

beyond Yunnan proper" (*waidi zhi yi*), and the "border tribals" (*yanbian zhi yi*) in southwestern Yunnan.[104]

Liu began by admitting that the difference between the barbarians of Yunnan proper and those of the border was purely geographic, and he subsequently lumped the two groups together as tribals of Yunnan proper. Liu's primary distinction was between those tribals who lived in *neidi* intermixed with Han populations and were under some form of direct administrative control and those who lived in *waidi*, who were under control "in name only but are not actually subordinated to us." These "wild people" (*yeren*) were in truth not under Qing control at all. Moreover, some groups who would technically be classified as border tribals because of their location, were actually *waidi* in administrative terms. The region of Gengma, a native chieftainship from 1585 to 1934, is categorized as "beyond Yunnan proper" (*waidi*), and Liu stated that consequently "the laws do not reach there." In Liu's experience, then, native chieftainships were operationally *waidi* and exerted little if any control on behalf of the dynasty over their extensive territories in southwestern Yunnan.[105]

Official references to "tribal territory" that do not explicitly tie indigenous peoples to the native chieftainship system seem intended to refer to these "wild" groups, who did not belong to any dynastic administration direct or otherwise. A number of sources from southwestern Yunnan define wild tribals as independent groups of indigenous peoples living in specific areas, both within and beyond Qing territory, and entirely free of any type of administrative incorporation by either the dynasty or its major regional rival, Myanmar. Despite this general consensus, the sources disagree whether wild tribals constitute a specific ethnic group. Some sources use the term to describe the political and social conditions of subdivisions within a major ethnic group, such as the Dai;

---

104. *Yongbei fu zhi*, 1:82b, 134a; Liu Bin, "Yongchang *tusi* lun," 3:2131b–32a. Li Genyuan's periodization of Liu's pieces as Ming dynasty works is in error, as demonstrated from internal evidence in all of Liu's essays cited herein and in Li's own compilation as well as biographical material from *Yongbei fu zhi*; *Yongchang fu wencheng*, vol. 12, 9:5a–7b.

105. Liu Bin, "Yongchang *tusi* lun," 3:2131b–32a.

others define "wild tribals" as an ethnonym distinct from the Dai and other major groups.[106] Whatever their precise status, wild tribals constituted a third, "wild" dimension, which could physically extend into the geographical space of Qing Yunnan, but remained beyond the province's operational administrative space. In consequence, local officials considered any problem involving peoples beyond prefectural *bian* to be largely or entirely administratively insoluble.

The terminological nuances of local administration in Yunnan reveal a concrete microcosm within the province in which distinctions between *neidi* and *waidi* refer not to borders between ethnically and politically distinct states but to boundaries between certain forms of ethno-geographically determined organization inside a single province of a particular state. These boundaries could form an acknowledged administrative middle ground, namely, chieftainship *jing*, within the ostensible confines of southwestern provinces that were at best semipermeable to imperial legislation and surveillance. They could also form interstitial wild spaces in or around any jurisdiction that would remain impervious to any sort of dynastic control; this lack of control rendered such spaces administratively "ungrounded." By the Daoguang period, the expansion of Han settlement within the southwest, although considerable, had yet to effect a thorough administrative transformation of both chieftainship and wild spaces into the more uniform, stable, and therefore more manageable ground of the *junxian* system.

Qing local administration was further limited by the fact that middle ground and ungrounded spaces were by no means restricted to regions at the extremities of Han expansion such as southwestern Yunnan. In another essay, devoted to stressing the importance of geography for control of the indigenous peoples throughout Yunnan, Liu Bin noted that whereas the prefectures of Dongchuan and Zhaotong had been transformed into units under control of the *junxian* system during Ortai's 1725 conversion operations, the two prefectures' vast expanses and deep mountains still concealed large numbers of indigenes who caused disrup-

---

106. See, e.g., accounts in *Shunning fu zhi*, 1:508–10; and *Yongchang fu zhi*, 332b.

tions.[107] Areas like these, which constituted the Yunnan side of the tri-provincial northeastern border with Sichuan and Guizhou, were the administratively ungrounded wild zones in which opium transgression proliferated at the interstices of provincial authority.

If the administrative structures of the *junxian* and native-chieftain systems were not perfectly congruent with the ethnic identity of the populations they were intended to control, these structures did determine the extent and degree of Qing bureaucratic control within a given area and were themselves initially determined in large measure by a locale's preponderant ethnicity rather than by territorial criteria.[108] As the rationales for, and the persistence of, conversion operations indicate, the *junxian* system was the center's preferred form of local administration for purposes of revenue collection, resource extraction, and often long-term local security. In general, areas under the domination of native chieftains remained at best partially under Qing bureaucratic control and surveillance throughout the eighteenth and nineteenth centuries.[109]

Of course, Liu Bin's ethno-geographic anatomies of Yunnan reflect the administratively determined perceptions of local Qing officials, rather than an objective situation permeating the entire prov-

---

107. Liu Bin, "Lun quan Dian xingshi," 3:2150a.

108. The case of the civilized Miao is problematic if, as maintained by Xu Jiagan, they consisted largely of Han who had gone native. It is not entirely clear, for example, whether a critical mass of such people was crucial for establishing the *baojia* and other *junxian* institutions in a particular locale. James Z. Lee ("Food Supply," p. 724) concludes from his examination of population records that "population registration [which was itself an indicator of a territory's incorporation into the *junxian* system] was mainly a function of territory, not, as has been thought, of ethnicity." This statement requires qualification insofar as the territories themselves were often ethnically determined and it was mainly due to immigration, which was often semilegal at best, that population registration began to transcend the boundaries of the Han ethnicity. Moreover, this contention ignores the determining role of malaria both demographically and politically. Actually, both territory and ethnicity were important in this process and difficult to separate in practice.

109. Lee, from the perspective of population registration, provides extensive evidence for the exemption of "land under native jurisdiction" and "areas with semiautonomous jurisdictions" from official surveillance through 1851 (see his "Food Supply," pp. 725–27).

ince. His essays may be taken as representative of a kind of southwestern semiofficial discourse ultimately intended to maintain, if not always expand, the province's administratively grounded spaces. The southwestern opium traffic was an immediate imperative for this expansion during the Daoguang reign, because many transactions took place in the middle-grounded and ungrounded spaces created and sustained by ethno-geographic diversity.

At the turn of the nineteenth century, the mines of the southwest, which had done so much to stimulate dynastic socioeconomic and political expansion in the region, went into an irreversible decline because of excessive production costs. Population growth slowed, and the economy stagnated. Large-scale interethnic feuding between Han and Hui, sometimes involving thousands, broke out in various areas of Yunnan, including the western prefectures of Shunning and Yongchang. Banditry, most notably by the Sichuanese Guolu gangs, increased and created further disruptions. Bandits were particularly active along the Yunnan-Sichuan border and, among other activities, became involved in opium smuggling.[110] Indeed, opium served as one important, possibly the most important, substitute for mining in the subsequently reduced economic circumstances of the southwest.[111]

Ethno-geographic diversity in the Qing southwest hindered the development of *junxian* structures in ways broadly similar to those found in contemporary Xinjiang, because it necessitated the establishment of non-Han administrative intermediaries, native chieftains rather than *begs* in this case, between the dynasty and its indigenous subjects. The motives for Qing penetration of the southwest, however, were primarily economic and of long stand-

---

110. For the disruptions in Shunning, Tengyue, and Yongchang, see *Shunning fu zhi*, 1:508–10, 513, 526. You, *Yunnan minzu shi*, pp. 566–67, gives a somewhat different account of the conflicts among native chieftainships in Shunning. For conditions in Sichuan, see Duan Yu, *Sichuan tongshi*, 6:1–6, 13–14. For factors leading to the socioeconomic and demographic stagnation of the southwest as a whole, see Lee, "Food Supply," p. 743.

111. For an argument that opium was the major form of capital formation in the southwest, defined as Guizhou and Yunnan provinces, from the second half of the nineteenth century through the Republican period, see Zhang Pengyuan, "Luohou diqu de ziben xingcheng," pp. 55–60, 64–67.

ing, whereas those of the northwest were largely strategic in character and relatively late in developing. It has been argued that the
southwest's general inability to pay for its own administrative incorporation was the major impetus for state economic development of the region during the Qing.[112]

One consequence of this difference in the administrative trajectories of the northwest and the southwest was the comparatively
more intensified colonization of the southwest, especially in the
form of conversion operations, which resulted in an almost continuous state of interethnic conflict. This ultimately caused a major
destabilization of Qing rule during the Panthay Rebellion (1856–73),
which saw the establishment of the Muslim Pingnan Sultanate under Du Wenxiu.[113] Perhaps even more disruptive for the central
government was the transethnic unity, which appears to have been
largely class based, that arose from contact between Han and the
locals. Such unity is visible in Zhou Shu's land dispute case and in
the presence of Han officials in the Pingnan Sultanate.

If the ethnic divisions embodied in the native chieftainship and
junxian systems created enclaves that were difficult for official investigators to penetrate, contact between ethnicities helped to
stimulate local opium production and commerce. This permitted
Han merchants to obtain opium from native chieftainships during
their trading excursions to these areas. Furthermore, the existence
of wild enclaves, especially in southwestern Yunnan, constituted a
safe zone outside all direct and indirect official control where traffickers and indigenous producers could freely mix.

In general the southwest was fatally linked to state policy in
both prosperity and disaster. State economic activism could and
did stimulate considerable regional development, but the withdrawal of vital state support swiftly reversed gains. Moreover, the
economic development of the southwest was quite uneven and focused primarily on urban areas and mining regions. Consequently,

---

112. Lee, *Political Economy of a Frontier*, pp. 30–31.

113. Liu and Smith, "The Military Challenge," pp. 212–14. "Panthay" is a Burmese term for the Muslims of Yunnan (Yule and Burnell, *Hobson-Jobson*,
pp. 669b–70a). Muslims would play an important role in the southwestern opium
traffic during the Daoguang period. See Chapter 6 for details.

positive state intervention generally did not occur in areas without towns, mines, or Han settlers. The opium traffic was in part a product of the instability that arose in southwestern peripheries having little or no access to the prosperity created by state development of the mining industry.

Uneven economic development combined with dynastic ethnic policy brought enormous disruption without ensuring long-term stability. The dynasty's motives for developing the southwest were based on the center's needs for monetary metals and on the necessity to clear provincial deficits, which constituted a drain on central revenues.[114] Fundamental policy decisions were thus made primarily in the interests of the center and only secondarily in those of the southwest. As a result of the irregular development engendered by this approach, many of the benefits of state intervention had disappeared by the mid-nineteenth century, and the turbulent legacy that remained exacerbated the regional opium problem and helped it to spread beyond the region.

Ethno-Geographic Diversity
and the Limits of Local Administration

The ethno-geographic diversity of the Qing empire both necessitated administrative diversification and made local control a more complex problem for the dynasty. The government attempted to respond by tailoring its regional administration to local conditions. Nevertheless, in many areas the center was ultimately interested in achieving a level of territorial incorporation that was attainable only through the imposition of the *junxian* system of administrative organization and control.

Such a system, however, was far from perfect, since it was vulnerable to innumerable forms of official malfeasance and indifference. Yet it did provide greater intelligence and access for official law enforcement than structures of indirect rule or wild zones, and the *baojia* system itself remained the primary medium for the

114. Lee, *Political Economy of a Frontier*, p. 196; Zhang Pengyuan, "Luohou diqu de ziben xingcheng," pp. 50–55.

implementation of the opium prohibitions among the populace. As subsequent chapters show, it also seems to have retarded illicit opium cultivation in several southeastern coastal provinces.

Of course, the *baojia* system was a tool of purely domestic enforcement and, as such, was unable to reach the Euro-American traffickers of the southeast coast. These and their Inner Asian counterparts in the northwest constituted wild zones of their own. Both groups, moreover, were able to establish spheres of quite localized control inside imperial territory itself in both Guangzhou and the Southern March. Finally, these domestic enclaves maintained links with India and Inner Asia, all of which were completely beyond the dynasty's reach. These inviolate areas would prove fatal for the dynasty's struggle to prohibit opium.

Qing authority was also limited inside the borders of the empire. As the structure of both the southwestern and the Xinjiang administrations shows, the prefectural borders of a Qing province did not necessarily delineate provincial administrative control. Aside from the obvious compromise of dynastic authority represented by the native chieftainship and *beg* systems, there existed large areas within some provinces and territories in which a Qing political vacuum existed for purposes of sustained local control. This condition is especially apparent in southwestern Yunnan, which would become the center of the empire's local cultivation problem during the Daoguang reign.

All these administrative blind spots arose as much from the success of Qing expansionism as from the weakness of Qing government. The dynasty steadily pursued an unprecedented course of territorial conquest, consolidation, and incorporation throughout much of the eighteenth century and attempted to continue the last two operations into the nineteenth. Specific plans for consolidation and incorporation of these territories, however, were fundamentally determined by the interests of the center, rather than those of the territories themselves. Consequently, state-sponsored administrative and economic development in these areas occurred only to the extent that the center benefited. The primacy of central interest thus created a military government in Xinjiang and uneven economic development in the southwest.

In terms of the opium problem, the primacy of central interests was significant because it created or exacerbated confrontations with indigenous peoples throughout the empire's western frontiers as well as created or perpetuated economic inequalities, all of which would later facilitate the opium traffic and hinder prohibition. Indeed, the sheer extent of the expanded empire's administrative responsibilities served to weaken an already overextended officialdom. These problems alone made prohibition an immense task and no doubt encouraged the dynasty to define the opium problem as one primarily of coastal urban smuggling. In short, the lineaments of Qing administration substantially determined the dynasty's perception of the opium problem and its consequent prescription.

The interaction between perception and prescription was also a product of the interaction between center and locality, the southeast coast in this case. The state's general prohibition policy was initially formulated on the basis of the southeast coast's experience with opium in the context of a *junxian* administration. The southeast coast thus remained the paradigmatic ground of Qing opium prohibition even after it became clear that the drug problem could not be regionally or administratively confined.

FOUR

The Han Core and
Policy Formation

The opium problem was clearly centered in China's southeast coastal provinces, a fact that influenced the court's formation of prohibition policy. To put the Qing government's actions in perspective, it is necessary to examine the interplay between the policymaking center in Beijing and the paradigmatic ground of implementation in the provinces of Fujian, Zhejiang, and Guangdong. This imperative arises because opium prohibition as the dynasty understood and practiced it was not aimed exclusively at Euro-American coastal traffickers. In fact, the central authorities saw them largely as indirect targets. Instead, the weight of dynastic prohibition fell on the poppy-growing, drug-smuggling, opium-smoking subjects of Qing China.

A focus on the state's formation and prosecution of these three major categories of opium offenses takes the analysis beyond the walls of Guangzhou's foreign compound and, ultimately, beyond the local administrations of the coastal provinces. This more general focus on prohibition permits an empirewide view of the Qing opium problem, the actual field of dynastic perception. By exploring the diversity of the problem rather than limiting ourselves narrowly to coastal foreign trafficking, we can understand how opium spread beyond its coastal origins to root itself throughout Qing soil.

I first present a general overview of opium prohibition as a product of the interaction between the imperial center and the drug problem's initial concentration in the southeast coastal region.

The succeeding sections of this chapter focus on important structural obstacles to the success of prohibition, drawing on examples from both central and local records. The scale of the analysis precludes a detailed account of every central policy decision on each violation committed in all the provinces and territories of the empire. Rather, the main intent is to present an account of the major elements of Qing prohibition as implemented primarily on the coast and secondarily in the rest of the Han core of China proper.

The Local Roots of Central Prohibition Policy

The Chinese historical experience with other addictive consumables such as tobacco, alcohol, and tea was useless in dealing with the disruption caused by opium. Although originally impelled by the addictive qualities of the drug, the state's confrontation with opium ultimately escalated to a full-scale conflict, which involved not only a domestic war on drugs but also an armed interstate conflict with Great Britain. Yet these struggles began in earnest only when the Daoguang emperor and his senior officials decided in the 1830s that an opium smoking epidemic was draining the country of silver, the lifeblood of state revenues and interprovincial commerce. Despite previous indications that opium trafficking and cultivation had spread to the interior, the early 1830s also mark the beginning of the period in which the government recognized that opium was no longer limited to the southeast coast and was becoming a transprovincial, multifaceted problem. The Qing court's conviction that the opium traffic was both causing the silver drain and spreading unchecked throughout the empire produced increasingly draconian policies, including capital punishment, intended to eradicate the drug from the empire.

The state's decision to implement an absolute prohibition arose within a historical context of two centuries of fitful bans. Although officials devoted no sustained attention to the opium problem over this time, the policies and practices of the 1830s were influenced by the dynasty's previous experience with opium as a contraband drug of overseas origin. The most important aspect of this historical legacy was the notion that there was an intimate relationship between foreign opium and the empire's southeastern coastal provinces, especially Guangdong, the drug's primary distribution and consumption center. This regionally circumscribed view of the opium problem thus determined the formation of central government prohibition policy even after it became clear that opium had spread into the imperial interior and literally taken root throughout the western frontiers of the Qing domain.

Despite the ethno-geographic diversification of opium, central government policy continued to focus on southeast coastal smuggling, which did indeed account for the bulk of the opium in Qing China in the 1830s, as the central problem. The questionable belief that the eradication of one particular aspect of the problem would automatically end all opium production, distribution, and consumption remained another important continuity in government policy formation. This belief also led the state to concentrate its prohibition resources on southeastern coastal suppression.

A single report during the sixth year of the Yongzheng reign in December 1728 laid the foundations for the state's conviction that the opium problem was essentially a matter of maritime trafficking. Su Mingliang, a regional military commander (*zhenzong bing*) in the Army of the Green Standard in Guangdong, proposed that punishments for various offenses be increased. One of these was a failure to detect the crime Su held to be a major source of Guangdong banditry, namely opium trafficking. Su charged that merchants from both Fujian and Guangdong were particularly active in the Fujian locales of Xiamen and Taiwan in the trade in crude opium, which was to be mixed with tobacco and smoked under the pretense it was for medicinal purposes. Su focused on traffickers mainly because he felt that prohibition of consumption would simply provide local officials with another pretext for extortion.[1]

Su's report and recommendations provided the basis for the first opium prohibition statutes, promulgated in 1729. In general, these laws reflected the regional character of the contemporary opium problem and were concerned almost exclusively with coastal trafficking in opium smuggled in from overseas. The punishment was the same as that for dealing in other contraband: a month in the

---

1. *Yongzheng chao hanwen zhupi zouzhe*, YZ 6.11.6, 13:848b–53b, cited in Wang Hongbin, *Jindu shijian*, pp. 20–21.

cangue and military exile for life. Exile in particular, as we shall see, was a problematic solution because it contributed to the spread of opium to the interior. Provisions were also made for the punishment of accessories, such as maritime customs superintendents (*haiguan jiandu*) guilty of malfeasance in connection with enforcing opium prohibition. These statutes were supplemented in 1730 by regulations that specifically targeted itinerant traffickers in Taiwan, who were to be returned to their native places on the mainland.[2] Both Han Chinese smokers and foreign, probably Portuguese, traffickers certainly existed on the island as early as 1723–24, as noted in several contemporary Chinese accounts.[3]

One of the few aspects of these regulations that was not explicitly connected with coastal trafficking but would become a defining characteristic of the most extreme prohibition policies was capital punishment, which in 1729 was exclusively reserved for opium den (*yapian guan*) operators. Death by strangulation, after a final review of the case during the annual autumn assizes, was prescribed for opium den operators, on the basis of an analogy with those who "deluded the populace" by spreading heterodox beliefs. The connection between the metaphorical and the mundane opium of the people is clearer in several reports linking Christianity with coastal opium consumption during the Jiaqing reign. An 1814 court letter from the emperor to senior Guangdong officials, for example, demanded a more active prohibition of these two harmful foreign imports.[4] Such formulations and attributions helped fix the foreign nature of opium in the mind of the state.

The only prosecution for violation of these new opium prohibitions during the Yongzheng era and the succeeding Qianlong reign

---

2. *Da Qing lü li tongkao jiaozhu*, pp. 621, 623. *HDSL*, 9:513a, 1013b, incorrectly and inexplicably notes the date the regulations were promulgated as the ninth year of Yongzheng (1731). A case from the seventh year of the Yongzheng emperor's reign makes it clear, however, that these prohibition regulations were already being enforced by mid-1729 (*Yongzheng chao hanwen zhupi zouzhe*, YZ 7.7.26, 15:901–2). Finally, there is some evidence that opium was originally banned in the late Ming; see Appendix A.

3. Spence, "Opium Smoking," p. 147.

4. *Qingdai waijiao shiliao*, JQ 12.11.16, 2:8a–9a, and JQ 19.5.4, 4:19a–b; *YPZZ*, JQ 19.5.4, 1:11–12, and JQ 20.3.23, 1:18–19.

that has come to light confirmed the coastal nature of the opium problem and also revealed the existing statutes to be seriously flawed. In August 1729 a merchant, Chen Yuan, was apprehended in Zhangzhou, Fujian, after he sold twenty kilos of opium to a police agent. It was eventually determined that this was legal medicinal opium, and this distinction saved Chen from exile. His arrest was overturned by the provincial governor with imperial concurrence. In order to avoid giving the populace the impression that the opium prohibitions were a dead letter, the prefect who arrested him was not punished for his mistake.[5]

Such an impression is, however, unavoidable given the complete lack of unambiguous cases from the official record for the next 75 years, between 1729 and 1806, even though the Yongzheng prohibitions were retained in the subsequent Qianlong-era code.[6] The considerable confusion over what constituted illegal opium may account for the dearth of cases.[7] The continued import of legal crude opium for medicinal purposes, which can be traced as far back as 1589 under the Ming dynasty, must have contributed to the legal muddle. Records from the Kangxi reign dated 1662 and 1687 confirm that medicinal opium was indeed being imported and taxed in Guangdong, whose senior provincial officials additionally affirmed the drug's legality throughout the Yongzheng and Qianlong periods during their 1836 review of the traffic. The continuation of opium's legitimate status after the formal promulgation of prohibition is also attested by trade records from 1755.[8]

In effect, legal opium and illicit opium mixed with tobacco existed simultaneously from 1729 until the first decade of the nineteenth century. Despite the apparent domestic suspension of

---

5. *Yongzheng chao hanwen zhupi zouzhe*, YZ 7.7.26, 15:901–2, and YZ 8.2.16, 17:943–44. This case has received considerable attention from scholars; see, e.g., *Yapian zhanzheng* 1:329–31; Spence, "Opium Smoking," pp. 156–57; and Wang Hongbin, *Jindu shijian*, pp. 18–20. It has even been translated into English; see Fu, *Documentary Chronicle*, 1:162–64.

6. *Da Qing lü li tongkao jiaozhu*, pp. 621, 623.

7. Edkins, *Historical Note*, pp. 45–46; Fu, *Documentary Chronicle*, 1:163, 519n; Spence, "Opium Smoking," pp. 148–49; Wang Hongbin, *Jindu shijian*, p. 19. All four authors, Edkins earliest among them, call attention to the confusion between medicinal and smokable opium. Wang provides the most recent analysis to date.

8. Edkins, *Historical Note*, pp. 25, 45, 49–51; YPZZ, DG 16.7.27, 1:205–6.

prohibition during the Qianlong era, European maritime traders for the East India Company took it seriously enough to discourage attempts to sell crude opium directly from Company ships in China between 1750 and 1782.[9] Their caution suggests the persistence of dynastic prohibition of the clandestine traffic in opium, but concrete Chinese evidence remains scant.[10] It is possible that prohibition was selectively enforced at key points of maritime contact, even though domestic bans were relaxed until the early nineteenth century because it was believed that opium had to be adulterated with other substances at coastal ports like Xiamen before it could be smoked.[11] Whatever the actual degree of enforcement, the court clearly took a dim view of opium. In a memorial from 1776, Cao Xuemin, a minister from the Court of the Imperial Stud (Taipu si), requested that "water tobacco" (*shuiyu*), which was used in hookahs, be prohibited and compared its harmful physical effects to those of "Fujian opium" (*Fujian yapian*). The tobacco was duly banned by imperial decree.[12]

Despite the numerous ambiguities in the record before the nineteenth century, the court clearly considered opium a minor irritant confined to coastal areas of Guangdong and Fujian. This attitude would change within a decade or so of the accession of the Jiaqing emperor in 1796, a change caused both by a shift away from the smoking of opium-tobacco mixtures to the smoking of

---

9. Edkins, *Historical Note*, pp. 49–51; Morse, *International Relations*, 1:174; Morse, *Trading to China*, 1:215, 288–89, 301, and 2:20, 77–78; Van Dyke, "Port Canton," chap. 2.

10. The single case of smoking from the Qianlong reign concerns a Zhejiang native caught smoking *yan* in Beijing. This term could have referred either to opium mixed with tobacco or simply tobacco itself; see Junji chajin, QL [year not given].8.13, #684.

11. *Yapian zhanzheng*, 1:538. For a longer discussion of the complexities and contradictions of the chronology of state policy on opium before the Daoguang period, see Appendix A.

12. Junji chajin, QL 41.10.17, #934–36. Cao seems to have been prompted by the personal disgust he experienced on returning to the capital after a stint in Rehe. The minister was dismayed to have his ears assaulted, as he traveled the streets at night, with the "particularly strange and hateful sound" of hookahs full of water tobacco, a term he also found "inelegant." This sound, described in one source as "rippling water," was characteristic of this type of smoking (Xu Ke, *Qingbai leichao*, 13:6355).

pure opium paste and the spread of this habit beyond the south-east coast.

Although some minor prohibition edicts were issued sporadi-cally in the first seventeen years of the Jiaqing reign, it was only in 1813 that the 1729 regulations were substantially revised. These revi-sions arose from a series of smuggling cases, several of which dem-onstrated that opium had begun to flow from coastal China, par-ticularly Guangdong, into the interior. The earliest case I have found occurred in 1806 in Fujian and involved the decoction and sale of opium, originally purchased from a Guangdong vessel, by a gambling den on the island of Haitan in Fuzhou prefecture. Two smuggling cases, attributed to coastal trafficking in Fujian and Guangdong, came to light in Beijing itself in 1808 and 1810 and trig-gered a decree to provincial officials to cut off opium at its source.[13] All these cases, and perhaps others like the 1808 discovery of opium in Xinjiang among exiles from Guangdong, served to reinforce the central government's conviction that the opium problem origi-nated in Fujian and Guangdong.[14]

The cases from the empire's interior were particularly ominous because they demonstrated that the problem was spreading beyond the southeast coast. An 1811 report from Hubei Governor Qian Jie describing local trafficking and consumption in what was almost certainly unadulterated opium paste not only confirmed the drug's penetration deep into the imperial interior but also described a new and more powerful form of opium.[15] The throne was alarmed enough by Qian Jie's report to issue a decree in April 1813, but the substance of the order was merely to intensify prohibition in

---

13. *Qingchao xu wenxian tongkao*, 53:8771b; Gongzhong jinyan, JQ 11.9.2; *YPZZ*, JQ 15.3.2, 1:1. For a translation into English of the imperial decree, which triggered a temporary intensification of opium prohibition in Guangdong and Fujian, see Fu, *Documentary Chronicle*, 1:380. The 1806 case may have triggered an 1807 decree (*QSL*, JQ 12.12.7, 30:500b–501a).

14. See Appendix A for an analysis of problems pertaining to the chronology of prohibition before the Daoguang era. For a discussion of the Xinjiang case, see Chapter 5.

15. Gongzhong jinyan, JQ 16.2.13. Space precludes a detailed treatment of the development of the opium problem in Hubei and Hunan through the Daoguang period; more than fifty documents relating to this issue, ranging in date from 1811 to 1844, are extant.

Guangdong, Fujian, Zhejiang, and Jiangsu to stop the flow of opium into the interior rather than a call for prohibition operations outside the southeast coast.[16]

An augmentation of the opium-prohibition statutes followed in August after the Board of Punishments concurred that stricter measures needed to be taken against all opium consumers, officials included, to stop the spread of the drug to the interior. Thus, the main focus of the newly promulgated statutes was the criminalization of consumption by both officials and commoners, offenses that had not previously been covered by formal regulations. All smokers were to be beaten and then put in the cangue for two months; officials who smoked were in addition to be stripped of their ranks.[17]

The explicit antismoking provisions in the augmented prohibition statutes of 1813, a major departure from previous regulations, opened a new front in the state's domestic struggle with foreign opium. Over the next two years, the foreign front witnessed a commensurate escalation in state antitrafficking provisions. As late as 1811, Guangdong officials were still relying on moral exhortation to deter foreign merchants. In 1814, as an immediate result of a case in Beijing involving a Guangdong tribute student and his servant, an imperial decree threatened to punish foreign drug suppliers in Guangzhou. In 1815 the throne warned Macao's foreign community that trafficking in opium, as well as Christian proselytizing, would result in permanent expulsion of the offenders from China.[18] These seem to have been the first specific punishments aimed directly at foreign traffickers by the Qing state.

Overall, the revisions of the prohibition law in 1813 represented a stronger commitment by the throne to eradicate opium at its source on the southeast coast. Successive cases during the rest of the Jiaqing reign, however, revealed an ongoing drug problem cen-

---

16. *QSL*, JQ 16.3.1, 31:233a–b. For a translation into English of this decree, see Fu, *Documentary Chronicle*, 1:381.

17. *YPZZ*, JQ 18.7.10, 1:5–6, and JQ 18.7.10, 1:7; *HDSL*, 9:1013b, 1015a; *QSL*, JQ 18.6.14, 31:655b.

18. *Qingdai waijiao shiliao*, JQ 16.5.13, 2:8a–9a, and JQ 19.5.4, 4:19a; *YPZZ*, JQ 19.5.4, 1:11–12, and JQ 20.3.23, 1:18–19; Inoue, "Shindai ahen mondai," pp. 62–63.

tered in coastal areas, especially Macao, but steadily spreading inland in all directions. Several maritime smuggling cases involving crude opium and opium paste were reported from Guangdong in 1816 and 1819 as was a case of official involvement in smuggling in 1818.[19] In addition, opium trafficking and consumption in Beijing in 1814 and 1815, Sichuan in 1816, and Shanxi in 1817 were linked to coastal sources of supply.[20]

All these cases, which arose as a result of the intensification of prohibition operations mandated in 1813, revealed the development of an empirewide opium-marketing system tying foreign smuggler-suppliers to imperial consumers through domestic distributors operating out of the southeast. Part of this system was exposed in a series of six cases from Anhui between 1816 and 1820. A regular smuggling route from Guangdong, used by at least seven traffickers, delivered paste north up the coast to a steady market in Anhui, which included at least one official. Crude opium was generally purchased by peddlers, mainly from Guangdong, from ships along the coast of their native province.[21] The peddlers then decocted the crude opium into a smokable paste, a process that often involved

---

19. Gongzhong jinyan, JQ 21.1.20 and JQ 23.6.2; Neige weijin, DG 1.7.5, #10066 (buben).

20. *Qingdai waijiao shiliao*, JQ 19.5.4, 4:19a; *YPZZ*, JQ 19.5.4, 1:11–12, JQ 20.1.10, 1:13–15, and JQ 20.1.10, 1:15; *Baxian dang'an*, JQ 21.5.6, 2:272. This document is a local public notice regarding the general prohibition of opium. For the full text of a public exhortation dated 1817 from Shanxi, see Appendix B.

21. It is difficult to make more than a rough estimate of the wholesale prices paid for opium in Guangdong, partly because a given quantity of crude opium could be sold wholesale several times before it reached the consumer. In 1822, for example, a Guangdong trafficker initially purchased crude opium for 19 silver taels per kilo, which he then resold to another trafficker for 24 silver taels, a jump of 26 percent in just a single transaction (*YPZZ*, DG 2.3.28, 1:40). A series of cases from the same year implies that 24 taels was an average wholesale price for that time locally, but that prices could range from 19 to 32 silver taels per kilo (*YPZZ*, DG 2.3.28, 1:40–43). During the 1822–23 trading season, the average price of a kilo of Bengal crude opium bought direct from foreign traffickers was roughly 28 silver taels, and 16 silver taels for a kilo of Malwa (see Table 2). Evidence from Anhui cited below, however, indicates that these 1822 figures are rather high; they work out to a retail value of a tael of crude opium of about 0.89 silver taels in Guangdong, 0.03 taels higher than the price of crude in Anhui around the same time.

boiling away as much as a third of the crude product, and transported it to Anhui, usually in amounts equivalent to several kilos. The "street value" of a tael (about 37 grams) of paste was fairly consistent: 1.8 silver taels versus 0.86 silver tael for the same amount of crude opium. This works out to a profit of about 36 percent on each tael of crude opium boiled, at a loss of a third of its weight, into paste. At these rates, a kilo of paste would sell for about 49 silver taels and a kilo of crude, which would yield about 700 grams of paste, would sell for about 23.5 silver taels.[22]

If these admittedly rough estimates are at all representative, they explain much of the financial incentive for the development of transprovincial distribution networks, which so disturbed officials in the opening decades of the nineteenth century. The street value of a single tael of opium paste in Anhui between 1816 and 1820, for example, was equal to 75 percent of the average price of a *shi*, or picul (about 84 kilos), of staple, second-grade rice (*gengmi*) in the Yangzi delta during the same period. Since an average adult would consume about 2–3 *shi* of rice per year, the cost of a tael of opium paste equaled between 25 and 38 percent of an individual's annual consumption of rice.[23] Such profits were also an incentive for the domestic production of opium. In 1831, Shandong Governor Ne-er-jing-e, for example, anticipated that cultivation would spread to new locations as extra-provincial traffickers began concluding purchasing contracts with local peasants for opium crops. [24]

---

22. Gongzhong jinyan, JQ 25.2.18. There are a few other documents on opium cases from Anhui, most of which provide statistics or details on individual cases of consumption by officials. The majority of the documents date from early 1839 to late 1840. The latest statistical report revealed that by the beginning of 1840 over 720 offenders had been arrested and 858 kilos of crude opium and paste had been confiscated (*Gongzhong DG*, DG 19.12.4, 10394a–95b).

23. There is a range of estimates concerning the actual weight of a *shi*, rice prices, and annual per capita consumption rates. For an average, modern equivalent of a *shi*, I have relied on Chuan and Kraus, *Mid-Ch'ing Rice Markets and Trade*, pp. 79–98; for rice prices, Yeh-chien Wang, "Secular Trends of Rice Prices," p. 44; for annual per capita consumption rates, Li and Dray-Novey, "Guarding Beijing's Food Security," p. 100n. The *Hanyu da cidian* (3:7777) estimates a *shi* at around 72 kilos. Differing estimates for annual per capita consumption rates, ranging from 1.74 to 5.5 *shi*, are given in Pomeranz, *The Great Divergence*, p. 319.

24. YPZZ, DG 11.7.2, 1:91–94.

It is, thus, not entirely coincidental that the discovery of domestic poppy cultivation in Qing China occurred around the same time the coastal smuggling traffic was entering a phase of rapid expansion, mainly because of the competition in India between Company-produced Bengal opium and native Malwa, as described in Chapter 2. The number of opium chests annually entering China tripled from 10,000 in the 1820s to 30,000 by the mid-1830s to 40,000 by the end of the decade.[25] These developments stimulated consumption and, beginning in the early 1830s, began to drive the Qing government toward active pursuit of absolute prohibition. Poppy cultivation within imperial territory stimulated both consumption and prohibition, since the transformation of opium from an expensive foreign to a cheaper domestic product could not be combated exclusively by pre-existing antitrafficking and anticonsumption measures.

The creation of a third category of opium offense necessitated a major ethno-geographic expansion in prohibition policy, as described in Chapters 5 and 6, when it became clear that the empire's primary poppy fields lay in isolated areas of non-Han habitation in western frontier locales, Yunnan chief among them. The court, however, initially proved incapable of expanding its localized notions about the opium problem. Beijing's immediate response to the first report of poppy cultivation in Yunnan in 1823 was to issue a decree ordering search-and-seizure operations at major southeastern ports to prevent coastal opium from spreading to the interior.[26]

The center could continue to insist that opium remained primarily a coastal problem during the 1820s in part because cultivation was also discovered in Fujian and Zhejiang, apparently as a result of the 1823 search-and-seizure operations.[27] Although some sort of anticultivation operations were apparently being implemented by local officials in both coastal provinces and in Yunnan at this time, these first poppy-eradication operations in Chinese history were quite ad hoc. Complaints by village elders in the Fujian prefecture of Quanzhou that poppy cultivation was interfering with

---

25. Greenberg, *British Trade*, pp. 112–13, 221.
26. *YPZZ*, 2.12.8, 1:48.
27. *Yapian zhanzheng*, DG 10.10.13, 1:161–62.

grain production, for example, seem to have been behind the official anticultivation operations.[28] The absence of systematized eradication reflects the fact that cultivation itself was not formally criminalized by the center, which merely fixed penalties for local officials who failed to report on and eradicate poppy fields from their jurisdictions.[29] In the view of central authorities, cultivation was a collateral offense, which arose from more serious crimes of imperial significance directly related to coastal trafficking of foreign opium and could be handled casually by local authorities.

By mid-1830, this view was substantially altered by the arguments of metropolitan Censor Shao Zhenghu, who asked for a reinterpretation of poppy cultivation as a crime commensurate with trafficking because of its ability to spread drug use beyond the coast. In his request for search-and-seizure operations on an imperial scale as well as revisions of the prohibition statutes to include formal criminalization of poppy cultivation, Shao described just how domesticated opium had become.

The environs of Taizhou in Zhejiang have the most numerous cultivators, and the numbers of those in the prefectures of Ningbo, Shaoxing, Yanzhou, and Wenzhou are not far behind. Types of local opium like "Tai juice" and "Kui juice" are no different from the opium that comes from overseas. Large numbers of peddlers sell it everywhere, and local officials have not been conscientious in investigation [of possible violations] and enforcement of the prohibitions, resulting in the spread of opium outside this region so that Fujian, Guangdong, and Yunnan all have cultivation and trafficking. Local opium is known as "Fu[jian] juice" and "Guang-[dong] juice" and "[a]*furong* paste," etc.[30]

On August 12, 1830, an imperial decree strongly affirming Shao's views inaugurated the first genuinely empirewide Qing prohibition operations against an augmented array of offenses, including poppy

---

28. Ibid.

29. The throne ordered the Boards of Personnel and Punishments to deliberate on regulations to ensure proper official handling of cases pertaining to a number of opium offenses not previously covered (*QSL*, DG 3.7.12, 33:971b–72b). The boards duly produced a group of regulations subsequently confirmed by imperial decree (*YPZZ*, DG 3.8.2, 1:51–52; Junji jinyan, DG 3.8.2, #1515–18). The order to eradicate poppy from Yunnan was also included in this decree.

30. Junji jinyan, DG 10.6.24, #1545–46.

cultivation. These operations also provided a context for similarly extensive anticonsumption investigations among yamen personnel, which were undertaken in 1831 as part of the intensified prohibition of consumption in general successfully requested by another metropolitan censor, Liu Guangsan.[31] The throne's enthusiasm for a comprehensive intensification of opium prohibition was undoubtedly further stimulated by a number of trafficking and consumption cases from Beijing that year, especially those involving palace eunuchs and a Muslim beile caught smoking together in the Yuan Ming Yuan summer palace.[32]

Anticultivation statutes in particular were heavily influenced by the input of senior coastal officials, particularly Governor-General Sun Erzhun of Min-Zhe (Fujian and Zhejiang). Sun both confirmed and augmented Censor Shao's account of poppy cultivation in his jurisdiction. He briefly described regional cultivation techniques and stated that the Zhejiang prefectures of Wenzhou and, especially, Taizhou were the main provincial centers of poppy cultivation, which had persisted mainly because of a lack of specific penalties for poppy growers. Sun proposed to raise the penalties for cultivation, as well as for the decoction of crude opium into paste, considerably and make them the same as those for trafficking offenses, exile for life. Moreover, all illegal poppy plots were to be confiscated by the state.[33] This considerable escalation against domestic producers was approved in its entirety by Grand Secretary Lu Yinbo in his joint memorial with the Board of Punishments to the throne on the subject. An imperial decree in early 1831 adopted their recommendations.[34]

The state's opium policies thus continued to reflect coastal influences, even though there were clear signs that the opium-

---

31. *QSL* DG 10.6.24, 35:643b–44a, and DG 11.6.16, 35:1010a–b; *YPZZ*, DG 11.5.15, 1:79–80.

32. ZZD, DG 11.10, pp. 123–30, DG 10.5, pp. 218–26, DG 11.6.2, pp. 33–36, DG 11.11, pp. 127–29, and DG 11.11, pp. 241–44; Junji jinyan, DG 11.7.10, #1621–22, 11.7.16, #1627–28, DG 11.10.8, #1645–52, and DG 11.11.4, #1667–69; *YPZZ*, DG 11.10.29, 1:102–4, and DG 11.11.5, 1:105.

33. *Yapian zhanzheng*, DG 10.10.13, 1:161–62.

34. Junji jinyan, DG 10.11.18, #1554–57, and DG 10.12.18, #1559–67; *YPZZ*, DG 10.12.18, 1:72.

marketing system was becoming regionally diverse. The equation of production and trafficking, both of which were still seen as almost exclusively coastal problems in the early 1830s, reinforced official perceptions of the empire's opium problem. Domestic production would soon require the state to confront new developments in the opium-marketing system outside the comparatively well ordered realm of urban coastal China proper, the main chokepoint for foreign opium. This fact was briefly and implicitly admitted by Governor-General Sun himself when he acknowledged that cultivation in wilderness areas of his own jurisdiction would be difficult for officials to detect.[35] This observation would prove an understatement for the understaffed, urban-based officialdom of the vast western expanses of Yunnan, Xinjiang, Sichuan, and Guizhou, all of which witnessed far more extensive poppy cultivation by their considerable non-Han populations by the end of the 1830s.

In effect, the revision of prohibition law in 1830–31, which was substantially driven by concerns over domestic drug production, was a declaration of war on opium throughout the empire, and the consequent investigations were commensurately extensive. The *baojia* system prevalent in areas of *junxian* administration was chosen as the primary medium through which the search for poppy cultivators as well as opium traffickers and consumers would be conducted throughout the empire from this time until the end of the reign in 1850.[36] During this investigative process, bonds certifying that no drug offenses had occurred were to be processed and forwarded by local officials to the central government as part of the annual system of *baojia* year-end reporting and submission of mutual responsibility certificates. It was hoped that extending the *baojia* practice of self-surveillance to cover investigation of violations and enforcement of the prohibition would lessen the burden on local officials.

---

35. *Yapian zhanzheng*, DG 10.10.13, 1:162.

36. *YPZZ*, DG 11.12.19, 1:194 (Jiangxi), and DG 11.12.20, 1:195–196 (Zhejiang); Gongzhong jinyan, DG 15.11.23 (Hunan) and DG 15.12.2 (Henan); Gongzhong baojing, DG 11.11.20 (Guangxi), DG 11.12.10 (Fujian), DG 20.12.10 (Fujian), DG 20.4.4 (Jilin), DG 20.11.28 (Shaan-Gan), DG 23.12.23 (Hubei), DG 24.11.27 (Shaan-Gan), and DG 29.12.7 (Hubei).

The *baojia* system was pervasive enough in the provinces of
Han-dominated China proper to act as the main administrative apparatus for prohibition enforcement. Indeed, reliance on the *baojia*
system was facilitated by the fact that three of the four provinces
identified by Shao Zhenghu as major sites of domestic cultivation
had *junxian* administrations. Officials from these provinces raced
to declare their poppy problems solved. Fujian led the pack because poppy cultivation there had already been declared eradicated,
probably some time soon after 1823, but for some inexplicable reason central government officials do not seem to have been informed until 1830.[37] Guangdong was next to rid itself of poppy,
which was reported to be restricted to Chaozhou prefecture and
declared eradicated in mid-1831.[38] Zhejiang took much longer, and
provincial officials did not declare the province free of poppy until
1835.[39] By this time, as noted in Chapter 6, poppy had also been
discovered in Guizhou and Sichuan, but the provincial and territorial administrations of the rest of the empire declared themselves
free of it in 1831–32.[40]

It remains unclear whether the poppy cultivation subsequently
discovered in Guangxi and Xinjiang in 1839 had been overlooked,

---

37. *Yapian zhanzheng*, DG 10.10.13, 1:161–62.

38. *YPZZ*, DG 11.6.29, 1:90–91. There is no record of any other instances of illicit cultivation in Guangdong.

39. *Gongzhong jinyan* DG 14.12.24. Unfortunately, no documents have come
to light concerning provincial cultivation between late 1830 and the eradication
declaration in 1835.

40. Initial reports of no cultivation for the eleventh year of the Daoguang
reign (Feb. 13, 1831–January 23, 1832) are extant for these eleven provinces; Gongzhong jinyan DG 11.2.8 (Shanxi), DG 11.3.8 (Hubei), DG 11.3.25 (Shaanxi), DG
11.4.10 (Anhui), DG 11.5.15 (Henan), DG 11.5.22 (Hunan), DG 11.5.29 (Guizhou),
DG 11.4.27 (Gansu), DG 11.12.19 (Sichuan), DG 11.12.19 (Zhili), DG 11.9.27 (Jiangxi).
There is also a separate report from Chengde prefecture in Zhili (Gongzhong jinyan, DG 11.12.21). Reports submitted after the eleventh year of the Daoguang reign
indicate that no cultivation was found in the three remaining provinces (Gongzhong jinyan DG 12.1.27 [Shandong], DG 12.2.7 [Jiangsu], DG 13.2.29 [Guangxi]).
This accounts for all the provinces of China proper. See Chapter 5 for reports of
no cultivation in Xinjiang by the Urumqi banner commander-in-chief. The existence of this report shows that the search for cultivation was also conducted outside China proper, but it is unclear whether all other imperial territories partici-
pated.

concealed, or appeared in the interim. The unquestionably gross inaccuracies in reporting during the 1830s, particularly in Shaanxi and Gansu (see Chapter 5), certainly justify the skepticism of local officials like Peng Songyu, whose doubts concerning provincial declarations of poppy eradication were noted in Chapter 3. His views make the revelations of poppy cultivation in a number of provinces all the more significant, if not miraculous, and are certainly an argument in favor of their basic veracity.

Whatever the local realities, the reported absence of poppy from most provinces was certainly a major reason why aspects of the empirewide intensification of opium prohibition began to lose momentum by the mid-1830s. By the end of 1835, many provinces and territories had been relieved of one or more of their obligations to conduct searches for cultivation or consumption by officials because no offenses had turned up in the preceding five years.[41]

The throne nevertheless remained concerned about opium, largely because of its conviction that the trafficking in and consumption of foreign opium were draining the empire of silver and consequently disrupting both commerce and tax revenues. Between 1829 and 1831, the authorities in Beijing became convinced that opium was responsible for the silver drain, also known as the "silver famine" (*yinhuang*), estimated at the time as a loss of several

---

41. Suspensions of investigations varied by time, place, and nature, but most seem to have been issued toward the end of the fifteenth year of the Daoguang reign (Jan. 29, 1835–Feb. 7, 1836) after approximately four years of investigations had turned up no official consumption or local cultivation in most areas. The suspensions themselves were rescripted onto an edict by the emperor who stated in effect that since no offenses had been detected, it was no longer necessary to memorialize on the subject. There does not seem to be much consistency to the suspensions, which sometimes stopped the investigation only of consumption by officials but not of cultivation (Gongzhong jinyan, DG 15.11.23 [Guangdong]). Other edicts seem to have suspended both (Gongzhong jinyan DG 15.11.23 [Hunan]). It is possible that surveillance continued in those areas where cultivation had originally been discovered. In response to an early 1836 report from Fujian, however, reaffirming the eradication of opium, the emperor suspended investigations both for consumption by officials and for cultivation (Gongzhong jinyan, DG 15.12.13). It also remains unclear whether investigations continued at the local level after the reporting requirement was lifted.

million taels annually.[42] It is almost certainly no coincidence that this date marks the Daoguang reign's first comprehensive overhaul of prohibition. In sum, the intensified prohibition of opium was the product of the Daoguang court's concern over the drug's financial impact, particularly on state revenues, rather than moral outrage over its effect on imperial subjects.[43]

Between 1831 and 1836, the court evaluated the results of its escalation of prohibition. A series of events during this period revealed the gravity of the drug's destabilizing spread across the empire. As noted above, domestic cultivation both along the coast and in the southwest was discovered during this period. Moreover, cases of trafficking and consumption continued to appear within and outside these two regions, including in Beijing itself.[44] Widespread opium smoking in the military was also brought to the court's attention. In 1832, an official investigation determined that Qing forces fighting Yao tribals in Guangdong were besotted with opium, and their commander, Liang-Guang Governor-General Li Hongbin, was cashiered. The emperor's action was also motivated by detailed reports from Metropolitan Censor Feng Zanxun regarding Li's failure to pursue prohibition vigorously and the spread of opium smoking to troops in Guangdong, Fujian, Zhejiang,

---

42. *YPZZ*, DG 9.1.24, 1:54–55, DG 9.12.16, 1:62–63, DG 11.5.24, 1:84–86. The outflow of silver and the inflow of opium were separate concerns during the Jiaqing reign, but the two were increasingly discussed together from 1822; see, e.g., *YPZZ*, JQ 19.1.25, 1:8–9, DG 2.2.12, 1:37–38, DG 9.1.25, 1:55–56, DG 9.10.28, 1:60–61, DG 11.5.24, 1:84–86, DG 13.4.6, 1:138–39, and DG 14.9.10, 1:157–59.

43. The direct relationship between the outflow of silver and the intensification of opium prohibition under the Daoguang emperor is well attested in the Chinese and Japanese secondary literature: see, e.g., Li Yongqing, "Youguan jinyan yundong," pp. 79–80; Ma Weiping, "Jinyan yuanyin bianxi"; Wu Yixiong, "Jinyan zhenglun," pp. 59–60; Zhu, "Yanguan de jinyan lun"; and Inoue, "Shindai ahen mondai," pp. 72–79.

44. Space precludes an exhaustive list of these cases, but the palace memorial opium-prohibition documents in the First Historical Archives of China contain numerous reports of trafficking and consumption cases from most provinces between 1831 and 1836. For Beijing cases, many of which involved consumption by bannermen and officials, see Gongzhong jinyan, DG 12.12.16; and Neige weijin, DG 12.4.5, #10102 (buben).

Yunnan, Guizhou, and Sichuan.[45] Li's successor, Lu Kun, was explicitly charged by the emperor to stop the spread of opium to the interior. In 1833 and 1834, more reports connecting opium and the silver drain, as well as continuing rumors about illicit taxation of the traffic by local officials in Guangdong, reached the throne.[46]

Taken as a whole, these events demonstrated that although prohibition was being pursued more vigorously, it was not stopping opium, which had clearly become an empirewide problem with serious security implications. The 1836 legalization debate consequently took place within the context of the court's greater cognizance of the transimperial scope of the traffic as well as its persistence in the face of intensified prohibition.

Dynastic concern over the silver drain was powerful enough for the emperor to sanction a debate over the legalization of opium in 1836 in response to a request by Vice Minister for the Court of Imperial Sacrifices Xu Naiji. Xu was only one of a group of Guangdong officials who had been working on legalization statutes since Governor-General of Liang-Guang Lu Kun cautiously raised the issue in 1834. Scholars from Guangzhou's famous Xuehai Tang academy helped to produce the proposed statutes submitted by Lu's successor, Deng Tingzhen, and Guangdong Governor Qi Gong at the beginning of the debate. All these proposals, which basically advocated a resumption of import duties on foreign opium and the toleration of domestic poppy cultivation, were predicated on the assertion that strict enforcement of the prohibitions was being used as a pretext for official extortion of innocent victims and was solving neither the opium problem nor the silver drain.[47]

---

45. Polachek, *Inner Opium War*, p. 109; *YPZZ*, DG 12.8.26, 1:123–24, DG 12.8.27, 1:125–26.

46. *YPZZ*, DG 13.4.6, 1:138–39, DG 14.9.10, 1:157–59.

47. The standard account of the legalization debate in English remains Chang, *Commissioner Lin*, pp. 85–92. Polachek, *Inner Opium War*, pp. 113–35, presents a more recent, alternative interpretation of the debate. Two excellent Chinese overviews of the debate are Tian and Li, "Sixiang qianqu," pp. 99–107; and Lin Youneng, "Chijin pai," pp. 20–21, 30–31. The pertinent primary sources may be found in *Yapian zhanzheng*, DG 14.10.3, 1:133–34; and *YPZZ*, DG 16.4.27 #3 and #4, 1:200–203, DG 16.4.29, 1:203, DG 16.7.27, 1:205–9.

The legalizers were probably inspired by their close ties to local merchants in Guangzhou. Common interests had united the region's two most powerful local groups on the opium question by the early 1820s and provoked what one scholar has called "the first opium debate," between Bao Shichen and Cheng Hanzhang. Bao, whose 1820 essay represents one of the earliest condemnations of the drug traffic as a drain on silver rather than as a simple vice, was an ex-official, essayist, and private advisor to senior provincial authorities in a number of coastal provinces. He wanted to enhance the rather ineffective prohibition operations against maritime traffickers by banning the coastal foreign trade altogether. This extreme proposal was soon answered by a representative of Guangzhou's official and mercantile elite. Around the time Bao's essay came out, Cheng was prefect of Guangzhou, and in 1822–23 he served briefly as the governor of Guangdong, all the while acting as a patron of the local academies that maintained intimate relations with the merchant community.[48]

Like Bao, Cheng also held opium to be a far greater economic than moral danger, but he warned in his essay that Bao's plan was impractical and could, moreover, lead to "continuous warfare and disaster, which will not be quelled for decades."[49] Cheng, however, had little to offer to counter what he admitted was a serious economic threat except more of the same ineffective prohibition operations against individual ships and traffickers.[50]

Cheng's views prevailed, but a decade and a half after his exchange with Bao the traffic had grown to the extent that it became impossible to ignore. Conditions had changed drastically enough that the Guangzhou elite put forward a radical solution, legalization. They were no doubt emboldened by the persistence of the opium traffic as well as the influence at court of one of their own number, former Liang-Guang Governor-General and Xuehai Tang Academy founder Ruan Yuan, who in 1836 was a grand secretary. In asserting what Inoue Hiromasa called a "Canton position on opium," the legalizers came into conflict with

---

48. Inoue, "Shindai ahen mondai," pp. 72–77.
49. Cheng, "Lun yang hai," 26:44b.
50. Ibid., 26:44a–b; Inoue, "Shindai ahen mondai," pp. 77–78.

prominent prohibitionists among the metropolitan censors, including the leader of the Spring Purification circle, Huang Juezi. The censors asserted what ultimately became the Beijing position on opium.[51]

Other vocal prohibitionists, including Vice Director of the Board of Rites Zhu Zun, Censor Xu Qiu, and Censor Yuan Yulin, objected on ethical grounds to legalization but sought primarily to demonstrate that opium legalization would not solve what all acknowledged to be the primary problem, namely, the silver drain. All three men successfully called for stricter enforcement of the existing prohibitions, especially against domestic traffickers, and for better supervision of local officialdom. This policy was the concrete result of the underlying philosophy of the antilegalization position, expressed in Xu Qiu's original dictum that one should "concentrate more on the domestic than the foreign; first rule yourself, then rule others."[52]

The debate between the prohibitionists and the legalizers was a complex conflict involving the political and economic interests created by the drug traffic. Legalization was not simply pushed by merchant-smugglers but also supported by a local community that had become economically dependent on the drug to maintain both legitimate and illegal activities, including the financing of regional administration through the illicit taxation of the traffic.[53] Nor was the critique of prohibition by advocates of legalization entirely cynical; the outbreak of war in 1839 justified Cheng Hanzhang's prophetic warning.

Similarly, prohibition was more than just a hypocritical by-product of an opportunistic Beijing faction. Although it exploited the opium issue, the Spring Purification circle did not manufacture the debate just as "the advocates of legalization seemed on the

---

51. Inoue, "Wu Lanxiu and Society in Guangzhou," 104–5, 112; Polachek, *Inner Opium War*, 116–17.

52. For punctuated versions of the memorials of Zhu Zun and Xu Qiu, see Tian and Li, "Sixiang qianqu," 103–7. For the memorial of Yuan Yulin, see *YPZZ*, DG 16.10.4, 1:213–17.

53. These relations are discussed in greater detail in the subsection "Qing Opium Dependency" in this chapter.

verge of success."[54] Not all the prohibitionists were circle members, but all were metropolitan censors, duty bound to distrust local officials. In arguing against a proposal to embrace an illicit and unsavory localized drug traffic, from which the legalizers were almost certainly profiting, and which appeared to be draining the country of its main medium of tax remittance, eroding its military capacity, and insidiously spreading despite six years of prohibition, a prohibitionist cabal seems superfluous.

The throne nominally accepted stricter prohibition in 1836 but did not explicitly condemn legalization until two years later.[55] Nevertheless, the initial imperial nod toward prohibition induced several prominent officials, such as Governor-General Deng Tingzhen and Governor Qi Gong, to distance themselves from legalization on the grounds that the main issue was not intensification or repeal of the opium prohibitions but stopping the outflow of silver abroad. The cause of legalization was also harmed by allegations of

---

54. Polachek, *Inner Opium War*, p. 113. Polachek presents about as much circumstantial evidence for his assertion regarding the imminence of legalization as Chang (*Commissioner Lin*, pp. 91–92) does for his contrary summation that Zhu Zun and Xu Qiu "spoke for the majority of officials" in Beijing. Nevertheless, it is hard to understand why any official beyond the coast, i.e., outside the circle of immediate beneficiaries, would be an active advocate of legalization; in contrast, the advantages of condemning the opium traffic on general principles would be obvious.

55. *YPZZ*, DG 16.8.9, 1:210. The Daoguang emperor expressed his final decision on the matter only when he demoted Xu Naiji, ostensibly because no provincial official supported legalization in the early stages of the New Regulations debate (*YPZZ*, DG 16.11.20, 1:220–22, DG 18.9.11, 1:391). Apparently for two years the emperor remained uncommitted to a policy either of strict enforcement or of legalization. Chang (*Commissioner Lin*, p. 92), however, concludes that Censor Yuan Yulin's November 1836 memorial convinced the emperor to decide firmly in favor of prohibition. Polachek (*Inner Opium War*, p. 124) makes a similar assumption, albeit based on several other factors besides Yuan's memorial. The imperial decree charging Governor-General Deng to conduct prohibition operations, however, stated: "Recently, advocates have been divided, with some requesting an adaptation of statutes to local conditions and others requesting strict enforcement of the prohibitions. The situation requires personal investigation, comprehensive planning, and sustained, unhindered action before it can be resolved" (*YPZZ*, DG 16.8.9, 1:210). I read this decree as a probationary rather than a decisive sanction of prohibition, as did Morse (*International Relations*, 1:191), who concluded that there was no "definite immediate settlement" of the issue.

hong merchant involvement in opium transactions in mid-1836.[56] Deng was to target the Chinese "fast crab" (*kuaixie*) and "scrambling dragon" (*palong*) smuggling boats, which moved silver and opium between the foreign receiving ships (*yapian tun*) at offshore locales like Lintin Island and the Chinese mainland, as well as the "brokerages" (*yaokou*) that sold opium wholesale.[57]

The ultimate outcome of the legalization debate was a policy of absolute prohibition directed almost exclusively against imperial subjects while leaving Western traffickers virtually untouched. This indirect assault on foreign smugglers through a direct attack on domestic traffickers drove the dynasty to increasingly draconian punishments of all imperial offenders. Meanwhile foreigners continued to operate with impunity, and opium offenses continued to spread and multiply.

Statistics make clear that the war on domestic traffickers had failed by 1838. Imports of foreign opium had risen from approximately 4,000 chests per year between 1800 and 1818 to over ten times this amount, or about 2.4 million kilos, enough to supply perhaps 3.5 million smokers using an average of 1.9 grams of paste per day.[58] Deng's increased antitrafficking operations in Guangdong had led to the capture of 692 offenders and the confiscation of around 5,144 kilos of crude opium and 137 kilos of opium paste. If Deng, as these fragmentary figures suggest, were seizing an average of about 1,285 kilos of crude opium per month, this represents

---

56. *YPZZ*, DG 16.6.23, 1:204–5.

57. *YPZZ*, DG 16.11.20, 1:220–22, DG 16.12.20, 1:223–24, DG 17.9.23, 1:239–41.

58. This rate is a rough estimate based mainly on a modification of figures from He Chengyuan ("Quanguo xidu renshu," pp. 7–8), who relies primarily on annual totals of imported chests converted into traditional Chinese measurements of fractions of a tael. There is, inevitably, a wide variation in estimates, particularly in numbers of smokers and their daily consumption averages. In 1838 Lin Zexu himself, for example, estimated a consumption rate that works out to about 0.8 grams/day for an indeterminate number of consumers (*YPZZ*, DG 18/8, 1:359). R. K. Newman ("A Reconsideration," pp. 783–86) estimates that eight million people were smoking what I calculate to be an average of 8.4 grams/day in 1879. Sir Robert Hart estimated in 1881 that two million smokers were consuming what would be about 11 grams/day on average (Inspectorate General of Chinese Customs, *Opium*, p. 3). One major reason for the differences is that Newman and Hart are using post-legalization figures whereas He uses pre-legalization ones.

less than one-tenth of 1 percent of the average monthly amount of opium estimated to have been smuggled into coastal China at this point.[59] Guangdong apparently had the highest rate of confiscation in the southeast during this period; even so the available fragmentary statistics for the entire region suggest an overall seizure rate of well under 1 percent.[60]

This lackluster performance no doubt inspired the famous and controversial memorial submitted by Minister of Rites Huang Jue-zi on June 2, 1838, which sparked the final great prohibition debate of the Daoguang reign. This debate has received extended attention from scholars, and it is unnecessary to deal with all its specifics in detail.[61] Its most immediate and important results were the promulgation of the New Regulations in mid-1839 and the appointment of Huguang Governor-General Lin Zexu as imperial commissioner in charge of overseeing the implementation of the prohibitions in Guangdong, the main theater of operations.

Huang's attempt to explain the most recent policy failure led him to the extreme of proposing capital punishment for all major categories of opium offenders, including, most controversially, consumers. He attributed the recent flood of foreign opium and a commensurate rise in the outflow of silver to an increase in the number of addicts, whose pivotal role, Huang held, had previously

---

59. The reported seizure figures cover only a four-month period from mid-January to mid-April 1839 (*Gongzhong DG*, DG 19.1.14, 8:737a–38a, DG 19.4.25, 8:258a–59a; *YPZZ*, DG 19.3.16, 1:522–24). Some previous cases are alluded to, running from the "spring of the seventeenth year of the Daoguang emperor" to the end of 1838, but no statistics are provided (*Gongzhong DG*, DG 19.1.14, 8:737a–38a).

60. Statistics for Jiangsu, which had confiscated only about 373 kilos during January 1839, indicate that the amounts seized were considerably less than those seized in Guangdong (*Gongzhong DG*, DG 18.11.9, 7:138a–b; *YPZZ*, DG 19.1.13, 1:491–92). Fujian authorities did much better, seizing 4,740 kilos of opium of all types and arresting 324 offenders up to May 1839, but these figures still fall short of the Guangdong statistics (*YPZZ*, DG 19.3.25, 1:538–39). No comparable statistics from Zhejiang have come to light.

61. In English, the definitive treatment remains Chang, *Commissioner Lin*, pp. 92–98. Yu, *Jinyan faling*, pp. 60–65, is a standard, if dated, Chinese work. Chinese revisionist scholarship, however, has produced a number of important articles, perhaps the most significant being Wu Yixiong, "Jinyan zhenglun." For the full text of the New Regulations, see *YPZZ*, DG 19.5.2, 1:564–86.

been overlooked because of the excessive focus on trafficking. Huang argued that capital punishment for addicts would eliminate the domestic market for opium by eradicating drug consumers, who were far more susceptible to state control measures than either foreign smugglers or domestic traffickers. Consumers would be given a grace period of a year, later increased to eighteen months, to break their habit; after that, capital punishment would ensue with no prospect of clemency.[62]

Although there was little objection to capital punishment for traffickers and cultivators among the 28 senior provincial officials involved in the New Regulations debate, only one fully supported Huang's call for the execution of opium consumers. In contrast, 21 favored an intensification of the existing antitrafficking operations in Guangdong, which included decapitation for convicted Han traffickers.[63] In effect, most officials were arguing that the eradication of coastal traffickers from Guangdong, and not the obliteration of imperial consumers, would eliminate the empire's opium problem. In the end, policymakers decided to combine both approaches, moderating the New Regulations with the grace period and an amnesty program that permitted offenders to surrender themselves and their contraband to mitigate or avoid punishment. These qualifications led to a rush by provincial officials to catch or amnesty as many offenders as possible before the full implementation of the New Regulations in 1841 resulted in an automatic death sentence upon conviction for major production, distribution, and consumption crimes.[64]

The flurry of enforcement that followed formal promulgation of the New Regulations in June 1839 was not limited to Guangdong or even the southeast coast. Consumption and trafficking offenses were discovered as far away as the Qing garrison in Tibet and in both Inner and Outer Mongolia. Opium arrived in these

---

62. Chang, *Commissioner Lin*, p. 92; Xu Haiquan, "Huang Juezi yu jinyan yundong," pp. 40–41.

63. Wang Licheng, "Jinyan juece pingxi," pp. 9–14.

64. Individual cases are too numerous to cite, but the chronological tables of contents in *YPZZ* volumes 1 and 2 provide an excellent overview of the expansion of enforcement operations from 1810 to 1841.

frontier areas almost entirely through the agency of Han commercial and military penetration.[65] Furthermore, opium from China was also flowing beyond the empire itself, most notably into Vietnam, where the southeast China drug traffic was being re-enacted by Qing merchant junks mainly from Guangdong. The Gialong emperor (r. 1802–20), the first ruler of the Nguyễn dynasty (1802–1945), had initially taxed opium in 1810 but banned it by 1818. His successor, the Minh-mang emperor (r. 1820–41), reiterated the ban on his accession to the throne. Vietnamese prohibition proved generally ineffective mainly because of the involvement of Vietnam's own politically influential Chinese merchant community in both the Chinese opium- and the Vietnamese rice-smuggling traffics, which were closely linked.[66] A similar cycle of coastal Chinese opium smuggling and state bans, beginning in 1813 and undermined by a resident Chinese merchant populace, was also occurring in Siam.[67]

The ban also failed in Qing China despite the shift to the last stage of absolute prohibition, completed by 1841, with the expiration of the grace period and the consequent full implementation of the New Regulations. Imperial confirmation of capital punishment for consumption became a routine matter at this point, as attested by the dozens of extant capital cases, mostly from Beijing, Zhili, and Guangdong, involving individuals using opium for ostensibly medicinal purposes, primarily pain relief.[68] Although it remains impossible to determine the fate of most opium offenders sentenced to death, some of whom were certainly pardoned, the many expressions of official concern indicate that such sentences were not taken lightly. From this perspective, the routine confirmation

---

65. For an extended treatment, see Bello, "Chinese Roots."

66. Woodside, *Vietnam and the Chinese Model*, pp. 269–70; Fujiwara, "Genchō no ahen."

67. Viraphol, *Tribute and Profit*, pp. 186, 221–22.

68. These cases, discussed in the Board of Punishment's routine memorials (*xingke tiben*), admittedly provide suspiciously uniform explanations for consumption. Expert witnesses before the Royal Commission on Opium in 1893, however, generally agreed that "the relief of pain and sickness was a major reason why people took up opium smoking" (Newman, "A Reconsideration," p. 776).

of capital sentences for opium consumption by the emperor was an ominous development.[69]

Although in 1843 the throne asserted its firm determination to continue the implementation of the prohibitions, large-scale operations had already been curtailed, probably because of the exigencies of war.[70] Nevertheless, selective and scaled-down prohibition continued throughout the rest of the Daoguang reign and into the succeeding Xianfeng reign, despite a brief spate of capital commutations to honor the imperial transition in 1850–51, until opium was legalized in 1858–59.[71] The first postwar legalization proposal was formally put to the emperor during the negotiations for the Treaty of Nanjing in 1843, but it was rejected by the throne, which reiterated its ineffective policy of concentrating on the prosecution of Han smokers to eliminate all drug offenses. Chinese and British interests, however, colluded in an informal local settlement that tolerated the continuation of the contraband coastal traffic in Indian opium without formally regulating it.[72] Coastal prohibition operations, particularly against foreign traffickers, were substantially suspended by this agreement.

Beijing, unwilling or unable to reverse itself publicly on a major issue like opium prohibition, nevertheless continued to mandate anticonsumption operations against Han smokers. The main administrative result of this selective persistence during the 1840s was the institution of empirewide lists of consumption cases, sub-

---

69. For evidence concerning the commutation of capital sentences for opium offenses, see Junji jinyan, DG 24.7.27, #145; QSL, DG 24.12.22, 39:175b; and Gongzhong jinyan, XF 4.12.21. For discussions of the issue of commutation in general, see Bodde and Morris, *Law in Imperial China*, pp. 134–43; and Lee, "Homicide et peine capitale." Authorities generally agree that only around 10–20 percent of those sentenced to "deferred execution" (*huan jue*), which was subject to confirmation during the annual autumn assizes review, were actually executed.

70. *Qingchao xu wenxian tongkao*, 53:8081a–b.

71. Neige weijin, DG 30.5.18 and DG 30.7.24, #10135 (buben); QSL, DG 30.1.26, 40:80b–83a. For a Xianfeng case list enumerating twelve cases of consumers on deferred execution, see Gongzhong jinyan, XF 4.8.3. For a study of opium legalization during the Xianfeng reign, see Fairbank, "Legalization." Poppy cultivation was legalized throughout China by 1891 (Madancy, *Troublesome Legacy*, p. 69n).

72. Fairbank, *Trade and Diplomacy*, pp. 145–51.

Table 3
Consumption Case Lists, 1843–49

Location[a]	1843	1844	1846	1848	1849
Anhui	1				
Fengtian			1		
Guangdong	1	2			
Huguang	6[b, c]	4[c]			
Jiangxi	2				
Khobdo			1		
Shanxi		5			
Sichuan	1[c]				
Yunnan	2				
Zhili	1[d]	1		1	
Beijing[e]	8[b]	1[c]	6[b, c]	8[c, d, f]	6[c, d]
TOTALS					
CASES	22	13	8	9	6
OFFENDERS	25	17	9	11	11

[a] Provincial location figures refer to autumn assizes.
[b] Includes female offender(s).
[c] Case(s) involving multiple offenders.
[d] Official offender(s).
[e] Imperial assizes.
[f] Includes the case of an imperial clansman.
SOURCE: *Daoguang Xianfeng liangchao chouban yiwu shimo buyi*, DG 23.intercalary 7.14, #58–60; DG 26.7.29, #153; DG 28.8.3, #207–9; *Junji jinyan*, DG 24.7.27, #136–44; DG 26.7.29, #157–62; DG 29.8.3, #229–41.

divided into the two categories of commoners and officials. A series of edicts to senior administrators, mainly in the Board of Punishments, issued in 1841 and 1842 mandated the compilation of these lists of smokers, who were arraigned at both the autumn and the imperial assizes, for the throne's perusal. Such lists are extant for the years 1843, 1844, 1846, 1848, and 1849 (see Table 3).[73]

Despite the center's attempt to acquire a more comprehensive view of consumption offenses through these lists, a comparison of the lists and extant routine memorials reveals that not all provincial cases were included. Consequently, these lists are probably repre-

---

73. For further details on these case lists, see Fairbank, "Legalization," pp. 223–26. In some instances, Fairbank's statistics do not entirely coincide with those in Table 3 due to a few errors in his text as well as the emergence of new sources.

sentative more of the throne's impression of the distribution of smoking offenses than of actual local conditions. Two consumption cases in Jiangxi during 1843 known through routine memorials do not appear on the official case list for that year or the year after.[74] In effect, if the emperor relied only on these case lists, he would have seen only half of Jiangxi's 1843 consumption cases at best. Fairbank notes that British observers gleaned some sixty cases involving smokers from the Beijing Gazette in 1845. In addition, 27 consumption cases between 1843 and 1850 from Shanxi, Shaanxi, Manchuria, Zhili, Guangdong, Sichuan, and Beijing are not on the case lists.[75]

Regardless of attempts to accumulate more information on offenses across the empire during the 1840s, no major prohibition statutes were issued after the promulgation of the New Regulations in June 1839. Despite the problematic nature of the official record, it is clear from the case lists in Table 3 and other sources that prohibition operations peaked in 1840 and rapidly tapered off.[76] This marked drop in operations roughly coincides with the end of the grace period for consumers, the disgrace of Lin Zexu in Guangzhou, and the disastrous conclusion of the first and most important phase of the Opium War on the southeast coast. An edict strictly prohibiting opium issued by the Xianfeng emperor upon his accession to the throne in 1850, possibly in response to a memorial by a Jiangxi education official, did not reverse this trend. Subsequently, only a few scattered offenses, including poppy cultivation by a Shanxi man in Fengtian in 1851, seem to have come to the attention of the central government.[77] The Qing state's loss of much of south

---

74. Neige weijin, DG 23.2.9 and DG 23.6.5, #10124 (buben).

75. For these 27 cases, see Neige weijin category under their appropriate years. For the 1845 cases, see Fairbank, *Trade and Diplomacy*, p. 241.

76. In Beijing's First Historical Archives of China, for example, there are 124 separate secret palace memorials concerning prohibition operations throughout the empire dated the twentieth year of the Daoguang emperor (Feb. 3, 1840–Jan. 13, 1841), but only 48 for the following year. Unfortunately, contradictions between extant memorials and the empirewide consumption case lists, which enumerate only some of the offenses reported in the memorials, preclude comprehensive analysis.

77. *Daoguang Xianfeng liangchao chouban*, DG 30.5.18, pp. 25–26; Fairbank, "Legalization," pp. 224–25.

China during the Taiping rebellion doubtlessly kept the limited amount of prohibition during the Xianfeng reign confined to north of the Yangzi, although the rebels themselves also banned the drug.[78]

Prohibition had begun as a few regulations intended to restrict the import of a physically harmful foreign drug into the urban ports of the southeast China coast. A survey of the development of prohibition policy between 1729 and 1843 demonstrates that the Qing administrative institutions through which prohibition was implemented could not keep pace with the transformations wrought by the production, distribution, and consumption of opium by imperial subjects and foreign traffickers. The power of the drug to destabilize social, political, and economic relations was directly related to the transformation of opium from a foreign to a domestic addictive consumable.

Opium as a Qing Addictive Consumable

Qing opium prohibition was a response to the uncontrollable power of opium as an addictive consumable, particularly in the form of a smokable paste. Indeed, smoking was the prerequisite for the criminalization of opium because its distinct physiological action within the human body ultimately produced a series of politically disruptive economic effects that resonated far beyond the individual consumer. Consequently, the act of opium smoking itself merits closer examination as the key link between individual consumption of an addictive consumable and that addictive consumable's social and historical consequences in Qing China.

Opium in various forms had a long history in China. It had been known since the Tang dynasty and during the Ming was ingested primarily as a treatment for dysentery, a preventive for malaria, and a stimulant. The standard Qing term for opium, *yapian*, also first appeared during the Ming as the layman's word for the pharmacological term *afurong*, which would subsequently refer primarily to poppy and its opium derivatives produced in south-

---

78. Fairbank, "Legalization," pp. 225–26; Shen, "Taiping tianguo de jin yapian"; Shih, *Taiping Ideology*, pp. 76–77.

west China during the Qing.[79] Of course, the connotation of "opium," whether *yapian* or *afurong*, during the Ming was consequently different from that of the Qing, which regionalized *afurong* and ultimately criminalized both terms. This shift from legitimate medicine to illicit drug was caused by the Qing practice of smoking, which escalated in potency from tobacco to a mixture of tobacco and opium and finally to a relatively pure opium paste. Smoking was the common mode of consumption of both tobacco and opium, and this activity was critical for the addictive properties and consequent criminalization of these drugs.

Smoking was certainly a familiar form of consumption during the Ming, but the addictive consumable of choice at this period was simply tobacco, which probably entered China from Luzon via southeastern coastal ports no earlier than 1560.[80] State prohibition followed no later than 1637 for reasons that are not entirely explicit but may have something to do with tobacco's physiological effects, described as making smokers "terribly confused to the point of collapse." Domestic cultivation grew rapidly and was very widespread by the end of the Ming dynasty, with the most expensive products coming from Fujian and Manchuria. At least part of tobacco's popularity in China came from its reputed medicinal properties of preventing malaria as well as "cold diseases," a major category of ailments in traditional Chinese medicine.[81]

The Manchus were also using tobacco for much the same reasons even before the final invasion of Ming China by Qing forces in 1644. The Manchu state responded in the same way as its Han counterpart, banning tobacco smoking a number of times between 1635 and 1641, in part because smokers were neglecting their dependents to sustain their own habits. The state's concern to control the production and consumption of a strategic commodity was also clearly an important motive for the tobacco bans. By the end

---

79. Li Gui, *Yapian shilüe*, p. 5517; Li Shizhen, *Bencao gangmu*, 23:14a–b. For a concise overview in English of opium in China prior to the Qing dynasty, see Fu, *Documentary Chronicle*, 2:518–19n. For a more extended discussion of pre-Qing opium use, see Edkins, *Historical Note*, pp. 1–40. *Yapian zhanzheng*, 1:322–24, 334, reprints a number of these sources in Chinese.

80. Hao Jinda, "Yancao chuanru," pp. 225–26.

81. Goodrich, "Early Prohibitions," pp. 648–53.

of this period, the Ming was relaxing its ban, and the Manchus had effectively abandoned prohibition.[82]

Nevertheless, the Qing state's attitude toward tobacco smoking remained equivocal, although the next attempt at prohibition, under the Kangxi emperor, who had smoked as a child, arose from significantly different motives. The few prosecutions I have come across during his ban, asserted in 1676 and reiterated in 1684, date from the late 1600s and were intended to prevent fires in the Forbidden City.[83] Whether out of filial piety or practical necessity, the Yongzheng emperor followed his father's example and reaffirmed the smoking ban in 1727, actually prosecuting at least one case in 1733.[84] The Yongzheng emperor's prohibition, however, was conveyed in terms mild enough to be cited against intensified prohibition by its opponents during the subsequent Qianlong reign, when some authorities viewed tobacco consumption as an epidemic.[85] The controversy over tobacco prohibition during this time arose out of wider economic debates, which included a proposed liquor prohibition, all of which were the results of comprehensive policy reviews upon the accession of the Qianlong emperor in 1735.[86]

The main argument against a tobacco ban was the ubiquity of tobacco smoking. Anecdote maintained that "during the Kangxi reign there was not one among the gentry who did not smoke tobacco, even down to the women and children, all of whom gripped

---

82. Spence, "Opium Smoking," p. 155; Benedict, "Hongtaiji's Tobacco Prohibitions," pp. 13–19.

83. Goodrich, "Early Prohibitions," p. 654; Spence, "Opium Smoking," pp. 155–56. For the criminal case records from 1683 and 1694, respectively, see *Qingdai Neige daku sanyi,* 11:61, 88. An apocryphal account from 1874 relates that the Kangxi emperor had a particular dislike of tobacco smoking and banned it after witnessing one of his senior officials burning his lips trying to use a pipe the emperor had bestowed on him during a southern tour (Chen Qiyuan, *Yongxian zhai biji,* 3:13a).

84. *Qingdai Neige daku sanyi,* 12:29–30.

85. QSL, YZ 5.3.3, 57:813b–15b; Junji chajin, QL 1.12.18, #822–28; Gongzhong jinyan, QL 3.12.11.

86. For the context and translations of major documents in the liquor prohibition debate, see Dunstan, *Conflicting Counsels,* chap. 5. On the roles of Chen Hongmou and Fang Bao in both the tobacco and the liquor debates of the Qianlong period, see Rowe, *Saving the World,* pp. 161–62.

a pipe in their hands. They could leave off food and drink, but never tobacco." The Yongzheng ban had not changed these consumption habits, which persisted into the Qianlong reign. By 1743 Governor of Jiangxi Chen Hongmou, an opponent of tobacco, estimated that 70–80 percent of the Chinese populace, including children, smoked.[87]

The considerable scale of domestic tobacco consumption had engendered domestic cultivation of commensurate scope, a fact acknowledged the same year by an imperial decree prohibiting the crop's cultivation on prime agricultural land while permitting it to be grown in limited quantities on marginal plots.[88] In 1737 the hard-line prohibitionist and eminent Neo-Confucianist foe of elite extravagance Fang Bao had taken advantage of the Qianlong policy review to express fear that agricultural resources would be wasted on the production of tobacco and grain alcohol, leaving no room to grow staple crops. Both Fang and Chen proposed an array of measures, including land and crop confiscations, to be enforced mainly through the *baojia* system. The aim was to radically curtail, if not entirely eliminate, the "wasteful" production of these addictive consumables in order to maximize production of staples. Significantly, Fang in particular noted that the main reason prohibition had slackened in the first place was because of the sheer number of cultivators, and prohibitionists generally acknowledged that some tobacco cultivation could continue, at least in fever-ridden malarial areas, as a sop to its popular use as a febrifuge.[89]

Officials favoring a more relaxed ban took greater cognizance of the fact that numerically significant numbers of the peasantry, upon whom the central government relied for a considerable portion of its revenues, were themselves dependent on tobacco cultivation. Vice Commander-in-Chief of the Bordered Yellow Banner Bu-lan-tai made precisely this point in his rebuttal of Fang's arguments. He also pointed out that the value of marginal agricultural resources was increased by the production on otherwise inferior

---

87. Xu Ke, *Qingbai leichao*, 13:6357; Gongzhong jinyan, QL 8.4.27.
88. *HDSL*, 2:1134a.
89. Junji chajin, QL 1.12.18, #822–28; Fang Bao, *Fang Bao ji*, 2:550–53; Gongzhong jinyan, QL 8.4.2.

soil of both grain alcohol from secondary cereals, such as sorghum, and tobacco. Bu-lan-tai's proposal was a kind of sustainable prohibition that took the economic interests of both the populace and the state into account. In practice this plan meant actively restricting the production of tobacco and alcohol grains to marginal agricultural resources while avoiding the numerous practical problems of imposing something approaching a total ban.[90]

Perhaps the most fundamental problem with any extreme form of prohibition was that it failed to address the situation in areas where natural conditions were not conducive to the production of staple crops. Bu-lan-tai's position was far more flexible in this regard and was soon vindicated in 1744 in Fujian. Acting Governor Zhou Xuejian reported that "strong" prohibition measures had "initially" been avoided because the conversion of land to grain production was impractical in the dry, mountainous areas of the province, where the peasantry was heavily dependent on tobacco.[91] By 1751 similar conditions had promoted a thriving cultivation of tobacco in Shaanxi, which was sending its produce beyond provincial boundaries to Shanxi and Henan. Local conditions like these seem to have effectively undermined arguments for the absolute prohibition of tobacco.

Bu-lan-tai's version of tobacco prohibition was sustainable for a number of reasons relevant to the failure of absolute opium prohibition a century later in the 1830s and 1840s. One critical point, also made in the 1830s by Censor Guo Baiyin in the context of southwestern poppy cultivation, was the determining role that the economic interdependency between the state and its agricultural subjects should play in the formation and implementation of prohibition policy. Bu-lan-tai had stressed that policy must be based on the fact that the state was dependent on tobacco production because a critical number of its agriculturalists were. Indeed, this interdependency was precisely why a total ban had failed in the first place, as Fang Bao himself recognized. From this perspective absolute prohi-

---

90. Gongzhong jinyan, QL 3.12.11. The major opponent of liquor prohibition, Sun Jiagan, made some similar arguments in 1739 (Dunstan, *Conflicting Counsels*, pp. 240–45).

91. Gongzhong jinyan, QL 9.4.16 and QL 16.7.12, 125b–26b.

bition was a futile and deluded autocratic reaction against superior popular material conditions. Sustainable prohibition acknowledged the dangerous vanity of such a reckless assertion of state power by fiat in opposition to the real basis of that same power.

The example of sustainable tobacco prohibition was raised during the discussions leading up to the absolute opium prohibition in the 1830s. In 1836, Xu Naiji used the dynasty's success with tobacco to bolster his antiprohibition argument to legalize opium consumption and poppy cultivation for the benefit of the domestic economy: "Formerly in the Ming, what is now called 'dry' tobacco came from Luzon. It was very powerful, and consumers became dizzy from it. It was thus prohibited initially, but subsequently the populace was permitted to smoke it. It was cultivated everywhere in China proper, and Luzon tobacco was no longer brought here."[92]

Revealing just how legitimated tobacco had become in the eyes of prohibitionists, one of Xu's most vigorous opponents, Zhu Zun, held that opium was not comparable to tobacco, which brought lower profits and did not require particularly rich soil for cultivation, as he believed opium did. Although Zhu would win the legalization debate, his policy of absolute prohibition of opium would fail, in large measure because of the dependency created by opium consumption, which was comparable to that created by tobacco.

Indeed, tobacco and opium were intimately linked, and possibly confused, in the Qing period. As late as 1830, the deleterious effects of opium were characterized as similar to those of tobacco, and both substances were confiscated during an antidrug operation on the Yangzi in Sichuan in 1839. To further confuse matters, there is also evidence of an uncertain date, but probably from the late Qing, that shows paste was being mixed with apparently legal tobacco to conceal clearly illegal opium consumption.[93] Individual official attitudes toward both drugs also seem contradictory. In 1811, for example, Liang-Guang Governor-General Song Yun expressed uncer-

---

92. *YPZZ*, DG 16.4.27, 1:202–3; Tian and Li, "Sixiang qianqu," p. 104. The term "dry tobacco" refers to the type smoked in a conventional pipe as opposed to a hookah.

93. *YPZZ*, DG 9.12.16, 1:62–63, DG 19.3.23, 1:532–33; Xu Ke, *Qingbai leichao*, 13:6358.

tainty as to the specific ingredients of opium then circulating in Guangdong but did know that it was boiled into a kind of "tobacco" (*yan*) whose addictive properties were harmful to health and property. This belief, however, did not stop the governor-general from accepting a gift of tobacco (*yangyan*) for distribution to his subordinates during his talks with foreign merchants regarding dynastic opium prohibitions.[94]

Many of these contradictions were no doubt based on the fact that the substance smoked from the early seventeenth century into the early nineteenth was almost exclusively a mixture of opium and tobacco, along with other vegetable matter, known to contemporary Westerners as "madak." The composite nature of this drug was reflected in its most common Chinese name during the Ming and Qing, *yapian yan*, a compound of the words for crude opium (*yapian*) and tobacco (*yancao*). The earliest official descriptions of madak clearly state that it is necessary to mix opium with tobacco, along with other vegetable material, prior to smoking it, but not all officials seem to have been privy to this knowledge. Indeed, the term *yapian yan* clearly meant different things to different people at different times. Chen Qiyuan, in his 1874 musings on the first prohibition case in 1728, revealed that he "could not help bursting into laughter" when he read that officialdom during the earliest stages of Qing prohibition made a legal distinction between medicinal opium and illicit opium mixed with tobacco. Chen asserted that there was no real difference between *yapian* and *yapian yan*, since tobacco was a superfluous additive. He concluded that people in the Yongzheng reign "had not known what opium is" because few actually smoked it.[95] Actually, it would be more accu-

---

94. *Qingdai waijiao shiliao*, JQ 16.5.13, 3:42a–43a. An English translation of this memorial gives the impression that Qing officials clearly understood that opium was being mixed with tobacco. The Chinese text, however, is too ambiguous for such a precise translation; see Fu, *Documentary Chronicle*, 1:381–83. Early Qing sumptuary laws had made tobacco consumption by non-elites a crime (Benedict, "Hongtaiji's Tobacco Prohibitions," p. 8). Similar conditions may have technically obtained in 1811.

95. Chen Qiyuan, *Yongxian zhai biji*, 8:14b–15a. Chen held opium to be "one hundred times more harmful than tobacco," which he seems to have considered more of a fire hazard than a potentially lethal narcotic (ibid., 3:13a).

rate to say that the people of the time did not know what opium paste was, probably because it had yet to be invented.

The practice of smoking madak probably began during the late Ming around the time tobacco smoking appeared. One Chinese account penned some time before 1626 concerning the use of snuff in Macao noted that opium was both smokable and illegal.[96] Qing records indicate that opium was flowing into the empire no later than the 1710s, either through the agency of Chinese maritime traders resident in the Dutch East Indian colony on Java or from the Dutch themselves during their control of Taiwan from 1624 to 1662.[97] The edition of the Taiwan prefectural gazetteer published in 1736 provides evidence for the Java transmission route. It states that the Dutch were responsible for the manufacture of madak and pushed it on the indigenous inhabitants of Java. Resident Chinese traders, the middlemen in the trade between the Dutch East Indies and China, began smoking it and smuggled the Javan drug to the Zhangzhou, Quanzhou, and Xiamen areas in Fujian. Transients from these areas then introduced madak to Taiwan and elsewhere.[98]

Whatever its ultimate origins, "opium" in China referred exclusively to madak until around the end of the eighteenth century. Neither pure tobacco nor opium was criminalized during this period, accounting for the Qing state's nearly unenforceable distinction between the legal, taxable medicine *yapian* and the illegal narcotic *yapian yan*. Around this time, the composition of *yapian yan* would undergo a crucial change into unadulterated opium paste. Paste was a far more powerful, and thus more profitable, derivative of crude opium. Opium paste yielded fifty times more morphia than madak, whose 0.2 percent morphia content probably made it no more potent than "a few inhalations of marijuana" despite ac-

---

96. Spence, "Opium Smoking," p. 147.

97. Lin Man-houng, "Qingmo shehui liuxing xishi yapian yanjiu," appendix 1; *Yapian zhanzheng*, 1:334. There are several Western accounts of local Chinese in Java ranging in date from 1602 to 1771; see Zheng, "Social Life of Opium," pp. 9–10; and Spence, "Opium Smoking," p. 147. Lo-shu Fu (*Documentary Chronicle*, 2:519*n*) cites a Xiamen gazetteer stating that smoking spread from Xiamen to Taiwan. For a history of opium in Java, see Rush, *Opium to Java*.

98. *Taiwan fu zhi*, 19:34a, 38a–b.

counts of addiction after only a few trials.[99] Although madak continued to be smoked as late as 1793, and no doubt beyond, consumers showed an increasing preference for paste.[100] The physical transformation of opium increased consumption dramatically and compelled the state to criminalize the possession of opium in any form during the first decades of the nineteenth century.

A comparison of descriptions of opium smoking reveals that the transition from madak to paste consumption began some time around the turn of the eighteenth century. The few early accounts from the 1720s and 1730s are quite important for their details about the consumption of madak, which clearly distinguish it from the later consumption of paste, a difference otherwise obscured by imprecise terms for opium in common use, especially *yapian yan*. One detail is, of course, the presence of tobacco, an infallible sign of madak. Another of equal importance is the vegetable matter, usually coir palm fibers, stuffed as tinder into the bamboo pipe prior to the insertion of the madak itself. Finally, the paraphernalia of madak smoking is less specialized than that of paste smoking.[101]

The earliest official account of madak smoking, submitted to the throne in 1728, does not use the term *yapian yan*. Instead, it describes the drug as being "decocted into a paste" (*paozhi cheng gao*), but this phrase does not refer to the pure opium extract (*gao*) common to accounts from around the end of the century. In this case, the paste was mixed with "shredded tobacco" (*yansi*) before being dried into *yan* and put in a bamboo tube stuffed with coir palm fibers for smoking. This description differs in a few impor-

---

99. Spence, "Opium Smoking," p. 148; *Yapian zhanzheng*, 1:324.

100. Spence, "Opium Smoking," p. 149; Edkins, *Historical Note*, pp. 51–52. Wang Hongbin (*Jindu shijian*, pp. 25–26) presents evidence for the appearance of pure opium smoking during the latter half of the eighteenth century and shows that some nineteenth-century Chinese authorities held the practice to have emerged in the closing years of the Qianlong emperor's reign. Despite strong evidence that paste smoking appeared during the Qianlong-Jiaqing transition, the specific details of when and how paste smoking came to China remain debatable.

101. On the significance of paraphernalia, see Wang Hongbin, *Jindu shijian*, p. 24.

tant respects from that of a private account published in 1736 by Regional Inspecting Censor for Taiwan (*xuntai yushi*) Huang Shujing. Huang did not use the term "paste" (*gao*) in his description of madak, nor do any other accounts I have come across. Instead, Huang said that tobacco, hemp, and other vegetable materials along with crude opium were "boiled into opium-mixed tobacco" (*zhucheng yapian ban yan*) before being smoked in the manner described above.[102]

Several accounts, dating from the late Qianlong or early Jiaqing periods, contain descriptions of opium smoking that resemble the more complicated process of using paste rather than the simpler procedures for madak. Most obvious is the omission of tobacco from the smoking preparations. Equally significant, however, are the more elaborate decoction or boiling process, the formation of the results into pills, and the employment of a lamp. The account of Yu Jiao, in a work compiled somewhat before 1800, is outstanding for its detailed explanations of all these distinguishing characteristics of paste smoking:

Opium comes from the various kingdoms beyond the seas and resembles horse dung colored a light green. It is soaked in three changes of water over as many nights, and the dregs are removed in progressively smaller amounts, leaving only the liquid. This is refined by flame into a paste (*huolian cheng gao*), like that used by physicians to treat lesions and toxins. The paste is apportioned into pills like grains, a lamp is placed near a couch, and a bamboo tube is grasped in the manner of a flute. One reclines and smokes. Smoking necessitates two to lie down and pass the pipe between them; the pleasure is thereby doubled. The smoke enters the belly and augments the vital principle so that no fatigue is experienced from sunset to dawn. If one continues on in this manner, after a few months it seeps into one's heart and spleen so that if one does not smoke daily on a regular basis, illness results. This is commonly known as crav-

---

102. Ibid., pp. 20–21; Spence, "Opium Smoking," p. 148. For Huang's text, see *Yapian zhanzheng*, 1:324. A brief section of this passage is translated in Fu, *Documentary Chronicle*, 2:518n. For the full text of the 1728 memorial, most of which was concerned with the suppression of four serious offenses in the author's jurisdiction, only one of which was opium trafficking, see *Yongzheng chao hanwen zhupi zouzhe*, YZ 6.11.6, 13:848b–53b.

ing (*yin*), which in extreme cases causes tears and mucus to flow and so debilitates the limbs that they cannot be raised.[103]

As paste smoking progressed, more sophisticated elements appeared, such as specialized utensils like metal pipe scrapers, and domestic varieties of opium, such as the home-grown "Tai juice" from Zhejiang, which was boiled in alcohol during the 1830s.[104] These were minor refinements to the final form of Qing opium, which, as shown by Yu Jiao's description, had surfaced at the end of the eighteenth century as a fully developed addictive consumable. It was around the same time that the premodern equivalent of the term "addiction," *yin* in the sense of a "craving," seems to have emerged in connection with opium smoking.[105]

Paste caused a new level of alarm among Qing officials. Qian Jie, in his 1811 report, provided an early official account of paste (*gao*) smoking involving a lamp (*deng*) passed from user to user, who proceeded to "drink smoke" (*yinyan*). The aspect of this process that most disturbed Qian Jie was the close relationship that passing the opium lamp produced among otherwise casual acquaintances, who, while smoking, "reveal their innermost feelings to one another as between elder and younger brother." They were thus emboldened to commit criminal acts both because of the drug's stimulant properties and because of the camaraderie that arose from the social character of its consumption. Qian had come to these conclusions through personal experience: he had previously dealt harshly but ineffectively with daylight break-ins in Guangxi and found that many young perpetrators were dying of withdrawal in custody. He asserted that their expensive addictions drove them to commit these brazen robberies and left them undeterred by punishment.[106]

Qian's report shows that the enhanced potency of paste, along with its particular mode of consumption, was giving new impetus

---

103. Quoted in Wang Hongbin, *Jindu shijian*, p. 25. Qin Heping (*Yunnan yapian wenti*, pp. 7–8) cites another Jiaqing-era source that provides a similar description of consumption and addiction.

104. Junji jinyan, DG 10.6.24, #1545–46; *Yapian zhangzheng*, pp. 161–62.

105. Howard, "Opium Suppression in Qing China," pp. 59–60.

106. Gongzhong jinyan, JQ 16.2.13.

and power to traditional forms of criminal behavior.[107] It also reveals why the particular composition of opium and its specific consumption practices were crucial for the exacerbation of the drug problem and the consequent intensified prohibition operations initiated in the Jiaqing years. The transformation of the drug from madak to paste not only removed ambiguities concerning the possession of opium but also increased both the consumption of the drug and the threat of smokers to the social order.

The ultimate state response to this threat was the extreme forms of absolute prohibition of opium operative during the 1830s and 1840s, which were fatally unrealistic in the context of the empire's overall historical experience with addictive consumables. The sustainable prohibition of tobacco, for example, was fundamentally conditioned by the empire's geographic diversity. In contrast, absolute prohibition sought to impose artificially uniform agricultural conditions on the sprawling Qing domains by assuming that agriculture was, or should be, the same everywhere. Indeed, this assumption was predicated on a moral judgment rather than experience, the basis of the practical statecraft underlying sustainable prohibition.

A bureaucratic ideology of an idealized uniformity, or "harmony," was a traditional and often effective mainstay of any Chinese state, but it could undermine bureaucratic control if taken too literally and uncritically. The sustainable prohibition of tobacco was not sacrificed to this kind of ideological consistency, but any form of absolute prohibition of addictive consumables was quite vulnerable in this regard. The effects of ideology on the state formulation and regional implementation of opium policy, as well as on the state's basic perception of the nature of opium consumption, are difficult to identify precisely, but they were important in justifying both the criminalization of the drug and the decisive shift to absolute prohibition.

---

107. Criminal activity by madak addicts, impoverished, if not emboldened, by the drug, was mentioned by Su Mingliang in 1728, but I have come across no specific claims of addict violence before Qian Jie's 1811 report; see *Yongzheng chao hanwen zhupi zouzhe*, YZ 6.11.6, 13:848b–53b.

The Ideology of Qing Prohibition

In the following analysis, "ideology" is the state-sponsored expression of the state's own motives for action, sincere or otherwise, on behalf of the commonweal. Such expressions are intended to achieve particular goals, all ultimately related to the perpetuation of the state itself, through the formation, or reformation, of the social identities of a critical mass of individual subjects. The analytical application of this definition to the specific historical context of Qing prohibition can be summarized as follows: the Qing government sought, through a number of measures, to persuade as many of its subjects as possible to actively reject all forms of opium; that is, to become spontaneous agents of prohibition whenever they encountered the drug and its adherents.

Although it is possible to understand many prohibition measures, such as the actual enforcement of specific criminal statutes, in the theoretical terms outlined above, I restrict my examination of Qing prohibition ideology primarily to the ethical and moral justifications for prohibition. It is certainly true that prohibition in practice was effected largely through the use of a small bunch of carrots and a big bundle of sticks, but state legitimacy rhetorically required something more than crude appeals to fundamental self-interest, which was in many cases being harmed by state prohibition policy.

Motivation based on self-interest was certainly not something the state wished to inculcate or promote in its officials, the primary agents of prohibition. Consequently, the state program for the formation of proper official identities, based substantially on various discursive techniques that can be abbreviated as "Confucianism," preferred to rely on ethical, that is, unselfish, justifications for actions, both public and private. The ideal state goal in this educational process was to produce officials who had fully internalized this key value, an achievement that would obviate the necessity for sustained state supervision by yet more unreliable and expensive officials. Proper officials would, in turn, transmit the value of unselfishness to the rest of society, and harmony would result. The price the state paid for this ideology was, of course, the necessity of at least appearing to adhere to the same value of unself-ishness toward all its subjects. From an ideological perspective, opium prohibition was the price paid by pervasive social vice, in the various forms of drug dependency, to the public virtue of har-mony (*he*) through unselfishness (*gong*) promoted by the state in order to legitimize and perpetuate itself.

Like the composition of opium itself, the ideology of dynastic drug prohibition changed over time, and these changes were in-strumental in determining the formation and implementation of state policy. Yet, just as madak use persisted even after the adoption of paste, earlier ideological constructs continued to be used along with later formations. The foundational ideological justification di-rected at the Qing populace for the prohibition of opium in particu-lar, as well as of many addictive consumables in general, was con-structed from the rhetoric of paramount state concern for the commonweal.

Chen Lihe, district magistrate of Taiyu, in Shanxi province, provided an unusually dramatic example of such rhetoric in 1817. Chen erected a stele inscribed with "a pledge to prohibit opium"; his goal was to have every member of the local population swear to refrain from opium consumption and, especially, trafficking. Although the immediate purpose of the stele seems to have been to issue a public warning that Chen would soon be conduct-ing prohibition operations in Taiyu, it was also intended to trans-form the officials and commoners of Taiyu into staunch observers of opium prohibition through the moral agency of the super-natural:

All merchants in the district who go to Fujian, Guangdong, Jiangsu, or Zhejiang to buy goods must pledge that they will not bring a single frag-ment of opium back to Taiyu for sale, to the great harm of its populace. If they render respectful adherence to their oaths of abstinence, the spirits will surely reward them. If they resume trafficking, the officials will cer-tainly punish them! And if official law cannot reach them, the spirits will surely lend assistance.

If any officials take bribes or connive to conceal trafficking, the spirits will surely punish them and beset them with calamity in the same way that they will do to traffickers and consumers! Ah! The people cannot possibly be harmed because the spirits cannot possibly be deceived.

Those of my merchants who travel to Fujian, Guangdong, Jiangsu, and Zhejiang on the sea desire that there be neither wind nor waves; those who travel on land desire that there be neither narrow passes nor dangerous defiles. When they are at peace, what profit can they not seek to gain? Must they violate the laws of the state and rouse the wrath of the spirits for such a thing as opium![108]

Admittedly, such hortatory tactics did not eradicate opium from Shanxi, where the drug problem persisted well beyond the Daoguang reign, but the material limits of local administration, implicit in Chen's appeal, made it necessary for officials to make a public case for the state's prohibition policy to the populace and their own subordinates.[109] The main ideological challenge facing

---

108. For the full Chinese text of Chen's stele, along with a very brief analysis, see Yang Kaida, "Yapianyan bei," pp. 27–28. The text is excerpted from Chen's biography in the Shibing district gazetteer, Chen's native place in Yunnan province. For a full translation of the text, which is one of a very few such documents for public consumption extant from before the Opium War, see Appendix B.

109. Although it is difficult to get a detailed picture of Shanxi's opium problem, it is clear that Taiyu district in Taiyuan prefecture was the most important center of the provincial traffic as early as 1821. This distinction was primarily due to the activities of merchants from this district, who were identified as the main culprits at this time by virtue of their extensive commercial intercourse with Guangdong and other southern coastal provinces (*Gongzhong DG*, DG 1.2.26, 1:173a–b). Indeed, there is much evidence to show that the Shanxi banks were heavily dependent on the coastal opium trade; see Chang, *Commissioner Lin*, pp. 37–39. Yet only one consumption and five trafficking cases, two from Taiyu, were reported before 1838 (Junji jinyan, DG 12.12.17, #1787–89; Gongzhong jinyan, DG 15.12.29; *YPZZ*, DG 11.12.30, 1:108–9). There were three other cases, however, involving Shanxi natives in Beijing during the year 1830–31 (ZZD, DG 10.5, pp. 219–26, DG 11.6.2, pp. 33–34; Junji jinyan, DG 11.7.10, #1621–22). Cases of consumption alone jumped to seventeen in 1838, and a month later, three major smuggling routes into the province—one from Tianjin, one from the southeast coast, and one from Sichuan—had been identified. Taiyu district alone reported the confiscation of 189 kilos of crude opium and paste, the single largest confiscation in the province (Junji jinyan, DG 18.10.28, #2080–82; *Gongzhong DG*, DG 18.11.28, 7:384a–85b). Around this time eleven Shanxi-related cases, six involving smugglers from Taiyu and one from Jiexiu in Shanxi, another important center, were discovered in Beijing (*Gongzhong DG*, DG 18.12.14, 7:556a–60a). At this point it appears that Tianjin, rather than Guangdong, was Shanxi's major source of southeastern coastal opium. By mid-1839 a total of 1,429 kilos of crude opium and paste had been confiscated, and 113 consumers and traffickers caught (*YPZZ*, DG 19.4.25, 1:560–61). There was a drastic decrease in confiscations shortly after this date. Between January and October

central policymakers was to justify to the rest of the empire an increasingly absolutist prohibition policy in the established terms of
benevolent government.

From the beginning of prohibition, the state's primary expression of benevolence was to defend all its subjects from the addictive power of opium, which was characterized as harmful to social
and individual mores in addition to being physically poisonous.
Occasionally, concern for consumption's debilitating effects on
family resources was also voiced. Such formulaic references perme-
ate the official record from the Yongzheng, Qianlong, Jiaqing, and
Daoguang reigns.[110] Yet, until 1813 no formal statutes fixing precise
punishments for opium consumption, which had been sporadically
punished with 100 blows of the heavy bamboo under a catch-all
statute of "violating imperial decrees" (*weizhi*), were promulgated.[111] Up until this date, no official conceptualization of an "addict," essentially a person held to have a socially dangerous, illicit
physical dependency on opium smoking, had emerged to stimulate
the active criminalization of opium consumption by the state.

Although Su Mingliang had offered the court a construction of
precisely such an addict in his foundational prohibition request of
1728, state power was directed almost exclusively against traffickers
and den operators until the early 1800s. Su himself suggested that
the prohibition of consumption would only encourage official
extortion, and this problem was obviously a main reason for the
omission of addicts from the statutes on punishment.[112] Another

---

1840, for example, only four kilos of crude opium and paste were confiscated.
Nevertheless, both Taiyu and Jiexiu remained foci of prohibition efforts (*YPZZ*,
DG 20.9.11, 2:449–50). Records from subsequent reigns show that opium persisted
in Shanxi well into the late Qing; see Li Sanmou, "Yapian zai Shanxi," 24–25. For
an outline of Shanxi's opium problem during the Daoguang period, see Lin Man-
houng, "Qingmo shehui liuxing xishi yapian yanjiu," pp. 77–78; and idem, "Yin
yu yapian," pp. 113–17.

110. For representative examples, see *Yongzheng chao hanwen zhupi zouzhe*, YZ
6.11.6, 13:848b–53b; Junji chajin, QL 41.10.17, #934–36; and *YPZZ*, JQ 16.6.26, 1:3,
DG 19.5.2, 1:565.

111. *YPZZ*, JQ 18.7.10, 1:5–6, JQ 18.7.10, 1:7; *HDSL*, 9:1013b. For information regarding catch-all statutes in Qing law, see Bodde and Morris, *Law in Imperial
China*, pp. 530–33.

112. *Yongzheng chao hanwen zhupi zouzhe*, YZ 6.11.6, 13:848b–53b.

less explicit reason is revealed in the original statutes themselves, which particularly condemn the den operators' "corruption of the sons and younger brothers of good families." Several subsequent reports clarify this vague, formulaic reference to status. An official report from 1807 condemned the Guangdong gentry for squandering its excessive wealth on, among other things, opium smoking, and in 1831 a metropolitan censor asserted that smoking had spread from "urban elites" (*chengshi fuhao*) to the general populace.[113] Unofficial sources indicate widespread smoking among the Qing urban elite, primarily as an aphrodisiac, and one account from the late eighteenth century claimed that only the peasantry did not smoke.[114] Despite the ire expressed in the official reports, the elite status of the vast majority of consumers of this expensive luxury good during the initial decades of prohibition may have helped delay the state's full criminalization of opium smoking until the later years of the Jiaqing reign. Indeed, one elite smoker was the Jiaqing emperor's successor, the Daoguang emperor, who praised what he called "the satisfier" during his minority.[115]

The Board of Punishments' revision of the prohibitions in 1813 was instrumental in the state's formal construction of the addict-offender. In the 1810 edict on the Beijing smuggling case ordering coastal officials to increase their antitrafficking activities, the Jiaqing emperor had declared that opium was a harsh stimulant that freed consumers from all moral and customary restraints.[116]

---

113. Ibid.; *HDSL*, 9.1013b; *Qingdai waijiao shiliao*, JQ 12.11.16, 2:8a–9a; *YPZZ*, DG 11.5.15, 1:80. There is also evidence of elite opium-eating in the Ming, when the drug was particularly expensive, by royalty and officialdom (Wang Hongbin, *Jindu shijian*, p. 15; Zheng, "Social Life of Opium," p. 8*n*). An English translation of a no longer extant local notice by Guangzhou's superintendent of maritime customs ("the Hoppo") implies that opium started at the bottom of the social hierarchy among "vagrants and disreputable persons" and worked its way insidiously upward (see Morse, *Trading to China*, 2:344), but given the expense of the drug during its early stages of consumption, smoking seems likely to have initially been an elite pastime.

114. Cited in Zheng, "Social Life of Opium," pp. 13–14.

115. Cited in ibid., p. 16.

116. *YPZZ*, JQ 15.3.2, 1:1. Lo-shu Fu (*Documentary Chronicle*, 1:380) provides an English translation of this edict that reads in part: "Opium has a very violent effect. When an addict smokes it, it rapidly makes him extremely excited and capa-

This basis for the state's construction of the criminal addict was substantially solidified by Hubei Governor Qian Jie's 1811 account of addict-robbers, which the Board of Punishments specifically cited in its 1813 deliberations. The board also asserted that opium consumption had spread beyond the coast among both market-place vagabonds and imperial bodyguards. Such smoking was a form of criminal "depravity" and lethally "contaminated people's minds" in exactly the same manner as "poison."[117]

The distinction between commoner and official addicts was also a creation of the Board of Punishments' deliberations at this time. Previously, government prohibition statutes were concerned only with administrative malfeasance, not consumption by officials. Subsequent major revisions of prohibition statutes generally included provisions for office-holding addicts, who clearly remained an ongoing problem, in part because officials were seen as models of proper behavior for the relatively unenlightened masses.

Addiction was felt to create particular problems for prohibition, a fact emphasized by Censor Liu Guangsan during his call for increased penalties for consumption in 1831. Liu specifically defined "addiction" (*yin*) as an illness contracted from extended opium smoking, which was fatal if not "satisfied" (*guo yin*) at the proper time. Liu argued that the deadly power of addiction was the main reason addicts would not reveal their sources of supply to officials, despite the threat of heavy punishment. Addict resistance was considered a major obstacle to prohibition and became the pretext for a further intensification of punishment for smokers, who were now to be sentenced to the far more serious punishment of three years' penal servitude as accessories to trafficking if they refused to reveal their drug suppliers.[118]

Prior to their explicit construction as state offenders in 1813, opium consumers were considered to be harming mainly themselves and their immediate families. The wider social effects of

---

ble of doing anything he pleases." There is no justification in the original text for Fu's use of the term "addict"; a literal translation of the original text would be "those who consume this [i.e., opium]."

117. *YPZZ*, JQ 18.7.10, 1:6.
118. *YPZZ*, DG 11.5.15, 1:79–80.

consumption, while touched on by some officials, were not considered serious enough to warrant special punishment. The state began to see consumers as criminals once smokers were reinterpreted as agents of the spread of opium both to the imperial interior and to lower levels of Qing society. By 1831, "addicts," especially those who were officials, had also become saboteurs of state prohibition policy. Enhanced criminalization of consumption was one consequence of the refusal or inability of addicts to internalize state ideological norms and transform themselves into prohibitionists willing and able to turn in their former suppliers or otherwise enforce the law.

The state transformation of opium consumers into criminal addicts was not entirely smooth. The general trend toward criminalization of consumption was temporarily interrupted by the legalization debate of 1836. Xu Naiji's proposals would have converted the criminal identities of most opium smokers and poppy cultivators into active defenders of the realm by legitimating the superior power of domestic consumers and producers to sustain a competitively cheaper form of opium and thus drive out foreign drug traffickers. Legalization would also transform traffickers of domestic opium into legitimate distributors. The only criminals left would be those who dealt in foreign opium, as well as officials and military personnel involved in consumption and administrative malfeasance.[119] Legalization would have reduced the number of opium offenses by decriminalizing a number of opium-related activities.

Prohibitionists responded to these particular arguments for legalization by asserting that opium-free officials and troops would, in the event of legalization, have to come from the opium-contaminated commoners.[120] In other words, legalization was in part predicated on impractical, idealized notions of identity-formation that would be fatal to the state in the long run. The triumph of this and other prohibitionist arguments had fatal consequences, for they persuaded the state to eliminate the people it could not change.

---

119. *YPZZ*, DG 16.4.27 #3 and #4, 1:200–203.
120. Tian and Li, "Sixiang qianqu," pp. 234–35.

By mid-1839 the state formally committed itself to eradicating addicts, as well as the other main criminal identities it had constructed by means of absolute prohibition. The Grand Council's memorial presenting the New Regulations for imperial approval summarized the evolution of the state's conceptualization of criminal addicts and connected it to a definitive argument for their elimination—they were the highest category of enemies of the state, traitors who enabled the opium traffic:

Smokers, who initially were fools seduced into smoking, are commonplace and unashamed. Their persistence in smoking in the face of widespread, public prohibition is simply defiance, and they can be considered a disorderly mob of rebels and corrupt people. Fools can be shown mercy; rebels and corrupt people cannot. Opium use attracts traffickers, and these are thus similar crimes. If both are treated with equal severity, then smokers will be too fearful to purchase opium, and the traffic will be extinguished for lack of buyers. Official malfeasance and the illicit activities of domestic merchants will also consequently be obliterated.[121]

This statement actually merged the identities of trafficker, which the memorialists ostensibly held to be the principal agent of the opium problem, and addict. In practical judicial terms, this discursive, abstract redefinition meant death sentences for consumers. The controversy that had preceded the 1839 promulgation of the New Regulations was largely fueled by a debate over whether these two identities were commensurate.[122] Although the majority of officials opposed to this idea generally advanced pragmatic reasons for their position, a few added ideological justifications. Shanxi Governor Shen Qixian, for example, criticized capital punishment for addicts as a Legalist atrocity incompatible with Confucian norms:

The onus of the large outflow of silver overseas will fall on the masses of opium smokers through the establishment of capital punishment to reprove them. I fear that these masses, whether they incur this punishment or not, will all guess that the severity of this law is based on financial calculation and is devoid of all compassion for the populace. . . . Promulgat-

---

121. *YPZZ*, DG 19.5.2, 1:565–66.
122. Wang Licheng, "Jinyan juece pingxi," p. 10.

ing the harsh laws of Shen Buhai and Han Feizi was not something done in the lenient age of Yao and Shun.[123]

There is no better statement of the fundamental ideological contradictions inherent in absolute prohibition or of the court's real motives for implementing it. Shen's invocation of the example set by the paradigmatic sage-emperors of Confucianism against the practice of the notorious Legalist minds behind the reputedly cruel and short-lived Qin dynasty may or may not have been sincere. It has been suggested that senior provincial opponents of capital punishment for addicts may simply have wanted to avoid the considerable administrative burden and risk of implementing the absolute prohibition mandated by the New Regulations in their jurisdictions. This observation is undoubtedly true, especially in light of reports of reservations expressed by local officials in Sichuan and Guizhou.[124] The considerable number of office-holding smokers also certainly reduced the enthusiasm for the execution of consumers. Nevertheless, objections to capital punishment were often not entirely self-interested and could combine ethical and practical elements, which were not necessarily mutually exclusive.

Officials like Scrutinizing Censor for Works Kuang Deng considered the potential effects of the New Regulations on morale serious enough to intensify efforts to clear all opium cases before the expiration of the grace period, which had six more months to run when he submitted his request in April 1840. Kuang feared that once capital punishment for consumers became operative in 1841, provincial officials would have no stomach to continue their investigations. Kuang reasoned that a sustained effort to catch all offenders needed to be made before 1841 in order both to save lives and to avoid burdening local officials with the choice of countenancing opium offenses or meting out grossly disproportionate punishments.[125] Such concerns were certainly the driving force behind the increased provincial prohibition efforts following the promulgation of the New Regulations in mid-1839.

---

123. *YPZZ*, DG 18.5.2, 1:260.
124. Wang Licheng, "Jinyan juece pingxi," p. 10. See Chapter 6 for examples of reservations from Guizhou and Sichuan.
125. Junji jinyan, DG 20.3.28, #3281–83.

A brief comparison of a few capital cases exposes a particularly cruel aspect of the legal distortions that validated views such as Kuang's. In January 1843, a Ms. Li, who was 40 *sui*, was sentenced to death by strangulation for opium smoking. She had been suffering from stomach pains and bought some 35 grams of opium paste from a neighbor as well as a pipe from an itinerant Guangdong peddler. She was cured but was subsequently ordered by her husband, Wang Er, 38 *sui*, to dispose of her paste and paraphernalia because of the prohibitions. Ms. Li instead buried these items in a rear courtyard and told her husband she had destroyed them. In 1842, Wang lost his job and decided to rent out his wife as a prostitute. Wang soon became a pimp for several other women and operated a brothel out of his residence. Around this time, Ms. Li experienced a relapse of her stomach pains and retrieved her opium and paraphernalia from the back courtyard. On the day she resumed smoking, officials on a vice raid entered her home and discovered her opium, pipe, and lamp.[126]

In grotesque contrast, Guangdong opium broker Tan Huanying's death sentence of decapitation was commuted to the maximum degree of exile because he had voluntarily ended his five-year career by turning over himself and 89 kilos of crude opium, upon discovering he was being sought by authorities in 1842.[127] Li's capital case involved minimal amounts of opium intended for short-term personal use and involved no trafficking on the scale of an opium brokerage. Tan's was, consequently, the more serious capital offense. This distinction between capital crimes was effected by the idiom of Confucian ideology, which considered physical mutilation, here Tan's decapitation as opposed to Li's strangulation, an unfilial violation of strictures to preserve the parental gift of the body intact.

Tan, however, whose mass-marketing activities had undoubtedly caused far more widespread harm, saved himself from a headless afterlife at the very bottom of the celestial hierarchy by his last-minute conversion to prohibition. The state expressed its approval of this supreme act of self-interest by preserving his life.

---

126. Neige weijin, DG 22.11.30, #10122 (buben).
127. Neige weijin, DG 22.7.19, #10122 (buben).

The profound ethical contradictions exposed by such cases, however, could not have escaped the presiding officials, Kuang Deng among many others.

A comparison of the cases of Li and Tan reveal a number of serious ideological contradictions that prevented many officials from becoming absolute prohibitionists. In effect, these cases demonstrate that, in the context of prohibition enforcement, smoking could be a far more serious offense than trafficking. This inversion was illogical even in terms of the New Regulations themselves, which held that traffickers produced addicts and hence were subject to more severe forms of capital punishment. In ethical terms, the operation of prohibition in these cases taught that harming oneself could be a far more serious offense than harming others. All these contradictions violated the norms on which the state justified absolute prohibition and can account for much of the official reluctance to implement it. It is probably no coincidence that the main objection to absolute prohibition was based on its indiscriminate application of capital punishment. There seems to have been no greater ideological contradiction than the prospect of state-sponsored executions of addicts justified in part by the state's frequently expressed concern for protecting the bodies of its subjects from the mutilating poison of opium.

The Li and Tan cases, as well as official objections as represented by Kuang Deng and Shen Qixian, reveal that the throne was obligated to act unselfishly, or benevolently, as the price of the reciprocal demand of loyalty made by the state on its subjects. The problem with absolute prohibition was that it could not be enforced benevolently, a fact that provided much of the impetus for policy conflicts like those over capital punishment for addicts. Expressed in terms more compatible with the ideological formations prevalent in Qing society, the inculcation of Confucian values by the state was all too often effected and affected by Legalist incentives of reward and punishment. In this spirit, Censor Liu Guangsan proposed to transform criminal addicts into cooperative informers through threats of penal servitude; when his suggestions proved impractical, the authors of the New Regulations sought to convert "rebellious" addicts and traffickers into loyal subjects with threats of execution. Even this final degree of absolute prohibition did not succeed with a critical mass of imperial subjects, the dubious conversion of offenders like Tan Huanying notwithstanding.

In no small measure, prohibition's failure from an ideological perspective was a vindication of Confucian principles of transformation through example, a fact recognized by another contemporary East Asian ruler of like convictions, the Minh-mang emperor of Vietnam. The emperor interpreted the initial defeat of Qing forces during the opening shots of the Opium War as a demonstration of the moral failure of Qing elites who openly indulged in the drug:

I am genuinely and greatly unsettled by this. Formerly the Red Hairs [Westerners] came to trade; hostilities broke out only because Lin Zexu discovered opium and confiscated ships' cargo. I have heard that the crown prince, the nobility, and the great civil and military ministers all smoke opium, as is also done publicly at town gates and marketplaces. If one's own state is so arranged, how can foreign states be ruled by its example?

It has moreover been heard that Lin Zexu's pipe is decorated with pure gold; thus he himself indulges in this evil. If one who is personally corrupt corrects others, all kinds of trouble will occur; how can this criminal still be relied on![128]

The Minh-mang emperor was unquestionably exaggerating the extent of opium smoking among the Qing elite, but he was quite precise about the consequences of elite hypocrisy for undermining the legitimacy of the Confucian state at home and abroad. For rulers like the Minh-mang and Daoguang emperors, opium smoking was immoral because it led to individual and collective practices that destabilized the ruling house.

As the Minh-mang emperor indicated, nothing was more dangerous than the spectacle of significant portions of the state addicted to opium smoking, except possibly an addiction to the revenue generated by drug consumption. Unfortunately, the Qing bureaucracy could not construct an identity of an "addict state" that could practically be targeted for transformation or elimina-

---

128. Cited in Woodside, *Vietnam and the Chinese Model*, pp. 121–22. The translation is mine.

tion without directing prohibition against itself. The inability of the state apparatus to reform itself, despite all attempts to suppress consumption and malfeasance among officials, merely transformed *junzi* (Confucian gentlemen) into *wei junzi* ("false gentlemen," i.e., hypocrites), and vitiated Confucian appeals to the populace. The state's dependency on opium deprived it of the ideological shield forged for just such a crisis and left only weapons of blunt coercion.

Qing Opium Dependency

The Qing state's substantial revisions and active enforcement of the opium prohibitions that began in the 1810s constituted an unprecedented threat to a number of previously unchallenged economic dependencies on opium among the imperial masses. This intensification also revealed that portions of the state administration itself were financially dependent on opium, in large measure because a critical number of imperial subjects in select localities were as well. Intensified prohibition, especially in its absolute form, exposed these dependencies, but it generally sought simply to eradicate them rather than to provide viable alternatives.

The resistance engendered both by new opium crimes and by the wider application of existing statutes revealed that some groups of subjects had been conditioned by lax prohibition to view opium as a legitimate source of income. One of the most striking examples of this attitude occurred in Taiwan's Danshui district in January 1814. Local shopkeepers who had been openly selling opium were confronted with a party of yamen runners sent to shut them down. Arrests and a brawl followed, in which one of the yamen runners sent to apprehend the miscreants was injured. This incident was followed by an attempt by the distributors' families to get all the shopkeepers of the town to shut down in protest against the arrests. The legitimate merchants proved immune to the power of the betel nut handed out by these families as an incentive, and the shutdown remained restricted to those shops that had been openly selling crude opium. With the arrest of several of the main perpetrators and the escape of the rest, what looks to have been

Danshui's first opium prohibition operation was brought to an ambiguous conclusion.[129]

The Danshui distributors were tenaciously defending what they must have thought were legitimate business operations, which were apparently so much a part of daily economic life that they thought they could enlist the help of the rest of the town's shopkeepers in a public protest. This act was an early indication of just how deeply opium distribution and consumption had penetrated the local economy of some areas by the mid-1810s. The experience of prohibition in Danshui should have made it clear to officials that an economic dependency on opium could create pro-opium constituencies among local community groups. The significance of such dependencies may have been tacitly recognized in a court letter issued about five months after the Danshui incident explaining to Guangdong officials that it was preferable to conduct prohibition operations at their ports because such operations would be far less disruptive than conducting them in China proper.[130]

Yet the formal criminalization of activities like poppy cultivation, which was occurring far from urban coastal ports, made such disruptions inevitable. Once cultivation was recategorized from an incidental violation of the general statutes governing the proper use of uncultivated land to a serious drug offense in 1831, officials were formally obliged to search out offenders for punishment.[131] As noted above, the criminalization of cultivation took prohibition beyond town walls into the countryside, where opium dependency constituted a much more extensive and complex web and threatened to undermine prohibition at the grassroots level.

Zhejiang, particularly the prefecture of Taizhou, proved exemplary in this regard. Anticultivation operations in the province were initiated in the early 1830s but had to be relaunched in 1839 when it became evident that the poppy persisted in spite of eradication operations because of the dependency of both local peasants and local officials on its cultivation.

---

129. Gongzhong jinyan, JQ 18.12.17.

130. *Qingdai waijiao shiliao*, JQ 19.5.4, 4:19a–b.

131. *Yapian zhanzheng*, DG 10.10.13, 1:161–62. For the statutes on the improper use of uncultivated land, see *Da Qing lü li tongkao jiaozhu*, p. 439.

Senior provincial officials, responding to the imperial edict of August 1830 to eradicate illicit cultivation, claimed that the opium poppy had been grown by peasants in the prefectures of Wenzhou and Taizhou since the inception of the Daoguang reign in 1821.[132] Cultivation, however, extended well back into the Jiaqing reign, when Taizhou poppies provided poetic inspiration:

> One hears of the poppy of Taizhou,
> which every house does grow;
> bringing gains pecuniary
> in excess of hemp or mulberry.[133]

This doggerel was more conventionally and precisely confirmed by Bao Shichen in his 1820 essay calling for intensified prohibition against maritime traffickers. He asserted that poppy had been cultivated for paste in Taizhou "from the Jiaqing emperor's tenth year [1805]."[134] In sum it seems that cultivation in Taizhou had been going on for at least 26 years by 1830, and it would not be eradicated by the anticultivation operations implemented at that time.

Five years passed before poppy was declared eradicated from Zhejiang at the end of 1835, but this assertion was to prove excessively bold. In early 1839, illicit poppies were rediscovered in the secluded, mountainous regions of Taizhou prefecture, the administrative unit identified by Shao Zhenghu in 1830 as the major site of coastal cultivation. Poppies were also subsequently detected in the adjoining prefecture of Wenzhou, which Shao's memorial had also previously exposed. Zhejiang Governor Wu-er-tai-e set to work, uprooting at least fifteen hectares of illicit fields in Taizhou, and declared eradication successful in August 1840.[135] The declaration came too late to avert the dispatch of two senior officials from Beijing to conduct an independent investigation of the matter when Censor Shen Peng charged that the persistence of Tai

---

132. *Yapian zhanzheng*, DG 10.10.13, 1:161–62.
133. Xu Ke, *Qingbai leichao*, 13:6360. Jeanette Barbieri assisted me with the translation.
134. *Yapian zhanzheng*, 1:538.
135. *YPZZ*, DG 19.1.10, 1:483–84; WJD DG 19.4.18, pp. 208–10; Gongzhong jinyan, DG 20.4.10.

juice was due to collusion between cultivators and opium-smoking local officials.[136]

The two investigators, Qi Junzao and the famous prohibitionist official Huang Juezi, confirmed the spirit, if not the letter, of Shen's suspicions. Qi and Huang noted that an incomplete eradication procedure had left the roots of the plants untouched and charged this oversight may have been a product of official design rather than official carelessness. Qi and Huang also reported that Taizhou officials tolerated poppy because illicit cultivators, unlike legitimate ones, did not resist the collection of grain for taxes.[137]

Direct evidence of a corresponding popular dependency on cultivation, implied by Qi and Huang's findings, had already surfaced in April 1840, when a group of 34 peasants in Taizhou's Tiantai district battled violently with official personnel sent to destroy their poppy plantings. Subsequent reports revealed that the peasants had been driven to poppy cultivation after a meager grain harvest in 1839 proved insufficient to sustain them. Illicit cultivation in this particular locale was facilitated by the fact that it was separated from the towns by mountains, so that "official investigations could not reach" into this area of the district. Initial success with a few small plots interspersed among regular fields encouraged expansion to about double the original area of cultivation and helped to lead to its discovery by locals hired by Tiantai District Magistrate Gao Zhenwan. Zhu Yongding, who was absent at the time of the raid, was identified as the major perpetrator, and his wife was detained while the poppies were uprooted. The eradication operations were obstructed by members of the Yang clan, who, like Zhu, had made such considerable investments in the enterprise that they feared ruin if the poppy crop were destroyed. An altercation ensued when Gao ordered further arrests, and some of his men were wounded by peasants wielding an array of agricultural implements. Upon the arrival of reinforcements from the magistrate's yamen, the peasants, including Zhu's wife, scattered. Poppy eradication

136. Junji jinyan, DG 20.3.20, #3244–#45; *YPZZ*, DG 20.3.20, 2:63.
137. *YPZZ*, DG 20.8.18, 2:346–48.

was completed and some arrests made, but eighteen peasant resistors, including Zhu Yongding, remained at large.[138]

Anticultivation operations in Taizhou had exposed a previously unacknowledged dependency linking peasants and local officials to poppy cultivation. This connection differed considerably from the normal forms of official corruption covered in dynastic prohibition statutes because the Taizhou officials were not simply being bribed by drug offenders to look the other way. Instead, the income derived from poppy cultivation played a fundamental role in the stabilization of local administration by harmonizing relations between the local populace and their immediate superiors, especially in sensitive times of economic hardship.

The reaction of the Tiantai peasants to anticultivation operations is also worthy of note, for it vindicated the permissive attitude of local officials toward poppy cultivation, which for them was clearly preferable to peasant violence. Such violence, just as in Danshui, strongly implies that opium prohibitions were considered illegitimate if they impoverished people. Of course, the popular sense of the legitimacy of poppy cultivation was only reinforced by the toleration, or even encouragement, of local officials. The collusion made opium legal in local practice if not in dynastic principle.

Not much seems to have been done about the dependency of local administration on poppy revenues, which, as detailed in Chapter 6, were discovered to be even more extensive in Yunnan. Before these revelations, the only comparable dependency brought to official attention was Censor Huang Zhongmo's 1822 accusation that the Guangdong superintendent of customs was taxing the drug traffic instead of suppressing it. The ensuing investigation cleared the superintendent, although central officials still suspected that the Guangdong administration had been corrupted by opium. The actions of the foreign merchant community in Guangdong vindicated these suspicions: in 1815, it established a "corruption fund" to defray the quasi-official costs of dealing in opium.[139] The Qing state

---

138. Gongzhong jinyan, DG 20.4.10 and 23.12.13.

139. *YPZZ*, DG 2.2.12, 1:37–38, DG 2.2.15, 1:38–39, DG 2.5.25, 1:44–45, DG 2.11.23, 1:46–47; Morse, *Trading to China*, 3:323.

did eventually deal with Guangzhou corruption through its emissary Commissioner Lin, but it never devised an equivalent solution to the problem of structural dependencies on opium like that exposed in Zhejiang.

The degree to which the privy purse was itself directly dependent on opium revenues through income derived from Guangzhou's customs remains an open question. Certainly it was a widely publicized notion among the foreign merchant community that the Qing government tacitly approved of the traffic as a means of supplementing the income of local governments.[140] The throne's ultimate support for prohibition suggests, however, that key policymakers had a more complex view of the fiscal significance of opium. Whatever the drug's immediate benefits to Beijing's coffers, a critical number of officials, as well as the emperor, finally concluded that Qing China would be better off without opium.

Opponents of absolute prohibition recognized that opium, by becoming an integral part of the quotidian economic life of the empire, had insinuated itself into the mutual dependency of the state and a critical mass of its subjects. This conviction was one of the principles behind the position paper on opium legalization, "Ending the Scourge," by a prominent education official in the Jianke Academy, Wu Lanxiu, in response to a request by Xu Naiji for a more articulate presentation of the argument for legalization:

I have heard of the order handed down to close the ports and cut off trade. The loss of over a million in taxes to preserve over ten million in silver is thus a small loss for a greater gain. This is uprooting the scourge and blocking its source. There have been merchant vessels of the states of the Western Ocean for over 1,000 years, and they have come to Macao for more than 200. Only the English traffic in opium. Now, shall the English be cut off, or shall all the states be ordered cut off? If all are cut off, there will be nothing with which to conciliate them. If one is cut off, then there will be nothing with which to restore relations.

If all the foreigners are made to leave, then the millions of people of the coast will lose their livelihoods all at once without any means to stay alive. This will be the only origin of calamity in the southeast: the petty will mass together and commit villainy; the great will be led to foment strife. One can then declare the scourge gone, but some island beyond

---

140. Chang, *Commissioner Lin*, p. 47.

Jiaomen [in Zhejiang, Ningbo prefecture] will be selected to set up shop and all the junks from Tianjin, Jiangsu, Zhejiang, Fujian, and Guangdong will be able to get there, and how then can they be followed to cut off the traffic?[141]

Wu's message that there were limits to state power and, consequently, to opium prohibition was rejected along with all the other arguments in favor of drug legalization. Nevertheless, the argument that absolute prohibition, advocated by legalization's most vocal opponents, made no provisions for various types of dependency continued to resonate among senior provincial officials. Perhaps the most visible manifestation of the persistent dissatisfaction with the shortcomings of absolute prohibition, especially regarding its provision of capital punishment for consumers, was the amnesty program.

The harsh penalties for consumers fixed by the New Regulations of 1839 were considerably softened by the inclusion of formal provisions for the voluntary surrender to authorities by offenders, which included the handover of all opium and paraphernalia, in exchange for amnesty.[142] This statute normalized a practice already common, if unevenly applied, throughout the empire, and amnesty could still be called an act of "extra-legal benevolence" by Scrutinizing Censor for Works Huang Lezhi as late as April 1839.[143] Amnesty and the eighteen-month grace period for consumers were recognitions that the sheer extent of Qing opium dependency

---

141. "Mi hai," in Liang, *Yifen wenji*, p. 9. For the social and intellectual context of Wu's position paper, see Inoue, "Wu Lanxiu and Society in Guangzhou."

142. *YPZZ*, DG 19.5.2, 1:571.

143. Junji jinyan, DG 19.3.3, #2454–56. The precise evolution of this important statute remains obscure, but for evidence of its implementation prior to the promulgation of the New Regulations, see *YPZZ*, DG 18.8.2, 1:356–58 (Hubei), DG 18.12.29, 1:477–79 (Guangxi), DG 19.1.9, 1:480–82 (Hunan), DG 19.3.25, 1:538–39 (Fujian), DG 19.4.25, 1:560–61 (Shanxi); and *Gongzhong DG*, DG 18.10.11, 6:867b–68b (Jiangxi), DG 18.11.9, 7:138a–b (Jiangsu), DG 19.1.14, 8:737a–738a (Guangdong). A memorial from Metropolitan Censor Ai-long-a dated January 6, 1840, stated that although some form of amnesty was being practiced in "every province," it had yet to be uniformly applied outside the capital, which contained the majority of participants in the handover program (Junji jinyan, DG 19.12.2, #2375–77). This lack of uniformity would account for regional and chronological gaps in the documentary record.

made the indiscriminate application of absolute prohibition impractical, even dangerous.

The implementation of amnesty itself was also fraught with peril, at least when applied to Western traffickers on the coast, who had to be blockaded inside their Guangzhou factories for 47 days by Commissioner Lin Zexu before they agreed to hand over an estimated 1,188,127 kilos of opium (about 21,603 chests). This confiscation was the culmination of Lin's operations, which actually stopped the coastal traffic for about five months. Unfortunately, this amnesty, which technically enabled the foreign traffickers to avoid being strangled under a special statute previously devised just for them by Lin, provided the British empire with a pretext for war.[144]

By 1839 at the latest, any plan for ending the scourge of opium had become a dangerous proposition in large measure because the drug had already become an integral part of the livelihoods of too many imperial subjects and too many local administrations. The eradication of opium meant the eradication of these same subjects and administrations, which in aggregate amounted to the eradication of portions of the state itself.

Prohibition and the Limits of State Power

The dynastic authorities' fatal overestimation of their ability to control opium was based on a simplistic confidence in the supremacy of state power. Rather than perceiving the effect of state power on the drug as contradictory, that is, as facilitating opium in some ways and hampering it in others, official elites generally assumed that absolute dependence on state power was their only recourse. They were either ignorant of the considerable evidence that such

---

144. Chang, *Commissioner Lin*, pp. 120–88; Wakeman, "Canton Trade," pp. 185–88; *YPZZ*, DG 19.4.6, 1:548–50, DG 19.4.29, 1:562–63. The British traffickers were only too happy to turn over their opium in the face of the market collapse, especially after British Superintendent Captain Charles Elliot assured them that the Crown would cover their losses. The traffickers handed over about $9 million worth of opium, pledging to turn over even more than they had in stock. This debt gave the British government a considerable incentive for war to recoup its losses.

power was itself contaminated by opium and even dependent on the drug trade in some locales or chose to ignore this. This dependency was not simply embodied in individual office-holding consumers; rather, it was inherent in the structure of some local administrations, Taizhou most obvious among them on the coast.

A naive assertion of state power was not the inevitable response to the challenge of an addictive consumable, as evidenced by the Ming and Qing approaches to tobacco. Opium provoked a different response from the Qing, but not until the authorities became convinced that dynastic revenues were threatened by the foreign drug's ability to generate domestic mass markets. Opium production, distribution, and consumption then became seen as direct threats to the roots of state power.

The state's ultimate response was absolute prohibition, a projection of what was hoped to be irresistible, uncompromising power against all three dimensions of the opium-marketing system. Unfortunately, this response was unrealistic in many respects. In terms of timing alone, the absolute prohibition came too late to stop opium from becoming part of the empire. It was only 80 years after the promulgation of the Yongzheng-era statutes against traffickers that the dynasty began the active and extensive pursuit of consumers in 1813, and poppy cultivation was not formally and systematically criminalized until a further seventeen years had passed.

Absolute prohibition might have been effective if enacted in the early stages of opium's infiltration into Qing China, but by the time it was pursued in earnest the state found itself overwhelmed. Even where successful, as it genuinely seems to have been at some points, the intensification of prohibition caused problems such as the overcrowded remand centers in Guangdong, Jiangxi, Anhui, Guangxi, and Guizhou.[145] Verification and disposal of the large

---

145. *YPZZ*, DG 20.3.11, 2:56–58 (Guangdong); DG 20.9.8, 2:442 (Jiangxi); DG 20.10.20, 2:531–32 (Guangxi); DG 21.1.18, 3:81–82 (Guizhou); WJD, DG 20.10.29, pp. 248–49 (Anhui). Lin Zexu submitted the first of these reports, which requested alterations in administrative procedure to speed the execution of sentence. He stated that the capture of over 1,400 offenders in one year, along with over 150 apprehended over the previous two months, necessitated an acceleration of processing. Most of those held were probably accomplices to various opium offenses awaiting transportation to their place of exile.

amounts of confiscated opium also presented a major challenge.[146] These breakdowns in the Qing administrative system, which further exposed the limits of state power, would not have occurred in the earlier stages of the drug's development. The construction of the criminal addict, which came to be the most ubiquitous offense, only exacerbated this situation.

A belated and extreme form of prohibition flung across a vast empire produced this overextension of the Qing administrative apparatus. The state's limited ability to deal with the sheer extent of this problem was tacitly acknowledged in the continued official assertions that the opium problem was centered within a single city's walls in the southeastern corner of a single coastal province. Unfortunately for the court, as early as the Jiaqing reign there was clear evidence that opium was not simply a problem confined to the Guangzhou waterfront or just an obstacle to the smooth functioning of Sino-British foreign relations but was already a domestic problem with its own dynamics, which would ultimately test the ability of the Qing state to enforce its will in places far from the empire's coastal zone.

Administrative resources were already being taxed to their limits in the relatively rich provinces of the coast, where, for example, Guangzhou officials had a difficult time controlling opium trafficking, let alone production and consumption. Provincial administrations barely succeeded in controlling poppy cultivation in the southeast, where it existed in relatively restricted and accessible areas. In the vast and ethnically diverse expanses of the west, this new offense was not confined to the corner of a single *junxian* pre-

---

146. Even before the implementation of the New Regulations, a proposal to transport all opium seized throughout the empire to Beijing for verification and disposal in order to avoid official overreporting was rejected as impractical, and personal supervision of disposal operations by senior provincial officials was substituted (*YPZZ*, DG 18.10.18, 1:410). The Daoguang emperor subsequently noted that he had heard of local officials' attempts to improve their confiscation statistics by manufacturing their own paraphernalia and bogus opium paste as well as of official pilferage for purposes of resale (*YPZZ*, DG 19.3.3, 1:520). He was probably referring to a list provided by Scrutinizing Censor for Works Huang Lezhi, who enumerated an array of abuses in the handover program, including the substitution of such substances as sugar, rice gruel, and rhubarb for opium (Junji jinyan, DG 19.3.3, #2454–56).

fecture, which could credibly declare poppy cultivation eradicated after a few months or years. Instead, western cultivators could conceal their poppy fields within thousands of kilometers of wilderness subject on paper to a handful of imported Qing officials and troops walled into a compound of an administrative town swamped by indigenous peoples governed mainly under their own forms of law and custom. Such ethno-geographic obstacles were the main reason why cultivation was never declared eradicated in places like Yunnan and Xinjiang. Moreover, the difference in the relative scales of east coast and western interior poppy cultivation remained fixed in the official mind well after the revelations of the 1830s, as when one censor in 1850 wrote of the paste-making and poppy cultivation in "the provinces of Yunnan, Guizhou and Sichuan" in the same line as that of "the Zhejiang prefectures of Wenzhou and Taizhou."[147]

The control of trafficking and consumption in western regions was difficult for similar reasons of geography and ethnicity, especially where smuggling routes passed beyond Qing boundaries into the territories of other states or tribal groups. The local Qing administration, especially outside *junxian* areas, simply could not transcend these lines, which indeed were its literal limits, unlike the opium-marketing system, which evaded them and extended far beyond them. One of the farthest of these places, in terms of both distance and culture, was Xinjiang.

---

147. *Daoguang Xianfeng liangchao chouban,* DG 30.12.15, p. 254.

FIVE

The Opium Problem
in Xinjiang

Xinjiang's status as an Inner Asian border territory rather than a province of China proper created a unique regional opium problem. This complicated Qing prohibition efforts, especially as foreign opium spread eastward. Xinjiang was the nexus connecting Inner and South Asian Muslim drug suppliers with Han consumers in China proper. The middlemen in this trade were the local East Turkestani and Han merchants, some of whom poured their own homegrown poppy sap into this eastward flow of foreign opium.

Neither the imperial drug traffic nor dynastic prohibition was conditioned solely by the involvement of Western smugglers along the coast. Rather, all non-Han smugglers, including Muslim opium smugglers in Xinjiang and their main sponsor, the Khanate of Kokand on the territory's western frontier, played a role. In this wider perspective, Qing prohibition policies that might appear designed to appease the Euro-American merchant community of Guangzhou, such as amnesty for traffickers, are revealed to have been standard procedures for dealing with foreign traffickers at both ends of the empire.

Moreover, Han and East Turkestani poppy cultivators posed problems of much greater scope and complexity than their coastal counterparts. In Xinjiang, rather than being limited to a few Han renegades within a single prefecture, poppy cultivation was spread throughout an enormous, rugged territory among an ethnically diverse populace. Anticultivation campaigns in the Northern March jurisdiction of Karashahr, for example, meant mounted patrols of an area roughly comparable in size to the entire province of Zhejiang, where most cultivation was confined to a few prefectures. Controlling the kind of cultivation that had taken root in Xinjiang, as well as in the southwest, presented a challenge to regional prohibition commensurate with the two offenses commonly assumed to define the opium problem: illicit distribution and consumption.

An examination of Qing prohibition diplomacy in Xinjiang can contribute to a more comprehensive understanding of how the dynasty confronted opium both within and beyond its borders. Qing negotiations with the Khanate of Kokand and tsarist Russia suggest that clashes between Chinese and Western notions of law, diplomacy, economics, and the like were not the main sources of difficulties between Britain and China in the 1830s and 1840s. Rather, the primary source of the disputes between China and all foreigners, Western and otherwise, was power in the form of commodified and addictive opium, which was singularly able to transcend all ethnic, geographical, and political boundaries.

The ethno-geographic diversification of the opium problem in the direction of Xinjiang reveals the existence of a northwest opium market, run by non-Westerners, which encompassed distribution and consumption as well as production. The development of this system meant that the largely British coastal traffic was only one part of the Qing empire's opium problem rather than its only opium problem.

The primacy of ethnic considerations was the defining characteristic of prohibition efforts in Xinjiang. Territorial authorities shared the general imperial consensus that traffickers were the main problem, but they did not intend to treat their traffickers in the manner prescribed by the New Regulations. This attitude reflected the general priority of avoiding major confrontations with Muslims in the territory in the context of opium prohibition. In practice, Muslim traffickers were treated with great leniency in comparison with their Han counterparts. Minimal resources were devoted to operations against consumers and cultivators. All in all, Xinjiang officials sought to dilute absolute prohibition, which had been adopted as imperial policy a few months before the discovery of an opium problem in the territory, in order to maintain interethnic harmony. Such harmony was necessary in part because Qing officials were dependent on East Turkestani *begs* to implement prohibition among all Muslims in Xinjiang. Moreover, both *begs* and Mongols manned the wilderness patrols intended to root out poppy cultivators regardless of ethnicity.

The overwhelming majority of all prohibition operations took place in late 1839 and January 1841. During this period of a little over a year, thousands of kilos of opium were seized and hundreds of people were arrested or turned themselves in across the territory. By coastal standards, however, the opium traffic officials uncovered in Xinjiang was small, amounting to a total of some 5,470 kilos (approximately 91 chests, 66 of which were voluntarily handed over) seized or turned in.[1] In contrast, the largely British coastal opium traders initially handed over what all involved considered a token amount of 1,000-odd chests, or approximately 60,000 kilos.[2] Nevertheless, Xinjiang's confiscation of almost 5,500 kilos in little over a year was among the highest in the interior; available evidence shows this amount was second only to the 12,573 kilos seized by officials in Yunnan over a period of sixteen months from January 1839 to April 1840.[3]

The relatively short duration of territorial prohibition operations also left a smaller documentary record for Xinjiang than for places where opium had been found much earlier such as Guizhou or for major sites of coastal trafficking and consumption like Guangdong. Xinjiang's prohibition efforts are, however, not the poorest-documented in the empire, and the dynastic authorities' concerns regarding the territory's opium problem generated considerable paper in a relatively short time. This proliferation of memorials on prohibition happened mainly because Xinjiang appears to have been the only place in the empire where local officials suggested modifications to the New Regulations before their

---

1. See Table 4 for a regional breakdown of official confiscation statistics.

2. Chang, *Commissioner Lin*, pp. 147–48. During a period of little more than a year and a half beginning in early 1837, over 8,700 kilos were seized in Guangdong alone (*YPZZ*, DG 18.12.8, 1:449–50).

3. Gongzhong jinyan, DG 20.4.19; see also Table 6 in this volume.

local implementation. The New Regulations had been developed with the provinces of China proper in mind, and this framework no doubt eliminated the need for much discussion between the central and the local administrations, which could integrate many aspects of prohibition into the regular functioning of the *baojia* security apparatus.[4] The throne's recognition that "Xinjiang is different from China proper (*neidi*)," however, officially sanctioned regional modification of the New Regulations.[5] As implied in this special dispensation from the throne, these differences would pose great problems in Xinjiang for the smooth implementation of prohibition, especially in its absolute form.

Whatever the disparities between prohibition in Xinjiang and that in China proper, opium in Xinjiang was a problem whose significance could not be measured in kilos, numbers of offenders, or memorials alone. In the northwest, Xinjiang opium, not the coastal drug, was the main problem. The opium market centered on Xinjiang became northwestern in scope when the drug began to flow eastward from the territory into China proper, and it was this fact that made Xinjiang opium a particular concern of the central government.

Adapting Imperial Prohibition to Xinjiang

Xinjiang was the last place in the Qing empire where opium was discovered during the promulgation of the New Regulations, and Beijing's attention was drawn to the territory only after Vice Minister of the Court of Judicial Review Hui-feng complained in August 1839 that he had seen no reports on opium cases there. His suspicions were rooted in his conviction that in the Chinese interior, "80–90 percent of officials, soldiers, and commoners are contaminated" with opium in some fashion. He held that this silence arose not because Xinjiang was "without traffickers and consumers but because its numbers of official and military personnel are few in comparison with China proper (*neidi*). People are scattered, the

---

4. This was noted, for example, in the imperial anticultivation decree of January 1831 (*YPZZ*, DG 10.12.18, 1:72).

5. *YPZZ*, DG 19.7.27, 1:678.

land vast; close surveillance is difficult." He concluded that if officials did not make concerted enforcement efforts, cases would continue to go undiscovered in Xinjiang, whose sheer size alone made
trafficking inevitable.[6]

Hui-feng recognized that the geographical obstacles to territorial
prohibition were only compounded by ethnic ones. Xinjiang's
"small roads of all sorts" connected the territory with foreign lands
and facilitated commerce with the "tribes" of Russia and Kokand,
including both Muslims and Mongols, all of whom mixed with the
Qing's itinerant merchant subjects. These subjects could not "avoid
an intimate familiarity with the consumption of opium." Hui-feng
warned that the "plots" arising from these transborder and multiethnic opium smuggling contacts were causing a loss of silver and
the enervation of border troops. The significance of these two factors made opium in Xinjiang more than a simple case of local drug
abuse. Hui-feng's accusations triggered an imperial decree, issued
on September 5, 1839, ordering Qing officials throughout the territory to launch investigations.[7]

Unlike the rumors of opium offenses in a particular locality
passed on by some metropolitan censors, Hui-feng's report was
based on personal experience. As Gansu's provincial surveillance
commissioner (*anchashi*) from November 1829 to February 1832, he
had handled cases of provincial trafficking in opium whose origin
was ultimately traced through Xinjiang to Kokandi traders from
Andijan, the khanate's main trade depot with the Southern
March.[8] It is possible that these cases had been considered of purely
local import at the time, and so there had been no formal notification of the central government.

This is the earliest date for foreign trafficking in the territory
that I have come across. The year 1832 is particularly significant because this is the date that En-te-heng-e, councilor of Yarkand, as-

---

6. Ibid., 1:675–77.
7. Ibid., 1:675–78.
8. Ibid., 1:676; Wei Hsiu-mei, *Qing ji zhiguan biao*, 2:875. In Qing documents,
Andijan is used to refer to both the town of that name in the eastern Ferghana
valley and the Khanate of Kokand itself; moreover, "Kokand" could also stand for
either the khanate or its capital (Saguchi, "Eastern Trade," pp. 67–68).

signed to the beginning of foreign trafficking in Xinjiang.[9] A group of foreign merchants had testified that they had begun to smuggle opium into Xinjiang only in 1838, when word arrived of high prices paid for the drug in China proper. This chronology was certainly wrong for the foreign traffic as a whole. Testimony from smuggling rings like Rong Jixiang's, the largest ever discovered in Xinjiang, demonstrated that foreign opium had been coming into the territory as early as 1834. Even before this information emerged, En-te-heng-e had concluded that Central and South Asian merchants began bringing opium through the checkpoints in the wake of the court's abolition of tariffs and inspections of foreign goods in 1832. This abolition had been one of the concessions to the Kokandis after their 1830 incursion into the Southern March.[10] Despite many ambiguities, foreign trafficking between Kokand and Gansu through Xinjiang was clearly established before 1832 when Hui-feng ended his official duties in Gansu.

As described in further detail below, 1832 was not the first time opium had come to official attention in Xinjiang. An 1808 case that revealed opium possession by a Guangdong exile in Ili triggered what was probably the territory's first search-and-seizure operation.[11] The Urumqi Banner Commander-in-Chief Chang-qing also searched for opium offenders in 1835 and 1836 as part of the ongoing empirewide search for opium cultivators and traffickers initiated in 1830. Chang-qing found no trace of opium activity in the region, and a vermilion rescript on his memorial suspended further investigation.[12]

By the time Chang-qing's prohibition reports, and his no doubt putative operations, were suspended in 1836, opium trafficking and consumption were certainly present in Xinjiang. Although Chang-qing's inquiries seem to have been restricted to the Eastern March,

---

9. An 1841 case provides testimony of opium trafficking and consumption in the jurisdiction of Urumqi as early as 1829, but the ambiguity of the text precludes an exact dating (WJD, DG 21.10.20, pp. 133–35).

10. Junji jinyan, DG 19.11.18, #3104–8; *YPZZ*, DG 19.12.22, 1:786, DG 21.7.29, 4:73.

11. Gongzhong jinyan, JQ 12.12.29.

12. Ibid., DG 14.12.2, 15.12.3. These reports were the last two in what was probably a series of reports initiated by Chang-qing's predecessor, Cheng-ge.

there is no evidence that opium was officially discovered anywhere in Xinjiang during the prohibition operations in the first half of the 1830s. In light of the subsequent evidence noted above, Chang-qing's investigations seem to have been perfunctory at best. The Kokand-Gansu traffic described by Hui-feng, for example, would have had to go to extraordinary lengths to avoid passing through Chang-qing's jurisdiction.

When active prohibition was resumed in September 1839 under the New Regulations, official laxity had given Xinjiang's opium traffic at least seven years, between 1832 and 1839, to develop relatively undisturbed. Beijing, however, acknowledged the decisive importance of Xinjiang's ethno-geographic diversity, which sufficiently distinguished it from China proper to hinder the implementation of the New Regulations. Specifically, the throne recognized that the territory's size and proximity to foreign states made it "difficult to guarantee that there are no incidents of foreigners smuggling opium through the checkpoints for purposes of sale and resale." These conditions required "modifications" (*biantong*), as suggested by the heads of the marches, in the imperial prohibitions. As noted above, this willingness to consider changes in the regulations appears to have been unique and is further evidence of the territory's unusual status. Despite this special consideration, Beijing had acted on only part of Hui-feng's message, for the court's reply was aimed exclusively at "foreign," that is, Central and South Asian Muslim, traffickers as well as consumers. Hui-feng's request for a separate decree prohibiting cultivation in Xinjiang was ignored.[13]

These priorities are indicative of the center's selective approach to prohibition and its belief that trafficking and consumption were more accessible to a territorial officialdom stationed in a few, scattered garrison towns. In this respect, the imperial decree of September 1839 was an assertion, directed toward Xinjiang, of the central government's conviction that trafficking and consumption were the primary causes of the drug problem throughout Qing China and that the eradication of trafficking would automatically eradicate the drug.

---

13. *YPZZ*, DG 19.7.27, 1:678.

In response to the throne's decree, the administrative heads of the three marches submitted preliminary reports, based in turn on reports from localities within their jurisdictions, on the implementation of prohibition and local modifications.[14] Reports were also submitted by Qing administrators in Uliassutai, namely, Qing Outer Mongolia, and Khobdo, a subadministrative region of this area on Xinjiang's northeastern border. Neither official reported trafficking cases, but both found it "difficult to guarantee no traitorous subject had been smuggling opium." Their uncertainty arose from the fact that they, like their Xinjiang counterparts, lacked the personnel necessary to conduct opium investigations in such a "vast territory."[15]

Xinjiang had a much more developed commercial system than Outer Mongolia, which brought many more people into the territory. It became clear from the preliminary reports that most of the complications in Xinjiang were linked to the large numbers of outsiders moving through the territory from both foreign lands and China proper and their sustained interactions with indigenous peoples of Xinjiang, particularly the East Turkestanis of the Southern March.

It is significant that the part of Xinjiang most integrated with China proper reported that implementation of the New Regulations required no special modifications. From Urumqi the Eastern March's Banner Commander-in-Chief Hui-ji's initial report on 37 cases of Han trafficking and consumption in his jurisdiction showed that operations were pursued almost exclusively through the *baojia* apparatus of the *junxian* system of districts and subprefectures, precisely as envisioned by the drafters of the New Regulations. Hui-ji's proposals for the eradication of opium from Xinjiang were

---

14. Reports came from the following administrative locales: Junji jinyan, DG 19.8.24, #2952–57 (Karashahr), DG 19.11.21, #3082–85 (Urumqi), DG 19.11.24, #3109–12 (Aksu); *YPZZ*, DG 19.12.19, 1:780–81 (Kashgar), DG 19.12.22, 1:785–89 (Yarkand), DG 19.12.13, 1:772–74 (Khotan), DG 20.1.16, 2:3–7 (Ili); Gongzhong jinyan, DG 20.1.11 (Tarbagatai), DG 20.1.27 (Turfan). Note that either all the major towns in Xinjiang did not submit reports, or, more likely, these nine are the only ones that have surfaced. There was no reason for the locales of Hami, Kucha, and Wushe not to respond to the July 7 decree, even if no opium had been discovered.

15. WJD, DG 19.10.16, pp. 137–39 (Uliassutai); *YPZZ*, 19.12.1, 1:749–50 (Khobdo).

likewise based on assumptions similar to those of the central government. Hui-ji's solution was to request that the Qing councilors in both Yarkand and Tarbagatai be instructed to interdict foreign smugglers and cut off their routes near the border. Traffickers would "then be without routes to bring in opium for sale and users will be without places from which they can purchase opium." Addicts would thus automatically disappear, and further official action would not be required. [16]

This formula was the Xinjiang version of a defining element of the central government's prescriptions for stopping the empire-wide opium problem, namely, cutting off foreign smuggling in Guangdong. The proposal also redirected the main brunt of prohibition onto the administrations of the other two marches, which did share Hui-ji's convictions regarding the centrality of foreign trafficking.[17] Unfortunately, it was not possible for senior officials in these jurisdictions to rely as heavily on the *baojia* system, which was difficult enough to employ among the large numbers of itinerant Han merchants moving through Urumqi. This system was, of course, useless for monitoring foreign merchants, East Turkestanis, Mongols, or Han poppy cultivators in wilderness areas in the Southern and Northern Marches.

The response to the September 1839 imperial decree from both these jurisdictions was, consequently, quite different from that of the Eastern March and served to emphasize the great contrasts that existed within the vast territory itself. Both En-te-heng-e in the Southern March and Yi-shan, the military governor of Ili in the Northern March, proposed lengthy modifications to the New Regulations. These memorials initiated a series of exchanges with central authorities over the propriety of particular modifications. As the communications continued into 1841, some of the legal is-

---

16. Junji jinyan, DG 19.11.21, #3082–85. I have come across only one of these reports, that of Turfan Unit Commander (*lingdui dachen*) E-le-jin-tai, who reported three cases of Han merchant trafficking and suspected that there were also foreign merchants actively moving opium into Turfan from western Xinjiang. Like Hui-ji, E-le-jin-tai reported there were no local obstacles to the implementation of the New Regulations (Gongzhong jinyan, DG 20.1.27).

17. *YPZZ*, DG 19.12.22, 1:785 (Yarkand), DG 20.1.16, 2:4–5 (Ili).

sues raised were so complex that the discussions outlasted the tenure, and nearly the lifespan, of En-te-heng-e.[18]

En-te-heng-e's insistence on eliminating capital punishment for both foreign traffickers and East Turkestanis dealing in "small amounts" of opium was primarily responsible for this protracted legal discussion with Beijing.[19] This perspective was not unique to the Southern March. It was instead, to judge from a similar proposal from Yi-shan, a territorial consensus on the appropriate way to deal with Xinjiang's Muslim offenders, most of whom, according to senior local officials, including En-te-heng-e's successor Tumingga, were caught carrying no more than four to eight kilos.[20] Yi-shan's argument began with the observation that foreign traffickers in Xinjiang were using

domesticated camels for transport; so smuggling is comparatively difficult, or else occurs in small quantities and, we believe, it does not amount to much. We find a great disparity between this situation and that of the coast, where ships are employed to carry immense loads that are stored for sale, and strongly feel that the establishment of uniform, generalized heavy punishments will obstruct the pacification of the foreigners.[21]

Although it clearly appreciated the security issues involved, the Grand Council, on behalf of the throne, did not entirely concur with these justifications of leniency for Muslim traffickers and restricted the commutation of capital sentences to those trafficking cases discovered within the grace period.[22] As is discussed in further detail below in the context of amnesty operations for foreign traffickers, however, in practice no Muslim traffickers were ever exe-

---

18. Gongzhong jinyan, DG 21.6.17. Dates for En-te-heng-e's tenure and that of his successor Tumingga can be found in Wei Hsiu-mei, *Qing ji zhiguan biao*, 2:537, 1144.

19. *YPZZ*, DG 19.12.22, 1:788, DG 20.3.27, 2:80–85. En-te-heng-e's stance included a number of qualifications. He did, for example, want to increase the punishment of East Turkestanis guilty of collusion with foreign merchants in stockpiling opium for sale to strangulation without judicial review. His reasoning is superficial, but it is possible that he wished to avoid overcrowding the jails with prisoners waiting for their cases to be reviewed during the autumn assizes.

20. Gongzhong jinyan, DG 21.6.17.

21. *YPZZ*, DG 20.1.16, 2:4.

22. *YPZZ*, DG 20.5.1, 2:114–19.

cuted. Special legal provisions were seemingly devised to prevent precisely the kind of disruptive incidents alluded to by Yi-shan.

The application of prohibition to Muslim offenders was the most important point of consensus between the Northern and Southern March administrators as well as one of the most important of Xinjiang's proposed modifications to the New Regulations. Nevertheless, as noted by En-te-heng-e, the "conditions in the Southern March differ from those of Ili and other locales of the Northern March."[23] Comparatively large-scale Han urban settlement in northern Xinjiang, with a corresponding absence of East Turkestanis, was perhaps the most important difference between the two marches. Han settlement is why Yi-shan, like Hui-ji, planned to rely on the *baojia* security apparatus to deal with drug offenses in the *junxian* areas of his jurisdiction.[24]

This option was not available to En-te-heng-e, who presided over a huge region deliberately devoid of large-scale Han settlement. *Baojia* controls in the Southern March were restricted to relatively small and mobile populations of Han merchants. Sparse Han settlement created unique problems for opium prohibition in the Southern March mainly because implementation was excessively dependent on the *begs*. Consequently, many of En-te-heng-e's proposed modifications, entitled "Regulations for the Prohibition of Opium in the Towns of Xinjiang's Southern March," were concerned with the role of these crucial mediators, who were unique to his jurisdiction, between the East Turkestani masses and the Qing state.

Begs unavoidably pervaded every level of prohibition in the Southern March, which was to be based on a restoration of the pre-1830 system of inspection for contraband to stop the transborder traffic. All foreign merchants would be escorted from the checkpoints to the towns where they wished to trade; their wares would then be inspected by the *hakim beg*, who would issue certificates that the inspection had been passed and obtain bonds that the merchants would refrain from opium trafficking. This system was intended to avoid "abuse" of foreign Muslims by non-Muslim

---

23. *YPZZ*, DG 19.12.22, 1:785.
24. *YPZZ*, DG 20.1.16, 2:6–7.

Qing personnel. The *begs* were also to keep the empire's own East Turkestani subjects, as well as foreigners, under surveillance by issuing road passes (*lupiao*) to merchants traveling between towns within Xinjiang and to assume most of the burden of policing the East Turkestani villages that dotted the Southern March. Many of these tasks involved translating the prohibitions into the local language and posting the notices at checkpoints, foreign hostels, and similar locations.[25]

En-te-heng-e was particularly concerned about the reliability of village *begs*, who constituted the entirety of officialdom in their numerous locales. On the assumption that these *begs* would not prove "very efficient in their inspections," he wanted to impose an additional layer of surveillance by dispatching other *begs* to conduct monthly inquiries and obtain mutual responsibility certificates.[26] En-te-heng-e's lack of confidence was justified in at least one instance, when the trafficking activities of one Yunus, from the village of Karghalik in the Yarkand jurisdiction, were exposed not by the actions of local *begs* but by statements of two foreign traffickers elicited during amnesty operations in Yarkand in December 1839. By the time Yunus was caught, put in the cangue, and finally remanded to hard labor in another Muslim hamlet, he had succeeded in selling most of his 51 kilos of opium to at least nineteen Han traffickers and consumers, some of whom had relayed their purchases to markets in the Eastern March.[27]

Even when *begs* did enforce the prohibitions, problems could occur when ethnic lines were crossed, as happened in the first case of cultivation discovered by officials in Xinjiang. In April 1839, shop owners Gu Mengxun and Zhao Deshou decided to make up for a slump in trade by getting into the lucrative business of poppy cultivation and paste production. The two went prospecting for a likely spot in the wilds east of their location in Kürla, a town of the Karashahr region in the Southern March. While looking around, Gu and Zhao ran into three other cultivators, one of whom, Ren Ju,

---

25. *YPZZ*, DG 19.12.22, 1:787. This was also done in the Northern March; see *YPZZ*, DG 20.1.16, 2:3.

26. *YPZZ*, DG 19.12.22, 1:787.

27. *Gongzhong jinyan*, DG 20.2.19.

had already begun sowing his plot approximately fifty kilometers east of Kürla. The five men decided to form a partnership, and a month later the group had cleared an acre or so of wilderness, planted their poppy, built some sheds, and were living near their new fields. They even hired a cook, at 500 cash per month, to serve them for the three months needed to tend their crop.[28]

Unfortunately for the group, the *hakim beg* of Karashahr, Tuo-hu-ta, and his patrol were out searching for poppy cultivators and ran across Zhao, who was on a supply run back to Kürla. Zhao's apprehension led to the arrest of the other five men, who were taken back to the town to await escort to the regional administrative center of Karashahr for trial. As the six arrived under guard in Kürla and were passing through crowds of onlookers in the Muslim section of town, they were approached by two associates, Li Yun and Old Man Liu, who got word to the prisoners of a plan to free them. Li and Liu got nine of their associates together and successfully ambushed the escort party on its way to Karashahr. The men rushed the transport carts shouting and brandishing clubs, scattering the Muslim escorts and freeing Gu and his five compatriots.[29]

This clash on the road to Karashahr pitting East Turkestani Muslims against Han Chinese was just the kind of confrontation Xinjiang officials were hoping to avoid in the process of enforcing territorial prohibition. Consequently, it was the Qing sergeant in command of the Kürla outpost, Zhao Zhongming, rather than Tuo-hu-ta, who was censured by decree for having failed to send troops to escort the prisoners from his jurisdiction to Karashahr.[30] As the senior administrators of both the Northern and the Southern Marches had warned, complex ethnic and geographic conditions made prohibition efforts particularly risky in Xinjiang.

Despite the focus on Sergeant Zhao, the authors of the decree recognized the structural effects of these complexities and echoed Hui-feng's original evaluation of the Xinjiang opium problem: "Incidents arise as a consequence of the fact that [Xinjiang's] towns are located amid desolate wilderness and wasteland. If investigations

---

28. Junji jinyan, DG 19.8.24, #2952–57.
29. Ibid.
30. *YPZZ*, DG 19.9.22, 1:715–16.

are not thorough, then it is impossible to avoid incidents of disloyal subjects aiming for illicit profit."[31] The territory's physical expanse was held to encourage official apathy, which was in turn enhanced by an excessive reliance on the *begs*.

Administrative limits to prohibition, however, were not merely functions of empty physical space, however vast. Specific aspects of Xinjiang's natural and human geography ensured that the territory would be plagued with all three major categories of opium offenses in a manner unique in the Qing empire.

The Ethno-Geography of Qiangtu

Opium's flow into, within, and out of Xinjiang was driven by the territory's position between Central and South Asian distributors and the consumers of China proper. In effect, opium moved from west to east through Xinjiang toward areas of large-scale Han settlement. But the movement was not reciprocal. Opium entered Xinjiang in response to a demand originally stimulated by the coastal traffic, but opium smuggled into southeastern China did not reach the territory in any commercial quantity. Instead, by 1839 at the latest, "Xinjiang" opium was supplying smokers within and well beyond the confines of the territory and had come to constitute a distinct, northwestern manifestation of the empire's opium market.

Censor Zhang Bingde provided a broad outline of the distribution of northwestern opium within China proper:

I have heard of a kind of opium from the Muslim frontier called *qiangtu*, smaller in size than that which comes from Guangdong. Its use in paste-making and smoking is no different from that of [Guangdong] opium. I, a native of Shanxi, have also heard that everyone from Xinzhou in Shanxi who goes to Xinjiang to trade smuggles back *qiangtu*. By way of various passes [connecting Xinjiang to Gansu], such as Jiayu and Hami, it secretly enters the interior and is sold in Shaanxi, Henan, and other places. It is, however, especially plentiful in Shanxi.[32]

---

31. Ibid.
32. *YPZZ*, DG 20.4.10, 2:96.

A modern scholar, Chen Zhao, has speculated that Xinjiang *qiangtu* was actually hemp or marijuana originating from "the Muslim frontier" (*Huijiang*), which he identifies as Xinjiang's Southern March, citing Zhang Bingde's report.[33] There are, however, a number of problems with this view.

One major problem is that Zhang's reference to the Muslim frontier cannot be restricted to a single march or ethnic group. In Qing sources, the Muslim frontier is not a consistent concept and so cannot be restricted geographically to a single contiguous area inhabited by one ethnic group within Xinjiang; rather, it more commonly refers to areas of substantial East Turkestani settlement, often intermixed with other ethnic groups, throughout the territory. Consequently, the area encompassed by the administrative handbook *Huijiang zeli* (Substatutes of the Muslim frontier) includes not only Yarkand in the Southern March towns but also Turfan in the Eastern March and Ili in the Northern March. Moreover, aspects of these substatutes, particularly the tribute schedules, also apply to Kazakhs and other nomads scattered throughout Xinjiang as well as to foreign states like Kokand.[34] The considerable variation among Qing sources as to the precise geographic extent and ethnic composition of the *Huijiang* often makes it possible to understand the term as a synonym for the whole of Xinjiang, excluding perhaps the major towns of Urumqi and Tarbagatai.[35] Consequently, the precise meaning of *Huijiang* is always sensitive to context and often difficult, as in Zhang's case, to determine.

The word *qiangtu* contains another imprecise ethno-geographic term. *Qiang* is a general ethnonym for a number of northwestern nomadic non-Han tribals used over centuries of Chinese contact with the region. There is no direct evidence among the Xinjiang prohibition documents that the term explicitly refers to the East Turkestanis of the Southern March or indeed any specific ethnic

33. Chen Zhao, "Wan Qing Xinjiang jinyan shulun," p. 26.

34. *Huijiang zeli*, 1:21a–22b; 4:12a–b.

35. James Millward, for example, cites an 1809 source that defines *Huijiang* as the region of Muslim clan settlement from Hami and Turfan to the eight main western towns (*Beyond the Pass*, p. 154). In this definition, Huijiang comprises all the Southern March and much of the Eastern March as well, but excludes the Northern March entirely.

group. Zhang Bingde's account seems to employ *qiang* as an ethno-geographic term for a northwestern location beyond Han-dominated China proper. It is certainly not, as Chen assumes, invariably a reference to East Turkestani Muslims when linked to the term *Huijiang*.

Chen's contention that *qiangtu* refers to marijuana is also unwarranted, if for no other reason than Zhang's explicit statement that the drug was consumed in the same fashion as opium paste. All Xinjiang prohibition documents employ the terms "opium" or "poppy."[36] Moreover, natural conditions were certainly conducive to poppy cultivation, for the plant had been legitimately grown in Xinjiang for ornamental purposes as early as 1770, as noted in the writings of exiled officials.[37] During the Daoguang prohibition, senior provincial officials identified three annual poppy crops, sown in spring, summer, and "winter."[38] More than one type of drug may have emerged from the territory, but, in light of similar examples of regional poppy products from the southeast coast and the southwest as noted in Chapters 4 and 6, it is more likely that *qiangtu* was a reference to opium produced from Central Asian poppy cultivated both within and beyond Xinjiang. Certainly officials like Zhang Bingde considered *qiangtu* no different from coastal opium, and consumers in China proper appear to have made no significant distinction between the two.

According to Zhang, itinerant Shanxi merchants were spreading *qiangtu* into China proper, but there is little confirmation of their participation. The case records for Xinjiang mention only a few minor traffickers from Shanxi, and those for Shanxi reveal instead the dominance of coastal trafficking from Tianjin and the southeastern provinces.[39] The records do, however, show that natives of

---

36. Junji jinyan, DG 19.8.24, #2952–57; *YPZZ*, DG 20.8.24, 2:387–88.

37. Hong, *Tianshan ke hua*, pp. 21a–21b; idem, *Yili jishi shi*, 18b.

38. Li Xingyuan, *Li Xingyuan riji*, DG 20.6.28, 1:96. Sources disagree on whether opium was planted in the fall. This may be a mere terminological distinction. Zeng (*Zhongguo jingying xiyu shi*, p. 607) describes fall sowing and states that young poppy plants were especially difficult to detect because of their resemblance to sprouts of winter wheat.

39. Gongzhong jinyan, DG 20.2.18 (Shanxi), DG 20.2.19 (Xinjiang); *Gongzhong DG*, DG 18.12.14, 7:556a–60a (Shanxi).

Shaanxi and Gansu provinces were quite active in the traffic, especially in running distribution networks through various business concerns they owned inside Xinjiang to move the drug east. In fact, most of the major traffickers captured in Xinjiang during the Daoguang reign were from one of these two provinces.[40]

Such men probably composed the majority of the merchant traffickers "from outside" mentioned in Shaan(xi)-Gan(su) Governor-General Yang Yuchun's four annual reports on trafficking in Gansu for the years 1831–34. Yang believed Gansu to be the route for traffickers operating between Xinjiang to the northwest and both Shaanxi and Sichuan to the southeast but did not specify the origins of the traffickers and their opium. His successor, Hu-song-e, expressed particular concern over the traffic with Xinjiang but provided essentially the same details.[41] As senior administrators of Shaanxi and Gansu, both must have been privy to the reports about *qiangtu* from Hui-feng, whose tenure as Gansu's provincial surveillance commissioner ended just after Yang began submitting his annual memorials on prohibition efforts. The throne's suspicions may have been lulled by Chang-qing's contemporary assurances that the Eastern March was free of opium or by the impression that northwestern opium was of coastal origin.

There was definitely evidence that coastal opium was being smuggled from Tianjin into Shaanxi, although points to the northwest of the province, namely Gansu and Xinjiang, were never included in these sweeping official reports, which were generally sparing of more specific geographic details.[42] Shaanxi, like several other interior provinces, appears to have been a watershed, with *qiangtu* dominating the market on its western side and coastal opium that on its eastern side.

The throne does not seem to have received geographically nuanced reports; it was certainly being told that the northwest's high mountains and frozen earth could not support poppy cultivation. This assurance arose from the unanimous and perfunctory conclusions of both Yang and Hu-song-e, who reproduced Yang's reports

40. Gongzhong jinyan, DG 20.2.19; *YPZZ*, DG 21.7.29, 4:72–76.
41. Gongzhong jinyan, DG 11.12.16; *Gongzhong DG*, DG 19.4.9, 10:59a.
42. *YPZZ*, DG 18.5.28, 1:301, DG 18.7.27, 1:351.

almost verbatim for the last time in 1836. Despite these assurances, which had led to the suspension of reporting requirements for a number of opium offenses, including cultivation, that same year, persistent rumors of provincial cultivation triggered another fruitless search of Gansu in 1839.[43] Eleven years later, a censor reported that he "had heard" of poppy cultivation in the southeastern Gansu prefecture of Pingliang.[44]

The outcome of these investigations might have been different had officials bothered to consult the 1780 gazetteer for Gansu's Ganzhou prefecture, where poppy was indigenous. Other works of local geography would have informed inquisitive local officials that Gansu had been producing not only poppies but also *afurong* as early as 1657 and as recently as 1819. Climatic conditions notwithstanding, Gansu would manage to produce 22,021 kilos of crude opium worth 18,464 silver taels in legitimate revenue by 1893. Shaanxi proved equally amenable to poppy, which was openly grown for similar purposes from the 1850s.[45] Ignorance or concealment of the northwest's potential for poppy cultivation seriously retarded regional anticultivation operations, which could have been implemented around 1830 rather than 1840.

At any rate, Beijing had missed the significance of early warning signs from Gansu. The center's wider perspective should have exposed the fact that by the early 1830s opium from the empire's northwestern and southwestern corners was converging on Gansu and then moving east farther into China proper. *Qiangtu* was probably quite cheaper than its coastal competitor in many regions of northern, and possibly even central, China.

---

43. Gongzhong jinyan, DG 11.12.16, 12.12.12, 13.11.29, 14.12.1, 15.11.28; ZZD, DG 11.2.15, pp. 176–82; *YPZZ*, DG 19.1.29, 1:500–501.

44. *Daoguang Xianfeng liangchao chouban*, DG 30.12.15, pp. 254.

45. *Ganzhou fu zhi*, p. 229; Junji zashui, GX 16.8.13, #1071–73, GX 16.8.13, #1074–76, GX 17.9.20, #1696–97, GX 18.2.17, #1851–53, GX 18.7.21, #2049–50; Li Sanmou, "Yapian zai Shanxi," p. 24. For citations from 1657 and 1819, see Lin Man-houng, "Qingmo shehui liuxing xishi yapian yanjiu," pp. 180–81. Waung ("Opium Cultivation," p. 211) cites a British source quoting an 1821 Chinese memorial requesting that opium cultivation be prohibited in Shanxi, but I have found no Chinese sources that support this contention. It seems unlikely, however, that poppy cultivation began in Shanxi during the 1850s.

The drug was certainly cheaper in Xinjiang. Although it is impossible to estimate the price of *qiangtu* in China proper, the prices for crude opium and paste inside Xinjiang can be roughly guessed from the handful of trafficking cases that contain figures. Crude opium sold for about 19 silver taels per kilo wholesale, and paste retailed for about 32 silver taels per kilo. Given a loss of about 25 percent by weight in processing, these prices meant a return of about 25 percent for Xinjiang traffickers. The returns probably increased the farther east *qiangtu* moved.[46] Using these admittedly inexact figures, we can calculate that even if *qiangtu* paste sold in Anhui for 20 percent below the rates estimated for imported Indian opium in Chapter 4, the profit on *qiangtu* would still be 39 percent, or nearly 15 percentage points more than in Xinjiang. Such profit ratios, if accurate, are why *qiangtu* began to flow into China proper.

The demand for opium can, of course, ultimately be traced to the drug's commodification by the British, but not much, if any, *qiangtu* was an import from British India. There were two types of *qiangtu*, a foreign product produced somewhere beyond Xinjiang's western border in the poppy fields of Central Asia or the northern subcontinent and a domestic product grown in the numerous isolated alpine regions of the territory itself. These conditions added poppy cultivation to the territory's already serious trafficking and consumption problems.

Inside Xinjiang, poppy fields were discovered in the Southern March jurisdictions of Aksu, Karashahr, Kucha, Ush, and Yarkand, along a line roughly paralleling the Tian Shan range, as well as the Northern March jurisdiction of Tarbagatai. No cultivation cases were apparently reported from the Eastern March during the Daoguang period, but not because natural conditions there precluded poppy planting. A number of locales in the Urumqi juris-

---

46. Gongzhong jinyan, DG 20.2.19. Determining the conversion rate between Qing imperial silver taels and the local copper currency of Altishahr, the *pul*, is an inexact science at best, especially because the rate seems to have differed from town to town, and the statistics are incomplete. Unfortunately, some figure is necessary since the few documents on the Xinjiang opium traffic that mention prices do so in *pul*. I have converted it at a rate of 200 *pul*/tael based on a loose interpretation of James Millward's figures (*Beyond the Pass*, pp. 68–75).

diction, for example, were "famous" for their poppy during the early Republican period, and migrants from both Gansu and Shaanxi were active in the cultivation of poppy and trafficking of opium in the Gucheng administrative region on the border with Gansu.[47] Lax enforcement or simply a failure to find cultivators hidden in the region's immense wildernesses, as well as gaps in the official record, could explain the absence of cases. Certainly Hui-ji expected to find cultivators in the alpine regions around his Eastern March headquarters of Urumqi on the initial sweeps of the mountains once the winter snows melted in early 1840.[48]

Poppy cultivation in Xinjiang was not determined by ethnicity. Cultivation was considered inevitable among Han civilian farmers in the agricultural colonies around Barchuk and Yarkand and among soldier-agriculturalists in those of Aksu and Ush.[49] It was also believed that East Turkestanis could be growing poppy "in various desolate places around cities and farms" throughout the Southern March. Both Han and East Turkestani planters had already been discovered in Karashahr and Kucha.[50] Even though poppies were clearly being grown by both groups, I have found no arrests of East Turkestanis for cultivation offenses. This absence suggests that if cultivation was not ethnically determined, anticultivation operations were.

Ethno-geographic factors are particularly visible in the operations against cultivators in Xinjiang. In September 1840 Mongol horsemen were secretly sent from Barluk with orders from the Northern March administrative center of Tarbagatai, about 110 kilometers to the northeast, to sweep the "winter alpine pastures" of the region in search of cultivators. The Mongols caught nine Han planters. One of them, Ji Shenglai, stated that the main perpetrators were four grain traders who worked in the area around the towns of Kur-Kara-Usu and Jing He, both approximately 570 kilometers southeast of Tarbagatai. The success of this operation

---

47. Zeng, *Zhongguo jingying xiyu shi*, p. 606; *Xinjiang zhi gao*, 2:48.
48. *Junji jinyan*, DG 19.11.21, #3082–85.
49. *YPZZ*, DG 19.12.22, 1:787, DG 20.8.24, 2:387–88.
50. *YPZZ*, DG 19.12.22, 1:787, DG 20.8.24, 2:387–88; *Junji jinyan*, DG 19.8.24, #2952–57.

convinced Tuan-duo-bu, the Tarbagatai councilor, of the necessity of random sweeps to keep the mountains free of cultivators.[51]

The distances covered by both enforcers and offenders were considerable, especially in the mountains of northern Xinjiang during fall. Anticultivation operations under these conditions were necessarily mounted operations and required Inner Asian horsemen, like the Mongols, who possessed the skills and stamina that Han troops did not. Anticultivation operations in Xinjiang were dependent on multiethnic cooperation among Han, Manchu, and Mongol troops, as well as East Turkestanis, who were involved in similar actions under *beg* leadership in the Southern March.[52] These ethno-geographic complexities distinguished prohibition efforts in Xinjiang from those in other parts of the empire, especially the moderate climes and Han-dominated urban areas of coastal China. The problem presented by distance alone was recognized, and deplored, at the state's highest levels.

The venomous course of opium intensifies, reaching into distant places like Xinjiang and spreading its pollution even more. It is truly detestable! Now, to have discovered in addition that there is poppy planting there is even more surprising. Incidents arise as a consequence of the fact that towns are located amid desolate wilderness and wasteland. If investigations are not thorough, then it is impossible to avoid incidents of disloyal subjects aiming for illicit profit from clandestine poppy planting.[53]

This decree, among others from the Daoguang emperor, imposed on territorial officials an immense task just in terms of preventing the local cultivation of *qiangtu*. But the sources of the drug were not confined to Xinjiang. Foreign *qiangtu*, which probably circulated in even greater quantities than the domestic product, was also moving through Xinjiang into China proper.

It is difficult to pinpoint the origin of foreign *qiangtu*. Most foreign traffickers exposed in Xinjiang came from Kashmir, Badakshan, Kokand, and "India," which could refer to any locale in the subcontinent within or beyond the sphere of British domination.[54]

---

51. *YPZZ*, DG 20.8.24, 2:388.
52. Junji jinyan, DG 19.8.24, #2952–57.
53. *YPZZ*, DG 19.9.22, 1:715.
54. *YPZZ*, DG 19.12.22, 1:786.

In the 1830s, Kokand was an independent state, Kashmir was under the domination of the Sikh empire in the Punjab rather than of British India, and Badakshan was independent of British rule. The understandable focus of Chinese nationalist scholarship on the Euro-American aspects of the opium trade, which attributes all opium in Xinjiang to the deliberate, imperialist machinations of either "British" or "Russian" traffickers, obscures facts showing the northwestern traffic had spread beyond direct European control, if it was ever subject to it, during the 1830s.[55]

It is possible, for example, that the "Indian" traders mentioned in Xinjiang prohibition reports were from the Punjab, which produced opium on its northeastern border with the independent Raj of Kulu, itself a producer and exporter of opium southward to India proper. Furthermore, even if there were traders from British India itself, it is not clear whether they brought opium with them or purchased it in either the Sikh empire or Kulu, where it was being openly sold in the 1820s.[56]

---

55. "British" opium is said to have been transmitted through Kashmir, Badakshan, and India as well as Kokand, which also acted as a conduit for "Russian" opium; see, e.g., Xinjiang Weiwuer zizhiqu, Jiaoyu weiyuanhui, Gaojiao lishi jiaocai bianxie zu, *Xinjiang difang shi*, pp. 190–91; Xinjiang shehuikexueyuan, Lishi yanjiusuo, *Xinjiang jianshi*, 2:2–3; and Zhang Zuoxi, "Shae dui Zhongguo de yapian maoyi," pp. 140–42. The general impression given in all these works is that Britain and Russia had a deliberate policy of using merchants to smuggle opium into Xinjiang to destabilize it. Although the opium trade in Xinjiang was certainly stimulated by the largely British coastal traffic, I have seen no evidence, from Qing sources or elsewhere, to suggest that it was being formally orchestrated by either European empire.

56. William Moorcroft and George Trebeck, British travelers in the Himalayan regions of the subcontinent during the 1820s, briefly described opium use in the Sikh empire: "There is considerable demand both for opium and the poppy in the Panjab, as the Sikhs, whose religious creed forbids the use of tobacco, supply its place by opium and an infusion of poppy heads, to both of which they are much addicted, the former being used by the more wealthy, the latter by the poorer people" (Moorcroft and Trebeck, *Travels*, 1:141). For information on Punjabi and Kulu opium production and sale, see ibid., 1:141, 171. In Kashmir itself, poppy was cultivated for production of narcotics before 1663, when the Mughal emperor Aurangzeb sought to prohibit the drug's cultivation. In the 1840s, poppy seeds were common enough to become an acceptable medium of tax remittance; see Sharma, *Kashmir Under the Sikhs*, p. 131.

Accounts of "Russian" trafficking are subject to similar qualification. No European Russian smugglers were ever caught in Xinjiang during the Daoguang reign, and, as described in more detail below, only one Muslim subject of the tsar, from Semipalitinsk, was ever apprehended by territorial authorities during this time. Although there is evidence, as early as 1834, of tsarist traders bringing small amounts of opium into northern Xinjiang, the origins of this "Russian" opium are not entirely clear. The drug may have been purchased, for example, from the independent Khanate of Bokhara, where it was produced in abundance.[57] Whatever overt Russian opium traffic there was before the 1850s seems to have been conducted at the main Sino-Russian trade depot of Kiakhta in Outer Mongolia and to a lesser extent in Manchuria, rather than in Xinjiang.[58]

It is unlikely that Qing officials were able, or inclined, to distinguish the jumble of independent states scattered over what was not yet either Russian Inner Asia or British northern India. Such complexities are probably why Xinjiang officials preferred to deal with a single Kokandi *hūda-i da* who represented all foreign traders, especially since the khanate controlled all the western trade routes into Xinjiang.[59] At any rate, the Qing authorities' knowledge of geographical and political conditions in India, the main source of foreign opium, was certainly deficient in both Xinjiang and Beijing. In a response to an urgent request for information from Beijing in 1841, En-te-heng-e reassured the throne, after conducting inquiries among his subordinates, that no overland routes connected Britain to Xinjiang that would permit traffickers to bring in opium and take out saltpeter to be used in gunpowder for the British war ef-

---

57. Zhongguo shehuikexueyuan, Jindaishi yanjiusuo, *Shae qin Hua shi*, p. 140; Fletcher, "Sino-Russian Relations," p. 328. For Bokhara, see Lal, *Travels in the Panjab*, p. 132. Even Chinese nationalist scholarship committed to demonstrating the direct complicity of Russian traders in the opium traffic acknowledges that "Russian" opium before the 1870s was exclusively produced in Turkey, Iran, Kokand, or Bokhara, none of which was under tsarist rule; see Zhang Zuoxi, "Shae dui Zhongguo de yapian maoyi," p. 142.

58. Mi, "Shahuang zhengfu zai Qiaketu diqu," pp. 47–50; Zhang Zuoxi, "Shae dui Zhongguo de yapian maoyi," pp. 140–41.

59. Saguchi, "Eastern Trade," pp. 109–10.

fort.[60] The court's query becomes slightly more comprehensible in light of a private statement made that same year by Ili's military governor, Yi-shan, that India, which he knew to produce opium, was adjacent to Britain.[61]

Some concrete intelligence on the foreign trafficking network, however, was reaching Qing officials in Xinjiang as a result of their prohibition operations. En-te-heng-e had been told by foreign merchants during his inquiries in December 1839 that opium "smoking" (xishi) was common in both Kashmir and India and that their opium had been produced "beyond the checkpoints" of Xinjiang in a region transliterated in Chinese as "Tui-yi-bo-te." These merchant traffickers, who hailed from Kashmir, Badakshan, and "India," stated that they had only recently initiated commercial relations with Tui-yi-bo-te for the purchase of opium.[62] This testimony implies that Tui-yi-bo-te lay somewhere between southwestern Xinjiang and the merchants' home territories, amid the intervening small and primarily Muslim principalities such as Wakhan, Kanjut, and Bolor.[63]

Officials also knew that the Eastern March was on the receiving end of the flow of both foreign and domestic qiangtu. As the Qing official primarily responsible for processing opium cases for this administrative area, Hui-ji was in a better position than any other official to detect currents in Xinjiang's opium flow. Privy to reports from officials in the other marches of Xinjiang, he found that opium was being smuggled into his jurisdiction from Tarbagatai in the Northern March and Yarkand in the Southern March. In other words, Urumqi was the confluence of the opium flowing from southwest and northwest Xinjiang eastward into China proper. Noting the absence of foreign merchants in Urumqi, where most of those arrested were "transient merchant subjects (shangmin)," Hui-ji concluded that Han merchants were buying opium from

---

60. WJD, DG 20.12.15, pp. 57–58; YPZZ, DG 20.8.4, 2:306–7, DG 20.12.5, 2:662.

61. Li Xingyuan, Li Xingyuan riji, 1:96.

62. Junji jinyan, DG 19.11.18, #3104–8.

63. Moorcroft and Trebeck, Travels, 2:259–73. Opium was certainly commonly consumed in at least some areas of this region. The inhabitants of Bolor, for example, had become "very fond" of opium no later than 1866 (Veniukof, "The Beolors and Their Country," p. 271).

foreign traders in the border towns and reselling it in the Eastern March to other Han consumers and traffickers.[64]

In general, smugglers were taking advantage of Xinjiang's main transprovincial transport routes, which were maintained by the dynasty for strategic purposes, as well as numerous minor and more local routes that enabled perpetrators to evade official patrols. The main routes most likely to have been employed by smugglers moving across Xinjiang between Kokand and China proper are depicted in Map 7.

Rong Jixiang's trafficking ring, which accounted for 10 percent of the 5,470 kilos confiscated in Xinjiang during the prohibition operations of the early 1840s, exemplifies the transterritorial character of the Xinjiang traffic. The apprehension and interrogation of Rong's business partner, Feng Yucai, by En-te-heng-e in Yarkand during the initial prohibition operations in the Southern March in early 1840 revealed that this ring was purchasing crude opium from both local and foreign traders in the town's Muslim quarter. The drug was then transported by Rong's associates across Xinjiang to locales throughout the Southern and Eastern Marches, including Aksu, Barchuk, Turfan, and Urumqi. The last two towns were about 4,000 *li*, or 2,000 kilometers, east of Yarkand, nearly the entire length of the territory.

The consensus of the official reports was that both foreign and domestic *qiangtu* flowed eastward out of Central Asia across a number of provinces into central China. This distance far exceeded that of the transprovincial networks of the coastal traffic that brought opium to Beijing or Yunnan or those of the southwestern traffic that carried the drug to Guangdong or Shaanxi. Some opium actually traversed the whole length of the empire from Guangdong into Xinjiang. Early 1840 reports from Ili revealed that some coastal opium was moving into Xinjiang, but no regional branch of Qing China's opium-marketing system, even that of the coast, was developed enough at the time to have sent the drug over such immense distances. Ironically, the Qing state itself possessed the only transport network extensive enough for such an accomplishment.

---

64. Junji jinyan, DG 19.11.21, #3082–85.

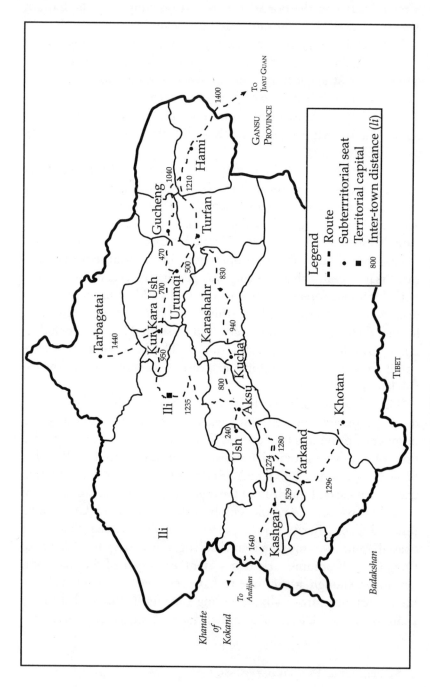

Map 7 Xinjiang, main transprovincial routes

The foundations of this transimperial enterprise were unintentionally laid by the routine functioning of the Qing legal system and further developed by the efficient execution of the opium-prohibition regulations. Specifically, the Qing system of penal exile for a variety of offenses, including a wide range of opium violations, inadvertently transported numbers of unreconstructed coastal traffickers and consumers to the Northern and Eastern Marches of Xinjiang, the empire's main destination for all serious criminals after 1759. Ili got the worst of this group.[65] The emergence of opium at both ends of the empire predated the serious revision of prohibition and enforcement measures under the Jiaqing emperor in 1813.

Guangdong natives Huang Shizong and Cao Shouren became members of the Northern March's convict population in 1808 for a variety of offenses unrelated to opium. Huang almost immediately succeeded in compounding his crimes of banditry, which had been perpetrated as a member of the notorious Heaven and Earth Society (Tiandi hui), by trying to poison a fellow Guangdong exile with opium paste. Huang had obtained the paste from yet another banished co-provincial, cashiered assistant brigade commander Cao Shouren, who had carried the drug from the coast for what were ultimately confirmed to be medicinal purposes and not for drug trafficking. This unsuccessful murder attempt got Huang decapitated, landed Cao in the cangue for three months, and moved Xinjiang's senior territorial administrator, Military Governor Song-jun, to conduct investigations for suspected traffickers among Ili's considerable exile community from Guangdong and Fujian.[66]

---

65. By 1761, Xinjiang was already becoming overcrowded with convicts, and this resulted in the establishment of a quota system to allocate criminal exiles among the various towns of the territory. Under this system the more serious the offense, the farther west one was sent, with the worst offenders ending up in Ili or Urumqi. Ili tended to get the bulk of this group (at a ratio of about 3:1) because, as explained in a 1766 memorial, "Ili is vast and they need people for reclamation work; so probably we should send more convicts there than to Urumqi" (Waley-Cohen, *Exile*, pp. 67–68).

66. Gongzhong jinyan, JQ 12.12.29. For a study of the Heaven and Earth Society, which was facing increased government repression in the Jiaqing and Daoguang years, see Qin Baoqi, *Tiandi hui*.

No further record of these operations has come to light, but it is almost certain, especially given the court's surprised reaction to revelations of opium in Xinjiang in 1839, that official vigilance was not maintained against drug offenses by exiles during the intervening thirty years. At this point, Song-jun's successor, Yi-shan, resumed the task of prohibition among Ili's coastal exiles, many of whom were now being transported to Xinjiang for opium offenses, on a much larger scale. Certain categories of drug offenders were being sentenced to exile in the territory no later than 1815. The implementation of the New Regulations added more exiles, particularly as military slaves, because of the increase in penalties for accessories to a number of capital drug offenses.[67] Thus a direct cause of the multiplication of opium offenses in Xinjiang was the penal exile of more and more offenders to the territory.

Yi-shan's conviction that the coast was ultimately responsible for generating the empirewide opium problem was influenced by his experience with exiled traffickers and consumers from that region. Although only about 5 percent of the 54 cases of trafficking and consumption uncovered by Yi-shan involved coastal exiles, he saw them as a distinct threat to prohibition in his jurisdiction: "Ili is where the banished are concentrated. Since those sent from Fujian and Guangdong are particularly numerous, it is difficult to guarantee there will be no incidents of smoking or selling opium."[68]

Moreover, unreformed consumers from throughout the empire were ending up in Yi-shan's jurisdiction, the majority of these as a result of having their capital offenses commuted to exile in Ili. Yi-shan called imperial attention to their plight and expressed fears that he would ultimately have to execute those who proved unreformable:

If the opium addiction is already deeply formed, we fear it is difficult to hope for an immediate emergence from the addiction. This is why the Imperial Decree's grant of a year and a half grace period, although truly a sage-ruler's gift of extra-legal benevolence, is still a small thread of clemency. The bodies of these kinds of banished criminals are only partially clothed, and their bellies are without food to fill them. Those so forlorn

---

67. *YPZZ*, JQ 20.1.10, 1:14; *HDSL*, 9:1014a, 1017a.
68. *YPZZ*, DG 20.1.16, 2:5.

are unable to shake their addiction, which is plainly deep and strong. They are actually without a way out, and one feels especially moved.[69]

This group of consumers had been transported to Xinjiang in order to quash demand for the drug. Instead, demand had simply been concentrated in the territory through the workings of the apparatus of prohibition itself, where it continued to sustain a territorial market for *qiangtu* as well as whatever small amounts of opium offenders could take with them into exile. Addict exiles also constituted a large group of potential capital offenders, in effect another transfer of an especially unwelcome part of the burden of absolute prohibition from China proper to Xinjiang. Yi-shan does not appear to have solved these problems. A December 1841 case involving consumption and trafficking by three exiles, two from Guangdong and one from Hunan, in the Urumqi jurisdiction in the Eastern March shows that violations by exiles from China proper continued beyond the expiration of the grace period and the confines of the Northern March.[70]

Exiled addicts and traffickers added to the already considerable and peculiar problems of prohibition presented by the intersection of geography and administrative practice in Xinjiang. As noted above, however, the main source of *qiangtu* and its attendant problems of trafficking and consumption lay to the west beyond imperial territory. This situation naturally constrained the prohibition of opium in Xinjiang, but it also permitted Qing authorities to avail themselves of another structure of control not normally available for use against domestic drug offenders. Diplomacy, consequently, became a crucial prohibition strategy in Xinjiang.

The Multiethnic Diplomacy of Xinjiang Prohibition

The southeast coast was not the only site of dynastic negotiations with foreign opium traffickers. The opium-marketing system uncovered in Xinjiang in 1839 was sustained primarily by transborder ties to Muslim merchants from India, Badakshan, Kashmir, and Kokand. The Qing, of course, did not maintain direct relations

---

69. Ibid.
70. WJD, DG 21.10.20, pp. 133–35.

with all these states; rather, it relied on Kokand to act as the representative of this cosmopolitan merchant community in much the same way the British did for Euro-American traders on the coast. This intermediary enabled the dynasty to notify Xinjiang's foreign merchants formally of prohibition regulations as well as to conduct various search-and-seizure operations among their ranks with relatively little opposition from either the merchants themselves or the government of Kokand.

Aside from Kokand, Xinjiang shared a border with another regional power in Central Asia, tsarist Russia, with which the Qing also maintained diplomatic relations. There was little need, however, for protracted negotiations between the two empires over Russian trafficking in Xinjiang since the tsarist empire sought to avoid incidents that would disrupt its more valuable trade in Chinese cotton and tea at Kiakhta.[71] The Russians had come to this conclusion after the Qing suspended trade for various reasons on fourteen occasions between 1762 and 1800. The last of these was also the date when opium was first listed as contraband in Russian trade regulations, evidence for Russian compliance with the Jiaqing court's ban on foreign opium. Tsar Nicholas I's government also cooperated in the inconclusive search for a Russian trafficker reputed to have sold opium to a Chinese smoker in the Kiakhta region in early 1839. Consequently, precedent for Russian acceptance of Qing opium prohibition was well established by the time the tsar issued a ukase on April 12, 1841, announcing formal compliance with the New Regulations.[72]

---

71. For general accounts of the Kiakhta trade, see, e.g., Khokhlov, "The Kyakhta Trade," pp. 66–105; and Zhang and Sun, *Qing qianqi Zhong-E guanxi*, pp. 215–308.

72. Mi, "Shahuang zhengfu zai Qiaketu diqu," pp. 48–50; Peskova, "China and Russia's Position," pp. 291–95; *QSL*, DG 21.6.29, 38:379b–80a. Mi's article is based on an examination of Russian archival sources, many of which are also cited by Peskova, and both concur, if not for the same reasons, that the tsarist empire made a genuine effort to comply with Qing prohibitions before the 1870s. Mi's article is a notable change from previous Chinese scholarship, exemplified by Zhang Zuoxi's 1979 article, which saw Russian compliance as a cynical ploy and made little distinction between Russian policy in practice before and after 1870; see Zhang Zuoxi, "Shae dui Zhongguo de yapian maoyi," pp. 141–42. Zhang does provide evidence, ignored by Mi, of fairly extensive Russian trafficking from the 1850s

In contrast to Kokand, tsarist Russia, which had no immediate territorial designs on the Qing empire and much to gain from co-operation, found accommodation to the opium prohibition relatively easy. This relationship explains the numerous references to Kokand and its clients in the Xinjiang prohibition documents between late 1839 and 1841 and the single incident of Russian trafficking, which involved no European Russians, recorded over the same period.

This case, which occurred in Tarbagatai in September 1840, was the only corroboration of Censor Hui-feng's assertion a year earlier that Russian smugglers were colluding with Xinjiang's domestic traffickers.[73] Tarbagatai's councilor, Tuan-do-bu, reported the apprehension of two Muslims and 419 kilos of opium. Of this amount, 373 kilos belonged to Ai-lin-bai, age 43, a Muslim trader from Kokand's main Russian trade depot of Tashkent. The other 46 kilos belonged to 58-year-old Nasir, from Semipalitinsk in the tsarist empire. Nasir was transporting his opium across Xinjiang's northern border with Siberia on behalf of an otherwise unidentified "Russian" when he encountered Ai-lin-bai, and they decided it would be safer to proceed together. If they had previously been ignorant of the Qing prohibitions, they were warned of them by some Kazakh tribesmen they subsequently met. Henceforth they passed themselves off as textile merchants, mainly in order to hire local bearers to assist them before they crossed the imperial frontier. The two planned to hide their opium until an opportune moment arose when they could move it across the patrol road that lay between them and their destination, but before they could conceal the contraband in a lakeside stand of reeds, they were apprehended by a Qing patrol.[74]

In his adjudication, Tuan-do-bu followed the standard procedure for handling foreign trafficking cases in Xinjiang. He cited the mitigating circumstance that both Tashkent and Semipalitinsk were too far to have received word of the Qing opium prohibi-

---

(p. 142). Mi does, however, show evidence that the tsar felt that Russian ability to enforce the prohibitions on its own subjects was limited (p. 48).

73. *YPZZ*, DG 19.7.27, 1:675–77.

74. *Junji minzu*, DG 20.8.24, #1030–34.

tions; consequently, both men were deemed first offenders trafficking in small amounts within the grace period. This argument had its usual persuasive effect on the emperor, who nevertheless demurred that 419 kilos was hardly a trifling amount. As a result, Nasir's and Ai-lin-bai's death sentences were commuted to two months in Tarbagatai's public cangues. A notification to the Russian and Kokandi "headmen" resident in Tarbagatai to send word of the prohibitions back to their native lands was the only act of interstate diplomacy arising from this incident.[75]

It is significant that Qing authorities ignored the fact that both traffickers had been aware of the prohibitions before they entered Qing territory. Tuan-do-bu even noted this fact in his adjudication, but apart from the comment that this deliberate act was "a serious violation of the law," he said nothing more about it. The emperor, who was clearly sensitive to the fine legal distinctions regarding quantity, followed suit. Such leniency was not an isolated act of extraordinary grace but part of a deliberate policy whose operation can be better observed through the Southern March's amnesties of Central and South Asian Muslims.

As noted in Chapter 3, the Qing had explicitly granted Kokand consular jurisdiction over the khanate's merchants in Xinjiang in 1835 as part of the treaty settlement in the wake of Kokand's invasion of the territory in 1830. It is unclear just when Kokand assumed similar authority over all foreign merchants operating in Xinjiang; nor is the extent of its authority clear, especially since the Qing court formally rejected a bid by the khanate to levy trade taxes on these groups in 1836.[76] Such authority was nevertheless operative by 1839 when Kokandi *hūda-i da* became, along with Qing *hakim begs*, important intermediaries in arranging amnesty for foreign merchants in the Southern March.

These opium handovers by Central and South Asian merchants were unique in the Qing empire in that they were managed by a troika of Kokandi, East Turkestani, and Manchu officials. The division of administrative labor was further ethnically determined, almost certainly to prevent interethnic strife arising from uninten-

---

75. Ibid.; WJD, DG 20.12.5, pp. 53–56.
76. Pan, *Zhongya Haohanguo yu Qingdai Xinjiang*, pp. 147–48.

tional or deliberate provocation. Most operations were conducted by the Muslim representatives of Kokand and those of the Qing with no direct participation by the dynasty's regular Manchu military administrators. Such was the case at Khotan in February 1840 when a group of "Andijani" merchants handed over 200 kilos of opium to the town's *hakim beg* Sha-mu-sha-mai-ma-te as regular Qing officials were processing thirteen cases of drug paraphernalia handed over by Han offenders. The handover proceeded smoothly as the Kokandi superintendent, "an ignorant foreigner unaware of the prohibitions," immediately ordered "the foreign Muslims" under his charge to turn in all the opium they had on hand to avoid punishment.[77]

As Table 4 shows, approximately 3,955 kilos, over 70 percent of the 5,470 kilos of opium confiscated by officials in Xinjiang and over 99 percent of the opium voluntarily handed in, was turned over in this manner between late 1839 and early 1841. These incomplete statistics suggest that amnesties for foreign merchants were the primary and most effective means of prohibition in the territory. They also exceed figures submitted by similar operations in the rest of the empire, with the sole exception of the more than one million kilos surrendered to Lin Zexu in Guangzhou. The Xinjiang operations, however, were conducted without serious confrontation.

The presence of an official Kokandi representative in Kashgar authorized to transmit correspondence between his government and that of the Qing was one reason violent confrontation over opium was avoided in Xinjiang. Superintendent Nu-lu-ba was duly informed of the dynastic opium prohibitions in January 1840 by the *hakim beg* of Kashgar, Zuo-huo-zi-dun, who was conducting inquiries similar to those under way in Khotan, Yarkand, and Aksu around the same time.[78] The *beg* received 84 kilos of opium from Kashgar's foreign merchant community along with Nu-lu-ba's formal acknowledgment of the prohibitions:

---

77. *YPZZ*, DG 20.1.29, 2:22.

78. Junji jinyan, DG 19.11.24, #3109–12 (Aksu); Junji minzu, DG 19.11.18, unnumbered *dapian* copy (Yarkand).

Table 4
Opium Confiscations in Xinjiang, December 1839–January 1841

Location	Number of seizures	Number of handovers	Opium seized (taels)	Opium handed over (taels)
Aksu*	5	0	1,500	0
Ili	7	47	356	-
Kashgar	7	40	400	3,136
Khotan	0	3	0	5,372
Tarbagatai	2	0	11,248	0
Turfan	3	0	-	-
Urumqi	37	3	-	-
Yarkand*	4	7	26,662	97,979
TOTAL (KILOS)			40,166 (1,498)	106,487 (3,972)
GRAND TOTAL (KILOS)				146,653 (5,470)

NOTES: Where possible, amounts of seized opium have been calculated from the traffickers' own reports of the amount they purchased wholesale, since the original quantity was subdivided and resold many times in a number of places across Xinjiang. This is especially true of the Rong Jixiang trafficking ring case, in which the opium was purchased in Yarkand but sold in Khotan and Turfan, where it was often locally resold. This resulted in complicated chains of dozens of small cases that are not counted in the table above.
*Other cases mentioned, but no details given.
SOURCES: Junji minzu, #1030–#34, DG 20.8.24, #1391–93, DG 20.12.29, #1394–95, DG 20.4.20; Junji jinyan, #3082–85, DG 19.11.21, #3104–8, DG 19.11.18, #3109–12, DG 19.11.24; Gongzhong jinyan, DG 19.12.19 (Section 11), DG 20.1.27, DG 20.2.19; YPZZ, DG 19.12.13, 1:772–74, DG 20.1.16, 2:3–7.

We heard of the intensity of opium investigations and arrests and are extremely afraid. We immediately sent a communication to the *beg* of Kokand and received the following response: since receiving notice of the Celestial Court's prohibition of opium, all tribes under Andijan's control have been notified by the *beg* of Kokand that, from now on, no one is permitted to smuggle opium through the checkpoints.[79]

---

79. YPZZ, DG 19.12.19, 1:780–81. The "*beg* of Kokand" was ruler Khan Muhammad Ali. It is probable that Nu-lu-ba also used the title "khan," and the term *beg* was substituted by Chinese translators. Such terminology was a very sensitive issue. Kokandi missions to Beijing had been suspended in 1809–10 because of Khan Alim's addressing of the Jiaqing emperor as "friend" in an official communication (Pan, *Zhongya Haohanguo yu Qingdai Xinjiang*, pp. 81–82).

From this time forward, all foreign merchants under Kokand's jurisdiction in Xinjiang were technically bound to refrain from opium smuggling by the khan's acknowledgment of the Qing prohibition. Anticipating a time lag in the spread of the news, Kashgar's highest Qing official, Unit Commander Fu-xing-a, personally informed all Muslims in Kashgar of the prohibitions and ordered them to notify their compatriots back home. He also assured the throne that subsequent violations could be handled in the same way.[80]

The largest amnesty operations occurred in Yarkand, which in June 1840 was designated the processing center for all foreign opium handed over or seized in the Southern March.[81] Yarkand had already concluded one large handover operation in December 1839. In all, 21 traders turned in 2,466 kilos of opium. Of this, almost 2,000 kilos came from nine Kashmiri traders, approximately 447 kilos from eleven "Indian" traders, and nearly 53 kilos from a lone Badakshani.[82] Within a month, 22 more merchants—five Kashmiris, four Badakshanis, four "Indians," one Kokandi, and several local and foreign merchants of indeterminate origin—handed in another 1,188 kilos of opium, the bulk of it again coming from the Kashmiris and the "Indians."[83]

These operations were managed by Yarkand's *hakim beg*, Ismail, acting under the orders of Councilor En-te-heng-e. Investigations of the transborder smuggling traffic were conducted simultaneously. Both groups of traffickers pleaded ignorance of the prohibitions, with those from the second group claiming that they dealt primarily with small Muslim settlements in the countryside around Yarkand, where news of the prohibitions was penetrating only slowly. En-te-heng-e expressed skepticism about many of the merchants' explanations, but this did not prevent him from recommending amnesty for all offenders, which the emperor granted.[84]

---

80. *YPZZ*, DG 19.12.19, 1:781.

81. *YPZZ*, DG 20.5.20, 2:137. Ili was designated the center in the Northern March, for the mostly Han offenders there.

82. Junji jinyan, DG 19.11.18, #3104–8.

83. Junji minzu, DG 20.1.29, #1391–93.

84. Ibid., DG 19.11.18, unnumbered *dapian* copy, DG 20.1.29, #1391–93; *YPZZ*, DG 19.12.23, 1:792–93, DG 20.1.29, 2:23.

In March 1840, En-te-heng-e had summoned over fifty merchants as well as Yarkand's *hūda-i da* and formally announced the
prohibitions. The merchants signed pledges not to engage in the
opium traffic and assured En-te-heng-e that they had sent word of
the prohibitions to their home territories. After collecting the
written pledges and warning the merchants that subsequent violations would bring total confiscation of their wares and permanent
expulsion from China, En-te-heng-e led them to witness the destruction of all the opium that they had turned over, a three-day
event analogous to the larger and more famous one presided over
by Imperial Commissioner Lin Zexu in Guangzhou.[85]

This action, with the exception of a few stints in the public
cangues meted out in Aksu in December 1839 and in Tarbagatai as
described above, is the most serious punishment on record inflicted
on foreign traffickers in Xinjiang during the Daoguang reign. Despite a standing imperial decree that foreign offenders would be
"severely punished," traffickers from across the border continued
to turn up and be spared because of their "ignorance" of the prohibitions.[86] In fact, it seems that the only way for the Qing to ensure
that foreign merchants were informed of the prohibitions was to
catch them trafficking, for news of En-te-heng-e's March 1840 an-
nouncement to Kokandi and other merchants had apparently not
been relayed to Ai-lin-bai in Tashkent by September of the same
year, although the same message had clearly reached the Kazakhs
along the frontier.

Such contradictions were almost openly asserted by the Grand
Council in its decisions regarding application of the New Regulations to the Southern March. In response to En-te-heng-e's attempt
to excuse Muslims from the full force of intensified prohibition on
the basis of ethnic difference, the council admonished Qing officials to treat foreign Muslim traffickers just as harshly as they did

---

85. Junji jinyan, DG 20.2.19, #3272–73. The memorial provides no specifics on
how the opium was destroyed, but judging from similar operations elsewhere, it
was probably mixed with "wood oil" (*tongyou*) and burned.

86. *YPZZ*, DG 20.1.29, 2:22; Junji jinyan, DG 19.11.24, #3109–12 (Aksu); Junji
minzu, DG 20.4.20, #1394–95 (Khotan), DG 20.8.24, #1030–34 (Tarbagatai), DG
21.10.29, #1396–402 (Kashgar).

Han traffickers. Yet, the Grand Council conceded that since the Muslims could not "quickly familiarize themselves with the prohibition regulations, all these cases will be seen as first offenses and punishment will be voided in accordance with the statutes on voluntary handovers within the grace period."[87] This qualification was a critical loophole, for grace period or not, foreign merchants who handed over their opium were always declared first offenders and spared further punishment.

This extraordinary leniency, in view of what befell Han traffickers at the time, was apparently not sufficiently appreciated by the Southern March's foreign merchant community, no matter how submissive their behavior in front of Qing officials. After another confiscation operation in the summer of 1841, complaints reached the ear of Khan Muhammad Ali of Kokand (r. 1822–42), who dispatched an emissary to deliver a formal protest to the Qing court. This protest was duly delivered to the new councilor of Yarkand, Tumingga, who had it translated into Chinese, checked it for "improper language," and forwarded it to Beijing in December. The khan was in evident physical distress: "I have heard from Muslim traders coming from Kashgar that a large and valuable quantity of opium was destroyed there without any recompense. Moreover, many of our people were taken into custody and cangued. What has been done has made my abdomen swell. Can this be proper?"[88]

Tumingga shot back a recitation of the Qing position on opium, which, as he emphasized, should already have been well known to the khan and his merchant subjects:

Opium is harmful to people and has therefore been strictly prohibited by the court. If there are traffickers, they will be beheaded at once. I, the grand minister consultant, was lenient with your little Muslims of Andijan because they were ignorant, and I memorialized the Great Emperor to permit them to avoid punishment by voluntarily handing over their opium.

The *hūda-i da* was charged two years ago to transmit a letter to you making known the decree that all your subjects would never be permitted

87. *YPZZ*, DG 20.3.27, 2:84–85.
88. Junji minzu, DG 21.10.29, #1396–402. The Kokandi original is extant.

to traffic in opium within the checkpoints. Your little Muslim traders should know the law and peaceably abide by it.[89]

This document apparently concluded the only diplomatic exchange between the Qing and Kokand concerning the Xinjiang opium traffic. Its severity was no doubt considerably reduced by the silver, red cloth, satin (both plain and purple-fringed), tea (including 100 catties of the Pearl Orchid variety), rice, wheat, and sheep distributed among the Kokandi party. At any rate I have come across no records of further communications.

What remains is, however, instructive in several respects, not the least of which is that this exchange confirms the confiscations of opium from Muslim traffickers in Xinjiang. Furthermore, these operations were still being carried out more than eighteen months after they had been initiated in the territory because these same traffickers and their government were disingenuously professing ignorance of the dynastic prohibitions. Qing officials continued to respond with irritated leniency. It is clear that the exchange constituted an accommodation between the two governments over Xinjiang's drug traffic.

The Kokandi position was reasonably straightforward. The khanate's merchants, along with their colleagues from Kashmir, Badakshan, and points south, were attracted by the demand for opium in Qing China and not deterred by rhetoric, the occasional confiscation, or a bit of painful public humiliation. The motives for the Qing's equivocal stance are less explicit than Kokand's, but they almost certainly reflect the dynasty's wish not to open a second front in the opium war in a strategic and unstable border area just to stop relatively small amounts of the drug from coming into the northwest. After all, Chinese silver was not hemorrhaging into Kokandi coffers to purchase opium. This stance both reinforced, and was reinforced by, the dynasty's official position that suppression of the coastal traffic would automatically eradicate opium from the rest of the empire.

The Qing's ethnically nuanced prohibition policy did not, however, simply appear after the outbreak of the Opium War with

---

89. Ibid.

Britain. The overall impact of ethnic factors on the implementation of prohibition, visible both among the Asian Muslims on the northwestern frontier and the Christian Euro-Americans on the southeast coast, was a manifestation of a fundamental dynastic policy. No foreign trafficker was ever sentenced to death, let alone executed, by the dynasty even when the most absolute forms of prohibition were being implemented against imperial subjects.

Ethnic grounds for the differential treatment of imperial subjects are also evident in the Grand Council's decision to leave minor offenses to the jurisdiction of *hakim begs*.[90] The authorities' questionable belief that East Turkestanis were not opium smokers is the most prominent example of how ethnicity influenced prohibition. East Turkestani traffickers were also treated differently, if not with as much leniency as their co-religionists from across the border. The six East Turkestani traffickers uncovered in the Yarkand village of Karghalik in early 1840, who are among the few East Turkestanis to appear in the official records on prohibition, initially received the same sentences as their Han counterparts. In the memorial reporting this case, En-te-heng-e requested permission to treat them differently, mainly because they, like the foreign traffickers involved in the case, were Muslims. All Muslims were ultimately able to avoid the full force of Qing law:

All these [six] Muslims are ignorant and are unaware of the prohibitions. Since those from beyond the checkpoints have been spared punishment, and since all six are first offenders for the same crime, it is asked that they be spared transportation. Instead, your servants will strictly charge that they be handed over to the *hakim beg* and cangued in the town's Muslim quarter for three months and exposed to the populace, so that the Muslim masses will all know fear. They will then be transported to a distant Muslim hamlet at hard labor under the strict supervision of the hamlet's *beg*, who will not permit them to cause further disturbances.[91]

En-te-heng-e was practicing a form of internal or domestic diplomacy commonly employed in Xinjiang when dealing with almost any question concerning the territory's indigenous Muslims. This approach was a tacit recognition that the ethno-geographic

90. *YPZZ*, DG 20.3.27, 2:85.
91. Gongzhong jinyan, DG 20.2.19.

realities of Xinjiang precluded "Han-style" control of a non-Han population that had greater cultural affinities with a neighboring and hostile power than it did with its putative Qing rulers. A dual system of external and internal diplomacy was a prerequisite for the implementation of territorial prohibition as part of the general maintenance of Qing rule in Xinjiang. Under these conditions, both *begs* and *hūda-i da* were Muslim ambassadors to the Qing.

Ethnicity was thus an even more complex determinant of the implementation of prohibition in Xinjiang than it was on the coast, where the authorities had to deal only with foreigners and Han. The modifications necessitated by the presence of both indigenous and foreign Muslim offenders, as well as Han addicts and traffickers, added to the problems inherent in the multiple administrative structures in Xinjiang, themselves a product of the territory's ethnic diversity. Ethno-geographic conditions in Xinjiang not only precluded the uniform enforcement of absolute prohibition but also imposed a selective, qualified enforcement as well as a tacit toleration of opium's continued ingress.

Opium in Qing Inner Asia

By the latter half of 1839, Qing officials in Xinjiang were confronting an interstate drug traffic, which was probably almost a decade old. It was also in the process of becoming indigenized through local poppy cultivation. Moreover, they had less time than their colleagues elsewhere in the empire to adapt and implement the revised prohibition regulations, which had not been formulated with Xinjiang in mind, before the onset of capital punishment for all major categories of drug offense. These problems alone would have made prohibition in the territory unusually difficult, even without the extra obstacles to enforcement produced by ethno-geographic diversity.

Opium prohibition in any Qing frontier territory would have encountered similar problems, and the dynasty made no comparable attempt to stop drugs in Tibet, Mongolia, or Manchuria. Only a few cases of consumption and trafficking surfaced among the Qing garrison at Lhasa, and no serious attempt at enforcement was made anywhere else in the territory, almost certainly because of the near-total absence of Qing administrative structures. Tibet was a protectorate of the Qing, which maintained only a small garrison there, rather than a full-fledged territory with a substantial dynastic military and civil presence.[92]

As in Xinjiang, some officials in a couple of jurisdictions in eastern Outer Mongolia, or Uliassutai, were also asked to propose modifications to the prohibitions, mainly to ensure proper control on Xinjiang's northeastern border with Mongolia.[93] They proposed no alterations in the policy, and their responses were entirely unrelated to the small number of offenses that occurred in other parts of Mongolia, for the most part in Zhili's northernmost prefecture of Chengde, also known as Rehe or "Jehol," beyond the Great Wall. During the empirewide search for poppy cultivation in the first half of the 1830s, the region's *baojia* security apparatus was employed at least twice, in 1832 and 1835, in a fruitless search for cultivators and traffickers. In 1838, seven traffickers and consumers were apprehended, and another trafficker was arrested in 1842, but the initial investigations of these cases seem never to have been followed up or expanded. There is no mention of Mongol offenders, and officials apparently conducted operations exclusively among Han settlements. A similar pattern emerged in Ulan Bator, where five more Han traffickers and consumers were also apprehended during what appears to have been the only search-and-seizure operation there.[94]

Operations in Qing Manchuria were more extensive than in either Tibet or Mongolia, in part because the throne was agitated by the penetration of opium into "the preserve of our dynasty's roots."[95] There are some indications that opium smuggling was integrated into the long-standing ginseng-smuggling networks of the area, as some offenders were caught with both contraband items at main commercial choke points such as Shanhai Guan. Unlike ginseng, however, opium was not a Manchurian product at this time.

---

92. Bello, "Chinese Roots," pp. 51–56.

93. WJD, DG 19.10.16, pp. 137–39; *YPZZ*, 19.12.1, 1:749–50 (Khobdo).

94. Gongzhong jinyan, DG 11.12.21; Junji jinyan, DG 15.12.26, #1887–88; QSL, DG 18.12.24, 37:959a–b; ZZD, DG 18.3, pp. 61–63; *Chouban yiwu shimo buyi*, DG 22.1.20, pp. 11–12.

95. *YPZZ*, DG 18.12.7, 2:243.

Southeastern coastal traffickers, operating from Tianjin, were initially suspected. A prolonged investigation confirmed that they, along with their counterparts from Shandong, were smuggling opium into the seaports of Fengtian (present-day Liaoning province). Traffickers, mainly from Shanxi, then purchased this opium for transport back to their native provinces. The drug seems not to have penetrated farther north, into Jilin or Heilongjiang, in any substantial quantity during the Daoguang period. Only one case of smuggling, involving 23 kilos of opium and four Jilin merchants, two men from Shandong, one from Shanxi, and one from Jilin, seems to have been discovered during the Daoguang reign. In effect, prohibition operations in Manchuria, which were pursued between 1834 and 1844, were almost exclusively directed at Han smugglers and consumers along the coastal fringes of Fengtian.[96]

Aside from a few vague references to "barbarian" traffickers in Tibet, there was no evidence that the indigenous peoples of Tibet, Mongolia, or Manchuria were participating in the traffic, and whatever opium was circulating in these three areas came exclusively from China proper.[97] Daoguang-era prohibition in these areas was, consequently, exclusively directed against Han traffickers and consumers either resident in or passing through these regions. This selective strategy obviated the necessity to adapt prohibition regulations for application among non-Han peoples. Prohibition operations in all imperial territories were thus ethnically determined in one way or another, but Xinjiang was the only locale in which prohibition was applied to both Han and non-Han.

Xinjiang was singled out for special treatment because opium was flowing through it toward China proper. Since opium made no fine distinctions of ethnicity, the situation required interstate diplomacy as well as the active assertion of dynastic control against indigenous peoples. Moreover, the appearance of poppy cultivation in Xinjiang itself, a unique problem among the empire's Inner

---

96. WJD, DG 14.9.5, pp. 22–23, DG 17.12.7, pp. 208–10; *YPZZ*, DG 18.9.7, 1:388–89, DG 19.1.10, 1:485–86; Junji jinyan, DG 18.3.14, #1938–41, DG 18.5.28, #1979–81; *Chouban yiwu shimo buyi*, DG 23.12.6, pp. 73–74. There are over 30 documents concerning prohibition operations in Manchuria during the Daoguang period.

97. Gongzhong shenban, DG 21.3.23. These foreigners were probably Tibetans, but this did not trigger a Qing response (Bello, "Chinese Roots," pp. 54–55).

Asian territories during the Daoguang era, necessitated a substantial commitment to antidrug operations.[98] Had these various trafficking and cultivation problems been confined to Xinjiang, the dynasty would probably have followed a minimalist prohibition plan against Han offenders like that operative in other territories, which were not channeling opium into China proper.

The appearance of *qiangtu* in the northwestern provinces of the Han core and rumors of its spillover into central China forced Beijing to impose absolute prohibition on Xinjiang, but the territory was no more amenable to prohibition than any other non-Han region. In fact, the long-term instability that arose from a discontented ethnic minority with close cultural ties to an expansionist power just across the border made Xinjiang the worst frontier territory in which to pursue prohibition.

The fact that prohibition had to be carried out through several ethnically determined, overlapping administrative systems, some of which were heavily dependent on these very minorities, made Xinjiang an undesirable ground on which to confront drug offenders. The improper functioning of these systems could result in the kind of collusion evident in many cases between Muslim and Han traffickers. Even when working properly, however, these structures could pit Han against Muslims, as in the Karashahr cultivation case.

The territory's role as the empire's main destination for exiles also worked against effective prohibition, since the routine functioning of the Qing penal system uprooted opium from the empire's eastern maritime zone and transplanted it in Xinjiang. As demonstrated by the experiences of Yi-shan in 1840 and of Song-jun in 1808, the successful judicial processing of opium offenders resulted in the state-sponsored transfer of opium traffickers from the coast to Xinjiang. These incidents reveal that one of the main goals of prohibition—stopping the spread of opium throughout the empire—was being undermined by the myopically successful application of the mechanisms of prohibition itself. There is perhaps no better example of the self-defeating consequences of the court's assumptions regarding the coastal, urban nature of the opium prob-

---

98. Cultivation did appear in Manchuria, for example, around 1860; see Wang Gesheng, "Dongbei zhong yingsu," p. 124.

lem. These beliefs, although theoretically intended to address other manifestations of the drug problem as well, tended in practice to subordinate all other aspects of opium prohibition to phenomena in the coastal ports.

The proximity and hostility of Kokand ensured that prohibition efforts in Xinjiang would achieve limited success at best. The khanate broke the monopoly on armed force that the Qing maintained throughout most of its dominions. As was more directly demonstrated on the coast, external military power, latent or overt, was a crucial factor in sustaining transgressive behavior. In Xinjiang this power produced the Kokandi consular system headed by *hūda-i da*, who played key roles in enabling Central and South Asian traders to escape the full force of Qing law. The manifestation of this power differed from that displayed on the coast during the Opium War in that it was not based on technological superiority but on military and commercial subversion, geographic position, and cultural affinity.

Ethnic diversity, however, did not preclude mutual understanding, nor did it always work to the disadvantage of the Qing state. The shared history between the Qing empire and the Khanate of Kokand did help to ensure that there would be no major confrontation comparable to that between the Qing and Great Britain in 1839. Moreover, Qing diplomacy with both Kokand and Russia during the 1830s almost certainly inhibited large-scale development of an opium market system centered on Xinjiang, where by 1874, during the Russian occupation of Ili, over 3,000 hectares of poppy were being cultivated for export to China proper.[99]

The mass production of opium on this scale for distribution throughout Chi`na would also arise in another part of the Qing western frontier. The southwestern province of Yunnan, along with Sichuan and Guizhou, would become the center of another opium market, which would ultimately dominate China during the second half of the nineteenth century.

In the empire's southwest, there was no coherent political entity such as the Khanate of Kokand with which to contend or negotiate. The history of prohibition in the provinces of the southwest

---

99. Zhang Zuoxi, "Shae dui Zhongguo de yapian maoyi," p. 143.

shows that the presence of a state independent of Qing control was, in itself, not a fundamental prerequisite for the maintenance of opium transgression. Instead, the mere absence of effective grass-roots administrative structures within the borders of Qing provinces themselves was sufficient to ensure that opium would continue to be produced, sold, and consumed throughout imperial domains.

SIX

The Opium Problem in Southwestern China

As in Xinjiang, the sale and consumption of southwestern opium would have been of only limited significance to the central government had it remained confined to its circumscribed places of origin. It was the flow of this opium, known as *afurong*, to the north and east and as far away as Guangdong, Shaanxi, and Beijing itself, that alarmed the authorities in the capital.

Yunnan, Guizhou, and southern Sichuan, which constitute southwestern China in my analysis, share two conditions that shaped them into a region with a distinctive opium problem. The first is the natural environment of the region, which is particularly conducive to the large-scale cultivation of the opium poppy. In the 1830s and early 1840s, this cultivation, disproportionately extensive in Yunnan, compelled the central government to implement systematic anticultivation operations throughout the region. Cultivation also produced income for peasants and revenue for local administrations; although illicit, this money proved indispensable to the regional economy.

The second condition, unlike the first, was not unique to these three provinces; namely, the presence of tribal settlements, both semi-incorporated and unincorporated. The native chieftain system was intended to administer the numerous, semi-incorporated indigenous minority peoples along lines broadly similar to those of the *beg* system in Xinjiang. These separate, indirect administrative jurisdictions, themselves a product of ethno-geographic diversity, provided spaces relatively free of routine central government surveillance not only for the production of opium but also for sales to Han traffickers for distribution elsewhere. The absence of surveillance was total, however, in the unincorporated, "wild" (*ye*) frontier zones, especially in southwestern Yunnan, inhabited by indigenous peoples under no recognized system of administrative organization, however indirectly connected to the dynasty. Indigenous settlements along provincial borders were particularly instrumental in facilitating the interprovincial dimension of the traffic, and this dimension in turn produced the southwestern opium problem.

The intersection of these administrative, geographic, ethnic, and economic relations within the confines of southwestern China produced a marked division of labor within a regional opium-marketing system broadly coincident with ethnically determined administrative boundaries. Poppy, feral or cultivated, grew in areas of indigenous settlement and was then acquired by Han traffickers, who transported crude opium sap to mainly urban and largely Han consumers within and beyond the southwest. Tribals also helped transport the drug at crucial points along distribution routes that ran through areas under their control adjacent to provincial borders. As the government became more aware of the nature and extent of the opium problem in the southwest, it discovered that the semi-incorporated and unincorporated areas were the main production and wholesale distribution centers for the regional opium traffic and that they were almost entirely immune to prohibition operations. This situation was decisive in the policy shift, advocated by many senior provincial officials, from anticultivation to antitrafficking measures.

The chronology of the implementation of the central government's prohibition policy in the southwest provides a general perspective from which to view both the special challenges presented by the distinctive geographic, ethnic, and economic aspects of the regional opium market and their influence on relations between center and locality. As we shall see, these aspects of the regional market were instrumental in the failure of Qing prohibition and the rise of the southwest as the world's largest producer and distributor of opium in the latter half of the nineteenth century.

Opium Prohibition Comes to the Southwest

Prohibition did not come to the southwest all at once, as it did in Xinjiang; rather, it progressed more gradually both geographically and chronologically. Although officials in Sichuan were aware of a trafficking problem in that province as early as 1816, documentation on prohibition operations in the interior during the Jiaqing period is sparse, probably because the center seldom paid attention to the area before the Daoguang reign. In 1823, several years before Censor Shao Zhenghu's August 1830 memorial triggered the empire's first systematic anticultivation operations, however, official reports of opium cultivation in Yunnan surfaced. Between 1831 and 1833 poppy cultivation was discovered in Sichuan and Guizhou as well and "rediscovered" in Yunnan. By the time the New Regulations were promulgated in 1839, regional anti-opium operations had been pursued after a fashion for nearly two decades, and the court was well aware of the existence of a large trafficking and cultivation problem in the southwest centered on Yunnan. Nevertheless, several years of intensified prohibition efforts proved fruitless, and the central government was unable to eradicate opium from the southwest.

An 1816 public proclamation from Ba district in Sichuan is the earliest known prohibition action in the southwest. This proclamation may, along with what appear to be ad hoc anticultivation operations in Yunnan at the close of the Jiaqing reign in 1820, have been connected to the throne's 1815 reiteration of the need to enforce prohibition at coastal ports of entry to prevent the spread of the drug to the interior.[1] Almost all of the scant information available suggests that prior to the Daoguang emperor's succession in 1821 prohibition was aimed against coastal trafficking to the virtual exclusion of all other aspects of the drug economy. The Daoguang court, however, was forced to alter this focus on the coast by an

---

1. *Baxian dang'an*, JQ 21.5.6, 2:272; *YPZZ*, JQ 19.5.4, 1:11–12. It is possible that Qing-bao, during his brief tenure as Yun-Gui governor-general in 1820, presided over some cultivation and consumption cases; see the vague reference in an 1831 official report by Yun-Gui Governor-General Ruan Yuan, *YPZZ*, DG 11.5.9, 1:77.

1823 report from Censor Yin Peifen that called official attention to poppy cultivation throughout Yunnan. In response to an imperial decree directing Yunnan provincial officials to investigate, Yun-Gui Governor-General Ming-shan confirmed that cultivation did indeed exist. By September 1823, the throne was ordering the senior provincial officials in the Yun-Gui region to implement the first formal anticultivation operations in Chinese history.[2]

The dearth of case reports from the 1820s, however, suggests that there was no sustained effort to eradicate opium from Yunnan, or anywhere else in the southwest, during this decade.[3] This is not surprising since even Censor Yin considered the ultimate source of the opium problem to be coastal smuggling, and he blamed maritime port officials' lack of diligence for the inland flow of the drug. Yin successfully proposed a very simple and standard series of measures to deal with Yunnan's cultivation and trafficking problems: stricter enforcement of existing prohibitions, including the provisions for official laxity or corruption, and confiscation and destruction of the local poppy.[4] The central government continued to focus on what was undoubtedly the much larger problem of coastal trafficking, which it considered the ultimate source of Yunnan's and Sichuan's drug problem.

Unfortunately, as Yin's memorial had revealed, opium had already rooted itself in the soil of the southwest, and the socioeconomic consequences would be decisive in defeating regional prohibition efforts in the 1830s. Poppy was unearthed in all three

---

2. Lin Man-houng ("Qingmo shehui liuxing xishi yapian yanjiu," pp. 184, 82) makes brief mention of the first imperial decree in response to Yin Peifen's initial report, as it is reproduced in QSL, DG 2.12.8, 33:817b, and quotes from Yin's first memorial of 1823, as reproduced in Dao, Xian, Tong, Guang si chao, pp. 72a–75a. See also QSL, DG 3.17.12, 33:971b–72b; YPZZ, DG 3.8.2, 1:51–52. See Chapter 4 for additional details on the evolution of anticultivation legislation.

3. I have come across only a single case for the 1820s; see Neige weijin, DG 8.5.22, #10092 (tongben). Of course, prohibition during this period may have been a purely local matter, thus obviating the need to submit reports to the central government. There is some suggestive evidence to this effect in subprovincial documents; see Baxian dang'an, JQ 21.5.6, 2:272 (Sichuan); and YPZZ, DG 11.5.9, 1:77–79.

4. Dao, Xian, Tong, Guang si chao, p. 74a–b; QSL, DG 3.7.12, 33:971b–72b.

southwestern provinces by 1833, often from fields in isolated areas along interprovincial boundaries and in tribal settlement areas.[5]

The initial approaches to these problems were typical in their reliance on the *baojia* system of surveillance and, to a lesser extent, on the native chieftain system. The Daoguang emperor was especially displeased with the cursory nature of the first report from Yunnan and complained that author Yun-Gui Governor-General Ruan Yuan had "merely used empty words to charge subordinates to investigate and prohibit opium." The emperor wanted to know how local officials would "actually carry out operations so that traitorous commoners will know fear." This reprimand produced a more detailed response dated June 18, 1831, which can stand as an outline of prohibition strategy in the southwest during the first half of the decade.[6]

Ruan Yuan proposed an overhaul of the "old" and admittedly weak prohibition policies of his predecessors, which relied on border checkpoints and seasonal field inspections by yamen personnel. In its place he recommended that the *baojia* system be used more vigorously to conduct inspections and to solicit bonds not to engage in poppy cultivation and that all land devoted to illicit cultivation be confiscated after the poppies had been uprooted. Supervising officials would be sent to monitor the overall progress of these intensified prohibition operations in *junxian* areas, and native chieftains would perform similar functions in their own tribal jurisdictions.[7]

The Daoguang emperor objected to Ruan's proposals, primarily because they depended on fundamentally unreliable auxiliary personnel. The emperor was particularly skeptical that poppies would be uprooted by unsupervised yamen underlings.[8] Although this, and other imperial objections, were reasonable, it is difficult to imagine what the average understaffed provincial administration

---

5. Junji jinyan, DG 10.6.24, #1545–46; *YPZZ*, DG 11.10.01, 1:99 (Sichuan); Junji, DG 12.12.16, #062220 (Guizhou).

6. *YPZZ*, DG 11.5.9, 1:77–79 (Yunnan), DG 11.10.01, 1:99–100 (Sichuan), DG 11.7.3, 1:95–96 (Guizhou).

7. *YPZZ*, DG 11.5.9, 1:78.

8. Ibid.

could have done. Indeed, the throne failed to offer alternatives and soon accepted virtually all of Ruan's proposals.[9]

It is difficult to evaluate the results of prohibition measures in the southwest. By mid-1832, for example, Ruan claimed that although some cultivation remained deep in the mountains, "70 to 80 percent" of Yunnan's homegrown product had been eradicated by the steady enforcement of the prohibitions. Ruan believed that his program of extensive confiscations of cultivators' land and judicious use of physical punishment was having the desired effect, and he stated categorically that opium could be eradicated despite the current persistence of poppy cultivation in isolated mountains and valleys.[10]

Provincial officials in both Sichuan and Guizhou were less sanguine. By early 1835 Guizhou Governor Yu-tai reached the much more qualified conclusion that, despite a marked decrease in the provincial opium caseload, the crime could probably never be fully eradicated. Yu-tai's caution may have arisen from the fact that his predecessor as governor of Guizhou, Song-pu, had ignorantly asserted in 1831 that arable land in the province was too scarce to raise both staple crops and cash crops such as opium and that the mountains of Guizhou were too rocky to grow poppy. In general, senior Guizhou officials limited their claims partly because they suspected their subordinates of colluding with local perpetrators to certify their jurisdictions free of opium.[11]

Reports from Sichuan in 1835 are also restrained in tone and state that numerous arrests were gradually decreasing the problem but admit that smoking had yet to be eradicated from the general populace.[12] By this time Ruan himself had already backed away from his earlier assertions. Near the end of 1834, he was still maintaining, based partly on covert inspections, that all the inhabitants of Yunnan proper, namely, those parts of the province under *junxian* administration, had "come to fear the law so that illicit cul-

---

9. *QSL*, DG 11.6.26, 35:1020a–b.

10. Junji jinyan, DG 12.2.9, #1746–49.

11. Ibid., DG 14.12.13, #195–97; *YPZZ*, DG 11.7.3, 1:95; Junji, DG 12.12.16, #062220.

12. *Baxian dang'an*, DG 14.2.13, 2:273.

tivation of poppy declines daily." Ruan was forced to admit, however, that illicit cultivation in native chieftainships, as well as in "many places in the mountains," was "inevitable" and, though declining, could not be fully controlled.[13]

But, as Ruan Yuan recognized, the eradication of poppy cultivation alone could not be equated with successful prohibition of opium in the southwest, because a decline in the amount produced locally would be offset by a commensurate inflow of coastal opium:

Opium smuggling from beyond the provincial border was initially unavoidable. Then, after local poppy began to be cultivated for sale, it was relatively cheaper and thus easy to sell so that opium that came from afar was more expensive. Profits became minimal, and traffickers gradually decreased in number. . . . Your servants especially fear that, as the domestic cultivation of poppy is gradually cut off, external trafficking in opium will reappear, as will laxity in enforcement as time passes.[14]

Prohibition policy in the southwest as it emerged during the early 1830s was thus intended primarily to eliminate both traffickers and cultivators, with operations against consumers relegated to a secondary role. The dual nature of southwestern trafficking and cultivation was broadly similar to that of Xinjiang and distinctly different from that of the coast, where foreign trafficking was the paramount problem. Widespread poppy cultivation, an unprecedented domestication of the opium problem, added to the burden of prohibition throughout the understaffed expanses of the empire's western border territories, which were already weighed down by problems with non-Han traffickers analogous to those of the coast.

The success of southwestern prohibition measures during this period is difficult to evaluate. Provincial case lists giving the number of offenders and the location and nature of their crimes were part of the intensification of antidrug operations in the southwest after 1830. Unfortunately, there was little if any standardization of the statistics on drug offenses. Moreover, the figures are problematic in that they are primarily relevant for *junxian* areas, especially

---

13. Gongzhong jinyan, DG 14.11.28.
14. Junji jinyan, DG 12.2.9, #1746–49.

those near provincial capitals, which were under fairly continuous and more dependable official surveillance. Nevertheless, some degree of prohibition was also implemented in at least some native chieftainships, as extant local documents dated 1831 from a Yunnan native chieftainship in Wuding department make clear.[15]

Whatever their limitations, these lists do show a radical decline from 27 cases in 1835 to 8 in 1836 in Yunnan and from 55 cases in 1834 to 21 in 1835 in Guizhou. There are no comparably detailed case lists from Sichuan, which seems to have reported an unusually low number of cases throughout this period—only eight or so trafficking and consumption cases between 1831 and 1836 and no new cultivation cases. Imperial rescripts appended to many memorials after the mid-1830s relieved officials of the necessity of submitting further reports due to the lack of new cases. Sichuan officials, for example, no longer had to submit memorials on poppy cultivation after February 1836. It is unclear whether officials continued prohibition operations after Beijing stopped requiring reports, but this suspension certainly accounts for the gap in reports on all three provinces between 1836 and 1838.[16]

Doubts about the efficacy of prohibition efforts in the southwest were, however, being raised around this time. In mid-1835 Metropolitan Censor Yuan Wenxiang called attention to what he claimed to be a growing number of incidents of opium consumption, the establishment of rural opium dens with official conniv-

---

15. Chuxiong Yizu wenhua yanjiusuo, *Wuding Yizu*, DG 11.3, #2–4, pp. 253–55. The document refers to those conducting grassroots operations by a term that identifies them as part of the *baojia* system of police enforcement. This term, *xiangbao*, actually refers to two officers (*xiangyue* and *dibao*) whose responsibilities, though not always clear, are connected with community policing; compare the contrasting explanations for *dibao* in Hsiao, *Rural China*, p. 63; and Huang Liuhong, *Fuhui quanshu*, p. 21. The summary from Maolian makes no mention of native chieftainships. It appears to have been drafted for circulation among the *baojia* of the *junxian* regions of the province and thus provides further, if indirect, evidence of the degree of separation between the *junxian* and native chieftain systems.

16. Junji jinyan, DG 12.12.8, #201–4 (Yunnan), DG 14.11.28, #198–200 (Yunnan); Gongzhong jinyan, DG 15.12.19 (Yunnan); Junji, DG 15.12.19, #69912, DG 12.12.16, #062220 (Guizhou); Junji jinyan, DG 14.12.13, #195–97 (Guizhou); Gongzhong jinyan, DG 15.11.23 (Guizhou), DG 14.12.21 (Sichuan), DG 15.12.20 (Sichuan).

ance, and the cultivation of poppy in Guizhou. These accusations were denied by Governor Yu-tai, who maintained that drug crimes were steadily being reduced in the province. Although the throne did order Guizhou to intensify its efforts, mainly through the *baojia* system, a few months later, in December 1835, it relieved provincial authorities of the requirement to submit reports on trafficking and consumption.[17]

Despite Yuan's allegations, and although no explicit official declarations were made, officials in both the southwest and Beijing apparently felt that the regional opium problem was effectively under control by early 1836 and that no further measures were necessary. Within three years, however, the throne was again ordering southwestern officials to investigate and report on the persistence and spread of opium offenses in their jurisdictions. Although the center's renewed attention to the southwest arose from the debates over opium legalization and intensified prohibition from 1836 to 1839, new revelations of the extent of the opium problem, particularly cultivation, were also attracting the throne's notice.

Beginning in December 1838, serious allegations were raised concerning the severity of Yunnan's opium problem. The throne had received information from "someone," possibly in Yunnan's Provincial Surveillance Commission. This person declared that poppy cultivation was common in all the border provinces, but it was particularly widespread in the mountainous wilderness of Yunnan. Furthermore, "50 to 60 percent" of the province's private secretaries, runners, students, merchants, soldiers, and commoners were smoking the drug, many of these in opium dens that operated openly. Such widespread official consumption prevented reports on the extent of the problem from reaching the center and left the local administration riddled with informers whose warnings to offenders pre-empted official prohibition efforts. Moreover, cheap Yunnan *afurong* was flowing out of the province to other regions of China, where it was successfully competing with the more ex-

---

17. Junji jinyan, DG 15.3.26, #1838–39; QSL, DG 15.3.26, 37:54b–55a; Gongzhong jinyan, DG 15.11.23. The rescript of suspension is somewhat vague, and it is difficult to determine whether reports concerning all cases of trafficking and consumption or just those involving official perpetrators were suspended.

pensive Indian imports found there.[18] These revelations were soon followed by Censor Guo Baiyin's memorial of January 16, 1839, calling attention to the pervasiveness of poppy cultivation throughout the southwest. A court letter had already been issued on November 20, 1838, to Yun-Gui Governor-General Ilibu and Yunnan Governor Yan Botao ordering an investigation; this marked the first major change in imperial policy in the southwest since 1830. Two months later, the throne reacted to Guo's memorial by demanding stepped-up efforts to eradicate poppy cultivation in Yunnan, Guizhou, Sichuan, and Guangxi.[19] Within this short period of time, prohibition operations in the southwest were resumed and intensified, primarily because of the persistence of regional poppy production after years of eradication operations.

The intensification of prohibition efforts produced disturbingly large drug seizures in both Yunnan and Guizhou in the space of several months. The emperor expressed some dismay at both the 828 kilos of crude opium and paste seized by Yunnan officials and the 1,098 kilos of crude opium and paste confiscated in Guizhou from 1,640 offenders (see Table 5). He correctly pointed out that such large figures revealed the extent and duration of the opium problem in the southwest to be greater than previously thought.[20]

---

18. Junji jinyan, DG 18.12.9, #2275. The provenance of this document is problematic. As with all such appended reports that have been separated from their original memorials, it lacks the name of the author. Qin Heping (*Yunnan yapian wenti*, p. 20) attributes authorship to Metropolitan Censor Guo Baiyin, but Qin relies on a memorial that merely identifies the author of the enclosure as "someone." Ilibu's own citation is merely a verbatim repetition of the emperor's original court letter (*YPZZ*, DG 18.11.4, 1:420, DG 18.12.18, 1:467). At the time the report and the court letter were drafted, Guo was metropolitan investigating censor for Shanxi, but the author of the enclosure clearly identified himself as attached to the Yunnan *zhisi*, which I have taken as a generic reference to the Provincial Surveillance Commission (Tixing anchashi si). This information was not included in the summary of the court letter cited by Qin. Moreover, Guo's official biography makes no mention of his ever having had any official connection with Yunnan; see *Qingshi liezhuan*, 14:4330–33.

19. WJD, DG 18.12.22, pp. 11–12; *YPZZ*, DG 18.11.4, 1:419–20; *YPZZ*, DG 18.12.2, 1:446.

20. *YPZZ*, DG 18.12.18, 1:468.

Table 5
Opium Offenses and Amnesties in Guizhou, Late 1838–February 1839

Location	Offenses		Opium seized (taels)		Amnesties granted	Opium handed over (taels)	
	Trafficking	Consumption	Crude	Paste		Crude	Paste
Anshun prefecture							
Qingzhen district	1	2	2		41	13	
Puding district			1,344		3	393	10
Anping district						436	
Guihua subprefecture	12	4	20	4	338	54	17
Zhenning department					21	52	
Langdai subprefecture					52		
Dading prefecture							
Prefectural seat		3			6		
Qianxi department			100			200	320
Bijie district					30		13
Weining department	2			17			21
Pingyuan department	32	2			206	418	
Duyun prefecture							
Prefectural seat					3		
Duyun district					2		
Libo district							
Dujiang subprefecture					15	35	18
Maha department					3	5	
Bazhai subprefecture					22		
Dushan department					2		
Guiyang prefecture							
Guizhu district	25	8	19,727	16			
Kai department	1	4	5	1	13		2

Guiding district	1				2	20	
Longli district					12	10	
Dingfan district					23	512	2
Guangshun department		1	10		20		
Liping prefecture							
Prefectural seat					121	500	30
Kaitai district					4		30
Guzhou subprefecture	1	6	40		38	700	200
Xiajiang subprefecture	6	4					
Pingyue department*							
Departmental seat		2			6	104	3
Meize district		3			8	254	
Yuqing district		2		38			
Weng'an district	2	1	350		7	100	4
Renhuai subprefecture*	1						
Subprefectural seat	1	5	164	42	1	13	
Shiqian prefecture							
Prefectural seat		3			40		
Sinan prefecture							
Prefectural seat					19	6	11
Yubing district	1	1	8		43	37	22
Wuchuan district						5	26
Songtao subprefecture*							
Subprefectural seat					15		
Tongren prefecture							
Prefectural seat						100	100
Tongren district							121

Table 5, cont.

Location	Offenses		Opium seized (taels)		Amnesties granted	Opium handed over (taels)	
	Trafficking	Consumption	Crude	Paste		Crude	Paste
Xingyi prefecture							
Prefectural seat	1	4	20	4	20	54	27
Xingyi district					1	63	31
Annan district						80	
Zhenfeng department					3		
Puan district	3	33	88		15	35	
Ceheng department					65	30	
Zhenyuan prefecture							
Zhenyuan district		2	20	8	40	231	32
Shibing district		4	20	10	53	70	
Taigong subprefecture						1	4
Huangping department	2		47		142	2,980	176
Zunyi prefecture							
Zheng'an department					11	80	
Huanyang district	4		8		2		
TOTALS	62	90	21,457	140	1,488	6,680	1,169
(KILOS)			800	5		249	44

NOTES: Subordinate jurisdictions are indented under their superordinate unit. Textual ambiguities have been omitted. This accounts for most of the discrepancies between figures given in Table 5 and original reports used to compile this table.

*Administrative level comparable to a prefecture.

SOURCES: *Gongzhong DG*, DG 18.10.28, DG 18.12.18, 77:485ob, DG 18.12.18, 30:568a–69b; *Junji jinyan*, DG 18.12.18, #2321–26.

Intensification of official scrutiny cannot by itself explain the enormous increase in offenders, particularly in Guizhou, the only southwestern province to submit extensive, detailed figures on number of offenders processed. Rather, the amnesty program, which added nearly 1,500 people to the list of Guizhou offenders, stands out as the major factor in this dramatic rise. Amnesty also contributed a considerable percentage of the total amount of opium confiscated by provincial officials and could be credited with 24 percent of the 1,049 kilos of crude opium and 90 percent of the 49 kilos of paste that fell into official hands. Finally, the amnesty program clearly contributed to the radical geographic expansion of Guizhou's prohibition operations, which now reached into every prefecture of the province. As Table 5 shows, 21 locales out of a total 52 reporting in late 1838 and early 1839 submitted amnesty figures exclusively.[21] For perhaps the first time in the history of Qing prohibition operations, the actual extent of opium production, trafficking, and consumption was being revealed to the court, and, at least in Guizhou, the amnesty program was responsible.

Prohibition in Sichuan continued to lag behind, possibly because Bao-xing held the post of governor-general of that province from 1838 to 1847 with only a brief hiatus. The governor-general's lax approach may have been related to the convictions of two of his sons, both of whom held official posts, for opium smoking some time before April 15, 1839, the date of an imperial decree of censure for his failure to control them. In May of the same year, the emperor also criticized Bao-xing for the perfunctory nature of his prohibition operations.[22]

What information Bao-xing did provide regarding the progress of prohibition operations in Sichuan confirms the role played by the amnesty program. The majority of the confiscations came from

---

21. He Changling's reports were compiled from statistics drawn from at least 56 locales, but textual ambiguities make any number extremely conjectural; see *Gongzhong DG*, DG 18.10.28, 7:4850b, DG 18.12.18, 30:568a–69b; Junji jinyan, DG 18.12.18, #2321–26.

22. *YPZZ*, DG 19.3.23, 1:532–33. See *QSL*, DG 19.3.2, 37:1003b, for the decree of censure and *Gongzhong DG*, DG 19.4.25, 8:262b–63a, for Bao-xing's memorial expressing gratitude for the emperor's leniency. The fact that Bao-xing was an imperial clansman may explain the emperor's decision.

voluntary handovers. In all, around 814 kilos of crude opium, with 57 percent coming from voluntary handovers in Chongqing and Chengdu, was confiscated from 33 offenders.[23]

Generally speaking, the intensification of prohibition in the southwest at the end of 1838 led to direct assaults on distribution networks as a means of indirectly attacking the relatively inaccessible cultivation sites. In Yunnan, this shift attempted to cut off the circulation of local opium after it had left its production sites. By focusing on the more accessible vectors of the opium infection, namely, urban-bound traffickers, senior provincial administrators hoped to destroy the system that carried the drug from rural regions of little or no official control into more densely settled, and thus better-monitored, areas. At the same time urban demand within the province, which constituted the major incentive for rural cultivation, came under more official pressure, partly through the stringent measures against consumers formulated by the center.[24] This shift in strategy was less clear in Guizhou and Sichuan, where cultivation appeared to have re-emerged, mostly in Chengdu prefecture.[25] Even though anticultivation operations continued throughout the southwest, the reports from all three provinces focused heavily on trafficking and consumption offenses in urban areas and along major communications arteries, an acknowledgment of the limitations of official writ in the countryside.

As shown in Table 7, after nearly three years of elaborate prohibition operations, only 1,932 kilos of crude opium and paste had been confiscated ("official totals" of opium both seized and handed over) in Guizhou, a mere 15 percent of the 12,573 kilos that would be confiscated in Yunnan (see Table 6). Sichuan's haul of 1,342 kilos of opium confiscated between 1839 and 1841 amounts to

---

23. *YPZZ,* DG 19.3.23, 1:532–33. Bao-xing reported a total confiscation of over 1,217 kilos, but 403 kilos of this amount was tobacco, which was not an illicit crop at the time. I have come across few references to tobacco confiscations during this period and conclude that such seizures were made only when it appeared that the tobacco was to be used in conjunction with opium. See Chapter 4 for a discussion of the lax nature of Qing tobacco prohibition.

24. *YPZZ,* DG 18.12.18, 1:466–69.

25. Junji jinyan, DG 18.12.18, #2321–26 (Guizhou); *YPZZ,* DG 19.3.23, 1:532–33 (Sichuan).

just under 10 percent of Yunnan's.[26] Although it is impossible to interpret these totals conclusively, they do suggest that a great deal of opium was being stockpiled in Yunnan. The official discovery of an extensive and sustained southwestern interprovincial traffic in 1840 revealed much of this stockpile was destined for consumers in southeastern Sichuan and points further to the north and east.

There had been a number of general reports that Yunnanese opium was flowing northward into southern Sichuan, but few specific details emerged before 1840, when the intensification of prohibition was in full swing. Metropolitan Censor Lu Yinggu was the first official to call formal attention to the problem in a memorial drafted on January 11, 1840: "Whereas the opium in the northern and southern provinces all comes from overseas, that in the border areas of Sichuan and Guizhou comes mainly from Yunnan, where the cultivation of poppy for the decoction of opium has been going on for many years."[27] Lu mapped out the smuggling routes used by "bandits," at least some of whom belonged to the Guolu gangs of Sichuan. These routes ran from southwestern Yunnan to the prefectures along its northern border with the southern Sichuan prefecture of Ningyuan. Merchant smugglers colluded with bandit gangs, which were often larger than the isolated garrisons of the interprovincial borders, along the fringes of tribal settlements. These groups then "fought their way through the passes," presumably back into Sichuan.[28]

Lu's solution reflected the shift to antitrafficking operations generally adopted during the late 1830s. He asserted that in order "to cut off the opium of foreign barbarians, first cut off the traffickers of China proper; to prevent these traffickers from colluding with the tribals, first prevent the Sichuanese bandits from entering Yunnan." The throne concurred and, on January 25, 1840, ordered local officials in both provinces to intercept bandit smugglers.[29]

---

26. Gongzhong jinyan, 20.7.28; Junji jinyan, DG 20.1.19, #3142–43; *YPZZ*, DG 19.3.23, 1:532–33, DG 21.1.25, 3:203.

27. *YPZZ*, DG 19.12.17, 1:774.

28. Junji diqin, DG 19.12.17, 267:11. For an account of the Guolu bandits' activities in the eighteenth century, see Cheng-yun Liu, "Kuo-lu."

29. *YPZZ*, DG 19.12.21, 1:784.

Table 6

Opium Confiscations in Yunnan, January 1839–April 1840

(taels)

Location	Seizures	Location	Seizures
Chuxiong prefecture		Qujing prefecture	
Prefectural seat	7,495*	Pingyi district	1,090
Chuxiong district	13,440†	Shunning prefecture	
Dali prefecture		Shunning district‡	14,860
Dengchuan department	3,100	Yun department‡	6,800
Zhao department	5,430	Mianning subprefecture	3,320
Taihe district	2,460†	Gengma NC	10,300†
Guangnan prefecture	3,510†	Mengmeng NC	2,416
Guangxi department**		Tengyue subprefecture	4,196
Departmental seat	13,580†	Wuding department**	
Shizong district‡	10,410	Yuanmou district	5,560
Jingdong subprefecture**	22,570	Yongbei subprefecture‡, **	
Kaihua prefecture		Subprefectural seat	12,140
Prefectural seat	3,125	Langqu NC	10,252
Wenshan district	2,080	Yongchang prefecture	
Lijiang prefecture		Wandian and Zhenkang NC	8,025
Lijiang district	4,106	Baoshan district	4,106
Haoqing department	9,387	Yunnan prefecture	11,080†
Lin'an prefecture		Zhaotong prefecture	11,000†
Jianshui district	2,120	Multiple locales§	59,843
Shiping department	1,520	Military regions	22,803

Menghua subprefecture**
   Subprefectural seat 43,900
   Zhanyi department 1,050

TOTAL 337,074

(KILOS) 12,573

NOTES: Subordinate jurisdictions are indented under their superordinate unit. Type of opium is unspecified unless otherwise noted. Due to textual ambiguities and gaps in the documentary record, the amounts listed for each location do not amount to the 387,290 taels (14,446 kilos), declared confiscated by Yan Botai throughout Yunnan between December 1838 and April 1840 (Gongzhong jinyan, DG 20.4.19). Another set of statistics submitted by Yun-Gui Governor-General Gui-liang in June 1841 covered confiscations all the way back to February 1840, which partially overlaps the period covered here. Gui-liang declared that a total of 48,500 taels (1,809 kilos) had been seized from over 500 offenders involved in 330 opium violations of various types (YPZZ, DG 21.4.27, 3:493–95). It is probable that the bulk of these confiscations dated from the early 1840s and are, consequently, included in the figures given above.

NC: native chieftainship *Paste only †Figures include both crude and opium paste ‡Figures probably include relatively small amounts from unspecified environs **Administrative level comparable to a prefecture §General confiscation statistics from 89 locales

SOURCES: Junji jinyan, DG 19.3.3, #2460–61, DG 19.4.29, #2603–4, DG 19.4.28, #2787–88; Gongzhong jinyan, DG 20.4.19, DG 20.4.19 (enclosure); YPZZ, DG 21.4.27, 3:493–95.

Table 7

Opium Offenses, Confiscations, and Amnesties in Guizhou, February 1839–September 1842

	Offenses			Opium Seized (taels)		Plots seized		Amnesties		Handovers		
Locale	(A)	(B)	(C)	(D)	(E)	F	G	(A & B)	(C)	(D)	(E)	(H)
Anshun prefecture												
Prefectural seat	1	1		6	4							
Anping district	1	3	2	4				18				
Guihua subprefecture	6	3	1					20		25	25	
Qingzhen district	1	2	10			4		233	5			1
Langdai department				10	1		14					
Puding district	2	8	1	4	2	1		2				
Yongning department				10								
Zhenning department		5	2			1		4		8		
Dading prefecture												
Prefectural seat	8	14	10	88	2	4	10	255	14	373		
Bijie district		14		2	1			3	10		24	
Pingyuan department	1	4	10	10			19	27	45	10		
Qianxi department	3	15	9	37	1	2	7	65	8*			
Shuicheng subprefecture		1		1						250	13	
Weining department	5	12		11	7				3		3	
Duyun prefecture												
Bazhai subdepartment								1				
Danjiang subprefecture	1	1										
Dujiang subprefecture	1	5	1									
Dushan department				2				3				
Duyun district	1	5						2				

Libo district	1	2					
Maha department		2		5	7	4	
Qingping district			2				2
Guiyang prefecture							
Prefectural seat	2	22	1				
Changzhai department	1	1	1	2			
Datang village	1	1		2			
Dingfan district	1	4	6	1	2		
Guiding district	3	5	12	5	2		
Guizhu district	45	82	26,755	387	7	300	
Guangshun department	3	3	153	1	1		
Kai zhou district	1	4	9	2	2		2
Longli district		1	1		1		
Luohu department		1	1	1			
Xiuwen district	2	1	6		1		
Liping prefecture							
Prefectural seat	3	7	5	5	1	8	
Guzhou ting district	5					5	
Kaitai district	1	3	5	2	1		
Xiajiang department	2	1	2		2		
Yongcong district		5					
Pingyue department†							
Department seat	2	1					
Meize district	1	2					
Weng'an district	1	2	150	1	4		4
Yuqing district	1						
Puan subprefecture†	1	7	142	144‡	40		
Renhuai subprefecture†	12	48	435	5	2	132	4

Table 7, cont.

Locale	Offenses			Opium Seized (taels)		Plots seized		Amnesties		Handovers		
	(A)	(B)	(C)	(D)	(E)	F	G	(A & B)	(C)	(D)	(E)	(H)
Shiqian prefecture												
Prefectural seat			1			1		1	1	4		1
Longquan district			7			7		1	6	8		6
Sizhou prefecture			1					28			12	
Sinan prefecture												
Prefectural seat	3	8	12	2	3	1					1	
Anhua district												
Wuchuan district					3							
Yinjiang district												
Yubing district								11				
Songtao subprefecture†	3	1		26								
Tongren prefecture												
Prefectural seat	10	2	4	127		4			22		22	
Tongren district		1		3								
Xingyi prefecture												
Prefectural seat		2	2					1				
Annan district	2	7	12	3				1				
Ceheng department	1	5	5									
Puan district			31			8			30			
Xingyi district	1	6	32	60		2		1				47
Zhenfeng department		4	1	10	2							
Zhenyuan prefecture												
Huangping department	2	13						1				

	A	B	C	D	E	F	G	H
Qingjiang subdepartment						1		
Shibing district	3		1					
Taigong subdepartment			4				2	
Tianzhu district			26			16		4
Zhenyuan district	4	27	7			9		
Zunyi prefecture								
Zunyi district	1	14	46	5		16*	1	17
Zheng'an department	1	5	9	3		1	9	1
Huanyang district	5	5	8	3		11		1
Tongzi district	1	5	48	7	3	2	3	2
TOTALS	152	345	771**	208	53	27,930	1,244	41**
(KILOS)				1,041	17			
OFFICIAL TOTALS	900§	1,828	N.R.	124		49,000	2,064	N.R.
(KILOS)				56	48			

COLUMNS: A: Trafficking B: Consumption C: Cultivation D: Crude E: Paste F: Number of plots G: Size of plots (*mu*)
H: Poppy plots voluntarily converted to cultivation of legal crops

NOTES: Subordinate jurisdictions are indented under their superordinate unit. Due to ambiguities and gaps in the documentary record, the "Official totals" for trafficking, consumption, and seizures of crude opium and paste do not correspond to the figures given in the table; they are based on He Changling's statement of the total opium seizures throughout Guizhou between January 1838 and October, 1840 (Junji jinyan, DG 20.9.15, #3433–34). The extant figures after the latter date add 108 traffickers and consumers; five cultivators, and 14 kilos of raw opium and paste to the previous totals. The figures for the amnesty program are even more problematic, and the total figures given above are based on those provided by He Changling on September 1, 1839 (Junji jinyan, DG 19.7.24, #2898–99). All totals for cultivation have been derived from information given in the table.

N.R.: Not reported *Families †Administrative level comparable to a prefecture ‡15 plots (11 mu) were seized from 14 tenant farmers on native chieftanship land **Figure excludes 24 families §Figure includes 372 cultivators and reported as "in excess" of 900 offenders

SOURCES: Junji jinyan, #2589–91, DG 19.4.29, DG 19.4.29, #2592–96, DG 19.4.29, #2770–72, DG 19.6.18, #2900–901, DG 19.7.24, #2902–3, DG 19.7.24, #3019–22, DG 19.11.2, #3072–73, DG 19.12.16, #3190, DG 20.1.19, #3331–34, DG 20.4.22, #3435–37, DG 20.9.15, #3435–37, DG 22.8.25; Gongzhong jinyan, DG 20.4.22; Gongzhong DG, DG 19.5.16, pp. 422b–244; YPZZ, DG 20.7.20, 2:286–89, DG 21.1.18, 3:79–81; Daoguang Xianfeng liangchao chouban, DG 22.1.22, #4.6–7.

Operations against cross-border opium banditry necessitated co-ordination between the provincial administrations of Yunnan and Sichuan. By March 12, Sichuan Governor-General Bao-xing had promised to work with Yunnan Governor Yan Botao, but he was not optimistic. Bao-xing's pessimism may have been influenced by the difficulties of enforcing the law across provincial jurisdictions. Such a problem had arisen by August 1840 when Censor Chen Xi warned that Guolu bandits were linking up with their tribal counterparts to raid the Han regions of the Yunnan-Sichuan border. Chen charged that the participation of tribals enabled local officials to avoid responsibility for suppression of the bandits, most likely because the indigenes were considered the responsibility of the native chieftains. The court considered this a major reason for the continuation of bandit activity along the Yunnan-Sichuan border and ordered Bao-xing to increase enforcement efforts.[30]

By this time, active coordination between the two provinces had begun, and three separate bands of armed Sichuanese merchant-smugglers were discovered operating in tribal territories in Yong-chang and Dali prefectures in western Yunnan, where they were purchasing opium for sale in their native province. The first group to be hauled in, consisting of sixteen dealers in jade, silk, and sundry merchandise in Yongchang, was led by Xu Hongshun. Business had been so bad they had decided to speculate in opium, which they knew brought a good price in Sichuan. They bought 44 kilos of crude opium at a price of about nine silver taels per kilo from "a tribal whose name they did not know."[31]

Around the same time a group of eighteen Sichuan silk merchants in the Midian tribal region of Dali prefecture, just north of Yongchang, led by Chen Wanshun, had come to the same conclusion.[32] Chen and his fellows bought 67 kilos at the bargain rate of

---

30. Junji jinyan, DG 20.2.19, #3194–95; SYDD, DG 20.7.24, 243.

31. Gongzhong jinyan, DG 20.7.28.

32. There is some confusion as to the exact administrative status of Midian, whose native chieftainship seems not to have survived the Ming dynasty (Gong, *Tusi zhidu*, p. 481). The area had a subdistrict police office (*xunsi*) to maintain surveillance over a local pass, but this office was gone by the beginning of the nineteenth century (*Jiaqing chongxiu yitong zhi*, 478:21a, 31:24447). It was probably a pass between Yunnan proper and wild territory at the time the merchant smug-

eight silver taels per kilo from another "tribal whose name they did not know." Soon after this transaction, a third group of four jade merchants, led by Dai Dabang, for much the same reasons as the first two groups, bought 11 kilos of crude opium at the bad rate of eleven silver taels per kilo from an equally unidentifiable tribal in the very same area where Chen Wanshun had found a bargain.[33]

Xu's and Chen's groups had met in Dali and decided to coordinate their attempts to cross back into Sichuan. In order to avoid detection by official forces on alert for smuggling in Han-administered areas (*neidi*), Chen suggested that each group cross through tribal territory (*yidi*). To defend themselves against attacks by locals, they purchased arms—hence their appearance as armed bandits when they were apprehended by Sichuan officials in Ningyuan prefecture. Chen's group remained at large. Although Bao-xing doubted that Chen had played a major role and suspected that this was not the merchants' first smuggling run, he did not question their route or the origin of their opium and duly notified Yan Botao of the incident.[34]

By January 5, 1841, this incident had become an armed insurrection, at least in the opinion of Metropolitan Censor Du Yanshi, who considerably amplified Lu Yinggu's warnings of two years earlier:

Your servant has heard that in Yunnan's Yongchang prefecture there are bandit gangs who traffic in opium. They abruptly appear several hundred strong, firearms in hand and each carrying a red banner inscribed with the phrases: "Throw Your Means into Profit; Risk Your Life for Wealth." They move back and forth between the prefectures of Shunqing and Ning-yuan in Sichuan, committing all sorts of outrages.

People of the border regions of Sichuan have long grown poppy for a living, from which they decoct opium, whose name they have altered to "*furong* paste." Half those who traffic in it are traitorous subjects from Sichuan who band together into bandit gangs. Local officials, fearing their

---

glers happened along. Whatever the region's exact status, it was definitely neither a native chieftainship nor part of the regular *junxian* administration. This case thus provides further evidence that "tribal territory" (*yidi*) refers to a wild frontier of Yunnan in the prohibition documents.

33. *YPZZ*, DG 20.10.28, 2:548–51.
34. Ibid.

ferocity, do not dare to investigate or arrest them, and in consequence, their ranks increase daily.[35]

Du also accused local officials in Yongchang of freeing a large number of bandit traffickers remanded there by Sichuan officials in Huili zhou. Du also accused Ilibu of falsely declaring poppy eradicated in Yunnan in his response to the imperial decree of January 25, 1840. The Yongchang incident enabled Du to question Ilibu's sincerity, and he charged both Ilibu and Governor Yan Botao with lax enforcement and inaccurate reporting.[36] The throne decreed an immediate investigation of these charges; the investigation in Yunnan was carried out by a new group of senior provincial officials, who had replaced the accused as part of the normal rotation of provincial officials during the course of 1840.[37]

Unsurprisingly, senior officials in both provinces denied Du's charges of laxity and mendacity. Yun-Gui Governor-General Guiliyang rejected most of Du's views, but he did concede that there was a serious transprovincial traffic in opium produced in the tribal areas of western Yunnan. He also claimed that 70–80 percent of trafficking cases handled in Yunnan to date involved Sichuanese bandits, who were adapting to the intensification of prohibition in areas under direct official control by using circuitous routes through the undersupervised wilderness areas of native chieftainships.[38]

Guiliyang also detailed the apprehension of several small groups of Sichuanese smugglers in Wuding department on Yunnan's

---

35. *YPZZ*, DG 20.12.13, 2:699.

36. Ibid. I have not found Ilibu's declaration that cultivation had been eradicated in Yunnan, which would have been an extremely reckless statement given the degree of official control in the countryside. Moreover, a figure for total offenses in Yunnan during 1840 and 1841 from the new Governor-General Guiliyang includes cultivation offenses (*YPZZ*, DG 21.4.27, 3:493–95). Du's assertion, however, seems equally reckless, but would account for the absence of cultivation statistics among the extant documents on Yunnanese prohibition operations from the late 1830s until Guiliyang's report, which was a direct response to Du's accusations. It remains impossible to dismiss even the more outlandish of Du's claims regarding banner-wielding opium smugglers, since these same rumors were repeated to Li Xingyuan by Su Yanyu, Sichuan's former provincial surveillance commissioner (Li Xingyuan, *Li Xingyuan riji*, DG 20.9.14, 1:108).

37. *YPZZ*, DG 20.12.30, 2:776–77.

38. *YPZZ*, DG 21.4.27, 3:493–95.

northern border. One group, led by Huang Yingcai, alias "Three Hemp Seeds" Huang, had resisted arrest in Yunnan, killed a soldier attempting to apprehend them, and fled to Huili zhou, where a joint Yunnan-Sichuan force caught them and sent them back to Yunnan.[39] Guiliyang recounted the case in some detail, perhaps because he felt that Du was repeating a garbled version of it.

Sichuan Governor-General Bao-xing came to the same conclusion about a case within his jurisdiction. Bao-xing asserted that Du had heard a garbled version of Xu Hongshun's and Dai Dabang's activities. Indeed, he said that the two merchant smugglers had "clearly" invented these tales of huge gangs of heavily armed insurgents to scare off small-scale official inquiries. Nevertheless, he was sending officials to southern Sichuan to make sure there were no large insurrectionary bands there. Bao-xing again stressed the need to seal the Yunnan-Sichuan border, but this action depended on the cooperation of local officials on both sides; unfortunately, their opposition to the severity of the New Regulations was, he felt, resulting in lax enforcement.[40]

There clearly was some attempt at coordination between Yunnan and Sichuan. Bao-xing, for example, confirmed that "Three Hemp Seeds" Huang had been arrested and extradited to Yunnan.[41] Cooperation between senior provincial officials was, however, apparently no substitute for the active support of prohibition operations by their subordinates. This morale problem, also noticed by He Changling in Guizhou, was caused by the expiration of the grace period: local officials seem to have unilaterally decided to veto Huang Juezi's program of capital punishment for consumers.[42]

Official cover-ups and insubordination were only a few of the obstacles senior provincial officials faced in their attempt to transform central government policy into effective local prohibition, an attempt that would fail before the mid-1840s. This chronology of southwestern prohibition has touched on many other practical difficulties, among them southwestern geography, ethnic policies, and

---

39. Ibid.
40. *YPZZ*, DG 21.1.25, 3:203–4.
41. Ibid.
42. *Chouban yiwu shimo buyi*, DG 22.1.22, #4, p. 6.

economic relations, that need to be examined in more detail in order better to understand the failure of Qing prohibition.

The Geography of Southwestern Opium

The fundamental geographic exercise of mapping the production sites and distribution routes of opium was a prerequisite for effective prohibition, and by the mid-1830s the authorities had such a map. Unfortunately for them, opium in one form or another had been present in the region for at least a century. Consequently, the map that officials produced depicted not an opium traffic in its formative and relatively vulnerable stages but a fully developed marketing system that extended all the way to the coast and even into north-central China.

A drug connection linking the southwet and the coast was certainly formed long before the 1830s prohibition campaign, but this connection was not simply one of the consumption of coastal opium by southwestern consumers. The few pieces of evidence from the eighteenth century suggest, rather, that Yunnan opium was moving eastward in response to coastal demand toward the close of the Qianlong era. The earliest reference to the drug, from a provincial gazetteer published during the inaugural year of the Qianlong reign in 1736, merely noted that *hafurong* was a term for opium (*yapian*) produced in the southwestern prefecture of Yongchang. There is no indication that *hafurong* was criminalized, probably because it was still legal to produce at this time in its medicinal form unmixed with tobacco. It is also unclear whether it was being transported out of Yunnan at this time.[43] Nevertheless, this legal local production of the 1730s was the foundation for the illegal local production formally, and belatedly, criminalized in the 1830s.

By the end of the eighteenth century at the latest, and almost certainly a decade or so earlier, *hafurong*, which would be called

---

43. Edkins, *Historical Note*, p. 46; Waung, "Opium Cultivation," p. 210. Edkins cites "a history" of Yunnan "published in 1736." Waung cites a British Indian government report from 1871. Both authors identify Yongchang as the prefectural site of poppy cultivation. The original Chinese source is *Yunnan tongzhi*, 27:10b. Waung's assumption, again predicated on the British 1871 report, that the 1736 entry refers to smokable opium is not supported by available evidence.

afurong during the nineteenth century, was no longer being described so ingenuously or used so parochially. The literatus Tan Cui also noted the production of Yongchang *hafurong*, in a geographical work on Yunnan written during the late eighteenth century, but in a way that revealed that conditions had changed since 1736. He described the substance as "opium, an aid to pleasure," which was "harming many inhabitants of Fujian by turning them into opium fiends (*yapian gui*)." Although Tan did not say directly that Yunnan opium was being transported to Fujian, the implication was there and was later confirmed. Bao Shichen, writing in 1820, stated that native chieftains in Yunnan had begun cultivating poppy after 1805 for the market in Xiamen, where he believed it underwent further processing before being sold as opium. Unfortunately, Bao did not specify the locales in Yunnan where poppies were being grown, but Yongchang, given its many large native chieftainships and the evidence from both the 1736 gazetteer and Tan Cui, is certainly the most likely spot. Some rumor may have reached Bao, an influential advisor to senior provincial officials in Sichuan and elsewhere, as a result of incipient anticultivation operations in Yunnan around the same time he was writing.[44]

In light of all this testimony, it is reasonable to assume that before Tan's demise in 1801, crude (*h*)*afurong* was being transported from tribal fields that lay just beyond the fringes of Yongchang's direct prefectural administration in southwestern Yunnan to urban consumers in coastal Fujian, where it was rendered into full-strength *yapian* paste. This long-distance flow that transformed western *hafurong* into eastern *yapian*, however, seems to have been hidden from officials, who remained convinced until the 1820s that all *yapian* flowed exclusively from southeastern sources.

As noted above, this conviction may have hindered early prohibition efforts in the southwest, between 1816 and 1820, toward the end of the Jiaqing reign. The problems encountered by Sichuan's Surveillance Commissioner Cao Liuxing, who issued the 1816 public notice decrying gatherings of vagabonds who smoked opium as a stimulant in local marketplaces and the growing number of traf-

---

44. Tan Cui, *Dian hai yu heng zhi*, 2:7a, p. 97; *Yapian zhanzheng*, 1:538; *YPZZ*, DG 11.5.9, 1:77–79.

fickers scrambling to supply their habit, may have been due in part to the fact that not all opium circulating in southeastern Sichuan came from the coast.[45] Sichuan's frontier resources were probably being deployed exclusively to controlling smuggling over routes that ran from the coast through southeastern areas of the province to the detriment of security for its southern connections with Yunnan, which had been producing opium for more than a decade by this time and would become a major opium supplier to Sichuan within another twenty years. In sum, before the 1820s, the southwestern opium problem was officially seen as coastal trafficking catering to urban consumers in southeastern Sichuan. If opium had ever actually been so circumscribed, it certainly did not long remain that way, even in the official mind.

When officials finally did discover poppy in Yunnan, it was no longer ostensibly limited to Yongchang prefecture. Within seven years of Cao's public notice, Censor Yin Peifen provided the throne with a very broad map of the geography of southwestern opium by declaring the existence of poppy plots in the "Eastern and Western Circuits," roughly three-quarters of the province.[46] Given the presence of poppy cultivation, legitimate or otherwise, in Yunnan during the bulk of the eighteenth century, Yin's claims were probably not greatly exaggerated. Indeed, the legal ambiguities surrounding opium during this period of transition from madak to paste certainly explain both the unhindered spread of provincial cultivation and the regularization of trafficking routes, also identified by Yin, connecting Yunnan to extra-provincial opium networks, which also carried legitimate commerce, running through both Guangxi and Vietnam to the coast. Yin had thus not only confirmed earlier indications from Sichuan regarding the coastal connections with the southwestern traffic but also, for the first time, linked the southwestern opium problem to locales beyond the confines of the Qing empire. He also revealed the exis-

---

45. *Baxian dang'an*, JQ 21.5.6, 2:272.

46. Circa 1820, the Eastern Circuit (Yidong dao) encompassed seven prefectures in eastern Yunnan: Chengjiang, Guangnan, Quqing, Kaihua, Dongchuan, Zhaotong, and Guangxi; the Western Circuit (Yixi dao) encompassed eight prefectures: Dali, Chuxiong, Shunning, Lijiang, Yongchang, Jingdong, Menghua, and Yongbei (*Jiaqing chongxiu yitong zhi*, 475:24247).

tence of extensive domestic poppy cultivation in Yunnan supplying the coastal demand, even as southwestern consumers were drawing on the coastal supply.[47]

Shao Zhenghu's memorial of 1830 initially focused attention on Yunnan, site of the only noncoastal poppy cultivation so far uncovered; around the same time reports on the newly discovered southwestern opium-marketing system began to come in from Yun-Gui Governor-General Ruan Yuan and Yunnan Governor Ilibu.[48] They confirmed that coastal opium was being smuggled in from Guangdong via Vietnam but did not go into further details about these routes. They also did not identify specific cultivation sites in Yunnan beyond noting persistent cultivation of poppy among tribals in border areas, as well as by Han subjects of Yunnan proper in secluded mountain valleys and other isolated areas. Statements in their memorial suggest that more exact information was provided in supplementary reports, but these have not yet come to light.[49] Whatever the deficiencies of the reports from Yunnan, reports reaching the throne from Sichuan and Guizhou provided a more detailed picture and showed that opium production, distribution, and consumption were pervasive throughout the region.

In 1831 officials in Guizhou and Sichuan confirmed reports that opium was entering the southwest via eastern and southern trade routes. In Guizhou, Governor Song-pu identified routes from neighboring Guangxi in the southeast. By 1838 clarification of these routes revealed that Guangdong smugglers were entering Guizhou via the important communications hub of Guzhou in the southeastern border prefecture of Liping as well as through the northeastern border prefecture of Tongren. Sichuan Governor-General E-shan pointed out that opium was flowing into his province from its eastern neighbor Hubei, as well as from the coastal provinces of Guangdong and Zhejiang. Finally, both Song and E-shan noted that opium was also coming into their provinces from Yunnan itself.[50]

---

47. *Dao, Xian, Tong, Guang si chao*, pp. 72a–75a. For further details on Chinese opium smuggling in Vietnam, see Chapter 4.

48. ZZD, 11.3, pp. 147–50.

49. *YPZZ* DG 11.5.9, 1:77.

50. *YPZZ*, DG 11.7.3, 1:95 (Guizhou), DG 11.10.1, 1:99 (Sichuan); *Gongzhong DG*, DG 18.12.18, 30:568a (Guizhou). Merchant smugglers and bandits from both

In 1839 Censor Lu Yinggu revealed that Yunnan opium was being transported from Wuding department into the tri-provincial border prefectures of Dongchuan and Zhaotong for transfer to the adjoining provinces of Sichuan and Guizhou.[51] He also identified specific smuggling routes along the Longchuan River in Yongchang prefecture as well as in Puer, Jingdong, Dali, and Yongbei prefectures that connected Sichuan consumers with poppy grown in both southwestern Yunnan and Ava in Myanmar.[52] These reports are particularly significant because they foreshadow Yunnan's position as the regional center of the opium market and the rise of a major trafficking route between Yunnan and Sichuan, which would be further explored by officials, prompted by Lu Yinggu's revelations, only in 1840. This route was a primary conduit for the export of southwestern opium, mainly from Yunnan, for markets both to the east and north.

The throne was clearly aware of the existence of the southern and eastern smuggling routes, which were probably directing bidirectional flows of expensive coastal opium into the southwest and of cheap southwestern opium toward the coast by the early 1830s. Around the same time, Beijing had also received preliminary reports, which would become more detailed by the end of the decade, of an additional flow of Yunnanese opium into Sichuan. The official record is silent, however, regarding the northern extremities of the southwestern trafficking network, which penetrated into the northwestern province of Shaanxi.

Li Xingyuan, Shaanxi provincial surveillance commissioner from May 26, 1840, to January 11, 1841, was in an ideal position to supplement deficiencies in the official record just as he had done for the Xinjiang traffic. Moreover, his stint as Sichuan's provincial surveillance commissioner for approximately six months after he left the Shaanxi post gave him an unusual opportunity to evaluate the traffic from both ends.[53] Li's diary entry for July 6, 1840, reveals that

---

Guangdong and Guangxi were an ongoing problem throughout Guizhou, smuggling amounts as large as 632 kilos of opium at a time (Junji jinyan, DG 30.10.25, #245–49).

51. Junji diqin, DG 19.12.17, 267:11.

52. *YPZZ*, DG 19.12.17, 1:774–75.

53. Li Xingyuan, *Li Xingyuan riji*, DG 21.8.24, 1:272.

opium was being smuggled into the extreme southwestern tip of Shaanxi, the district seat of Ningqiang zhou in Hanzhong prefecture, from Sichuan's northeasternmost prefecture of Baoning across the provincial border. He also noted that little opium had been seized and that checkpoints to intercept smugglers had not yet been established in Shaanxi. A colleague, Su Yanyu, Li's predecessor as Sichuan's provincial surveillance commissioner from 1833 to 1838, provided Li with information that extended this leg of the southwestern traffic all the way into Yunnan. Su stated that the farther opium traveled from Yunnan, the more it could be sold for; at the northern end of the route in Shaanxi it fetched a price equivalent to 100 silver taels per kilo.[54] These accounts of Li and Su document the existence, by no later than the end of the 1830s, of connections between southwestern opium and northwestern demand.

Smuggling networks were only one dimension, albeit a physically enormous one, of the southwest opium market. An equally important aspect was widespread local poppy cultivation. Censor Shao Zhenghu's 1830 memorial identified Yunnan's indigenous poppy as *furong*. The same term was used by another metropolitan censor to describe Guizhou opium in 1835. A report submitted six years later by Yun-Gui Governor-General Guiliyang related that the original name for the poppy itself was *afurong*; shortened to *furong*, a word that had come to refer to all opium products derived from its sap. He asserted that this term had a long history in Yunnan. Curiously, and perhaps significantly, no nineteenth-century document I have seen uses the term *hafurong*, a name that appears to have been current in Yunnan only during the eighteenth century.[55]

---

54. Ibid., DG 20.6.8, 1:77, DG 20.9.14, 1:107–8. Li's explanations account for the lack of documents from Gansu and Shaanxi, for which his diary constitutes the bulk of the evidence. One of the two memorials known to me from Shaanxi for the entirety of 1839 and 1840 recounts that from December 1838 to January 1840 a total of 234 traffickers and consumers were apprehended along with 1,228 kilos of crude opium and paste (Junji jinyan, DG 20.2.10, #3184–85). When compared to the 1,828 kilos seized in Guizhou between February 1839 and September 1842 from 824 traffickers, consumers, and cultivators, the amount impounded from Shaanxi does not seem particularly small. Li is probably comparing his operations to those of the coast, where these figures would have represented small amounts.

55. Junji jinyan, DG 10.6.24, #1545–46, DG 15.3.26, #1838–39; YPZZ, DG 21.4.27, 3:493–95. The term *afurong* first appears in the Yunnan prohibition documents in

Afurong did not remain restricted geographically, and with the discoveries of poppy in Sichuan in 1831 and in Guizhou two years later it was clear that *afurong* was synonymous with opium grown in the southwest.

The plantings uprooted in the early 1830s revealed more extensive cultivation in the southwest than in the various coastal provinces, thus making the southwest the empire's center of poppy production. As prohibition intensified, officials began to obtain more specific information on cultivation sites. Reports by senior provincial officials in Guizhou and Sichuan substantially augmented the picture of southwestern poppy cultivation first sketched by Yin Peifen in 1823. Poppy plots were reported in Huili zhou, in Sichuan's southernmost prefecture of Ningyuan and bordered on the south and east by the Yunnanese prefectures of Wuding and Dongchuan, respectively.[56]

As Table 8 indicates, cultivators were also operating on the Guizhou-Yunnan border in Puan district in Xingyi prefecture, where twelve cultivators were apprehended in a mountainous area by Acting Governor Lin Qing. These arrests were part of a larger provincial sweep in early 1833 that ultimately resulted in 89 cases of cultivation and trafficking. In an instance of rare but crucial transprovincial coordination undoubtedly facilitated by the Yun-Gui government-general administration, Lin had been tipped off by a secret communication about the Puan cultivators from Ruan Yuan, who was based in Yunnan's provincial capital. In his evaluation of the operation, Lin concluded that trafficking was inevitable given Guizhou's geographical position as a crossroads between Sichuan, Hunan, Yunnan, and Guangxi.

In contrast and despite intelligence assistance from Yunnan, Lin considered cultivation Guizhou's problem since it fell entirely within his jurisdiction, spread rapidly, and was "particularly injurious to the local garrisons." Further discoveries of poppy plots in

---

an 1831 memorial by Ruan Yuan (ZZD, DG 11.3, pp. 147–51). As noted in Chapter 4, *afurong* had been the general pharmacological term for opium during the Ming.

56. *YPZZ*, DG 11.10.01, 1:99. For information on the eight native chieftainships in the Huili zhou region, see Gong, *Tusi zhidu*, pp. 381, 384–87.

Table 8
Traffcking and Cultivation Offenses in Guizhou,
ca. February 1833

Location	Trafficking and cultivation offenses*
Anshun prefecture	13
Prefectural seat	0
Puding district	5
Qingzhen district	8
Dading prefecture	19
Prefectural seat	0
Bijie district	4
Qianxi department	11
Weining department	4
Guiyang prefecture	23
Prefectural seat	6
Dingfan department	2
Guizhu district	12
Xiuwen district	3
Puan subprefecture	10
Shiqian prefecture	2
Prefectural seat	0
Longquan district	2
Xingyi prefecture	20
Prefectural seat	1
Puan district	18†
Xingyi district	1
Zhenyuan prefecture	2
TOTAL	89

NOTES: Subordinate jurisdictions are indented under their superordinate unit.
*No distinction made between offenses in original report.
†All offenses identified as cultivation offenses in original report.
SOURCES: Junji, #062220, DG 12.12.16.

Qianxi department in Dading prefecture, near Guizhou's north-western tri-provincial boundary with Sichuan and Yunnan, con-firmed Lin's fears that Puan was not the only place in Guizhou's ex-tensive, secluded mountainous terrain where "petty commoners who think only of profit" were concealing fields of *afurong*.[57] By

---

57. Junji, DG 12.12.16, #062220.

early 1839 poppy fields had been detected in the Guizhou prefectures of Zunyi, Dading, and Anshun, as well as Xingyi—in other words, along almost the entirety of Guizhou's western and northwestern borders with its provincial neighbors Yunnan and Sichuan.[58]

As prohibition intensified after 1830, officials began to obtain more specific information on areas of cultivation in Yunnan. The results are tabulated in Table 9. By 1836, illicit poppy had been detected in the western border prefectures of Yongchang and Shunning; the eastern border prefectures of Guangnan, Guangxi, and Qujing; the northern border prefectures of Chuxiong and Wuding; the western prefectures of Dali and Menghua; and the central capital prefecture of Yunnan. Out of 24 known cultivation cases, eight occurred on Yunnan's eastern border with Guizhou; seven were reported from Yunnan's western and southwestern tribal frontier zones; and four came from Wuding department, along Yunnan's northern border with Sichuan and another area of tribal habitation. The distribution of these cases provides further evidence of cultivators' preference for the interstices of official jurisdictions. Subsequent reports from joint provincial prohibition operations on the Yunnan-Sichuan border during the early 1840s reveal particularly extensive networks connecting the poppy fields of western and southwestern Yunnan with the urban consumers and communications hubs of southeastern Sichuan.

Extant records show that urban areas seem to have been the ultimate destinations for the wholesale distribution of opium to consumers and retailers. Yunnanese case lists covering drug offenses from 1832 to 1836, for example, list 46 trafficking and consumption cases; 33 of these occur in Yunnan prefecture, site of the provincial capital.[59] It is surely correct that, as Ilibu observed in 1839 during his tenure as Yun-Gui governor-general, a large number of merchants were drawn to Yunnan's provincial capital because of its comparatively high population, which ensured that there would be more trafficking there than anywhere else in the province.[60] Ilibu's

---

58. Junji jinyan, DG 18.12.18, #2321–26.
59. See Table 9.
60. Gongzhong DG, DG 18.11.9, 7:129b–30a.

observation is certainly borne out by arrest statistics, as we shall see below.

Case lists from Guizhou, the most complete and detailed among extant southwestern records, also indicate a disproportionate number of trafficking and consumption offenses were being uncovered in Guiyang, the provincial capital, and its surrounding prefecture of the same name. Statistics submitted during sweeps in 1833 show that almost a third of trafficking and cultivation cases were occurring in Guiyang prefecture (see Table 8). It is difficult, however, to draw firm conclusions, since the original report does not distinguish these two offenses. Later statistics, compiled from reports submitted between late 1838 and early 1839 (see Table 5), make explicit distinctions between all offenses and provide information on the amounts of crude opium and paste seized during prohibition operations. Over 90 percent of these seizures, about 736 kilos, came from Guizhu, the district of the provincial seat, where 40 percent of the trafficking offenses occurred. Only about 9 percent of consumption offenses were perpetrated in the district, but the eight cases from the provincial seat itself is exceeded only by 33 cases in Xingyi prefecture's Puan district, apparently a favorite haunt of drug offenders of all types.[61]

As prohibition operations progressed, Guiyang prefecture continued to garner a disproportionate share of opium offenses, albeit at reduced levels. Another set of statistics, compiled from reports covering arrests throughout Guizhou between February 1839 and September 1842 (see Table 7), shows that opium confiscations in Guizhu district dropped to 55 percent of the approximately 1,828 kilos of opium seized throughout the province during this period of three and a half years. About 30 percent of the period's trafficking offenses also surfaced in the district, and a further 8 percent occurred at other locales in the prefecture. The metropolitan prefecture's share of 38 percent of Guizhou's trafficking cases was a definite drop from the previous high of 44 percent, but the number of

---

61. The figures given are derived from totals in official reports, which I have assumed to be more accurate if not unambiguously correct.

Table 9
Opium Offenses in Yunnan, March 1832–February 1836

Location	Cultivation offenses	Trafficking offenses	Consumption offenses	Trafficking and consumption offenses *
Chuxiong prefecture				
Chuxiong district		1		
Dayao district	1			
Zhennan department				1
Dali prefecture				
Yunnan district	1			
Zhao department	3			
Guangnan prefecture				
Baoning district	1			1
Guangxi department†		1		
Shizong district	4			
Kaihua prefecture				
Wenshan district		1	1	
Menghua subprefecture†	2			
Qujing prefecture				
Luliang department	3			
Luoping department		1		
Nanning district		1		
Xundian department		1		
Zhanyi department			1	
Shunning prefecture				
Yun department	1			
Wuding department†	3			
Luquan district	1			1
Yongbei subprefecture†				2
Yongchang prefecture				
Baoshan district	1			
Yunnan prefecture				1
Chenggong district	2			2
Fumin district				2
Kunming district		7	15	
Kunyang department				2
Lufeng district		1		
Puning department				1
Songming department	1			1
Yiliang district			1	
TOTALS	24	14	18	14

Table 9, cont.

NOTES: Subordinate jurisdictions are indented under their superordinate unit.
*No distinction made between offenses in original report.
†Administrative level comparable to a prefecture
SOURCES: Junji jinyan, DG 12.2.9, #1746-49, DG 14.11.28, #1825-27; Junji chajin, #062372, DG 12.12.8, #069912, DG 15.12.19.

cases in Guiyang prefecture had more than doubled, from 27 to 57, throughout this period. Consumption offenses detected in the capital prefecture, however, increased dramatically from 14 percent to 35 percent, with Guizhu district accounting for 68 percent of the prefecture's consumption offenses. Despite the general reductions, especially in its share of opium seizures, Guiyang's position as Guizhou's drug capital was still unchallenged, as is made apparent by comparison with statistics from the prefectural runners-up in the three categories of trafficking, consumption, and opium seizures for 1839–42. Dading prefecture was the next highest unit for both provincial trafficking and consumption offenses with 11 percent and 17 percent of the totals, respectively. Of greatest significance, however, is the fact that Renhuai subprefecture accounted for under 1 percent of the 1,828 kilos of opium paste seized, a far-distant second to Guiyang.

Evidence from Sichuan, the province with the least complete records, at least partly confirms the urban attraction to opium. Although specific data are virtually nonexistent, the overwhelming majority of extant trafficking and consumption cases come from the trade center of Chongqing and its environs, with a few other cases from Sichuan's other major city, the provincial capital of Chengdu.[62] The vagueness of the reports makes it impossible to determine the origins of most of the 1,342 kilos of opium confiscated in Sichuan between 1839 and 1841, but the majority of the few recorded cases involve smugglers intercepted in less urbanized areas. Nevertheless, many of these smugglers seem to have been heading for

---

62. *Baxian dang'an*, DG 11, 2:272, DG 14.2.13, 2:273, DG 17.8.23, 2:274; *YPZZ*, DG 21.11.19, 4:485–89. The date of the initial report for the case summarized in the DG 11 memorial is DG 11.10.4.

southeastern Sichuan or moving out of this area along the Yangzi toward more easterly river ports.[63]

Of course, the administrative hubs of all three southwestern provinces would naturally maintain a greater level of official surveillance; the higher numbers of arrests and the greater amounts confiscated in these areas might therefore be interpreted as an artifact of higher levels of administrative surveillance rather than proof of a greater opium problem. Certainly, however, both the economic attractions and the administrative resources of provincial capitals played determining roles. The influence of both factors is apparent in the seizure of 919 kilos, around 50 percent of Guizhou's total known confiscations of about 1,828 kilos, in a single May 1839 operation conducted by Guizhu District Magistrate Feng Shaopeng in the vicinity of the provincial capital.[64]

Despite its affinity for urban centers, the southwestern opium market was quite widespread in terms of distribution and consumption. Moreover, its span kept growing because of the spread of opium poppy cultivation. In mid-1835 Censor Yuan Wenxiang sought to account for the existence of *afurong* by accusing merchant smugglers from Fujian and Guangdong of introducing coastal poppy seeds into Guizhou and Yunnan, a superfluous action given poppy's eighteenth-century pedigree.[65] Yuan may have been trying to blame coastal culprits, who were among those identified by Lin Qing in 1833 in his attempts to explain the appearance of cultivation in Guizhou. Lin claimed that merchant-smugglers from "outside" had spread poppy sap–gathering techniques to Guizhou, but he did not single out any one provincial group from his roster of main offenders from Hunan, Lingnan, Sichuan, and Yunnan.[66] Guangxi Governor Liang Zhangjun pared Lin's list of suspects to Yunnan smugglers and added those from Guizhou itself when he asserted in mid-1840 that poor border areas of his province were attracting numerous cultivators from these two neighboring provinces. His con-

---

63. Gongzhong jinyan, 20.7.28; Junji jinyan, DG 20.1.19, #3142–43; *YPZZ*, DG 19.3.23, 1:532–33, DG 21.1.25, 3:203.

64. WJD, DG 19.4.29, pp. 330–32.

65. Junji jinyan, DG 15.3.26, #1838–39.

66. Junji, DG 12.12.16, #062220.

viction arose from the mid-1839 discovery of extensive poppy cultivation in three of Guangxi's western prefectures bordering on
Vietnam, Yunnan, and Guizhou. Although poppy was declared
eradicated from the province after little more than five months, a
subsequent report in May 1840 revealed another 22 cultivation cases
necessitating the eradication of over 129,500 poppy plants.[67] If Liang was correct, southwestern cultivation was spreading eastward
toward the coast. *Afurong* trafficking was certainly flowing westward beyond imperial territory into Myanmar, possibly as early as
the 1830s.[68]

Testimony from the provinces reveals that no aspect of the
southwestern opium market was confined to a single province, or
even Qing territory, by the end of the 1830s. Aside from the obviously transprovincial nature of trafficking, poppy plots, which may
have first been established during the eighteenth century in Yongchang, were lining the provincial borders of Yunnan no later than
1831 and had spread beyond the southwest eastward into Guangxi
no later than 1839. In the majority of cases, cultivation was occurring in tribal settlements and along interprovincial borders, both
areas of Qing administrative ambiguity, weakness, or absence.

By the mid-1830s, officials had produced the basic map of southwestern opium smuggling routes and regional production sites. By
revealing that coastal opium was coursing throughout the southwest both through the intervening imperial provinces and through
Vietnam, these official reports demonstrated that the Qing state's
attempt to contain opium at its coastal points of entry during the
Jiaqing reign had failed. This failure must have occurred at least
partially because, as eighteenth-century records show, not all
contraband opium was foreign in origin, a fact that no officials
seem to have known until the 1820s. The greatest failure of prohibition exposed by the southwest's drug map, however, was that the
regional circulation of indigenous southwestern opium, fully exposed by the early 1830s, had shortly become extra-regional. South-

---

67. *Gongzhong DG*, DG 19.3.21, 6:80b–81b; Junji jinyan, DG 19.8.27, #2904–5;
Gongzhong DG, DG 19.3.21, 6:80b–81b; Junji jinyan, DG 19.4.26, #2581–84; SYDD,
DG 19.4.26, 52; Gongzhong jinyan, DG 20.4.10.

68. Yule, *Mission to the Court of Ava*, p. 148n.

western poppy was apparently spreading despite the explicit anticultivation policies of the 1830s.

The expansion of southwestern production effected a major change in the opium traffic. Coastal merchant-smugglers had initially directed a flow of relatively expensive Indian opium into the southwest; this main flow was reversed between 1820 and 1832 when cheaper southwestern opium, particularly from its primary source in Yunnan, began to wash back north and east.[69] The counterflow of opium from the interior toward the coast alerted the court to the existence of an alternative, domestic source of the drug. Thus, the central government subsequently perceived Yunnan's opium problem chiefly as one of local cultivators and regional smugglers, rather than of long-range drug trafficking by coastal merchants. This perception was reinforced with the discovery of extensive distribution networks connecting the poppy fields of southwestern Yunnan with traffickers and consumers in major regional urban communications hubs in southeastern Sichuan. From these points, Yunnan and Sichuan opium was transferred north and east to Beijing, Shaanxi, Henan, and Hunan.[70]

The discovery of these distribution networks concentrated official attention on the more northerly smuggling routes connecting Yunnan and Sichuan rather than on the more southerly ones connecting the southwest with Lingnan, which have recently drawn scholarly attention as important vectors for the transmission of the bubonic plague pandemic that spread throughout Asia and parts of Euro-America from Yunnan during the early nineteenth century. Consequently, during the 1830s and 1840s, the Qing central government saw Yunnan's overland links with Sichuan, which was the initial contact site between local and extra-regional distributors of southwestern opium, rather than its relatively distant connections with Lingnan as the more immediate problem.[71] The imple-

---

69. Junji jinyan, DG 12.2.9, #1746–49.

70. *YPZZ*, DG 21.7.13, 4:32, DG 21.11.19, 4:485 (Beijing); Junji jinyan, DG 20.2.19, #3194–95 (Henan); Gongzhong jinyan, DG 21.9.9 (Hunan); Li Xingyuan, *Li Xingyuan riji*, DG 20.6.8, 1:77 (Shaanxi). The ultimate destination of at least some of this opium was probably Guangdong.

71. Benedict, *Bubonic Plague*, pp. 51–71. Although there is certainly contemporary evidence that coastal opium was being smuggled into the southwest, official

mentation of a strategy of disrupting the Yunnan-Sichuan link, which included simply tightening inspections at all provincial borders, may also have been easier to coordinate since only two provincial administrations were involved. A full concentration on the more southerly routes out of Yunnan, for example, would have involved coordination with Guizhou, Guangxi, and Guangdong as well as with Vietnam, an unimaginably unwieldy proposition from an administrative point of view.

The Qing state's strategy of targeting smugglers, and later urban consumers, was substantially determined by the regional geography of opium. The map of southwestern opium revealed a terrain unfavorable for state suppression of indigenous cultivation, and the obstacles were at least as much ethnic as geographical. Reports from Yunnan, Sichuan, and Guizhou showed that Han traffickers were obtaining poppy from areas of indigenous settlement.

The Ethnography of Southwestern Opium

Poppy and ethnicity were associated throughout the history of the southwestern opium traffic. In 1820, Bao Shichen first linked the two, and twenty years later, in 1841, merchants operating in tribal territory in Yunnan's Jingdong subprefecture were popularly assumed to be involved in the opium traffic.[72] Whatever the actual conditions adumbrated by these general and unofficial views, by the Daoguang reign, tribal participation in the southwestern opium market was not limited to cultivation. Yi tribal peoples, and probably Dai and Miao as well, were active in the southwestern opium market both as poppy cultivators and as wholesalers of crude opium to Han merchant-smugglers rather than as distributors of crude opium and paste to Han consumers. Some of these groups may even have smoked opium regularly.

------

statements give few details. Nevertheless, routes running through Lingnan and Vietnam, as well as those linking all three southwestern provinces, are mentioned; see *Gongzhong DG*, DG 18.12.18, 7:568a; *Dao, Xian, Tong, Guang si chao*, 72a–75a; *YPZZ* DG 11.5.9, 1:77, DG 11.10.1, 1:99, DG 18.5.28, 1:301; Junji diqin, DG 19.4.13, 267:11.

72. *Yapian zhanzheng*, 1:538; Neige weijin, DG 21.7.13, #10119 (buben).

Tribals were not the only minority peoples involved in the opium market. Chinese Muslims also acted as smugglers and were, perhaps, the main actors in the Yunnan side of the Yunnan-Sichuan traffic. The man who initially exposed that traffic, Censor Lu Ying-gu, certainly believed Muslims to be the primary instigators; many Yunnanese traffickers, he said, were "evil Muslim youths" based in Yuanmou district in Wuding department and were active from Yunnan's northern prefectures along the Sichuanese border to the southwestern prefecture of Shunning.[73] Unfortunately, arrest records rarely identify Muslim offenders; one exception is a Muslim (Huimin) cultivator caught in Wuding department.[74] It is, consequently, impossible to determine, for example, whether southwestern Muslim networks were in any way associated with East Turkestani Muslim networks in Xinjiang.

If Hui had been the only ethnic minority involved in the southwestern opium market, prohibition would have been facilitated, for there were no vast and relatively inaccessible areas under the relatively exclusive jurisdiction of local Muslim officials. The adverse effects of this system on prohibition in Xianjiang are noted in Chapter 5, but these problems had less to do with the specific ethnic identity of the indigenous inhabitants of these enclaves than with the fact that the Qing dynasty permitted such enclaves to exist as a concession to many non-Han ethnic groups. Consequently, the dynasty encountered a similar problem of local control in the native chieftainships of the southwestern tribal peoples, particularly those of the Yi.

The involvement of Yi native chieftainships can frequently be inferred, if not unequivocally determined, from reports from all three southwestern provinces. Memorialists' precision regarding the ethnic identity of offenders, particularly en masse, is generally questionable; an 1838 report from Guizhou, for example, links "Miao" tribals to cultivation scattered over nearly the entirety of the province's prefectural borders with Sichuan and Yunnan.[75]

---

73. Junji diqin, DG 19.12.17, 267:11.

74. Junji, DG 12.12.8, #062372.

75. Junji jinyan, DG 18.12.18, #2321–26. Cultivation was detected in the prefectures of Dading, Zunyi, Xingyi, and Anshun, all of which had diverse tribal popu-

Nevertheless, in certain cases it is possible to identify the precise groups involved. The growers caught, for example, in Guizhou in early 1833 were almost certainly Yi. Four offenders, including a tribal headman, were arrested in the Dading district of Weining, home to at least eight separate Yi native chieftainships at one time or another.[76] The Yi were the traditional landowning group among the locals, which included Miao and Hui, as well as Han Chinese, and Weining itself was characterized as lying "entirely within tribal frontiers" during the Daoguang period.[77] The traffic was thus orchestrated or at least sanctioned by Yi leaders, regardless of the specific ethnicity of each participant.

Yi native chieftainships in Yunnan were also being searched for opium offenders in the early 1830s, and cultivation was certainly found in the Maolian native chieftainship in Wuding department on the Yunnan-Sichuan border. Headman Na Zhenxing made a personal inspection of hamlets in his area around March 1831 in response to a complaint by provincial authorities regarding his dilatory enforcement of the opium prohibitions. Na claimed that his jurisdiction was generally free of poppy cultivation, with the exception of two plots cultivated by a kinsman of his. These were uprooted, apparently without incident, in front of an official sent to supervise the operation. Not all anticultivation operations in Maolian proceeded so smoothly; Na related the story of one Zhou Yushun, who stoutly refused to uproot his poppies and claimed

---

lations. Moreover, discrepancies in the sources preclude definitive identification. For example, the memorial explicitly identifies cultivation by Miao in several districts of Anshun prefecture, and such Miao habitation is confirmed by an important Daoguang-era administrative work on Guizhou, Luo Raodian's *Qiannan zhifang jilüe* (pp. 282–83, 285). Gong (*Tusi zhidu*, pp. 834–51), however, records that many of Anshun's native chieftainships in these same districts were headed by Yi clansmen, an ethnicity not mentioned by Luo as living in Anshun.

76. Junji, DG 12.12.16, #062220; Gong, *Tusi zhidu*, pp. 818–20.

77. Of course, not all four offenders were necessarily Yi. With the exception of the headman, the other three could have been any of the above-mentioned ethnicities. Han Chinese, for example, worked many of Weining's lead mines and rented land from Yi elites. Indeed, one of Weining's ten villages was entirely composed of these "guests" (*kemin*). The rest were generally of mixed or native populations and run by a headman (*tumu*); see Luo Raodian, *Qiannan zhifang jilüe*, p. 300.

that the Na family had no jurisdiction over him. Zhou threatened to reopen an old lawsuit against the Na family on the grounds that they were harassing him. A rescript appended to Na's report ordered that Zhou be detained at once, but his ultimate fate, as well as his ethnicity, remains unclear.[78]

Since its initial discovery in Sichuan in 1831, poppy cultivation was also associated with Yi chieftainships; cultivators were thought to be active in areas adjacent to the "tribal frontier" (*fan jie*) across the border from Maolian in Ningyuan prefecture. All but one of the nine native chieftainships in the prefecture were under the control of a Yi family. The sole exception was headed by a Dai family.[79] Yi tribals along the Yunnan-Sichuan border certainly did not restrict themselves to cultivation. Yi enclaves in Ningyuan sat astride the main interprovincial smuggling route and were in an ideal position to participate profitably in all aspects of the considerable traffic between Yunnan and Sichuan. They acted as escorts for smugglers once they had passed into Sichuan and apparently sold and consumed the drug as well.[80] Most vague references to "tribals" by officials attempting to control the Yunnan-Sichuan route probably concern the Ningyuan Yi enclaves or unincorporated wild territories.

Yi tribal areas along the boundaries of the three southwestern provinces were clearly centers of poppy cultivation and related illicit activities by the mid-1830s. Something about these areas was obviously conducive to opium production, distribution, and consumption. Although it is probable that geographic factors explain the affinity of the Yi for opium-related activities, they do not fully explain why smugglers preferred to move through tribal territories,

---

78. Chuxiong Yizu wenhua yanjiusuo, *Wuding Yizu*, DG 11.3, #1, p. 252. The introduction and appendices to this volume contain supplementary information on the native chieftainship, whose history under several clans spans the Yuan period into the twentieth century. For a concise genealogical outline of Maolian, see Gong, *Tusi zhidu*, pp. 724–25.

79. *YPZZ*, DG 11.10.01, 1:99. For information on the nine native chieftainships in the Huili zhou region, see Gong, *Tusi zhidu*, pp. 381, 384–87.

80. Li Xingyuan, *Li Xingyuan riji*, DG 21.2.23, 1:175. The precise nature of tribal consumption, however, remains unclear in light of an account from the 1890s asserting that Yunnan tribals had only recently switched from opium eating to opium smoking; see Carey, "A Trip to the Chinese Shan States," p. 390.

as they clearly did. Administrative factors were also decisive in the choice of route. The testimony of Yunnan-Sichuan traffickers arrested in 1840 revealed that smugglers preferred to move through tribal areas (*yidi*) along the border rather than through areas of regular provincial administration (*neidi*) because of "the intensity" of the search-and-seizure operations then being pursued in the regular jurisdictions.[81] In this situation, the more relaxed implementation of prohibition regulations in native chieftainships caused the opium traffic to detour through tribal territory.

Admittedly, adequate implementation of the prohibitions by native chieftainships would have necessitated relatively large-scale eradication operations well beyond village fields in order to eliminate feral poppy, a "natural" source of crude opium. Native chieftainships appear to have been reactive at best in this regard. In the early months of 1827, two merchants, Ma Wen and Zhou Fachun, were traveling in Shunning prefecture to purchase raw cotton for sale 300 kilometers to the northeast in Yunnan prefecture. There, in the Gengma native chieftainship, a Dai clan area, they discovered a stand of what seem to have been feral poppies growing in a secluded area on the banks of the Gengma River. Ma, who was "quite familiar with" the production of opium from "*furong* capsules," gathered about four kilos of sap to take back with him for decoction and sale. A month or so later, they reached Yunnan district in Dali prefecture, where they stayed at an inn in the village of Mafang. Lacking funds to continue to their destination, Ma decocted some opium from the sap in order to raise some money. He was seen, however, and was soon confronted by a gang of six men led by Huan Jinsheng, a local resident aged 43 *sui*. Huan accused Ma and Zhou of trafficking in opium and tried to search their baggage as a prelude to handing them over to local authorities. An altercation ensued when Ma refused and drew a knife. Huan smashed Ma's head in with an iron flail. Homicide was a capital offense, and this helped to ensure the case's otherwise unlikely preservation in the historical record when Yunnan Governor Ilibu submitted an official report to Beijing on July 3, 1828.[82]

---

81. *YPZZ*, DG 20.10.28, 2:550.
82. Neige weijin, DG 8.5.22, #10092 (tongben).

The ultimate resolution of this case is unknown; there is no question, however, that Ma and Zhou were guilty of trafficking in opium. One of the points that Ilibu clarified was the provenance of their opium. He affirmed that the opium had come from feral poppies in the jurisdiction of the Gengma native chieftainship, a problematic conclusion given the ultimate human origins of all opium poppies, noted in Chapter 1. No supervised eradication of the poppies had taken place, however, because Ilibu declared the chieftainship too far from "Yunnan proper" (*neidi*) for local officials (*difang guan*) to keep under surveillance.[83] It consequently fell to the Gengma native chieftain Han Sipei to investigate the matter and eradicate the opium.[84]

The Ma and Zhou case is certainly unusual in many respects; it is, for example, both the only detailed record of southwestern opium from the 1820s and the only recorded use of feral poppy by traffickers known to me. Feral poppies grew not just in Shunning but throughout considerable areas of Yunnan as well as the other southwestern provinces, where medicinal poppies had previously and legitimately been cultivated, and it was clearly a simple matter to make use of them for the casual production of crude opium.

Locating and eradicating stands of feral poppy would have been difficult enough for provincial authorities within their own jurisdictions, but such operations were rendered extraordinarily difficult by the fact that ostensibly feral poppy stands existed in tribal areas beyond the reach of local officials from Yunnan proper. Given *Papaver somniferum*'s dependence on humans, only the eradication of cultivated fields would permanently eliminate feral stands of poppy. Moreover, human-poppy dynamics are such that the existence of feral stands in native chieftainships was proof that poppy cultivation either had occurred within a few years or was still occurring; in either case, state conflict with tribals was inevitable. Senior provincial officials in Guizhou admitted that poppies were being grown "where officials do not set foot."[85] But in the face of central pressure to intensify anticultivation operations in

---

83. Ibid.
84. Ibid.
85. Junji jinyan, DG 18.12.18, #2321–26.

early 1839, Ilibu, Ruan Yuan's successor as Yun-Gui governor-general since 1835, reiterated that native chieftainships were beyond the reach of regular Qing officials. Although official personnel could conduct crop-eradication operations in Yunnan proper without restraint, they could not enforce prohibition in native chieftainships, where such activities would inevitably lead to clashes with the locals. He was thus compelled, as usual, to conduct prohibition indirectly, through the tribal chieftains.[86]

The reliability of native chieftains was, however, questionable. Aside from various indications of collusion with opium traffickers noted above, incidents like Ma and Zhou's casual and undeterred harvest of crude opium in tribal Gengma as well as Na Zhenxing's encounter with the defiant Zhou Yushun in Wuding indicate that native chieftains themselves had limited control over their territories and charges. Even Qing officials themselves admitted that native chieftainship territory was too vast to keep under effective surveillance.[87] Eradication of opium from the southwest would have required much more proactive, sustained efforts by chieftainship administrations. An absence of deliberate malfeasance on the part of tribal authorities was not enough for effective prohibition. Active enforcement by native chieftainships was especially necessary because, as the Ma and Zhou case demonstrated, a concerted, deliberate effort to cultivate poppies was apparently not necessary for small-scale opium production. If conditions in Gengma in 1827 were in any way indicative of general conditions throughout the southwest, native chieftainships were acting, consciously or not, as natural refuges for poppy.

Subsequent events were to demonstrate that simply ordering the native chieftain to eradicate local poppy had not solved Gengma's problem. On July 30, 1839, the emperor awarded Gengma native chieftain Han Sipei the Blue Feather (rank of Junior Guardsman) for having seized nearly 310 kilos of crude opium and paste in the wake of the promulgation of the New Regulations.[88] Indeed,

---

86. *YPZZ*, DG 18.12.18, 1:466–69.
87. *YPZZ*, DG 21.4.27, 3:494.
88. *YPZZ*, DG 19.6.20, 1:641.

Gengma tribal authorities would turn over a total of 384 kilos between December 1838 and April 1840, about 3 percent of total provincial confiscations of 12,573 kilos of crude opium and paste during this period. Gengma led the other three native chieftainships participating in these confiscation operations. Mengmeng native chieftainship, also in Shunning, turned in about 90 kilos of opium; Wandian and Zhenkang native chieftainships in Yongchang prefecture jointly handed over about 299 kilos; and Langqu native chieftainship in Yongbei subprefecture, part of Yunnan's northern border with Sichuan, about 382 kilos. In all, confiscations from native chieftainships in western Yunnan accounted for about 8 percent of total provincial seizures (see Table 6).

The confiscation statistics and the few reports extant from Maolian show that some native chieftainships were actively pursuing prohibition operations by the late 1830s, and a few, such as Gengma and Maolian, appear to have been doing so at or before the start of the decade. An indeterminate number of unidentified Sichuan native chieftainships reported a complete absence of cultivation in their jurisdictions, at least during 1834–35.[89] Of course, no such operations were being conducted in any wild frontier zone. Regular Qing officials understood the limitations of prohibition in all areas of tribal settlement and knew that such areas would persist as important production centers of *afurong*. Indeed, Gengma's vigorous pursuit of prohibition was considered unusual, even unique, by Yunnan Governor Yan Botao in 1839: "The Gengma *tusi* was quite able in his handling of search and seizure in his jurisdiction, capturing over 8,000 taels. If other *tusi* were able to be as diligent, routes for *furong* smuggling would be cut off in no more than a year or two, and the breaking of Yunnan's opium habit would quickly follow."[90]

Yan's statement also testifies to the importance of tribal enclaves to the southwestern opium market. Censor Lu Yinggu, a native of Yunnan, also affirmed the relative inviolability of native enclaves: Yunnan's local officials, he stated, could not prevent the cultivation of opium in any of the "tribal territories" (*yidi*) as easily as

---

89. Gongzhong jinyan, DG 14.12.21, 15.12.20.
90. Junji jinyan, DG 19.4.28, #2787–88.

they could in Yunnan proper. The tribal territories on his list of cultivation sites included native chieftainships and wild territory in Shunning and Yongchang. Shenhu Guan, in western Yongchang, for example, formed part of the outer provincial boundary and lay on the "borders of the wild people" (*yeren jie*), but it was not a functional part of any jurisdiction. In contrast, Mengding, in the extreme south of Yongchang, was a native chieftainship under the control of a Dai clan.[91]

As demonstrated by both indigenous cooperation and resistance, the successful implementation of the central government's prohibition in the southwest was heavily dependent on tribal authorities, not all of whom were cooperating with the Qing government. Excessive dependence on tribals fatally compromised and ultimately precluded a sustained and serious attempt by provincial officials to eradicate opium in areas of tribal settlement, which were generally considered not susceptible to Qing administrative control, whatever their nominal status. Although still engaging in anticultivation operations, provincial authorities seem to have focused on distribution and consumption, which were much more vulnerable to the urban-based administrations of Han-dominated *junxian* jurisdictions. As prohibition intensified, however, it became apparent that substantial sections of the provincial economies of the southwest were directly or indirectly dependent on opium.

The Economy of Southwestern Opium

As shown in Chapter 4, concern over the economic effects of the opium traffic on the empire's supply of silver was the main motive for the opium prohibition during the Daoguang period. Beijing, however, appears to have been much less worried about the economic implications of these policies for localities that had become dependent on the income generated by opium. Widespread dependency on the economic rather than the physiological effects of *afurong* extended from peasant cultivators into the local administrations charged with implementing prohibition. The ensuing

---

91. *YPZZ*, DG 19.12.17, 1:774–75; *Jiaqing chongxiu yitong zhi*, 498:9a.

contradictions proved overwhelming for already overtaxed provincial administrations in the southwest.

Southwestern Yunnan's hot, humid climate is especially suited to poppy cultivation, but the plant can be grown throughout the southwest. Despite considerable regional variation, during the Qing, poppy was generally sown in the fall, sprouted in about twenty days, bloomed in March of the next year, and was scraped for sap in the summer.[92] The peasantry often also used the poppy to supply daily necessities, pressing the seeds for lamp oil and, in Guizhou, even eating the plant's roots. As in Xinjiang and elsewhere in China, poppies were also used for decorative purposes. These legitimate usages presented several practical problems for poppy eradication, for it was, of course, often impossible to determine whether they were being cultivated for illegal purposes. At least one case of "illicit cultivation," subsequently found to be trumped up by a yamen runner for purposes of extortion, arose from a Guizhou merchant's failure to get rid of the potted poppies decorating his establishment. In addition to the opportunities for this kind of official abuse, such ambiguities provided cover for drug cultivators, who grew poppy "under the guise of gathering poppy seeds to press for oil." Arrests were actually made in Guizhou for mere possession of poppy seeds in 1839.[93]

Authorities also confronted problems associated with the medicinal uses of the drug, particularly because people in the southwest smoked opium to prevent malaria, a fact of existence in the region. Since all medicinal uses of the drug involved consumption, they blurred distinctions between licit and illicit utilization of the poppy to an even greater extent than the other common uses made of the plant. Consequently, otherwise legitimate preventative measures against malaria became crimes in the eyes of officials like Governor of Yunnan Yan Botai, who saw it, like poppy-seed gathering, as just another cover for illicit activity: "In the regions beyond Yunnan's border, malaria is easily contracted, and both the

---

92. *YPZZ*, DG 11.5.9, 1:77; Qin Heping, *Yunnan yapian wenti*, p. 13.

93. *Gongzhong DG*, DG 19.5.16, pp. 421b–23a; Junji, DG 13.5.28, #064234, DG 12.12.16, #062220; *YPZZ*, DG 11.5.9, 1:77.

commoners and the barbarians vie to become contaminated by opium consumption, ostensibly to prevent the disease."[94]

Generally speaking, although officials did recognize that poppy, and even opium itself, had legitimate uses, it was clear to them that opium was doing more harm than good to the state. Moreover, since it was largely impossible to distinguish licit from illicit poppy and opium in practical administrative terms, officials like Guizhou Governor He Changling concluded that "although not all opium is cultivated for opium production, this is no reason for lax prohibition, which would promote abuse. Eradication must be total."[95] The inability of authorities to make fine distinctions among consumers incriminated anyone who continued to rely on the poppy and its products for any reason. Indeed, there was little room for ambiguity or leniency in such matters, as a provisional official of Zhao zhou, in Dali prefecture in Yunnan, discovered. District Magistrate Xu Shijie was impeached in 1832 for reversing his predecessor's verdict of illicit cultivation and acquitting several individuals who claimed that they were using poppy for fuel and medicine.[96]

The blanket criminalization of possession and consumption of all poppy products would certainly have posed difficulties for some groups but by itself would probably not have seriously affected the progress of prohibition in the southwest. The criminalization of poppy cultivation was a different matter, since it had a much more profound and immediate effect on the lives of many more peasants who depended on the crude opium scraped from their poppy fields as a source of income, especially in poor rural areas.

Peasant devotion to the production of addictive consumables at the expense of edible grains and vegetables had drawn official cen-

---

94. Gongzhong jinyan, DG 20.1.18. For a modern discussion of regional disease during the nineteenth century, see Benedict, *Bubonic Plague*, chap. 1. Western sources confirm that opium was held to be a febrifuge in many malarial regions of China (Spence, "Opium Smoking," p. 144; and Newman, "A Reconsideration," p. 776). The Dutch in Java also used it as a remedy against various tropical diseases (Edkins, *Historical Note*, p. 29).

95. *Gongzhong DG*, DG 19.5.16, p. 422a.

96. Gongzhong jinyan, DG 12.9.1.

Table 10

Area of Poppy Cultivation in Guizhou, June 1839–October 1840

Locale	Number of cultivators arrested	Area cultivated (*mu*)	Average area per cultivator (m²)
Anshun prefecture	6	14	929
Dading prefecture			
Case #1	3	3	398
Case #2	8*	13	647
Case #3	3	3	398
Case #4	9	18	797
Case #5	4	8	796
Case #6	8	8	398
Puan subprefecture†			
Case #1	14	11	312
Case #2	1	1	398
Renhuai subprefecture†	3	1	133
Sinan prefecture	3	3	398
Tongren prefecture	22	22	398
Xingyi prefecture	69	33	190
Zunyi prefecture	9	3	133
TOTALS**	154	141	364
OFFICIAL TOTALS	290	128	124

NOTES: Discrete totals from lower administrative levels are recorded separately as "cases" under their respective superordinate administrative levels. Discrepancies between the table and official totals are partly due to the exclusion of family statistics from the former. There are also probably overlaps in some of the statistics reported.
*Families
†Administrative level comparable to a prefecture
**Family figures excluded from these totals
SOURCES: Junji jinyan DG 19.4.29, #2589–91, DG 20.4.22, #3331–34, DG 20.9.15, #3437, DG 19.7.24, #2898–99; Gongzhong DG 19.5.16, pp. 422b–24a.

sure during the tobacco debates of the late 1730s (see Chapter 3). A century later, in mid-1835, Censor Yuan Wenxiang expressed similar concerns regarding the effect of Guizhou's mass production and consumption of opium on provincial grain prices, which would rise dramatically in the event of a large-scale local shift from grain to opium cultivation. There was little financial incentive, however, for peasants to stick to grain, for, as Yuan himself recognized,

Guizhou's opium crop was "several times more profitable than grain cultivation without the labor of plowing or weeding."[97]

This observation notwithstanding, poppy cultivation was quite labor-intensive in comparison with many other crops but far more profitable. Indeed, reports from the southwest during the early 1830s acknowledged that peasant cultivation of poppy would be stimulated by the profitability of opium. By the end of the decade, opium was said to bring in "ten times" the profit poor peasant farmers could acquire from rice in Yunnan.[98] Poppy was, like tobacco before it, probably valuable enough to be profitably grown in small patches. Estimates I have derived from the fragmentary statistics tabulated in Table 10 reveal poppy plots ranging in average size from 124 to 929 square meters. It became apparent during the 1830s that rural peasants had become addicted to opium not as consumers but as producers.

An incomplete statistical record makes it impossible to determine how profitable *afurong* was to traffickers. The few details available indicate that in the late 1830s and early 1840s the "wholesale" price of a kilo (or about 27 taels) of southwestern crude opium sold in Guizhou and Yunnan for between eight and eleven silver taels and could sell in regional urban areas for about sixteen silver taels.[99] It is clear, however, that southwestern opium, particularly the Yunnan product, was generally much cheaper to smoke than its imported coastal competitor, small amounts of which cost Chongqing smokers in 1816 up to a full silver tael per day. Indeed, the relative cheapness of *afurong* was held to be the main reason it

---

97. Junji jinyan, DG 15.3.26, #1838–39. It is somewhat unclear whether the text merely refers to opium mixed with tobacco or both opium and tobacco. I have not encountered the term "opium tobacco" (*yapian yancao*) in any other document. Internal evidence from the memorial suggests that this term is synonymous with *afurong*.

98. Qin Heping, *Yunnan yapian wenti*, p. 13; YPZZ, DG 11.7.3, 1:95, DG 11.5.9, 1:77; Junji jinyan, DG 18.12.9, #2275.

99. In an 1840 case from Guizhou's provincial capital of Guiyang, crude opium was sold for sixteen silver taels per kilo (Gongzhong jinyan, DG 20.4.22). In another case from Guizhou's Anshun prefecture in 1838, it was sold between friends for nine silver taels per kilo (Neige weijin, DG 19.7.24, #10116 [buben]). Sichuanese smugglers were paying eight to eleven silver taels per kilo of crude to tribals in southwestern Yunnan around the same time (YPZZ, DG 20.10.28, 2:548–51).

began to circulate beyond the southwest.[100] Extra-regional distributors were instrumental in making *afurong* cultivation profitable by connecting it with markets outside the southwest. An early 1839 report from Guizhou revealed that merchant-smugglers from "beyond the province" were contracting with provincial peasantry for their poppy harvests. These drug entrepreneurs provided seed money to peasants and then arrived in the fields when the poppy had just begun to sprout in order to fix a price for purchase of the expected harvest. This sum was paid in silver in advance.[101]

These transactions represented more than pure peasant greed, which most officials involved with prohibition regarded as axiomatic. Narrow and superficial attributions of greed as the sole motive for peasant action blinded most officials to the fact that although the economic attractions of poppy cultivation for peasants presented considerable obstacles to prohibition, this attraction was actually a dependency rather than simple avarice. In other words, poppy cultivation could not simply be eliminated; it would have to be replaced. Shanxi Circuit Investigating Censor Guo Baiyin was one official who understood that successful prohibition required more than the eradication of poppy. On January 16, 1839, Guo articulated this idea in a memorial expressing doubts about the coastal, urban assumptions of the central government's prohibition policy. Guo's position was succinctly formulated in his assertion that "provinces like Guangxi, Sichuan, Yunnan, and Guizhou are places where barbarian ships cannot reach and foreign opium cannot penetrate. All these places come by opium from the locals' poppy planting and paste making."[102]

Guo's argument was that opium's impact in western China, where it was produced from locally cultivated poppy, was different from that in the eastern urban coastal regions, where it was smuggled in from overseas by foreign merchants. Although foreign opium drained silver and wasted the wealth of the populace, the effect of the homegrown *afurong*, which Guo called "little dirt"

---

100. *Baxian dang'an*, JQ 21.5.6, 2:272; Junji jinyan, DG 12.2.9, #1746–49, DG 18.12.9, #2275.

101. Junji jinyan, DG 18.12.18, #2327–28.

102. WJD, DG 18.12.22, pp. 11–12.

(*xiaotu*), was more insidious. The unique power of little dirt lay in its dual ability to exhaust the soil of China and to deprive the Qing state of legitimate tax revenue through the covert nature of its production. Guo argued that these qualities made it a serious problem in its own right because of the impact on the agricultural revenues of the state, the mainstay of Qing taxes.[103]

Guo was alerting the throne to the southwestern agricultural economy's dangerous dependence on opium and the consequent vulnerability of state revenues if poppy was precipitously eradicated under the scheduled implementation of the New Regulations' anticultivation measures. Indeed, Guo predicted that eradication would only be hampered by intemperate action. Guo observed that the New Regulations' anticultivation provisions would go into effect in many rural regions in the spring of 1839. By then the poppy plants would already have sprouted, and peasants would be more likely to resist eradication operations because of their heavy investments in the crop. Although the poppy crop would be destroyed, it would be too late for these peasants to plant a crop of grain; thus taxes would continue to be lost, and peasants would suffer considerable hardship.[104]

Guo's insistence that peasant interests be taken into account during prohibition echoes Bu-lan-tai's defense of tobacco cultivators during the legalization debates of the late 1730s (see Chapter 4). Of course, unlike Bu-lan-tai, Guo was not advocating the complete decriminalization of cultivation. Nevertheless, common to both men's approaches was the conviction that the production, distribution, and consumption of certain agricultural products created an intricate interdependency between the peasantry and the state and that this should have a determining effect on the formulation and implementation of central government policy. Moreover, implicit in Guo's argument was the idea that there was a significant difference between peasant cultivators and opium smugglers in their relation to the state and in their socioeconomic functions. Ultimately, the state was dependent on a harmonious relationship with peasants, whose labor and skills were required to feed the empire;

103. Ibid.
104. Ibid.

parasitical smugglers fulfilled no such role and, hence, could be eliminated without undue consequence. It would be inimical to the state's interests to equate peasant cultivators with smugglers and subject them to the same punishments, as envisioned by the New Regulations.

In the case of tobacco, the Qing state acknowledged the importance of its interdependency with peasant cultivators; in the case of opium, the state ignored this relationship. Guo's appeal did not succeed in persuading the throne to reconsider its timetables. Indeed, despite its original intent, his memorial refocused the attention of the court on the southwestern cultivation problem at a point when its attitude toward all opium offenses was hardening and indiscriminate solutions were gaining favor. Guo succeeded only in generating an imperial decree to accelerate search-and-seizure operations in Guizhou and Yunnan.[105] The 1836 arguments of legalization's prime opponent, Zhu Zun, may have been influential in the throne's 1839 decision to proceed with the immediate implementation of the revised anticultivation measures. Zhu had claimed that the mountains and wilds of Yunnan were full of cultivators and that this domestic production had done nothing to stem the flow of silver abroad, which was the prime rationale for Xu Naiji's proposal to legalize the drug.[106] Silver was considered more important than regional agriculture.

Guo's message was not heard in Beijing, but it may have found a receptive audience in Guizhou. In response to the imperial decree generated by Censor Yuan Wenxiang's revelations, the administration of Governor Yu-tai seems to have employed conventional police measures of confiscation and punishment against provincial cultivators.[107] These actions certainly did not eliminate the problem, as Yu-tai's successor, He Changling, discovered. Governor He did not uncritically implement anitcultivation operations in early 1839 along the heavy-handed lines demanded by strict prohibitionists in Beijing. Instead, He designed his measures to address the

---

105. *YPZZ*, DG 18.12.2, 1:446.

106. For Zhu's October 1836 memorial, see Tian and Li, "Sixiang qianqu," pp. 100–101, 103–5.

107. Gongzhong jinyan, DG 15.11.23.

dependency of the provincial peasantry on poppy constructively. In Guizhu district, the governor's administration employed crop substitutions of wheat instead of plot confiscations and arrests in more than ten villages of "Tanka" coastal immigrants, possibly from Guangdong.[108] Other reports from Guizhou are somewhat more ambiguous, but 41 families or individuals voluntarily converted 58 plots to either grain or cotton cultivation between January 1838 and September 1842. Cotton was another attempt at sustainable crop substitution by Governor He, who hoped to reduce Guizhou's large expenditures on imports of raw cotton textiles from Huguang by distributing free seeds to those who had voluntarily uprooted their poppy. Other aspects of Guo's arguments may have influenced He, since he noted that the springtime sowing of cotton, just at the time poppy began to sprout, would enable both a quick eradication of poppy and a relatively smooth transition to a legitimate crop. Governor He also established bureaus to educate peasants about cultivating the new crops and improving the textiles derived from them.[109]

Guizhou seems to have been the only province in which crop substitution was seriously attempted, and it did not succeed in weaning peasants off poppy cultivation. The relative profitability of opium, in comparison with any other crop that could be grown in the southwest, certainly was the most obvious cause of this failure, but there were also other significant, if less apparent, factors. Given the extent of the regional opium marketing system, for example, crop substitution within a single southwestern province was inadequate. As Peng Songyu noted, "Since the people of Yunnan consider opium a necessity of life, they necessarily treat opium like grain. If poppy cultivation is not permitted within provincial frontiers, they certainly will look for a supply from the frontiers of other [provinces]. If it is not cultivated in China, it will be purchased from foreign barbarians."[110] Officials would have to scale crop substitution to a multiprovincial region rather than a single province to be effec-

---

108. Junji jinyan, DG 18.12.18, #2327–28.

109. WJD, DG 19.4.29, pp. 330–32; He Changling, *Naian zuoyi*, 2:589–93, 635–39. For statistics, see Table 7.

110. Peng, *Yu chou ji tan*, p. 68.

tive under these conditions. This task was far beyond even the extended jurisdiction of a governor-general and would have required an altered form of multiprovincial integration.[111]

Despite formidable barriers to its implementation, crop substitution was critical for successful prohibition no matter how lenient or draconian because of the subsistence requirements of the peasantry. According to one unofficial account concerning the Daoguang-era prohibition campaign in Menghua subprefecture in Yunnan, for example, the local magistrate, in an attempt to avoid additional administrative burdens and opportunities for corruption arising from prohibition, apparently decided on his own initiative to confiscate the opium without meting out further punishment to offenders. This relatively lenient measure drove the cultivators, now "without a livelihood," into banditry and provoked the armed resistance of traffickers on a scale sufficient to intimidate and paralyze the local authorities.[112]

Peasants needed to produce sufficient means not only for their own subsistence but also for their financial obligations to the state, which was dependent on their produce in the form of taxes generally paid in silver. As peasants knew from their transactions with drug traffickers, opium was easily converted into money and indeed occasionally functioned as a currency.[113] The drug thus proved an ideal medium of exchange between the peasantry and local officials, who also had tax obligations to the provincial and central governments, again payable in silver, to fulfill. The illicit source of some southwestern administrations' revenues was known to higher officials. Xi'an Regional Defense Commander Tai-yong, who had spent a great deal of time in Yunnan, privately informed Li Xingyuan, for example, that there were extensive poppy fields in the prefectures of Dali, Yongchang, Zhaotong, and Yunnan, where local officials, unable to prohibit cultivation, taxed it instead.[114]

---

111. Some type of hybrid structure does seem to have integrated select parts of northern and eastern Xinjiang with the Shaanxi-Gansu government-general administration through Zhenxi prefecture (see Chapter 3).

112. Peng, *Yu chou ji tan*, pp. 55–56.

113. See, e.g. *Baxian dang'an*, DG 17.8.23, 2:274.

114. Li Xingyuan, *Li Xingyuan riji*, DG 20.6.28, 1:83.

In early 1840 Censor Lu Yinggu exposed this relationship and its fatal effects on prohibition in the southwest. As a supplement to his information on the Yunnan-Sichuan traffic, Lu submitted a memorial attacking the professed ignorance of Yunnan's local officials regarding the extensive conversion of bean and wheat fields to poppy cultivation in some of the province's more outlying prefectures, subprefectures, departments, and districts such as Mengzi, Guangnan, Kaihua, Jingdong, Zhao zhou, and Menghua.[115]

The purpose of Lu's memorial was to identify the convergence of interests between local officials and their peasant charges that not only permitted cultivation to continue but actually encouraged it. He asserted that the main cause of the problem was

that the profit obtained from poppy cultivation among the populace is fairly substantial. In consequence, tax quotas can be fulfilled quite early, and local officials benefit from the ease of revenue collection and are concerned only with their performance evaluations; they are heedless of the benefit or harm done to the populace. Thus, they permit the people to cultivate and do nothing to prohibit it.[116]

Lu reasoned that production would increase in response to market demand, which would eventually drive prices down and make the drug more readily available to a wider range of consumers, which would include both military and official personnel.[117] In many ways an extrapolation of Guo's arguments, Lu's analysis demolished the justification for the central government's suppression policy, which was largely predicated on the urban, coastal, and mercantile nature of the traffic. Of most immediate significance for the government's strategy was Lu's observation that transprovincial smuggling of *afurong*, primarily by Muslims in the Yuanmo district of Wuding department in Yunnan, was the main

reason why smokers in these places [along the tri-provincial boundary between Yunnan, Sichuan, and Guizhou] need not look to foreign barbarians for aid. If the free circulation of gangs through neighboring provinces

---

115. Junji diqin, DG 19.12.17, 267:11. There is some ambiguity about the authorship of this memorial. I follow Qin Heping, *Yunnan yapian wenti*, p. 20, in attributing it to Lu Yinggu.

116. Junji diqin, DG 19.12.17, 267:11.

117. Ibid.

is not detected and arrested and eradication operations not intensified, then even if opium from overseas is cut off, that produced in China proper will be limitless and its legacy of harm unspeakable.[118]

In these few lines Lu Yinggu captured the essence of the problem facing the central government in the southwest by the end of the 1830s. A self-sustaining opium market had appeared in the southwest, and the local administrative structures that could be mobilized to destroy the system had become dependent on it. This insight is particularly valuable because it explains how what began as an alien opium trade became rooted in the quotidian domestic practice of the imperial economy. It was the mutual dependency between the traffic and local socioeconomic structures, rather than greedy merchants, an irrational and venal bureaucracy, wild tribals, or a benighted population of addicts, that ensured the failure of the central government's belated prohibition policies.[119] Like the peasant cultivators on whom they depended to fulfill central government tax quotas, local officials were also addicted to opium production.

The Imperial Significance of the Southwestern Opium Market

Administrative, geographic, ethnic, and economic factors had combined by the end of the 1830s to create a pervasive and abiding opium dependency in the Qing southwest that absolute prohibition could not eliminate. The failure of prohibition had an empirewide significance because domestic southwestern *afurong*, not Indian Malwa or Bengal, would become the source of 60 percent of all opium produced in Qing domains during the second half of the nineteenth century and would largely replace Indian imports. By 1897, Yunnan, Sichuan, and Guizhou were the top three opium-producing provinces in the empire. This advantage was based not only on the natural conditions of soil and climate but also on the

---

118. Ibid.

119. Qin Heping ("Yunnan de jinyan wenti," pp. 61–63) has also called attention to the significance of Lu's explanation for an analysis of the opium problem in general.

socioeconomic conditions brought about by the nature of Qing incorporation of the region.[120]

The southwestern opium market drew much of its strength from local roots. Suitable natural conditions for cultivation were enhanced by legitimate opium cultivation during the eighteenth century and the belatedness of the discovery of this cultivation and its criminalization by the state around a century later. Even when operating with this heightened sense of awareness, the existing administrative structure, substantially determined by ethnicity, still left large expanses of ostensibly Qing territory under weak or illusory control. Coastal conditions were not as accommodating for the domestication of opium. Coastal officials presiding over areas of illicit cultivation, all of which apparently occurred in *junxian* areas, could not complain of their limited authority or reluctance to intervene in the affairs of an alien, hostile people. The few instances of coastal cultivation discovered in 1830 were rapidly brought under control or remained very limited in scale where they persisted due in no small measure to the relatively unrestricted access enjoyed by local officials to poppy fields; there were no areas of absolute inviolability to official surveillance comparable to those in the southwest. If the *junxian* system could not prevent administrative incompetence or corruption, it did deprive officials of an excuse for inaction and facilitated intervention.

Of course, the greater number of agricultural and commercial alternatives to poppy cultivation in the more economically dynamic southeast also undoubtedly limited its appeal in the face of vigorous state prohibition and, hence, its spread. The existence of economic alternatives is precisely why crop-substitution programs, if implemented throughout the southwest in combination with ongoing prohibition operations, could have been used to reduce poppy growing among the peasantry, who generally appear in the official prohibition records as attracted to opium primarily as a

120. Yang Kaiyu and Liao, *Guizhou zibenzhuyi*, p. 83; Owen, *British Opium Policy*, pp. 265–68; Lin Man-houng, "Qingmo shehui liuxing xishi yapian yanjiu," pp. 208–11; Su, *Zhongguo dupin shi*, pp. 182–95. For a book-length regional study of the opium problem in Yunnan from 1840 to 1940, see Qin Heping, *Yunnan yapian wenti*.

source of income rather than as an article of consumption. Although crop substitution would not have removed the incentive for urban consumers to smoke, it could have removed the primary motivation for domestic rural producers to grow poppies. Successful crop substitution would have rendered consumers far more dependent on trafficking networks linked to the coast, and prohibition could then have been more reasonably and efficaciously confined to coastal smuggling.

It is difficult to escape the impression that the central government's lack of a genuine commitment to the material well-being of its southwestern population precluded the implementation of a comprehensive crop-substitution program as an integral part of a sustainable regional prohibition policy. Unfortunately, as seen in the selective reaction to Guo Baiyin's memorial, immediate eradication for the benefit of central coffers, not gradual transition for the benefit of local economies, was the state's explicit policy.

Yet any sort of effective action against opium at the local level, whether crop substitution, port surveillance, or the arrest of consumers, required a considerable degree of comprehensive local control, but the experiences of the southeast coast, the southwest interior, and Xinjiang suggest that the common cause of the opium problem throughout the empire was precisely a lack of such control over crucial geographic spaces. In the southwest, tribal settlements constituted these crucial spaces; in the southeast, the absence of Qing control over its coastal waters was decisive. Xinjiang, due to the extremely complex nature of its internal administrative apparatus and to the presence of the Khanate of Kokand, suffered from problems akin to both those of the southwest and those of the coast; its territorial administration did not control either its overland border checkpoints or the unincorporated hinterlands that lay just behind them.

Unlike Xinjiang or the coast, however, the southwest was under no direct threat from any foreign state capable of resisting the projection of Qing power into its sphere of influence. Instead, problems manifested themselves exclusively in the form of weaknesses in the structures of intra- and interprovincial local control. The contradictions of Qing ethnic policy contributed substantially to these weaknesses as the state schizophrenically pursued both quarantine and colonization with an absolute minimum of administrative overhead to maximize the extraction of regional wealth. This approach left large regions of the southwest ostensibly incorporated but actually impoverished and recalcitrant, as the massive uprisings of various ethnic minorities that rocked the southwest throughout the second half of the nineteenth century amply demonstrate.[121]

Such instability only served to enhance the regional dependency on opium. During the largest of the southwestern uprisings, the Panthay Rebellion (1856–73), there were reports that the financial structures of the local opium market constituted the only reliable source of credit for trade in Yunnan.[122] Whatever problems arose as a result of the repeated clashes and collusion between indigenous peoples and Han merchants and settlers, the continued benefits of opium revenues to official coffers rendered *afurong* effectively legitimate.

---

121. This problem can also be seen in the Qing incorporation of Taiwan; see Shepherd, *Taiwan Frontier*.

122. Newman, "A Reconsideration," p. 793.

SEVEN

Opium and
Qing Expansionism

Intensified prohibition, despite some apparent initial successes, ultimately did not eradicate opium from the southwest, Xinjiang, or
any other part of the Qing domain. This failure is, perhaps, the
greatest reason for the dearth of attention to the internal dynamics
of opium prohibition in China. The simple, persuasive explanation
generally given for this failure—the incompetence and irrationality
of an outmoded dynastic system—serves only to contribute to
scholarly complacency. This explanation is an updated version of
the traditional narrative of dynastic decline periodically invoked to
explain historical changes of all sorts. Although the Qing system
was seriously plagued by both corruption and inefficiencies, an un-
critical reliance on these factors as causal explanations obscures the
larger significance of the history of Qing prohibition efforts, which
reveals such factors to be as much effects as causes. The systemic
problems encountered in the prohibition campaign owed far more
to the vast expansion of dynastic territory, and consequently of the
entity and concept of "China," from the seventeenth through the
eighteenth centuries.

The ethno-geographic diversity that resulted from this expansion was a direct cause of the administrative decline that in turn
served to encourage governmental corruption and inefficiency,
both of which are rather relative and problematic terms.[1] Corrup-

---

1. On the fluidity of the concept of corruption in eighteenth-century China,
see Park, "Corruption," pp. 968, 975, 985. Although relatively clearly defined in

tion can be understood as a bureaucratic response to the contradictory demands arising from the consequences of the destabilizing territorial and demographic expansion. In effect, the center dictated that there be no increase in the tax burden commensurate with such expansion while expecting local administrations to continue to extract enough revenue to cover the state's increased costs of territorial incorporation as well as those of regular administration. Moreover, there was to be no major increase in official personnel, which would have further driven up administrative costs.

The response of the central bureaucracy and the court to these challenges was, fiscally, a fatal increase in centralization. As a result of the Qing refinement of the Ming "single-whip" system of taxation, pursued most intensely during the fiscal reforms of the Yongzheng reign, the center officially gained control of all "legitimate income" derived from the three most important regular sources of revenue, the land tax, the head tax, and duties on salt, tea, and imports.[2] These reforms deprived local governments of most of the revenues upon which they had previously relied. It was this increase in centralization, more than individual malfeasance, that created serious deficits in subprefectural and even provincial administrations and encouraged local officials to rely on "informal

---

the statute books, corruption in practice was often difficult to distinguish from the collection of "customary fees" and other quasi-regularized sources of official revenue at the local level (ibid., pp. 979, 983–85). As for questions of efficiency, it is easy to see the central bureaucratic advantages of such measures as the conversion of various taxes in kind and labor to silver payments as occurred under the single-whip systems of the Ming and Qing, but the rational appeal of these schemes is less evident for a peasantry whose access to money of any kind was quite limited in general and subject to exploitation where practicable. Inefficiencies in poor localities caused by uniform enforcement of single-whip practices were numerous. For an example, see Zelin, *Magistrate's Tael*, p. 40.

2. Madeline Zelin's work on eighteenth-century dynastic fiscal policy has revealed the underlying structural imperatives for corruption at the local level, which was deprived of revenue adequate for its expenditures by the centralizing reforms of the Yongzheng period. The effect of these reforms was to divert funds from the locality to the center, thus forcing the former to search for less conventional methods of meeting its ever-increasing administrative obligations; see *Magistrate's Tael*, pp. 4, 9, 42.

networks of funding," such as meltage and other extra-statutory "customary fees."[3]

Much of the revenue diverted to the center was used to pay for the militarily successful extension of Qing authority into places such as Inner Asia and the southwest. The very success of the operations against the Zunghars, the Three Feudatories, and the native chieftains of the southwest ensured the empire's overextension when the Qing sought to consolidate its administrative control through territorial incorporation.

Aside from the considerable limitations on its assimilation of newly conquered territories, the state could not even enhance its control over the Han core. The financial impossibility of an intensification of incorporation in core areas already under *junxian* administration has long been noted by scholars. G. William Skinner has estimated that in order to maintain the ratio of population per administrative unit prevailing circa 1730, when there were 1,360 districts in place, the Qing government of 1850 would have had to expand this number to 8,500, a figure that he concludes was beyond the communications and control infrastructure of any agrarian bureaucracy.[4] It has been estimated that this expansion would have consumed the whole of the land- and head-tax revenues, the two primary sources of central government income, for the entire eighteenth century.[5]

The dynasty's administrative overextension was not due solely to the radical increase in population, which undoubtedly increased instability. Increases in both the empire's territorial extent and the

---

3. Ibid., pp. 18, 26, 46–54. Zelin has in particular emphasized that the motive behind many such informal networks was not simple greed or corruption in a crude sense, but a magistrate's response under general conditions of fiscal deficit to a structural imperative to alleviate a pressing problem of local administration with funds set aside for another contingency (ibid., p. 70).

4. Skinner, "Urban Development," pp. 19–20. Skinner also notes that the average area of districts, which "should have declined over centuries," was gradually increasing so that "the total area incorporated within" the 1,360 districts of 1730 "was far greater that that incorporated within the 1,235 counterpart units a millennium earlier" (ibid., p. 19). See Yeh-chien Wang, *Land Taxation*, p. 58, for data on the expense of the administrative expansion that did occur.

5. Zelin, *Magistrate's Tael*, p. 306. Zelin bases her estimate on Skinner's population-to-district ratios quoted above.

diversity of its subjects played equally important roles. The fact that most major social upheavals occurred in sparsely populated frontier or interprovincial border areas, that is, precisely where administrative surveillance was weakest, rather than in densely populated core regions is suggestive of the pivotal role of expansionism in imperial destabilization. This expansionism, which includes demographic and spatial increases as well as greater ethnic variation and new conceptual constructions to help accommodate these changes, both detracted from the court's ability to maintain control in core areas and opened up new zones of instability. As Susan Naquin and Evelyn S. Rawski have observed,

certain kinds of decline were actually associated first—and in the eighteenth century almost exclusively—with the peripheries of regions and not with the cores. It was in these regions, and especially those of the newly colonized highlands of south and central China, that we find disorder and rebellion, conditions caused not by a collapsing state but by the inability of government and elite institutions to incorporate new populations and new territory. The problems encountered by the state bureaucracy as it tried to cope with a growing population and an increasingly complex economy were quite different in the peripheries than in the cores. Not until the late Qing did breakdown and the devolution of power in the cores become a serious problem.[6]

Expansion and the consequent administrative instability provided fertile ground for the opium traffic. The mere fact of Qing expansion into several opium-producing regions ensured that Han settlers, when economically motivated by core demand, would become involved in production through contact with the natives. This dynamic was clearly operative both in the southwest and in Xinjiang. Moreover, Han traffickers became vectors for the spread of the drug because of the consolidation of imperial authority in places like Tibet, Mongolia, and Manchuria, as well as through existing trade relations with neighboring states such as Vietnam and Siam.

This basic ethno-geographic diversification of opium soon developed to a new level through the contradictions of dynastic

---

6. Naquin and Rawski, *Chinese Society*, p. 226. See also pp. 223–24 for a reevaluation of the expansion of Qing population as an explanation for instability.

revenue-extraction policy, which the opium traffic, as a superlative "informal network" of local funding, proved well suited to resolve.[7] As recognized by Censor Guo Baiyin, an almost singular voice among the official clamor of the late 1830s, large portions of the populace in southwestern China were dependent on opium cultivation, which was more profitable in many areas than were conventional crops, because it enabled them both to provide for their own subsistence and to meet their heavy financial obligations. The evidence provided by Guizhou Governor He Changling in early 1839 of coastal traffickers contracting with the local peasantry for the seasonal opium crop confirms Guo's observations and reveals that cultivation had become regularized as part of the socioeconomic structure connecting rural peasants and urban merchants. Furthermore, resistance, documented in Taiwan, Zhejiang, and Yunnan, also confirmed Guo's fears concerning the negative effects of precipitous eradication on the peasant economy and attests to how important opium was to both peasants and small merchants.

Guo's memorial also addresses several important issues ignored by the central government's prohibition program and adumbrates an alternative model of prohibition that was never implemented on a transprovincial scale. The most salient point was his suggestion regarding crop substitution, which seems to have been seriously adopted only by Guizhou Governor He Changling, the great proponent of Qing statecraft studies. Because of its restriction to a single province, however, crop substitution failed to sever the regional and imperial market relations that connected Guizhou to other poppy-producing and opium-trafficking locales. As Peng Songyu implied (see Chapter 6), measures like crop substitution had to be transimperial, even as he inadvertently acknowledged that success would convert the opium problem into a truly foreign one more in conformity with the assumptions of central Qing prohibition policy.

---

7. On the development of these informal networks of opium production into regularized forms of legitimate local administrative revenue in the southwest from the late Qing into the Republican period, see Zhang Pengyuan, "Luohou diqu de ziben xingcheng," pp. 55–60.

A sincere examination of the merits of crop substitution by central policymakers would almost certainly have resulted in more regionally appropriate prohibition regulations, in at least some areas. Systematized implementation of appropriate crop substitution across the empire's interdependent provinces and territories could have helped to stimulate the local economies of many underdeveloped regions, which were attracted to opium cultivation as a source of adequate, stable currency and not as a recreational drug.

During his reconquest of Xinjiang from Yakub Beg's indigenous regime in 1878, the famous Qing official Zuo Zongtang claimed to have implemented just such an effective anticultivation program in Xinjiang, as he had done during his administration of Gansu. In Xinjiang, these operations included the suppression of foreign smugglers as well as crop substitution, mainly cotton, to provide economically viable alternatives for local opium cultivators. Zuo noted with satisfaction in an 1881 memorial that his ban on poppy cultivation had been successful and peasants along the Xinjiang-Gansu border were prospering because of their new crops.[8]

Whatever the truth of his contentions, and they are almost certainly exaggerated in light of official reports beginning in the 1890s discussed below, Zuo did acknowledge the critical significance of peasant poppy cultivation for successful prohibition, as opposed to consumption or even trafficking.[9] Moreover, his antitrafficking

---

8. Zou, "Zuo Zongtang," p. 30; *Guangxu chao Donghua lu*, GX 7.1, 1:1032. Whatever the immediate truth of Zuo's contentions, they did not outlast the dynasty. Despite some efforts to eradicate the drug in the first few years of the Republican period, local officials, now transformed into warlords, remained financially tied to the traffic, which persisted through the 1930s (Zou "Jindai Xinjiang jin yapian," pp. 39–43). On the re-emergence of the drug problem in Xinjiang, ostensibly in the wake of the PRC's economic reforms, see Xu Xifa, "Xinjiang jindu wenti." Ethnicity remains an important component of the drug trade. I personally witnessed Uighur restaurateurs in Xi'an selling hashish to consumers around Shaanxi Normal University in 1987, and as of 1999 it was still possible to catch the occasional whiff of consumption near Uighur restaurants in Beijing. I have heard "urban legends" from Han Chinese to the effect that hashish is a basic ingredient of the Uighur cuisine on offer at these eateries.

9. Zou, "Zuo Zongtang," p. 30. Zuo himself acknowledged that cultivation would inevitably persist off Gansu's beaten paths despite the province's rigorous prohibition operations (ibid., p. 31).

operations gave due consideration to the economic, as opposed to the recreational or analgesic, attractions of the poppy for peasant cultivators. In some key areas of the empire, this economic attraction almost certainly predated the criminalization of opium smoking, for example, in Yunnan's Yongchang prefecture, where crude opium, if not madak, was being produced during the eighteenth century. Of course, as the case of Zhu Yongding in Zhejiang demonstrated (see Chapter 4), peasants could also be driven to open cultivation of illegal poppy when they could no longer make ends meet through the cultivation of regular cereal crops.

The Zhu case is just one of many important pieces of evidence that peasants produced opium for basic income, not for personal use. Under these conditions, crop substitution would have been a reasonable response to poppy cultivation. Although effective crop substitution would not have discouraged urban consumers from smoking, it would have eliminated much of the incentive for rural producers to grow opium. The state would then have been able to free resources for the suppression of urban trafficking and consumption, aspects of the problem that it was in a much stronger position to prohibit. It might also have prevented opium from becoming fully domesticated.

Unfortunately, aside from requiring an unknown but probably large amount of scarce resources appropriately distributed across the empire, such a program was predicated on the assumption that the center was genuinely interested in the economic well-being of all the localities under its authority as an end rather than as a means to increase the court's revenues. In light of the timing of the court's full commitment to prohibition following the growth of its conviction that opium was the cause of the silver drain and was decreasing its revenues, a sincere engagement with local economic development seems unlikely. The impression of court indifference is only reinforced by the poor implementation record of the Jiaqing reign, whose prohibition rhetoric revolved entirely around the throne's putative concern for the physical well-being of its subjects. The court's refusal or inability to deal with the opium problem in a comprehensive fashion commensurate with the drug's socioeconomic and ethno-geographic variegation bound policymakers to a rigid, narrow view of prohibition that promoted a sin-gle-track strategy of penal escalation targeted almost exclusively against the Han majority in coastal urban areas. This official de-pendence on urban administrative centers for effective prohibition persisted into the twentieth century.[10]

This situation was the logical outcome of a prohibition policy predicated on the notion that the eradication of the coastal traffic would eliminate opium from the rest of the empire by blocking the main source of supply. The bureaucratic mentality, by no means re-stricted to Qing or Chinese society, that produced this strategy was instrumental in the failure of prohibition. The appearance of exten-sive poppy cultivation in both Xinjiang and the southwest invali-dated the main Qing strategy because opium was no longer exclu-sively a foreign import restricted to a particular region.

Legalization was simply another facet of centralized, monolithic thinking rather than an alternative policy, for this policy, too, was unconcerned with the alleviation of economic need in underdevel-oped localities. These areas were instead exploited for the benefit of the central coffers, an approach to opium little different from that of the warlord period. It is precisely this concern for the stabi-lization of central government revenues at the expense of all other considerations that links dynastic legalization and prohibition policies.[11] Both policies failed to address the underlying economic problems of which the opium traffic was a symptom, not a cause.

Of equally serious import was the fact that the economic bene-fits of the poppy were not restricted to commoners. For all Guo's insight into the rural dynamics of opium, he failed to articulate fully the relations that circumscribed and motivated peasant action, as well as those that bound peasants and local officials to the center. In contrast to Guo's argument that clandestine opium cultivation deprived the state of revenue from legitimate crops, Metropolitan Censor Lu Yinggu and Xi'an Regional Defense Commander Tai-

---

10. R. Bin Wong, "Opium and Modern Chinese State-Making," p. 193.

11. Official concerns over revenue were decisive for the informal taxation of opium in various coastal ports in the years immediately before legalization in the late 1850s as well as for legalization itself; see Fairbank, "Legalization," pp. 232, 258–63.

yong provided evidence that opium could not be eradicated precisely because of its significant contribution to revenues at the subprovincial level. The accounts of both men provide evidence that by the end of the 1830s at the latest southwestern opium cultivation had become part of the network of informal funding that had arisen since the 1720s to compensate for the diversion of revenue from locality to center.[12]

On the coast, Qi Zuncao's and Huang Juezi's investigations of the Zhejiang cultivation problem also uncovered evidence of official toleration of peasant cultivators, who were said to be much more amenable to taxation than the average farmer. Moreover, the illicit taxation of contraband opium had been in place in select ports since at least the latter half of the Qianlong reign, and rumors to this effect had been reaching the throne at least since the Jiaqing era.[13] By the 1850s, in the years prior to formal legalization, informal taxation of opium in coastal ports became fairly open.[14]

Opium would continue to be a crucial source of revenue for both the central and the local governments. Between 1885 and 1905, for example, opium taxes constituted approximately 6–7 percent of the Qing state's total revenues, a figure that jumped to 14 percent in 1906 when these various taxes were consolidated.[15] One twentieth-century observer subsequently confirmed the fundamental connection between opium and revenue in his reflections on the generally effective implementation of empirewide prohibition between 1906 and 1911: "The problem before officials, and more espe-

---

12. The southwest was particularly prone to the use of such networks since its revenues from the land- and head-taxes were quite low, especially in Yunnan. As early as 1727, Yunnan had already formally added to its regular tax collections a surcharge specifically intended to cover local government operating expenses (Zelin, *Magistrate's Tael*, p. 48). Xinjiang, was, if anything, a more extreme case because of the high costs of its military garrisons and its lack of a sufficiently large tax base to pay the territory's bills. The result was an excessive reliance on transfer payments from other provinces and a commensurate "fiscal vulnerability" for the Qing Central Asian empire (Millward, *Beyond the Pass*, pp. 44–45, 235). Transfer payments did not, however, preclude a plethora of schemes by local officials to increase the territory's revenue (Millward, *Beyond the Pass*, chaps. 2 and 3).

13. *YPZZ*, JQ 18.7.10, 1:7.

14. Fairbank, "Legalization," pp. 232–58.

15. Zhou, *Anti-Drug Crusades*, p. 30.

cially those of the western provinces, is to find a source of revenue to take the place of that formerly derived from opium."[16]

Administrative dependence on opium revenue was the major long-term obstacle to prohibition into the twentieth century. Significantly, the most successful prohibition effort launched by the dynasty, the anti-opium campaign of 1906–11, occurred in large measure because Britain agreed to reduce and eventually end Indian drug exports to China, in part due to the trade's diminished significance for Indian revenues. Domestically the Qing state was forced to raise taxes on a variety of goods and transactions, including the purchase of opium.[17] Furthermore, eradication was pursued mainly through coercive measures that included the militarization of anticultivation operations against peasants.[18]

Whatever the immediate achievements of the anti-opium campaign of 1906–11, they did not outlive the dynasty, and once again revenue was a major reason for the legal resurrection of the drug. During both the warlord period and the Nanjing decade, opium production, distribution, and consumption reappeared with the active support of governments throughout China, all of which depended on opium as a crucial component of their revenues. This situation did not fundamentally change even with the initiation of the largely futile Six-Year Opium Suppression Plan (1935–40) by the Nationalist government, which sought prohibition only as a

---

16. Wilson, *A Naturalist in Western China*, 2:80. For additional evidence from Sichuan, Shanxi, Shaanxi, and Gansu, see R. Bin Wong, "Opium and Modern Chinese State-Making," p. 192.

17. Zhou, *Anti-Drug Crusades*, pp. 28, 30; Madancy, "Poppies, Patriotism, and the Public Sphere," pp. 237–38, 243–44. Although these works show that Chinese nationalism played a significant role in the 1906–11 campaign, their perspective is primarily that of urban elites. Rural populations experienced a different reality: the militarization of anticultivation operations against a peasantry that clearly did not wish to give up poppy cultivation for the sake of the modern nation-state (Bianco, "Response of Opium Growers"; Madancy, *Troublesome Legacy*, chap. 8).

18. Military force seems to have been the state's standard eradication strategy; see, e.g., Hosie, *Trail*, 1:4. Hosie conducted an evaluation of Qing prohibition policy in western China during 1910–11. Although he did find that cultivation had been substantially reduced throughout the region, even eliminated in some provinces such as Sichuan, he noted that poppy cultivation remained undisturbed over considerable areas, particularly in the northwestern provinces of Gansu and Shaanxi (ibid., 1:123–30, 267–71).

device to consolidate its power by cutting off the revenues of regional warlord governments. The plan was largely undermined by
halfhearted implementation, local resistance, and the Japanese invasion. Indeed, the plan was not much more than a plot by Chiang
Kai-shek to secure his own undisputed monopoly of the drug.[19]

The revelations concerning the taxation of opium cultivators by
local officials in Yunnan and the levying of illicit customs duties
on opium smugglers in Guangdong exposed the state's complicity
in the failure of the Qing opium prohibitions. Just as the imperial
system of penal exile helped to spread the coastal opium problem
to Xinjiang, so the state's contradictory demands on its local officials and its common subjects provided the motivation for them to
persist in the production, trafficking, and consumption of opium.
An 1877 report by Board of War Senior Vice Minister Guo Songtao
confirmed that illicit taxation remained a staple of local official
revenue in western China:

In Sichuan, Yunnan, Gansu, and Shaanxi, the primary motive for cultivation is tax revenue. Your servant has heard that the produce of a single
mu of poppy fields is many times that of a field of conventional crops. . . .
Consequently, provinces, subprefectures, and districts increase their [ex-
tra-statutory] customary fees and thereby collect an illicit tax on crude
opium, which also is many times greater than regular tax revenue. Since
both official and commoner profit thereby, opium spreads everywhere.[20]

Venal or addicted individual officials were also obstacles to the
local implementation of prohibition. The drug dependency of
entire local administrations was a less obvious but more critical ob-
struction to prohibition in no small measure because only a wholesale, and quite impractical, overhaul of the empire's field administrative system would have eliminated it. The complexity and scope
of this system also tended to obscure the fact that large areas of
territory were under imperial control only for very limited purposes. Although some cultivators were fortuitously discovered in

---

19. Zhou, *Anti-Drug Crusades*, pp. 39–92; Slack, *Opium State and Society*, chap.
4. Qin Heping (*Yunnan yapian wenti*, pp. 311–17) argues that the Six-Year Plan was
not entirely ineffective in central areas of China proper, but much more problematic in poor and frontier areas.

20. *Guangxu chao Donghua lu*, GX 3.4, 1:394.

the Xinjiang wilderness or around southwestern *junxian* administrations, officials openly admitted their limited abilities to project government power extensively and continuously into rural or wilderness areas, particularly in the absence of Han Chinese. Structures of local control were signally absent in the wild zones of Yunnan, where prohibition was apparently not even attempted.

The fact that opium persisted in areas under both direct and indirect Qing rule diverts attention from an important difference between these two ethnically distinct administrative spaces, a difference that becomes more clearly visible only with the onset of the twentieth century. Prohibition operations during the Republic encountered much more difficulty in areas where Han administrative structures were weak or nonexistent. Hill tribals in Yunnan, for example, were still growing poppy in 1939 as their main cash crop.[21] These areas consequently became centers of opium trafficking, which was increasingly linked in official eyes to minority peoples and their settlements.[22] Such constructions of minority traffickers can also be glimpsed during the Qing.

Many of the Xinjiang dispatches, and a few of those concerning the southwest, exposed considerable Muslim participation in the regional opium traffic. The Xinjiang record makes it abundantly clear that Muslims, both foreign and domestic, were the primary source of opium for Han traffickers in the territory and that the Muslim state of Kokand was the main geographic conduit for the flow of Central and South Asian opium into Xinjiang. In the southwest the evidence for the centrality of Muslim participation in the traffic is less extensive, but it is implied by the Arabic origins of the term for regional opium, *afurong*. More concrete evidence was offered by Censor Lu Yinggu, who not only identified the center of Yunnan's Muslim trafficking operations but also elucidated their central role in the interprovincial smuggling operations across the Yunnan-Sichuan border.

An examination of the key roles played by Muslims, both imperial subjects and foreigners, in the southwestern and Xinjiang traffics reveals that government prohibition tactics were substantially

---

21. Yan Deyi, "Pu-Si yanbian," p. 35.
22. Kuang and Yang, "Shaoshu minzu diqu de yapien duihai wenti."

determined by ethnicity. The dynasty was as hesitant to prosecute Muslim offenders vigorously as it was to punish coastal Euro-American traffickers. Since the brunt of prohibition, even in its antitrafficking dimensions, fell almost entirely on Han offenders, the court's leniency shows that ethnicity was an important factor in the criminal identities constructed by Qing prohibition.

This fact has been obscured by narratives that portray Euro-Americans as the only non-Han participants in the opium traffic. Further problems have been created by the Euro-American traffickers' constructions of themselves as victims of oriental despotism. In practice, the dynasty largely avoided the stringent enforcement of opium prohibition on its own minority subjects as well as on foreigners, whether from Europe or Central Asia. There is little doubt that this policy was a general one of enlightened self-interest pursued in order to avoid interethnic strife between Han and non-Han throughout the empire, an objective specifically alluded to in its Xinjiang context by both Yi-shan and En-te-heng-e.

Despite such attempts to take the empire's ethno-geographic diversity into account and what appear to be genuine prohibition efforts on the part of senior officials in many places, the drug policies of the Daoguang period did not prove effective for long. Even in places like Xinjiang, where opium diplomacy and conscientious officials like En-te-heng-e made progress, the Qing state clearly failed to eradicate opium. A Russian expedition in 1876–77, for example, reported that opium was being exported *to India* from the Southern March administrative and trade center of Yarkand in exchange for products from the subcontinent. In 1873–74, "700 horseloads at 18 ducats" per load amounting to a total of 12,600 ducats was hauled out of Yarkand by Indian merchants.[23] This Russian report was submitted just a few years before Zuo Zongtang declared his 1878 anticultivation operations in Xinjiang a success. Yet, just over a decade later, in 1890, local officials submitted an estimate of the revenue Xinjiang opium could generate. Nearly twenty

---

23. Kuropatkin, *Kashgaria*, p. 88. Currently, opium, along with heroin and cannabis, is flowing back into Xinjiang, mainly from the northern subcontinent and Central Asia; 24,958 kilos of opium alone were confiscated in 1993 (Xu Xifa, "Xinjiang jindu wenti," p. 14).

years later in 1908, tsarist Muslim traffickers were being apprehended along the Xinjiang-Russian border.[24]

The 1890 official inquiry into the revenue potential of Xinjiang opium concluded that it was negligible since little poppy was produced or bought by the East Turkestanis of the Southern March, "who, being Muslims, customarily had no taste for it and did not cultivate it." Nevertheless, in the Northern March, where Han people "lived mixed together with Muslims," there was reportedly small-scale cultivation for personal use. Such cultivation for "subsistence" smoking may explain why there was so little demand for the official product.[25] At any rate, Islam was certainly no absolute barrier to opium use; Muslim emperors of Mughal India such as Akbar (r. 1556–1605) and his successor, Jahangir (r. 1605–27), were casually noted as opium consumers in official histories. Observers in British India also noticed opium consumption, sometimes almost exclusively, by Muslims.[26] In 1868–69, the predominantly Muslim inhabitants of Kashgar were generally characterized in a report by a Muslim operative of the Raj as "opium eaters."[27] In light of such evidence, more research is required to re-evaluate late Qing official claims concerning poppy eradication and almost nonexistent consumption levels among East Turkestanis, particularly because distinctions between opium eating and opium smoking remain vague.[28] Nevertheless, the regularization of poppy cultiva-

---

24. Junji zashui, GX 16.9.6, #1139–41; *Xinjiang tuzhi*, 3:1994–95.

25. Junji zashui, GX 16.9.6, #1139–41. An 1891 financial report from Xinjiang Provincial Governor Wei Guangdao revealed that all opium revenue was being derived from drug shipments entering Xinjiang from China proper, since there was no taxable indigenous production (ibid., GX 17.12.21, #1771–72). This is a strange assertion given the extent of the Russian opium farms in the Northern March noted by Chinese scholars. It is possible that provincial officials were submitting gross underestimates of opium revenues in an attempt to retain them for local use.

26. Watt, *Dictionary of the Economic Products of India*; 6:34; Winther, *Anglo-European Science*, p. 204. Consumption in the Mughal period was limited to eating and drinking opium since, according to Watt (6:41), smoking was a "modern" Chinese import to India.

27. Montgomerie, "Report of the Mirza's Exploration," p. 197.

28. The Chinese scholarly consensus is that large-scale opium cultivation in Xinjiang only occurred as a result of the Russian occupation of Ili after 1871, when a system of opium farms was established in the occupied area of the Northern

tion in the northwest, however rudimentary, is clear evidence that by the late nineteenth century the informal opium network had become a legitimate source of official revenue.[29]

Yunnan and Sichuan proved to be exceptionally well suited for the establishment of an informal opium network and the ideal ground to effect Chinese control of its own domestic opium market. Although the large-scale Muslim uprisings during the Xianfeng reign may have disrupted the region's opium market, they also provided the immediate incentive for the taxation of poppy by local officials with the support of the central government. Yun-Gui Governor-General Lao Chongguang successfully proposed an opium tax to generate revenue for provincial military expenses incurred during the Muslim uprisings. This policy was continued in the wake of legalization and subsequently expanded empirewide under the Guangxu emperor (r. 1875–1907) and was instrumental in the expansion of the southwestern opium market.[30]

Production for extra-regional mass consumption was the ultimate result in these prime opium-producing areas of southwestern China, which in the second half of the nineteenth century surpassed the original production sites in India to make China the largest producer of opium in the world.[31] By the early twentieth

---

March; see Zhongguo shehuikexueyuan, Jindaishi yanjiusuo, *Shae qin hua shi*, p. 236; Zhang Zuoxi, "Shae dui Zhongguo de yapian maoyi," pp. 142–43; and Xinjiang shehuikexueyuan, Lishi yanjiusuo, *Xinjiang jianshi*, 2:165–66. As the Kuropatkin report demonstrates, however, there was also extensive trafficking in the Southern March, of which the Russians seem to have been unaware as late as 1876. It is, of course, possible that this export trade was enabled only by the Russian-sponsored cultivation in the north, which ostensibly produced opium for the Chinese mass market.

29. Informal funding networks were often quite systematized in their operations, which no doubt encouraged the conversion of some of them into formal structures of official revenue (Zelin, *Magistrate's Tael*, p. 69).

30. Qin Heping, *Yunnan yapian wenti*, p. 22.

31. Guizhou and Yunnan emerged as major production sites of domestic opium in the 1830s, and Yunnan was the center of China's production by 1869. It would be replaced by Sichuan in the 1870s. By 1879 at the latest, sales of Chinese domestic opium had surpassed those of Indian opium. By 1906 China produced 87 percent of the world's opium and consumed 93 percent of it; see Waung, "Opium Cultivation," pp. 211, 217; Lin Man-houng, "Qingmo shehui liuxing xishi yapian yanjiu," pp. 189, 192–93, 453.

century, the economic pre-eminence of the drug was assured in provinces like Sichuan, where an observer asserted that "no other crop even remotely approximating the pecuniary value of opium can take its place."[32]

Regional varieties of opium began to appear in Yunnan; "horse turd" (*mashi*), for example, was produced in the southeastern and southwestern parts of the province for the Guangdong market; "stuffed buns" (*baozi*) in the west, including Gengma, for the Sichuan, Hubei, and Shanghai markets; "tall boys" (*gezi*) in the east for the Guizhou, Hunan, and Guangxi markets, and "lumps" (*kuaizi*) in the mid-west for the Wuhan and Guangxi markets.[33] This variety is indicative of a highly refined domestic production and distribution system that could supply a wide spectrum of tastes across China. Ironically, the sophistication of southwestern production helped the Chinese merchant-traffickers to best their Euro-American competitors. During the latter half of the nineteenth century, Chinese producers and distributors were able to corner their home market. A similar process had occurred in India, as Bombay merchants edged Europeans out of the trade.[34] The trade had become "nativized."

Domestic dynamics, however significant they were to become, were not the initial stimuli that engendered the cycle of opium in the Qing empire. The activities of foreign elements were prerequisites for the establishment and development of both the regional and the empirewide Chinese opium market systems. The Euro-American traffickers, whose sponsorship of the traffic is most evident, most extensive, and most crucial, as well as the South and Inner Asian traffickers, were all critical actors in the history of opium in China. The links established by these groups with various Qing subjects, Han and otherwise, provided these subjects with a form of power, commodified opium, whose source was almost entirely beyond the throne's control. The indirect quality of Qing rule, especially in Xinjiang where it was of relatively recent

32. Wilson, *A Naturalist in Western China*, 2:81.

33. Qin Heping, *Yunnan yapian wenti*, p. 15. The translations are mine.

34. Farooqui, *Smuggling as Subversion*, chap. 6; Trocki, *Opium, Empire and the Global Political Economy*, chap. 6.

establishment, made these links particularly difficult, even dangerous to sever. As a result, the Khanate of Kokand was able to impose its own system of extraterritoriality on the Qing in southern
Xinjiang and use it to conduct an opium traffic in defiance of Qing
prohibitions. This influence was established, albeit on a smaller
scale, more through geographic proximity and cultural affinity
than through any kind of superiority in technology or organization, as has been held to be the case on the coast.

Using different methods, both the British and the Kokandis succeeded in establishing inviolate spaces on the borders of imperial
territory from which they could sustain their trafficking operations.[35] Whether launching their operations from the town of Andijan or from Lintin Island, smugglers were able to co-opt or evade
Qing security apparatuses. The ability of criminal groups from two
very different states to establish much the same trafficking systems
implies that both were exploiting the same weakness of their intended target, the Qing empire. The experiences of the southeast
coast, the southwest interior, and Xinjiang suggest that a common
cause of the opium problem throughout the empire was a lack of
control over crucial geographic spaces. In the southwest, tribal settlements constituted these crucial spaces; in the southeast, the absence of Qing control over coastal waters was decisive. In Xinjiang,
both Muslim settlements and wilderness areas were critical.

Local administrative weakness, while manifesting itself in a
uniquely Qing way, was not unique to the Qing, however. The
limited geographic span of administrative control, especially when
faced with the challenge of a commodified addictive consumable,
seems to be characteristic of the bureaucratic structures of this period. The inability of the East India Company to prohibit the production, transport, and sale of Malwa in its Indian domain was at-
tributable to factors generally similar to those that caused the

---

35. Considerable evidence has been presented by scholars that reveals the construction of similar inviolate spaces during the warlord period. This construction
in many areas appears to have been enabled largely or exclusively by opium. See,
e.g., Gao, "Xi'nan junfa yu yapien maoyi"; Li Longchang, "Lüetan Guizhou de
yanhuo"; Yang Kaiyu, "Jindai Guizhou de yapien liudu"; Lin Shourong and Long,
"Sichuan junfa yu yapianyan"; and Wu Xiaogao, "Zhengshou yapien teshui de
neimu."

failure of absolute prohibition in Qing China, insofar as local administrative conditions are concerned. The British lacked the ability in the early nineteenth century to impose administrative uniformity throughout the Indian subcontinent sufficient to gain full control of the entire process of opium production, distribution, and consumption. The dynamics that arose from this ungovernable diversity rendered even limited prohibition "irrational" from an economic and political if not from an ethical perspective. If, as has been said of China, controlling opium was "very much an issue of defining power and authority relations" between the center and its various localities, then neither the Qing nor the Company imperial states carried sufficient weight on their respective grounds during the first half of the nineteenth century.[36]

Under such conditions, it is not surprising that prohibition was a failure for both the Qing and the Company. Because of their respective positions in the opium-marketing system, however, their responses were radically dissimilar. In the wake of British India's failure to prohibit the marketing of Malwa, it was able to shift the cost of its failure to the Qing through a deliberate expansion of the Chinese drug market. British India could accomplish this shift by virtue of its position as a major producer and distributor for China. In effect, the Company abandoned prohibition and acquiesced more fully to comparatively modern market mechanisms driving overseas trade, which it had done a great deal to oppose, in order to protect a traditional monopoly at home in India.

Qing China did not have this option, since its market role was primarily defined by consumption, a seemingly impossible condition to adapt to the protection of a traditional socioeconomic order. China's status as the ultimate destination for the overwhelming bulk of the opium produced in India ensured that the Qing state could not simply ignore or placidly accept the consequences of its indirect and incomplete control of its own territory or turn these weaknesses into profit as British India had done. Any profit to the Qing state would have been extracted from the bodies of its own consumer-subjects and ultimately from the Qing privy purse.

---

36. R. Bin Wong, "Opium and Modern Chinese State-Making," p. 206.

Moreover, the problems arising from domestic consumption could not be solved simply by eliminating obstacles to the free-market circulation of opium. Guo Songtao, during his 1877 reflections on the legacy of the Daoguang reign's opium problem, noted that the flood of opium in mid-reign caused a general social decline and resulted in continuing banditry and other calamities, all of which fed on one another. Guo concluded not only that opium was harmful to the health and wealth of the populace but that it was "the decisive factor for the stability or disruption of the state."[37] These symptoms of an addicted state and society initially appeared during the escalating prohibition campaign but persisted long after opium consumption and distribution had been legalized and the drug's cultivation encouraged.

The significance of the Qing opium problem cannot be limited to its coastal manifestation, just as the commodified power of opium was not restricted to the drug's immediate producers and consumers. The goal of stabilizing revenues indifferently extracted from a uniform populace of pliant subjects was common to both the Qing and the British imperial administrative bureaucracies and was the main impetus for all state attempts to control opium, even in defiance of market forces. Whatever its attitude toward the drug at any given point, the state's addiction to an idealized exercise of power gave opium a transcendent appeal and ensured its persistence into the twentieth century.

The source of this appeal ultimately lay in the psycho-physical response of people to opium in and around the British Indian and Qing empires, but the drug's power was not restricted to the dimension of mere physical addiction. Opium's ability to create dependency enabled producers to transmute drug consumption into political and economic power over other groups of people, whether or not they smoked opium. In this sense, opium, in the form of economic and political power, was as psychologically compelling to merchant-capitalists, bureaucrats, and politicians as it was physically compelling to drug consumers. Producers, consumers, and all the beneficiaries of the relationship between the two were in this way united in their addiction to power.

---

37. *Guangxu chao Donghua lu*, GX 3:49, 1:397.

Appendixes

APPENDIX A

Dynastic Opium Policy Before
the Daoguang Reign

This appendix aims to clarify the chronology of pre-Daoguang opium policy in an attempt to resolve a few basic contradictions in the historical record of prohibition prior to the 1820s.

It is first necessary to separate a fanciful Jiaqing edict from the factual ones. A number of sources hold that an important prohibition edict was issued in the first year of the reign in 1796. In 1879, for example, Wang Zhichun (*Qingchao rouyuan ji*, pp. 165–66) cited the text of a memorial by Liang-Guang Governor-General Jiang Youxian regarding the formulation of a new set of prohibition regulations. This conviction outlasted the dynasty and was reasserted by Yu Ende in his influential 1934 chronological analysis of Qing opium policy (*Jinyan faling*, p. 22). Yu provided both additional citations and an explanation of the absence of any specifics of the 1796 prohibitions in primary dynastic sources. Citing both an edition of the *Guangzhou Gazetteer* and evidence from East India Company records provided by H. B. Morse, Yu concluded that the text of the decree promulgating the new prohibitions was no longer extant.

It was certainly necessary to find new evidence for the 1796 prohibition edict, since the memorial cited by Wang was actually submitted on May 2, 1815, by Governor-General Jiang in the twentieth year of the Jiaqing reign. This memorial has been translated into English from an entry in the *Qingshi lu* (QSL, JQ 304:18a–b; Fu, *Documentary Chronicle*, 1:399–400). The errors of nineteenth-century annalists like Wang had been passed on to those of the twentieth century, such as the compilers of the important 1920s administrative work *Qingchao xu wenxian tongkao*. This work also cited Jiang's memorial as the document that initiated Jiaqing-era prohibition in 1796 (*Qingchao xu wenxian tongkao*, 53:8077a–b). The 1815 anachronism has been noted by Wang Hongbin (*Jindu shijian*, p. 35), who inexplicably does not identify the original source and who still maintains that the 1796 prohibitions were promulgated.

H. B. Morse's account of the East India Company's China trade is the main evidence presented by both Yu Ende in 1934 and Wang Hongbin in 1997 for the existence of the 1796 prohibitions. Unfortunately, Morse himself did not believe in their existence and used the same East India Company evidence cited by Yu and Wang to show that no such edict had been issued at that time (*Trading to China*, 2:316). Company records for 1798 explicitly state that "no Edict has lately been issued," but they do say that an intention to do so was communicated to "private" residents of Guangzhou. This informal warning was what apparently prompted Company officials to repeat their order that no Company ships should bring opium to China at this time. A year later, in 1799, a provincial order reiterating prohibition, mainly for imperial subjects, was sent from the governor of Guangdong through the Guangzhou superintendent of trade to the hong merchants, who, in their capacity as intermediaries, informed the foreign merchant community (Morse, *Trading to China*, 2:326, 344–46). This 1799 communication, presented in a contemporary English translation and identified by Morse as the "Hoppo's Edict of Dec. 2, 1799," was not actually a formal imperial edict but an intraprovincial notice similar to that issued in Sichuan in 1816 (Morse, *Trading to China*, 2:327n; cf. *Baxian dang'an*, JQ 21.5.6, 2:272).

The ultimate source of this provincial edict may have been a 1799 memorial by Liang-Guang Governor-General Ji-qing. Unfortunately, I have come across only an indirect reference to this document, which advocated the formal criminalization of opium trafficking. During the 1836 legalization debate, Liang-Guang Governor-General Deng Tingzhen asserted that opium prohibition had begun in 1799, when the throne formally adopted his predecessor Ji-qing's proposed solution to the silver drain. Deng also reported that up until this point, opium had been legally imported as a medicine throughout the Yongzheng and Qianlong reigns (*YPZZ*, DG 16.7.27, 1:205–6). Deng's chronology, which completely omits the Yongzheng-era prohibition statutes of 1729, is certainly inaccurate, but not entirely so. It is likely Ji-qing did submit a request for the criminalization of trafficking, but that the throne contented itself with a mere reiteration of the existing statutes by the governor of Guangdong.

The nature of the 1799 communication explains why there is no Chinese record of major imperial prohibition edicts between 1796 and 1813 corresponding to a number of extant English translations of prohibition communications issued to Guangzhou's foreign merchant community over this same period. Such communications were part of the local and more fragile administrative archive, which was not nearly as well preserved as that of the central government. They were not, moreover, formal imperial edicts marking significant changes in prohibition policy, and this critical distinction has generally been ignored.

It seems reasonable to conclude that the materials concerning 1815 deliberations have been systematically mistaken as evidence for a formal 1796 prohibition, for which no direct evidence has come to light. Citations from dynastic records themselves have proved impossible to confirm; Yao Weiyuan's (*Yapian zhanzheng shishi kao*, p. 12) unverifiable generalized assertion that the *Donghua lu* contains entries concerning the criminalization of nonmedicinal opium and paraphernalia in 1780 and the drug's total prohibition in 1796 is one such example. Although it remains possible that an intraprovincial communication reiterating prohibition was issued by provincial authorities in 1796, no imperial decree to affirm or intensify prohibition was promulgated at this time.

The Jiaqing emperor's own Board of Punishments made no mention of any 1796 or 1799 prohibitions during the first major revision of the opium statutes in 1813, in the eighteenth year of the reign. The board's review of previous regulations consisted of nothing more than the 1729 laws and a minor edict issued in 1811 concerning coastal traffic (*YPZZ*, JQ 18.7.10, 1:5–6). Two other edicts, in 1807 and 1810, were apparently considered too insignificant for the board to mention. All were directed primarily at coastal officials and ordered them to intensify their enforcement of existing prohibition statutes in their jurisdictions. These facts undermine Morse's unsupported chronology in which the 1729 prohibitions were intensified in 1796 and the "final step" in Jiaqing-era prohibition was taken in 1800 with an edict prohibiting poppy cultivation and the importation of foreign opium (Morse, *International Relations*, 1:175).

The minor edicts of the Jiaqing era were responses to isolated offenses and simple reiterations of the necessity for enforcing preexisting prohibitions rather than entirely new laws. That of 1810, for example, arose from a Beijing smuggling case that impelled the emperor to demand better control of opium at its coastal ports of entry (*YPZZ*, JQ 15.3.2, 1:1; Fu, *Documentary Chronicle*, 1:380). The result of this order to enforce prohibition actively was apparently a moral appeal to foreign traffickers in Guangdong by local officials (*Qingdai waijiao shiliao*, JQ 16.5.13, 2:8a–9a) in 1811.

It is important to note that the 1810 decree did not explicitly mention foreign traffickers; specific penalties had yet to be enumerated for their offenses. The 1799 notice, for example, threatened to punish only hong merchant-guarantors of foreign merchant-traffickers rather than the traffickers themselves (Morse, *Trading to China*, 2:346). Indeed, the standard dynastic statutory handbooks are devoid of imperial pronouncements directed at foreign traffickers. The overview of dynastic prohibition law in the *Qing huidian shili*, for example, does not mention a single regulation prohibiting foreign trafficking. In other words, these handbooks exclusively concern Qing prohibition law for imperial subjects.

The informal nature of the prohibition of foreign trafficking can explain much of the contradiction between Western accounts of periodic warnings from local officials and an absence of corresponding imperial decrees in the official record. In fact, these ambiguities disappear with the inauguration of formal provisions for the punishment of foreign offenders in 1814–15 (*YPZZ*, JQ 19.5.4, 1:11–12, JQ 20.3.23, 1:18–19). Contradictions between the Chinese and the English records prior to this period are an artifact of the adoption of an analytical perspective uncritically based on that of the foreign merchant-traffickers rather than that of the Qing administrators. A more accurate chronology of Qing prohibition should, rather, be critically based on a Qing-centered foundation that uses foreign sources to buttress or retouch, rather than construct, the narrative edifice.

An improved chronology of prohibition can also help to explain apparent contradictions within the Chinese record. The local and somewhat informal character of coastal prohibition before 1814–15 can partly account for the unusual chronology of prohibition between 1662 and 1820 presented in 1838 by Jiangnan Governor-General Tao Shu. Tao may have exchanged this information with his contemporary, then Board of Revenue Vice-Minister Qi Junzao, who wrote down an essentially identical chronology in an unofficial account some time after 1838 (*Zhongguo jindu shi ziliao*, pp. 245–46). Tao stated that the prohibitions on "South Seas opium" (*nanyang yapian*) had been relaxed under the Kangxi emperor in 1685, and opium was thenceforth taxed as a medicine until it was formally banned in 1810 under the Jiaqing emperor (*YPZZ*, DG 18.6.19, 1:317). In other words, in Tao's view, opium of some sort was under a Qing ban more than forty years before the ostensible inaugural prohibition in 1729 and was never prohibited again until the end of the first decade of the nineteenth century.

Tao's account is augmented by some evidence scattered throughout Ming and Qing materials for a pre-1729 ban on opium. The earliest reference to such a ban occurs in a Xiamen gazetteer some time before 1626 (Spence, "Opium Smoking," p. 147). The Yongzheng emperor himself noted in response to Su Mingliang's initial 1728 memorial that a decree concerning opium had "already . . . been promulgated" (*Yongzheng chao hanwen zhupi*, YZ 6.11.6, 13:853b, cited in Howard, "Opium Suppression in Qing China," pp. 76–77n).

Tao's chronology clearly omits the Yongzheng statutes of 1729 as well as the pre-1810 prosecutions of cases in Fujian, Beijing, and Xinjiang. He also exaggerated the significance of the 1810 prohibition edict. His assertion regarding opium prohibition before 1685, however, has yet to be conclusively disproved. It is possible that

Tao merely chose to focus on edicts he considered to be of imperial, rather than of merely regional, significance. This would at
least explain Tao's focus on the 1810 Beijing case, which proved
opium was circulating beyond the coast into the capital. Moreover,
Tao may have been ignorant of the Xinjiang case, which does not
appear to have generated an imperial decree in response.

Tao's chronology does have the merit of explaining the dearth
of cases from 1729 through the whole Qianlong reign and into the
first decade of the nineteenth century. This would not necessarily
be contradicted by Western accounts of Qing opium prohibition
during the same period, for the dynasty may have relaxed domestic
prohibition while maintaining restrictions on foreigners, a policy
that would not have been accurately reflected in the statute books.
Although there are clearly problems with this interpretation, my
more comprehensive examination of material that has come to
light suggests that the dynasty may have maintained some such
dual policy during much of the eighteenth century.

Translation of Shanxi Taiyu District Magistrate Chen Lihe's "Opium Prohibition Pledge" Stele

The court established officials to govern the people, with every prefecture, subprefecture, department, and district possessing its own offices. There is, moreover, an order to the worship of the spirits, and it is commanded that these offices offer seasonal sacrifices, paying their respects on the first and fifteenth of each month. This is done in order that they may avail themselves of the mystical sense for upright conduct that is possessed by the spirits. From the depths of the netherworld, good is rewarded and evil punished, and nothing can match this netherworld in assisting officialdom in its punishment of crimes.

Thus, among the people of every department and district, those who act as traitors and transgress the law, bringing generations of harm to their localities, will doubtless be detected by the eyes and ears of the spirits.

Opium is produced beyond the seas, but its poison flows into China. Those who buy it and consume it break their families, harm their own lives, and violate the law. Treachery, licentiousness, robbery, and brigandage all arise from it. Both the young and vigorous and the old and weak die from it. Wealthy and luxurious houses are impoverished by it. Brave and bright sons and younger brothers are made stupid and unfilial by it. People who dwell in peace in their houses well stocked with delicacies feel the heavy blows of the bamboo and the weight of the cangue because of it; they also suffer strangulation, exile, and banishment at the hands of the law because of it.

As for its injurious effect on custom, opium destroys the five natural relationships, and its harmful effect on individual character is even more unspeakable.

When [Chen] Lihe came here as an official, he sought to preserve what was beneficial to the region and get rid of what was harmful to it. Last year, before he had arrived at his post, he heard rumors of local fools who liked to consume opium and become full of hidden sorrows and disquiets therefrom. After two months here, although no incidents have been substantiated, inquiries still must be made. As a shepherd of the people, going about making surprise arrests without having first made the prohibitions known is something I, Lihe, cannot bear to do.

To eradicate a great scourge, its source must first be cleansed. If the district were without traffickers, from where would my people buy opium? If there were no traffickers outside its boundaries, from where would my district buy opium? This is why the prohibition of trafficking is the first task in eradicating the source of opium.

That which has already come in is difficult to pursue, but in future it will be necessary to abstain from bringing it in. We will use this house of self-cleansing and vegetarianism to gather the people to pray to the spirits. Henceforward, all merchants in the district who go to Fujian, Guangdong, Jiangsu, or Zhejiang to buy goods must pledge that they will not bring a single fragment of opium back to Taiyu for sale, to the great harm of its populace. If they render respectful adherence to their oaths of abstinence, the spirits will surely reward them. If they resume trafficking, the officials will certainly punish them! And if official law cannot reach them, the spirits will surely lend assistance.

If any officials take bribes or connive to conceal trafficking, the spirits will surely punish them and beset them with calamity in the same way that they will do to traffickers and consumers! Ah! The people cannot possibly be harmed, because the spirits cannot possibly be deceived.

Those of my merchants who travel to Fujian, Guangdong, Jiangsu, and Zhejiang on the sea desire that there be neither wind nor waves; those who travel on land desire that there be neither narrow passes nor dangerous defiles. When they are at peace, what profit can they not seek to gain? Must they violate the laws of the state and rouse the wrath of the spirits for such a thing as opium?

If some say that the Way of the Spirits is obscure and incredible, that they will not know if merchants violate the law and will not ask if officials bend the regulations, that the mystical sense for upright conduct will not manifest itself, let all merchants respectfully give ear to me and together pray for the spirits' mystical intelligence to shine forth!

Reference Matter

Character List

Entries are alphabetized letter by letter, ignoring word and syllable breaks, with the exception of personal names, which are ordered first under the surname and then under the given name.

afurong 阿芙蓉
Ai-long-a (n.d) 愛隆阿
aiman 愛曼
akhund (Ch. a-hun) 阿渾
amban 大臣
anchashi 按察使
Annan district 安南縣
Anping district 安平縣
Anshun prefecture 安順府
aogao 熬膏

Ba district 巴縣
banshi dachen 辦事大臣
bao 保
Bao Shichen (1774–1855) 包世臣
baojia 保甲
Baoning district 寶寧縣
Baoshan district 保山縣
baoshe 保社
Bao-xing (1777–1848) 寶興
baozheng 保正
baozi 包子
Bazhai subprefecture 八寨廳
bazong 把總
beg (Ch. bo-ke) 伯克
Beilu 北路

bian 邊
bian Miao 變苗
biantong 變通
bianwai 邊外
Bi-chang (d. 1854) 壁昌
Bijie 畢節
bitieshi (M. bithesi) 筆帖式
bu 部
buben 部本
Bugur 布古爾
bujin zichu 不禁自除
Bu-lan-tai (d. 1752) 布蘭泰
Bu-yan-tai (1791–1880) 布彥泰

canzan dachen 參贊大臣
Cao Liuxing (n.d.) 曹六興
Cao Xuemin (1718–87) 曹學閔
Ceheng department 冊享州
Chang-qing (d. 1856) 長清
Changzhai subprefecture
　　長寨廳
Chaozhou 潮州
Chen Hongmou (1696–1771)
　　陳弘謀
Chen Lihe (1761–1825) 陳履和
Chen Shen (1641–1722) 陳詵

Chen Xi (n.d.) 陳熙
Cheng Hanzhang (1762–1832)
　程含章
Chengde prefecture 承德府
chenggao 成膏
Cheng-ge (n.d.) 成格
Chenggong district 呈貢縣
Chengjiang prefecture 澂江府
chengshi fuhao 城市富豪
chengshou ying 城守營
chengshou ying dusi 城守營
　都司
chengshou ying qianzong 城守營
　千總
chijin pai 弛禁派
Chongqing prefecture 重慶府
chuantu 川土
Chuxiong district 楚雄縣
Chuxiong prefecture 楚雄府

da chen 大臣
Dading prefecture 大定府
Daizu 傣族
Dali prefecture 大理府
Danjiang subprefecture 丹江廳
Danshui district 淡水縣
Dayao district 大姚縣
deng 燈
Deng Tingzhen (1775–1846)
　鄧廷楨
Dengchuan department
　鄧川州
diantu 滇土
dibao 地保
difang guan 地方官
Dihua department 迪化州
Dingfan department 定番州
Dongchuan prefecture 東川府
Donglu 東路
Du Yanshi (n.d.) 杜彥士
Dujiang subprefecture 都江廳
Dushan department 獨山州

dutong 都統
Duyun district 都勻縣
Duyun prefecture 都勻府

E-le-jin-tai (n.d.) 額勒金泰
En-te-heng-e (?–1842) 恩特亨額
E-shan (1770–1838) 鄂山

Fang Bao (1668–1749) 方苞
fan jie 番界
fanmai 販賣
Feng Shaopeng (n.d.) 馮紹彭
Feng Zanxun (fl. 1820) 馮贊勛
Fumin district 富民縣
furong, see afurong
Fu-xing-a (n.d.) 富興阿
Fuzhou prefecture 福州府

gaitu guiliu 改土歸流
ganjie 甘結
gao 膏
Gao Zhenwan (n.d.) 高振宛
Gengma native chieftainship 耿馬
　土司
gengmi 粳米
ge sheng dufu 各省督撫
gezi 格子
gong 公
gonghang 公行
Guangnan prefecture 廣南府
Guangxi department 廣西州
Guiding district 貴定縣
Guihua subprefecture 歸化廳
Guiliyang (Gui-liang; 1785–1862)
　桂良
Guiyang prefecture 貴陽府
Guizhu district 貴筑縣
Guo Baiyin (?–1884) 郭伯蔭
Guo Songtao (1818–91) 郭嵩燾
Guolu 啯嚕
guo yin 過癮
Guzhou subprefecture 古州廳

hafurong 哈芙蓉
haiguan jiandu 海關監督
Haitan 海壇
Han Sipei (fl. 1824) 罕思沛
hang 行
Hanmin bian Miao 漢民變苗
Hanzhong prefecture 漢中府
Haoqing department 鶴慶州
he 和
He Changling (1785–1848) 賀長齡
hezhuang 合樁
Huang Juezi (1793–1853) 黃爵滋
Huang Lezhi (n.d.) 黃樂之
Huang Shujing (?–1756) 黃叔璥
Huang Zhongmo (fl. 1809) 黃中模
Huangping department 黃平州
huan jue 緩決
Huanyang district 緩陽縣
hubao ganjie 互保甘結
hūda-i da 呼岱達
Hui-feng (d. 1851) 惠豐
Hui-ji (d. 1845) 惠吉
Huijiang 回疆
Huili zhou 會理州
Huimin 回民
Huitun 回屯
huolian cheng gao 火煉成膏
Hu-song-e (d. 1847) 瑚松額

Ilibu (Yi-li-bu; d. 1843) 伊里布
Ili jiangjun 伊梨將軍
Ili jiu cheng 伊梨九城

jasak (Ch. zha-sa-ke) 札薩克
jia 甲
Jiang Youxian (1766–1830) 蔣攸銛
Jianshui district 建水縣
jiaoyan 繳煙
jing 境
Jingdong subprefecture 景東廳
Jingni jiangjun 靖逆將軍
jitun 集囤

juntun 軍屯
junxian 郡縣
junzhang 君長
junzi 君子

Kai department 開州
Kaihua district 開化縣
Kaihua prefecture 開化府
kaishe yaokou 開設窯口
Kaitai district 開泰縣
kemin 客民
Khoja (Ch. Hezhuo) 和卓
kuaixie 快蟹
kuaizi 塊子
Kuang Deng (n.d.) 況澄
Kunming district 昆明縣
Kunyang department 昆陽州

Langdai subprefecture 朗岱廳
Langqu native chieftainship 滾蕖
    土司
Lao Chongguang (1802–67) 勞崇光
Li Hongbin (d. 1846) 李鴻賓
Li Xingyuan (1797–1851) 李星沅
Li Zhiguo (n.d.) 李治國
Liang Zhangju (1775–1849) 梁章鉅
Liangjiang 兩江
liangwu ting 糧物廳
liang yuan 糧員
lianhuan qiejie 連環切結
Libo district 荔波縣
Lifan yuan 理番院
Lijiang district 麗江縣
Lijiang prefecture 麗江府
Lin Qing (1791–1846) 麟慶
Lin Zexu (1785–1850) 林則徐
Lin'an prefecture 臨安府
lingdui dachen 領隊大臣
Lingnan 嶺南
Liping prefecture 黎平府
Liu Guangsan (n.d.) 劉光三
liuyu minren 流寓民人

Longchuan River 龍川江
Longli district 龍里縣
Longquan district 龍泉縣
lu 路
Lu Kun (1772–1835) 盧坤
Lu Shiyi 陸世儀
Lu Yinbo (1760–1839) 盧陰簿
Lu Yinggu (d. 1857) 陸應穀
Lufeng district 祿豐縣
Luliang department 陸涼州
Luohu department 羅斛州
Luoping department 羅平州
lupiao 路票
Luquan district 祿勸縣

Maha department 麻哈州
Maolian 茂連
mashi 馬屎
Meize district 湄澤縣
Mengdian 猛甸
Mengding 猛定
Menghua subprefecture 蒙化廳
Menglian 猛連
Mengmeng native chieftainship
　孟孟土司
Mengzi 蒙自
menpai 門牌
Mianning subprefecture 緬寧廳
Miaojiang 苗疆
Miaozu 苗族
Midian 米甸
Min-Zhe 閩浙
Mingshan (Ming-shan; d. 1834)
　明山
mu 畝
Mujangga (Mu-zhang-a; 1782–1856)
　穆彰阿

Na Zhenxing (n.d.) 那振興
Nanchang 南昌
Nandian 南甸
Nanlu 南路

Nanning district 南寧縣
nanyang yapian 南洋鴉片
Na-yan-cheng (1764–1833) 那彥成
Ne-er-jing-e (d. 1857) 訥爾
　經額
neidi 內地
neidi zhi yi 內地之夷
Ningbo 寧波
Ningqiang zhou 寧羌州
Ningyuan 寧遠

Ortai (E-er-tai; 1680–1745)
　鄂爾泰

pai 牌
palong 爬龍
paozhi cheng gao 炮制成膏
Peng Songyu (n.d.) 膨崧毓
pengmin 棚民
Pingliang prefecture 平涼府
Pingyi district 平彝縣
Pingyuan department 平遠州
Pingyue independent department
　平越直隸州
Pizhan 辟展
Puan district 普安縣
Puan subprefecture 普安廳
Puding district 普定縣
Puer prefecture 普洱府
Puning department 普寧州

Qi Gong 祁憤
Qi Junzao (1793–1866) 祁寯藻
Qian Jie (1760–1812) 錢楷
qiangtu 羌土
Qianxi department 黔西州
Qianzhou 乾州
Qingjiang subprefecture 清江廳
Qingping district 清平縣
Qingzhen district 清鎮縣
Quanzhou 泉州
Qujing prefecture 曲靖府

Renhuai subprefecture 仁懷廳
Ruan Yuan (1764–1849) 阮元

Shaan-Gan 陝甘
Shaan-Gan zongdu 陝甘總督
shangmin 商民
Shao Zhenghu (n.d.) 邵正笏
Shaoxing 紹興
Shen Qixian (?–1839) 申啓賢
sheng Miao 生苗
Shengjing (i.e., Mukden; present-
   day Shenyang) 盛京
Shenhu guan 神護關
shi 石
Shibing district 施秉縣
shicha 失察
Shiping department 石屏州
Shiqian prefecture 石阡府
Shisan hang 十三行
Shizong district 師宗縣
Shuicheng subprefecture 水城廳
shuli 書吏
shu Miao 熟苗
Shunning district 順寧縣
Shunning prefecture 順寧府
Shunqing prefecture 順慶府
Sinan prefecture 思南府
Sizhou prefecture 思州府
Song-yun (1754–1835) 松筠
Songming department 嵩明州
Song-pu (d. 1846) 嵩溥
Songtao subprefecture 松桃廳
Su Mingliang (n.d.) 蘇明良
Su Yanyu (n.d.) 蘇延玉
sui 歲
suiyu 水漁
Sun Erzhun (1770–1832) 孫爾準
Sun Jiagan (1683–1753) 孫嘉淦

Taigong subprefecture 台拱廳
Taihe district 太和縣
Taipu si 太僕寺

Tai-yong (n.d.) 台湧
Taizhou 台州
Tan Cui (1725–1801) 檀萃
Tanka (Ch. Tanren) 蛋人
Tao Shu (1779–1839) 陶澍
Tengyue subprefecture 騰越廳
Tiandi hui 天地會
Tianshan 天山
Tianzhu district 天柱縣
Tixing anchashi si 提刑按
   察使司
tongben 通本
Tongren district 銅仁縣
Tongren prefecture 銅仁府
tongyou 桐油
tongzhi 同知
Tuan-duo-bu (n.d.) 湍多布
tubian 土弁
tuguan tusi zhidu 土官土司
   制度
Tui-yi-bo-te 推依博特
tujia zu 土家族
tuman 土蠻
Tumingga (Tu-ming-a; d. 1847)
   圖明阿
tumu 土目
tuntian 屯田
tusi 土司

waidi 外地
waidi zhi yi 外地之夷
Wandian native chieftainship 灣甸
   土司
wangdi chengwen 妄遞呈文
Wei Guangdao (n.d.) 魏光燾
weijin xiahai 違禁下海
wei junzi 僞君子
Weining department 威寧州
weizhi 違制
Weng'an district 甕安縣
wen na toushou 聞拿投首
Wenshan district 文山縣

Wenzhou 溫州
Wu Lanxiu (1789–1837) 吳蘭修
Wuchuan district 婺川縣
Wuding department 武定州
Wu-er-tai-e (d. 1842) 烏爾泰額

Xiajiang subprefecture 下江廳
Xiamen 廈門
xiangbao 鄉保
xiangyue 鄉約
xiaotu 小土
xiedou 械斗
xingfan 行販
Xingyi district 興義縣
Xingyi prefecture 興義府
Xinjiang nanlu ge cheng chajin
    yapian zhangcheng 新疆南路
    各城查禁鴉片煙章程
xishi 吸食
Xiuwen district 修文縣
Xu Naiji (fl. 1809) 許乃濟
Xu Qiu (fl. 1831) 許球
Xu Shijie (n.d.) 許士杰
Xuehai Tang 學海堂
xun 汛
Xundian department 尋甸州
xunsi 巡司
xuntai yushi 巡台御史

yan 煙
Yan Botao (d. 1855) 顏伯燾
yanbian zhi yi 沿邊之夷
yancao 煙草
Yang Yuchun (1761–1837)
    楊遇春
yanghang 洋行
yangyan 洋煙
yanjin 煙禁
yanjin pai 嚴禁派
yanju 煙具
yansi 煙絲

Yanzhou 嚴州
yaokou 窯口
yapian 鴉片
yapian guan 鴉片館
yapian gui 鴉片鬼
yapian ni 鴉片泥
yapian tun 鴉片圖
yapian yan 鴉片煙
yapian yancao 鴉片煙草
Yarkand canzan dachen 葉爾羌
    參贊大臣
ye 野
yeren 野人
yeren jie 野人界
yeyi 野夷
Yi 彝
yidi 夷地
Yidong dao 迤東道
yifang 夷方
Yiliang district 宜良縣
yin 癮
Yin Peifen (n.d.) 尹佩棻
yinfang zhangjing 印房章京
yinhuang 銀荒
Yinjiang district 印江縣
yinyan 飲煙
Yi-shan (d. 1878) 奕山
Yixi dao 迤西道
Yongbei subprefecture 永北廳
Yongchang prefecture 永昌府
Yu Jiao (n.d.) 俞蛟
Yuan Wenxiang (n.d.) 袁文祥
Yuan Yulin (n.d.) 袁玉麟
Yuanjiang department 元江州
Yuanmo district 元謀縣
Yubing district 玉屏縣
Yun department 云州
Yunnan district 雲南縣
Yunnan prefecture 雲南府
Yuqing district 余慶縣
Yu-tai (1788–1851) 裕泰

Zhang Bingde (fl. 1820)
　張秉德
Zhanxi County 盏西縣
Zhanyi department 沾益州
Zhao department 趙州
Zhaotong prefecture 昭通府
Zhenfeng department 貞豐州
Zheng'an department 正安州
zhengjiao 政教
Zhenkang native chieftainship
　鎮康土司
Zhennan department 鎮南州
Zhenning department 鎮寧州
Zhenxi independent subprefecture
　鎮西直隸廳
Zhenyuan district 鎮遠縣

Zhenyuan prefecture 鎮遠府
zhenzong bing 鎮總兵
zhiqing shouji 知情受寄
zhishang tanbing 紙上談兵
zhisi 識司
Zhou Shu (n.d.) 周澍
Zhou Xuejian (d. 1748) 周學健
Zhu Zun (d. 1862) 朱嶟
zhucheng yapian ban yan 煮成鴉
　片拌煙
zongjia 總家
Zunyi district 遵義縣
Zunyi prefecture 遵義府
zuo duyushi 左都御史
Zuo Zongtang (1812–85) 左宗堂

Works Cited

Aibida 愛必達. *Qiannan shilüe* 黔南識略 (Guizhou administrative primer). 1749. Reprinted—Guiyang: Guizhou renmin chubanshe, 1992.

A-la-teng-ao-qi-er 阿拉騰奧其爾. *Qingdai Yili jiangjun lungao* 清代伊犁將軍論稿 (Qing military governors of Ili). Beijing: Minzu chubanshe, 1995.

Baojia shu 保甲書 (Baojia handbook). Comp. Xu Dong 徐棟. In *Muling shu* 牧令書 (The local magistrate's handbook), comp. Xu Dong. 1848. Reprinted—Yangzhou: Jiangsu Guangling guji keyinshe, 1990.

Bayly, C. A. *Indian Society and the Making of the British Empire.* Cambridge, Eng.: Cambridge University Press, 1988.

Beeching, Jack. *The Chinese Opium Wars.* New York: Harcourt, Brace, Jovanovich, 1975.

Bello, David A. "The Chinese Roots of Inner Asian Poppy." *Cahiers d'études sur la Méditerranée orientale et le monde turco-iranien* 32 (July-Dec. 2001): 39–67.

———. "Opium in Qing Xinjiang and Beyond." In *Opium Regimes: China, Britain and Japan, 1839–1952*, ed. Timothy Brook and Bob Tadashi Wakabayashi, pp. 127–51. Berkeley: University of California Press, 2000.

———. "The Venomous Course of Southwestern Opium: Qing Prohibition in Yunnan, Sichuan and Guizhou in the Early Nineteenth Century." *Journal of Asian Studies* 62, no. 4 (Nov. 2003): 1109–42.

Benedict, Carol. *Bubonic Plague in Nineteenth-Century China.* Stanford: Stanford University Press, 1996.

———. "Hongtaiji's Tobacco Prohibitions and the Construction of the Early Qing State, 1630–42." Paper presented at the Association for Asian Studies Annual Meeting, New York, Mar. 29, 2003.

Berridge, Virginia, and Griffith Edwards. *Opium and the People: Opiate Use in Nineteenth-Century England.* London: Allen Lane / St. Martin's Press, 1981.

Bianco, Lucien. "The Response of Opium Growers to Eradication Campaigns and the Poppy Tax, 1907–1949." In *Opium Regimes, China, Britain and Japan, 1839–1952*, ed. Timothy Brook and Bob Tadashi Wakabayashi, pp. 292–319. Berkeley: University of California Press, 2000.

Bodde, Derk, and Clarence Morris. *Law in Imperial China*. Philadelphia: University of Pennsylvannia Press, 1967.

Bowen, H. V. "British India, 1765–1813: The Metropolitan Context." In *The Oxford History of the British Empire*, vol. 2, *The Eighteenth Century*, ed. P. J. Marshall, pp. 530–51. Oxford: Oxford University Press, 1998.

Brewer, John, and Roy Porter, eds. *Consumption and the World of Goods*. London: Routledge, 1993.

Burnett, John. *Liquid Pleasures: A Social History of Drinks in Modern Britain*. London: Routledge, 1999.

Carey, Fred W. "A Trip to the Chinese Shan States." *Geographical Journal* 14, no. 4 (1899): 378–94.

Chang, Hsin-pao. *Commissioner Lin and the Opium War*. Cambridge, Mass.: Harvard University Press, 1964. Reprinted—New York: Norton, 1970.

Chaudhuri, K. N. *The English East India Company*. New York: A. M. Kelly, 1965.

Chen Hua 陳樺. *Qingdai quyu shehui jingji yanjiu* 清代區域社會經濟研究 (Studies of regional socio-economies in the Qing). Beijing: Zhongguo renmin daxue chubanshe, 1996.

Chen Qiyuan 陳其元. *Yongxian zhai biji* 庸間齋筆記 (Notes from the Yongxian Studio). 1874. Reprinted—Shanghai, 1925.

Chen Wangcheng 陳旺城. "Zhanggeer shijian zhi yanjiu" 張格爾事件研究 (A study of the Jahangir Incident). Master's thesis, Zhengzhi University, 1992.

Chen Zhao 陳趙. "Wan Qing Xinjiang jinyan shulun" 晚清新疆禁煙述論 (Overview of late Qing opium prohibition in Xinjiang). *Xiyu yanjiu* 3 (1996): 22–28.

Cheng Hanzhang 程含章. "Lun yang hai" 論洋害 (Concerning the foreign scourge). In *Qing jingshi wenbian* (Collected writings on statecraft from the Qing dynasty), 3 vols., ed. He Changling 賀長齡, 1:654a–55b. 1887 ed. Reprinted—Beijing: Zhonghua shuju, 1992.

Chia Ning. "The Lifanyuan and the Inner Asian Rituals in the Early Qing (1644–1795)." *Late Imperial China* 14, no. 1 (June 1993): 60–91.

Chou, Nailene Josephine. "Frontier Studies and Changing Frontier Administration in Late Ch'ing China: The Case of Xinjiang, 1759–1911." Ph.D. diss., University of Washington, 1976.

Chouban yiwu shimo (Xianfeng chao) 籌辦夷務始末咸豐朝 (Comprehensive account of the management of foreign affairs [Xianfeng reign]). 8 vols. 1867. Reprinted—Beijing: Zhonghua shuju, 1979.

Chouban yiwu shimo buyi 籌辦夷務始末補遺 (Supplement to *Chouban yiwu shimo*). Taibei: Zhongyang yanjiuyuan, Jinshi suo, 1968.

Chowdhury, Benoy. *Growth of Commercial Agriculture in Bengal, 1757–1900.* Calcutta: Indian Studies Past & Present, 1964.

Ch'ü, T'ung-tsu. *Local Government in China Under the Qing.* Cambridge, Mass.: Harvard University Press, 1962. Reprinted—Stanford: Stanford University Press, 1969.

Chuan, Han-sheng, and Richard A. Kraus. *Mid-Ch'ing Rice Markets and Trade: An Essay in Price History.* Cambridge, Mass.: Harvard University, East Asian Research Center, 1975.

Chuxiong Yizu wenhua yanjiusuo 楚雄彝族文化研究所, ed. *Qingdai Wuding Yizu Nashi tusi dang'an shiliao jiaobian* 清代武定彝族那氏土司檔案史料校編 (Edited compilation of Qing dynasty archival materials related to the Na line's Yi native chieftainship in Wuding department). Beijing: Zhongyang minzu daxue chubanshe, 1993.

Cranmer-Byng, John L., and John E. Wills, Jr. "Trade and Diplomacy Under the Qing." In *China and Maritime Europe, 1500–1800*, ed. John E. Wills, Jr. Cambridge, Eng.: Cambridge University Press, forthcoming.

Daoguang Xianfeng liangchao chouban yiwu shimo buyi 道光咸豐兩朝籌辦夷務始末補遺 (Supplement to *Chouban yiwu shimo* [Daoguang and Xianfeng reigns]). Taibei: Zhongyang yanjiuyuan, Jinshi suo, 1982.

Dao, Xian, Tong, Guang si chao zouyi 道咸統光四朝奏議 (Memorials from the four Qing reigns of Daoguang, Xianfeng, Tongzhi, and Guangxu). Taibei: Taiwan shangwu chubanshe, 1970.

Da Qing lüli tongkao jiaozhu 大清律例通考校注 (Annotation of *Da Qing lüli tongkao*). Ed. Ma Jianshi 馬建石 and Yang Yutang 揚育棠. Ca. 1778. Reprinted—Beijing: Zhongguo zhengfa daxue chubanshe, 1992.

Dermigny, Louis. *La Chine et l'Occident: le commerce Canton à au XVIIIe siècle, 1719–1833.* Paris: S.E.V.P.E.N., 1964.

Diamond, Norma. "Defining the Miao: Ming, Qing and Contemporary Views." In *Cultural Encounters on China's Ethnic Frontiers*, ed. Stevan Harrell, pp. 92–116. Seattle: University of Washington Press, 1995.

Di Cosmo, Nicola. "Qing Colonial Administration in Inner Asia." *International History Review* 20, no. 2 (June 1998): 287–309.

Ding Mingnan 丁名楠 et al. *Diguozhuyi qin Hua shi* 帝國主義侵華史 (A history of the imperialist aggression against China). 6th ed., vol. 1. Beijing: Renmin chubanshe, 1992.

Dunstan, Helen. *Conflicting Counsels to Confuse the Age: A Documentary Study of Political Economy in Qing China, 1644–1840.* Ann Arbor: University of Michigan, Center for Chinese Studies, 1996.

Edkins, Joseph. *Opium: Historical Note or the Poppy in China.* Shanghai: Inspector General of Customs, 1881.

Elliott, Mark C. "Bannerman and Townsman: Ethnic Tension in Nineteenth-Century Jiangnan." *Late Imperial China* 11, no. 1 (June 1990): 36–74.

Fairbank, John K. "Legalization of the Opium Trade Before the Treaties of 1858." *Chinese Economic and Political Science Review* 17, no. 2 (July 1933): 215–63.

———. *Trade and Diplomacy on the China Coast.* 2 vols. Cambridge, Mass.: Harvard University Press, 1953. Reprinted—2 vols. in 1, Stanford: Stanford University Press, 1969.

Fang Bao 方苞. *Fang Bao ji* 方苞集 (Fang Bao's collected works). 2 vols. Shanghai: Shanghai guji chubanshe, 1983.

Fang Yingkai 方英楷. *Xinjiang tunken shi* 新疆屯墾史 (A history of the colonization of Xinjiang). 2 vols. Urumqi: Xinjiang qing shaonian chubanshe, 1989.

Farooqui, Amar. *Smuggling as Subversion: Colonialism, Indian Merchants and the Politics of Opium.* New Delhi: New Age International Publishers, 1998.

Fisher, Michael H. *Indirect Rule in India, Residents and the Residency System, 1764–1858.* New Delhi: Oxford University Press, 1991.

Fletcher, Joseph. "Ch'ing Inner Asia c. 1800." In *The Cambridge History of China*, vol. 10, *Late Ch'ing, 1800–1911, Part I*, ed. John K. Fairbank, pp. 35–106. Cambridge, Eng.: Cambridge University Press, 1978.

———. "The Heyday of the Ch'ing Order in Mongolia, Sinkiang and Tibet." In *The Cambridge History of China*, vol. 10, *Late Ch'ing, 1800–1911, Part I*, ed. John K. Fairbank, pp. 351–408. Cambridge, Eng.: Cambridge University Press, 1978.

———. "Sino-Russian Relations, 1800–62." In *The Cambridge History of China*, vol. 10, *Late Ch'ing, 1800–1911, Part I*, ed. John K. Fairbank, pp. 318–50. Cambridge, Eng.: Cambridge University Press, 1978.

Fu Lo-shu. *A Documentary Chronicle of Sino-Western Relations.* 2 vols. Association for Asian Studies Monographs and Papers, no. 22. Tucson: University of Arizona Press, 1966.

Fujiwara Riichirō 藤原利一郎. "Genchō no ahen kinrei ni tsuite" 阮朝の アヘン禁令について (Nguyễn dynasty opium prohibition). *Shisō* 8 (1960): 32–41.

Gagliano, Joseph A. *Coca Prohibition in Peru.* Tucson: University of Arizona Press, 1994.

Ganzhou fu zhi 甘州府志 (Gazetteer of Ganzhou prefecture), ed. Zhong Gengqi 鍾賡起. 1780. Reprinted—Lanzhou: Gansu wenhua chubanshe, 1995.

Gao Yanhong 高言弘. "Xi'nan junfa yu yapian maoyi" 西南軍閥與鴉片貿易 (Southwestern warlords and the opium trade). *Xueshu luntan* 2 (1982): 74–76.

Gardella, Robert. *Harvesting Mountains: Fujian and the China Tea Trade, 1757–1937*. Berkeley: University of California Press, 1998.

Giersch, C. Pat. "'A Motley Throng': Social Change on Southwest China's Early Modern Frontier, 1700–1880." *Journal of Asian Studies* 60, no. 1 (Feb. 2001): 67–94.

Goldstone, Jack A. *Revolution and Rebellion in the Early Modern World*. Berkeley: University of California Press, 1991.

Gong Yin 龔蔭. *Zhongguo tusi zhidu* 中國土司制度 (China's native chieftain system). Kunming: Yunnan renmin chubanshe, 1992.

Goodman, Jordan. *Tobacco in History: The Cultures of Dependence*. London: Routledge, 1993.

Goodrich, L. Carrington. "Early Prohibitions of Tobacco in China and Manchuria." *Journal of the American Oriental Society* 58, no. 6 (1938): 648–57.

Greenberg, Michael. *British Trade and the Opening of China, 1800–42*. Cambridge, Eng.: Cambridge University Press, 1951.

Grousset, Rene. *The Empire of the Steppes: A History of Central Asia*. Trans. Naomi Walford. New Brunswick, N.J.: Rutgers University Press, 1970.

Guangxu chao Donghua xu lu 光緒朝東華續錄 (The Donghua records of the Guangxu reign). 5 vols. Ed. Zhu Shoupeng 朱壽朋. 1909. Reprinted—Beijing: Zhonghua shuju, 1984.

Guo Yunhua 郭蘊華. "Qing zhengfu tongyi Xinjiang de lishi yiyi" 清政府統一新疆的歷史意義 (The historical significance of the Qing government's unification of Xinjiang). In *Zhungaer shilun wenji* 准噶爾史論文集 (Anthology of articles on Zunghar history), ed. Zhungaer shilüe bianxie zu 准噶爾史略編寫組, 2:314–22. Beijing: Zhongguo shehuikexueyuan, Minzu yanjiusuo, 1981.

Hami zhi 哈密志 (Hami gazetteer). Ed. Zhong Fang 鍾方. 1846. Reprinted—Taibei: Chengwen chubanshe, 1967.

Hanyu da cidian suoyin ben 漢語大辭典縮印本. Shanghai: Hanyu da cidian chubanshe, 1997.

Hao Jinda 郝近大. "Dui yancao chuanru ji yaoyong lishi de kaozheng" 對煙草傳入及樂用歷史的考證 (The history of the transmission of tobacco and its medicinal use). *Zhonghua yishi zazhi* 17, no. 4 (1987): 225–28.

Hao, Yen-p'ing. *The Commercial Revolution in Nineteenth-Century China: The Rise of Sino-Western Mercantile Capitalism*. Berkeley: University of California Press, 1986.

He Changling 賀長齡. *Naian zouyi* 耐菴奏議 (The memorials of He Changling). 1882. Reprinted—Taibei: Chengwen, 1968.

He Chengyuan 何程遠. "Yapian zhanzheng qianxi quanguo xidu renshu yu xidu jiceng de kaocha" 鴉片戰爭前夕全國吸毒人數與吸毒階層的考察 (An inquiry into the number of addicts nationwide and their class backgrounds on the eve of the Opium War). *Lishi jiaoxue* 4 (1989): 7–10.

Herman, John E. "Empire in the Southwest: Early Qing Reforms to the Native Chieftain System." *Journal of Asian Studies* 56, no. 1 (Feb. 1997): 47–74.

Hevia, James. *Cherishing Men from Afar: Qing Guest Ritual and the Macartney Embassy of 1793*. Durham, N.C.: Duke University Press, 1995.

Hong Liangji 洪亮吉. *Tianshan ke hua* 天山客話 (Anecdotes from a traveler in the Tian Mountains). 1843. Reprinted—Beijing: Zhongguo shuju, 1993.

———. *Yili jishi shi* 伊犁紀事詩 (A poetic chronicle of Ili). Ca. 1800. Reprinted—Ed. Zhongyang minzu xueyuan tushuguan 中央民族學院圖書館. Beijing: Zhongyang minzu xueyuan tushuguan, 1983.

Hosie, Alexander. *On the Trail of the Opium Poppy: A Narrative of Travel in the Chief Opium-Producing Provinces of China*. London: G. Phillip & Son, 1914.

Howard, Paul Wilson. "Opium Suppression in Qing China: Responses to a Social Problem, 1729–1906." Ph.D. diss., University of Pennsylvania, 1998.

Hsiao, Kung-ch'üan. *Rural China: Imperial Control in the Nineteenth Century*. Seattle: University of Washington Press, 1960.

Hu Qiwang 胡起望. "Qian Jia Miaomin qiyi canjiaren gongdan jianshu" 乾嘉苗民起義參加人供單簡述 (A brief discussion of the confessions of participants in the Qianlong-Jiaqing Miao uprising). In *Miaozu yanjiu luncong* 苗族研究論叢 (A collection of research articles on the Miao), ed. Hu Qiwang and Li Yangui 李廷貴, pp. 193–212. Guiyang: Guizhou renmin chubanshe, 1988.

Hua Li 華立. "Qingdai baojia zhidu jianlun" 清代保甲制度簡論 (A brief discussion of the Qing *baojia* system). In *Qingshi yanjiu ji* (Anthology of studies in Qing history), ed. Zhongguo renmin daxue, Qingshi yanjiusuo 中國人民大學清史研究所, pp. 87–121. Beijing: Guangming ribao chubanshe, 1988.

Huang Jianhua 黃建華. "Qing zhi Minguo shiqi Xinjiang Weiwuerzu zhasake zhi yanjiu" 清至民國時期新疆維吾爾族札薩克制研究 (A study of the *jasak* system among the Uighurs of Xinjiang from the Qing to Republican periods). *Xibei minzu yanjiu* 1 (1992): 149–57.

Huang Liuhung 黃六鴻. *Fuhui quanshu* 福惠全書 (A complete book concerning happiness and benevolence). Trans. Djang Chu. 1694. Reprinted—Tucson: Arizona University Press, 1984.

(*Qinding*) *Huijiang zeli* 欽定回疆則例 (Imperially commissioned collection of the substatutes of the Muslim frontier). 1842. Reprinted as (*Qinding*) *Menggu lüli, Huijiang zeli* 欽定蒙古律例回疆則例 (Collection of the substatutes of Mongolia and the Muslim frontier). Ed. Zhongguo bianjiang shi di yanjiu zhongxin 中國邊疆史地研究中心. Beijing: Quanguo tushuguan wenxian suowei fuzhi zhongxin, 1988.

Huijiang zhi 回疆志 (Gazetteer of the Muslim frontier). 1772. Reprinted—Taipei: Chengwen chubanshe, 1968.

Impey, Elijah. *A Report on the Cultivation, Preparation and Adulteration of Malwa Opium and Appendix.* Bombay: Opium Department, 1848.

Inoue Hiromasa 井上裕正. "Shindai Kakei Dōkō ki no ahen mondai ni tsuite" 清代嘉慶道光期のアヘン問題について (The opium problem during the Jiaqing and Daoguang periods). *Tōyōshi kenkyū* 41, no. 1 (June 1982): 58–83.

———. "Wu Lanxiu and Society in Guangzhou on the Eve of the Opium War." *Modern China* 12, no. 1 (Jan. 1986): 104–14.

Inspectorate General of Chinese Customs. *Opium.* Shanghai: Inspectorate General of Customs, Statistical Department, 1881.

Jiaqing chongxiu yitong zhi 嘉慶重修一統志 (Jiaqing revision of the *Comprehensive Gazeteer of the Qing*). Comp. Mujangga 穆彰阿 et al. 35 vols. 1842. Reprinted—Beijing: Zhonghua shuju, 1986.

Jin Yijiu 金宜久, ed. *Yisilanjiao shi* 伊斯蘭教史 (A history of Islam). Hebei: Zhongguo shehui kexue chubanshe, 1992.

[U.S.] Justice Department. Drug Enforcement Administration. Intelligence Division. *Opium Poppy Cultivation and Heroin Processing in Southeast Asia.* Washington, D.C., 1993.

Kangxi chao Hanwen zhupi zouzhe huibian 康熙朝漢文朱批奏摺匯編 (Combined [Beijing and Taibei] edition of the Kangxi court's Chinese-language vermilion rescripts). Zhongguo diyi lishi dang'anguan 中國第一歷史檔案館, ed. Beijing: Dang'an chubanshe, 1984.

Khokhlov, A. N. "The Kyakhta Trade and Its Effects on Russian and Chinese Policy in the 18th and 19th Centuries." In *Chapters from the History of Russo-Chinese Relations, 17th–19th Centuries,* ed. S. L. Tikhvinsky, pp. 66–105. Trans. Vic Schneierson. Moscow: Progress Publishers, 1985.

Kuang Haolin 況浩林 and Yang Liqiong 楊麗瓊. "Jindai woguo shaoshu minzu diqu de yapian duhai wenti" 近代我國少數民族地區的鴉片

毒害問題 (The opium scourge in China's ethnic minority areas during the modern period). *Zhongguo jingji shi yanjiu* 4 (1986): 131–42.

Kuhn, Philip A. *Soulstealers, The Chinese Sorcery Scare of 1768.* Cambridge, Mass.: Harvard University Press, 1990.

Kuropatkin, A. N. *Kashgaria, Eastern or Chinese Turkestan: Historical and Geographical Sketch of the Country, Its Military Strength, Industries and Trade.* Trans. Walter E. Gowan. Calcutta: Thacker, Spink and Co., 1882.

Lai Yongbao 賴永寶. "Qing Qian, Jia, Dao san chao zhili Huijiang xisicheng zhi yanjiu" 清乾嘉道三朝治理回疆西四城之研究 (A study of the administration of the Muslim frontier's four western towns during the Qianlong, Jiaqing, and Daoguang reigns). Master's thesis, Zhengzhi University, 1981.

Lal, Mohan. *Travels in the Panjab, Afghanistan and Turkistan, to Balk Bokhara, and Herat; and A Visit to Great Britain and Germany.* 1846. Reprinted—Patiala: Punjab, Language Department, 1971.

Lapidus, Ira M. *A History of Islamic Societies.* Cambridge, Eng.: Cambridge University Press, 1990.

Lee, James Z. "Food Supply and Population Growth in Southwest China, 1250–1850." *Journal of Asian Studies* 41, no. 4 (Aug: 1982): 711–46.

———. "Homicide et peine capitale en Chine à la fin de l'empire: analyse statistique préliminaire des données" (Homicide and capital punishment in late imperial China: a preliminary statistical analysis of the data). *Études chinoises* 10, no. 1–2 (Spring–Autumn, 1991): 113–33.

———. "Law and Ethnicity in Late Imperial Southwest China: A Code, a Case, and Their Connotations." Paper presented at conference on Ethnicity, Politics, and Cross-Border Cultures in Southwest China: Past and Present, Lund University, Center for East and Southeast Asian Studies, Lund, Sweden, May 25–28, 2000.

———. *The Political Economy of a Frontier, Southwest China, 1250–1850.* Cambridge, Mass.: Harvard University Press, forthcoming.

Legrand, Jacques. *L'Administration dans la domination sino-mandchoue en Mongolie Qalq-a: Version mongole du "Lifan Yuan Zeli"* (Administration in the Sino-Manchu dominion of Khalka Mongolia; the Mongol version of the *Lifan yuan zeli*). 2 vols. Paris: Collège de France, Institut des hautes études chinoises, 1976.

Li Gui 李圭. *Yapian shilüe* 鴉片事略 (Overview of opium). In *Biji xiaoshuo daguan* 筆記小説大觀 (Collectanea of miscellaneous writings and novels), series 10, vol. 9. 1895. Reprinted—Taibei: Xinxing shuju, 1975.

Li, Lillian M., and Alison Dray-Novey. "Guarding Beijing's Food Security in the Qing Dynasty: State, Market, and Police." *Journal of Asian Studies* 58, no. 4 (Nov. 1999): 992–1032.

Li Longchang 李隆昌. "Lüetan Guizhou de yanhuo" 略談貴州的煙禍 (A brief discussion of Guizhou's drug disaster). *Guizhou wenshi congkan* 2 (1983): 21–26.

Li Pengnian 李鵬年, Liu Ziyang 劉子揚, and Chen Qiangyi 陳鏘儀, eds. *Qingdai liubu chengyu cidian* 清代六部成語辭典 (A dictionary of the administrative terminology of the Six Boards of the Qing dynasty). 1842 ed. Reprinted—Tianjin: Tianjin renmin chubanshe, 1990.

Li Sanmou 李三謀. "Yapian zai Shanxi de weihai" 鴉片在山西的危害 (The opium scourge in Shanxi). *Puyang xuebao* 6 (1990): 24–26.

Li Shizhen 李時珍. *Bencao gangmu* 本草綱目 (Compendium of *materia medica*). 1596. Reprinted—4 vols. Beijing: Renmin weisheng chubanshe, 1975.

Li Shuyuan 李書源. "Guanyu 'qinding yanjin yapianyan tiaoli' de pingjia wenti" 關於欽定嚴禁鴉片煙條例的評價問題 (Problems concerning the evaluation of the imperial regulations on the strict prohibition of opium). *Shixue yuebao* 5 (1985): 119–20.

Li Xingyuan 李星沅. *Li Xingyuan riji* 李星沅日記 (The diary of Li Xingyuan). Ed. Yuan Yingguang 袁應光 and Tong Hao 童浩. 2 vols. Beijing: Zhonghua shuju, 1987.

Li Yongqing 酈永慶. "Youguan jinyan yundong de jidian xin renshi" 有關煙運動的幾點新認識 (A few points of new understanding concerning the opium prohibition movement). *Lishi dang'an* 3 (1986): 79–86.

Liang Tingnan 梁廷楠. *Yifen wenji* 夷氛聞記 (An account of the barbarian invasion). 1874. Reprinted—Beijing: Zhonghua shuju, 1997.

Lin Dunkui 林敦奎 and Kong Xiangji 孔祥吉. "Yapien zhanzheng qianqi tongzhi jieji neibu douzheng tanxi" 鴉片戰爭前期統治階級內部斗爭探析 (Analytical inquiry into the struggle within the ruling class during the early stages of the Opium War). *Jindai shi yanjiu* 3 (1986): 1–19.

Lin En-hsien 林恩顯. *Qingchao zai Xinjiang de Han-Hui geli zhengce* 清朝在新疆的漢回隔離政策 (The Qing dynasty's Han-Hui segregation policy in Xinjiang). Taibei: Taiwan shangwu yinshuguan, 1988.

———. "Qingdai Xinjiang huanfang bingzhi zhi yanjiu" 清代新疆換防兵制之研究 (Research on the garrison rotation system in Qing Xinjiang). *Bianzheng yanjiusuo nianbao* 8 (1977): 159–213.

Lin Man-houng 林滿紅. "Qingmo shehui liuxing xishi yapian yanjiu: gongjimian zhi fenxi, 1773–1906" 清末社會流行吸食鴉片研究: 供給面之分析 (A study of the spread of opium smoking in late Qing society: a supply-side analysis, 1773–1906). Ph.D. diss., Taiwan Normal University, 1985.

———. "Yin yu yapian de liutong ji yin gui qian jian xianxiang de quyu fenbu (1808–1854); shijie jingji dui jindai Zhongguo kongjian fangmian zhi i yingxiang" 銀與鴉片的流通及銀貴錢賤現象的區域分布 (1808–1854): 世界經濟對近代中國空間方面之一影響 (A case study of the spatial impact of the world economy on China; the circulation of silver and opium and the regional distribution of the silver appreciation phenomenon, 1808–54). *Zhongyang yanjiuyuan, Jindaishi yanjiusuo jikan* 22, no. 1 (June 1993): 89–135.

Lin Shourong 林壽榮 and Long Dai 龍岱. "Sichuan junfa yu yapianyan" 四川軍閥與鴉片煙(Sichuan warlords and opium). *Sichuan daxue xuebao* 3 (1984): 101–6.

Lin Yongkuang 林永匡 and Wang Xi 王熹. *Qingdai xibei minzu maoyi shi* 清代西北民族貿易史 (Foreign trade with northwestern ethnic groups during the Qing dynasty). Beijing: Zhongyang minzu xueyuan chubanshe, 1991.

Lin Youneng 林有能. "Guanyu chijin pai de jige wenti" 關於弛禁派的幾個問題 (Several questions concerning the lax prohibition clique). *Lishi jiaoxue wenti* 4 (1987): 20–21, 30–31.

Lindesmith, Alfred R. *Addiction and Opiates*. Chicago: Aldine, 1968.

Liu Bin 劉彬. "Lun quan Dian xingshi" 論全滇形勢 (On the overall situation in Yunnan). In *Qing jingshi wenbian* 清經世文編 (Collected writings on statecraft from the Qing dynasty), ed. He Changling 賀長齡, 3:2150a–51b. 1887 ed. Reprinted—Beijing: Zhonghua shuju, 1992.

———. "Yongchang *tusi* lun" 永昌土司論 (On the native chieftainships of Yongchang [prefecture]). In *Qing jingshi wenbian* 清經世文編 (Collected writings on statecraft from the Qing dynasty), ed. He Changling 賀長齡, 3:2131b–33b. 1887 ed. Reprinted—Beijing: Zhonghua Shuju, 1992.

Liu, Cheng-yun. "Kuo-lu: A Sworn Brotherhood Organization in Szechuan." *Late Imperial China* 6, no. 1 (June 1985): 56–77.

Liu Fengyun 劉風雲. *Qingdai Sanfan yanjiu* 清代三藩研究 (A study of the Three Feudatories of the Qing dynasty). Beijing: Zhongguo renmin daxue chubanshe, 1994.

Liu, Kwang-Ching and Richard J. Smith. "The Military Challenge: The North-West and the Coast." In *The Cambridge History of China*, vol. 11, *Late Ch'ing, 1800–1911, Part 2*, ed. John K. Fairbank, pp. 202–73. Cambridge, Eng.: Cambridge University Press, 1980.

Liu Xiusheng 劉秀生. "Qingdai guonei shangye jiaotong kaolüe" 清代國內商業交通考略 (Overview of domestic commercial communications routes in the Qing dynasty). *Qingshi luncong* (1992): 1–20.

Lombard-Salman, Claudine. *Un Exemple d'acculturation chinoise: la province du Gui Zhou au XVIIIᵉ siècle* (An example of Chinese acculturation: Guizhou province in the eighteenth century). Paris: École française d'Extrême-Orient, 1972.

Lu Ren 陸韌. *Yunnan duiwai jiaotong shi* 雲南對外交通史 (History of Yunnan's extra-provincial overland communications). Yunnan minzu chubanshe, 1997.

Luo Raodian 羅繞典. *Qiannan zhifang jilüe* 黔南職方紀略 (Summary of the main administrative aspects of Guizhou). 1847. Reprinted—Guiyang: Guizhou renmin chubanshe, 1992.

Luo Yunzhi 羅運治. "Qingdai Xinjiang kalun de tantao" 清代新疆卡倫的探討 (Examination of checkpoints in Qing Xinjiang). *Zhongguo lishi xuehui shixue jikan* 18 (1986): 187-217.

Ma Dazheng 馬大正 and Cai Jiayi 蔡家藝. "Zhungaer guizu dui Nanjiang de tongzhi" 准噶爾貴族對南疆的統治 (The rule of the Zunghar nobility in southern Xinjiang). In *Zhungaer shilun wenji* 准噶爾史論文集 (Anthology of articles on Zunghar history), 2:290-301. Beijing: Zhongguo shehuikexueyuan minzu yanjiusuo, 1981.

Ma Mozhen 馬模貞, ed. *Zhongguo jindu shi ziliao* 中國禁毒史資料 (Historical materials on drug prohibition in China). Tianjin: Tianjin renmin chubanshe, 1998.

Ma Ruheng 馬汝珩 and Ma Dazheng 馬大正, eds. *Qingdai de bianjiang zhengce* 清代的邊疆政策 (Qing dynasty border policy). Beijing: Zhongguo shehui kexue chubanshe, 1994.

Ma Weiping 馬衛平. "Qing Daoguang 1838 nian jinyan yuanyin bianxi" 清道光 1838 年禁煙原因辨析 (Critical analysis of the reasons for the Daoguang emperor's 1838 opium prohibition). *Zhongshan daxue yanjiusheng xuekan* 1 (1990): 75-80.

Madancy, Joyce A. "Poppies, Patriotism, and the Public Sphere, Nationalism and State Leadership in the Anti-Opium Crusade in Fujian, 1906-1916." In *Opium Regimes, China, Britain and Japan, 1839-1952*, ed. Timothy Brook and Bob Tadashi Wakabayashi, pp. 228-47. Berkeley: University of California Press, 2000.

———. *The Troublesome Legacy of Commissioner Lin: The Opium Trade and Opium Suppression in Fujian Province, 1820s to 1920s*. Cambridge, Mass.: Harvard University Asia Center, 2003.

Maher, John T. *Opium and Its Derivatives: A Lecture*. A special report prepared at the request of the U.S. Department of Justice Drug Enforcement Administration National Training Institute. September 1976.

Mao Haijian 矛海建. *Tianchao de bengkui* 天朝的崩潰 (The collapse of the celestial dynasty). Beijing: Shenghuo, Dushu, Xizhi sanlian shudian, 1995.

Marshall, P. J. *Bengal: The British Bridgehead, Eastern India, 1740-1828*. Cambridge, Eng.: Cambridge University Press, 1987.

————. *Problems of Empire: Britain and India, 1757–1813*. London: George Allen Unwin, 1968.

Merlin, Mark David. *On the Trail of the Ancient Opium Poppy*. Toronto: Associated University Presses, 1984.

Mi Zhenbo 米鎮波. "Lun Yapian zhanzheng qianhou Shahuang zhengfu zai Qiaketu diqu jinzhi yapien zousi de zhengci" 論鴉片戰爭前後沙皇政府在恰克圖地區禁止鴉片走私的政策 (On the Czarist Russian government's policy of prohibition of opium smuggling in the Kiakhtia region before and after the Opium War). *Nankai xuebao* 1 (1996): 47–50.

Miao Pusheng 苗普生. *Boke zhidu* 伯克制度 (The *beg* system). Urumqi: Xinjiang renmin chubanshe, 1995.

————. "Qingdai Weiwuerzu renkou kaoshu" 清代維吾爾族人口考述 (Inquiry into the Qing dynasty's Uighur population). *Xinjiang shehui kexue* 1 (1989): 70–80.

Michie, Alexander. *An Englishman in China during the Victorian Era: as Illustrated in the Career of Sir Rutherford Alcock . . . Many Years Consul and Minister in China and Japan*. Edinburgh, 1900.

Milligan, Barry. *Pleasures and Pains: Opium and the Orient in 19th-Century British Culture*. Charlottesville: University Press of Virginia, 1995.

Millward, James. *Beyond the Pass: Commerce, Ethnicity and the Qing Empire in Xinjiang, 1759–1864*. Stanford: Stanford University Press, 1998.

Mintz, Sidney W. *Sweetness and Power: The Place of Sugar in Modern History*. New York: Viking Penguin, 1985.

Montgomerie, T. G. "Report of the Mirza's Exploration of the Route from Caubul to Kashgar." *Proceedings of the Royal Geographical Society of London* 15, no. 3 (1870–71): 181–204.

Moorcroft, William, and George Trebeck. *Travels in the Himalayan Provinces of Hindustan and the Panjab; in Ladakh and Kashmir; in Peshawar, Kabul, Kunduz and Bokhara from 1819 to 1825*. 2 vols. London: John Murray, 1841. Reprinted—New Delhi: Asian Educational Services, 1989.

Morse, Hosea Ballou. *The Chronicles of the East India Company Trading to China 1635–1834*. 5 vols. Oxford: Clarendon Press, 1926–29.

————. *The International Relations of the Chinese Empire: The Period of Conflict, 1834–1860*. New York: Longmans, Green and Co., 1910.

Mou Anshi 年安世. *Yapian zhanzheng* 鴉片戰爭 (The Opium War). Shanghai: Shanghai renmin chubanshe, 1982.

Mui, Hoh-cheung, and Lorna H. Mui. *The Management of a Monopoly: A Study of the English East India Company's Conduct of Its Tea Trade, 1784–1833*. Vancouver: University of British Colombia Press, 1984.

Naquin, Susan. *Millenarian Rebellion in China: The Eight Trigrams Uprising of 1813*. New Haven: Yale University Press, 1976.

Naquin, Susan, and Evelyn S. Rawski. *Chinese Society in the Eighteenth Century*. New Haven: Yale University Press, 1987.

Newman, R. K. "Opium Smoking in Late Imperial China: A Reconsideration." *Modern Asian Studies* 29, no. 4 (1995): 765–94.

Niu Pinghan 牛平漢. *Qingdai zhengqu yange zongbiao* 清代政區沿革綜表 (Summary tables of changes in Qing administrative regions). Beijing: Zhongguo ditu chubanshe, 1990.

Nutt, David J. "Neuropharmacological Basis for Tolerance and Dependence." In *Drug Addiction and Its Treatment, Nexus of Neuroscience and Behavior*, ed. Bankole A. Johnson and John D. Roache, pp. 171–86. Philadelphia: Lippincott-Raven, 1997.

Owen, David Edward. *British Opium Policy in China and India*. New Haven: Yale University Press, 1934. Reprinted—Hamden, Conn.: Archon Books, 1968.

Pan Zhiping 潘志平. *Zhongya Haohanguo yu Qingdai Xinjiang* 中亞浩罕國與清代新疆 (The Central Asian khanate of Kokand and Qing dynasty Xinjiang). Beijing: Zhongguo shehui kexue chubanshe, 1991.

Park, Nancy E. "Corruption in Eighteenth-Century China." *Journal of Asian Studies* 56, no. 4 (Nov. 1997): 967–1005.

Peng Songyu 彭崧毓. *Yu zhou ji tan* 漁舟記談 (Conversations recorded from a fishing boat). 1862. Reprinted—Taibei: Dahua yinshuguan, n.d.

Peskova, G. N. "The Opium Trade in China and Russia's Position." In *Chapters from the History of Russo-Chinese Relations, 17th–19th Centuries*, ed. S. L. Tikhvinsky; trans. Vic Schneierson, pp. 274–300. Moscow: Progress Publishers, 1985.

Philips, C. H. *The East India Company, 1784–1834*. Manchester: Manchester University Press, 1961.

(*Qinding*) *Pingding Zhungaer fanglüe* 欽定平定準噶爾方略 (Imperially commissioned campaign history of the pacification of the Zunghars). 1772. Reprinted—4 vols. Quanguo tushuguan wenxian suowei fuzhi zhongxin, 1990.

Polachek, James. *The Inner Opium War*. Cambridge, Mass.: Harvard University, Council on East Asian Studies, 1992.

Pomeranz, Kenneth. *The Great Divergence: China, Europe and the Making of the Modern World Economy*. Princeton: Princeton University Press, 2000.

Prakash, Om. *European Commercial Enterprise in Pre-Colonial India*. Cambridge, Eng.: Cambridge University Press, 1998.

———. "Opium Monopoly in India and Indonesia in the Eighteenth Century." *Indian Economic and Social History Review* 24, no. 1 (1987): 63–80.

Qin Baoqi 秦寶琦. *Qing qianqi Tiandi hui yanjiu* 清前期天地會研究 (Studies on the Heaven and Earth Society of the early Qing). Beijing: Zhongguo renmin daxue chubanshe, 1988.

Qin Heping 秦和平. "Qingdai Daoguang nianjian Yunnan de jinyan wenti ji jinyan shibai zhengjie de fenxi" 清代道光年間雲南的禁煙問題及禁煙失敗癥結的分析 (The opium problem in Yunnan during the Daoguang period and an analysis of the crux of the failure of the opium prohibitions). *Zhongguo bianjian shidi yanjiu* 4 (1996): 57–63.

———. *Yunnan yapian wenti yu jinyan yundong* 雲南鴉片問題與禁煙運動 (Yunnan's opium problem and prohibition movement). Chengdu: Sichuan minzu chubanshe, 1998.

Qingchao wenxian tongkao 清朝文獻通考 (Encyclopedic collation of the institutions of the Qing). 2 vols. 1936. Reprinted—Taibei: Shangwu yinshuguan, 1987.

Qingchao xu wenxian tongkao 清朝續文獻通考 (Supplement to *Qingchao wenxian tongkao*). 1921. Reprinted—4 vols. Taibei: Shangwu yinshuguan, 1987.

Qingdai Neige daku sanyi Manwen dang'an xuanbian 清代內閣大庫散佚滿文檔案選編 (An edited selection of Manchu archival documents scattered throughout the main holdings of the Qing Grand Secretariat). Liaoning minzu guji lishi lei, vols. 11 and 12. Ed. and trans. Liaoning shehui kexue yuan, Lishi yanjiu suo 遼寧科學院歷史研究所 et al. Tianjin: Tianjin guji chubanshe, 1991.

Qingdai waijiao shiliao 清代外交史料 (Historical materials related to Qing foreign relations). Ed. Guoli Gugong bowuyuan 國立故宮博物院. Taibei: Guoli Gugong bowuyuan, 1932.

Qing jingshi wenbian 清經世文編 (Collected writings on statecraft from the Qing dynasty). Ed. He Changling 賀長齡. 1887 ed. Reprinted—3 vols. Beijing: Zhonghua Shuju, 1992.

Qingshi liezhuan 清史列傳 (Official biographies [prepared] for *Qingshi*). 20 vols. 1928. Reprinted—Beijing: Zhonghua Shuju, 1987.

Rawski, Evelyn S. "Presidential Address. Reenvisioning the Qing: The Significance of the Qing Period in Chinese History." *Journal of Asian Studies* 55, no. 4 (Nov. 1996): 829–50.

Ray, Rajat Kanta. "Indian Society and the Establishment of British Supremacy, 1765–1818." In *The Oxford History of the British Empire*, vol. 2, *The Eighteenth Century*, ed. P. J. Marshall, pp. 508–29. Oxford: Oxford University Press, 1998.

Reed, Bradley W. *Talons and Teeth: County Clerks and Runners in the Qing Dynasty*. Stanford: Stanford University Press, 2000.

Richards, J. F. "The Indian Empire and Peasant Production of Opium in the Nineteenth Century." *Modern Asian Studies* 15, no. 1 (1981): 59–82.

Rowe, William T. *Saving the World: Chen Hongmou and Elite Conscious-ness in Eighteenth-Century China.* Stanford: Stanford University Press, 2001.

Rush, James R. *Opium to Java: Revenue Farming and Chinese Enterprise in Colonial Indonesia, 1860–1910.* Ithaca: Cornell University Press, 1990.

Saguchi, Toru. "The Eastern Trade of the Khoqand Khanate." *Memoirs of the Research Department of the Tōyō Bunko* 24 (1965): 47–114.

Scarborough, John. "The Opium Poppy in Hellenistic and Roman Medicine." In *Drugs and Narcotics in History*, ed. Roy Porter and Mikulá Teich, pp. 4–23. Cambridge, Eng.: Cambridge University Press, 1995.

Shammas, Carole. "Changes in English and Anglo-American Consumption from 1550 to 1800." In *Consumption and the World of Goods*, ed. John Brewer and Roy Porter, pp. 1220–25. London: Routledge, 1993.

———. "The Revolutionary Impact of European Demand for Tropical Goods." In *The Early Modern Atlantic Economy: Essays on Trans-Atlantic Enterprise*, ed. John J. McCusken and Kenneth Morgan, pp. 163–85. Cambridge, Eng.: Cambridge University Press, 2000.

Sharma, Dewan Chand. *Kashmir Under the Sikhs.* Delhi: Seema Publications, 1983.

Shen Jiarong 沈嘉榮. "Taiping tianguo de jin yapian jinjiu he jin zaigeng niu" 太平天國的禁鴉片禁酒和禁宰耕牛 (The Taiping prohibition of opium, alchohol, and plow oxen). *Lishi zhishi* 1 (1983): 21–22.

Shepherd, John Robert. *Statecraft and Political Economy on the Taiwan Frontier, 1600–1800.* Stanford: Stanford University Press, 1993.

Shih, Vincent C. Y. *The Taiping Ideology, Its Sources, Interpretations and Influences.* Seattle: University of Washington Press, 1967.

Shunning fu zhi 順寧府志 (Gazetteer of Shunning prefecture). 2 vols. Comp. Zhu Zhanke 朱占科 et al. 1904. Reprinted—Taibei: Chengwen chubanshe, 1968.

Skinner, G. William. "Introduction: Urban Development in Imperial China." In *The City in Late Imperial China*, ed. idem, pp. 3–31. Stanford: Stanford University Press, 1977.

Slack, Edward J., Jr. *Opium State and Society.* Honolulu: University of Hawai'i Press, 2001.

Smith, Kent Clarke. "Ch'ing Policy and the Development of Southwest China: Aspects of Ortai's Governor-Generalship, 1726–1731." Ph.D. diss., Yale University, 1971.

Smith, Paul J. *Taxing Heaven's Storehouse: Horses, Bureaucrats and the Destruction of the Sichuan Tea Industry, 1074–1224.* Cambridge, Mass.: Harvard University, Council on East Asian Studies, 1991.

Spence, Jonathan. "Opium Smoking in Ch'ing China." In *Conflict and Control in Late Imperial China*, ed. Frederic Wakeman, Jr., and Carolyn Grant, pp. 143–73. Berkeley: University of California Press, 1975.

Spuler, Bernard. "Central Asia from the Sixteenth Century to the Russian Conquests." In *The Cambridge History of Islam*, vol. 1A, *The Central Islamic Lands from Pre-Islamic Times to the First World War*, ed. P. M. Holt, Ann K. S. Lambton, and Bernard Lewis, pp. 468–94. Cambridge, Eng.: Cambridge University Press, 1970.

Su Zhiliang 蘇智良. *Zhongguo dupin shi* 中國毒品史 (A history of drugs in China). Shanghai: Shanghai renmin chubanshe, 1997.

Taiwan fu zhi 臺灣府志 (Gazetteer of Taiwan prefecture). Comp. Fan Xian 范咸 et al. 1747. Reprinted in *Taiwan fu zhi sanzhong* 臺灣府志三種 (Three gazetteers from Taiwan prefecture), ed. Jiang Yuying 蔣毓英 et al. Beijing: Zhonghua shuju, 1985.

Tan Chung. "The British-China-India Trade Triangle (1771–1840)." *Indian Economic and Social History Review* 21, no. 4 (Dec. 1974): 411–31. Reprinted in idem, *Triton and Dragon* (q.v.), pp. 22–44.

———. *China and the Brave New World*. Durham, N.C.: Carolina Academic Press, 1978.

———. *Triton and Dragon: Studies on Nineteenth-Century China and Imperialism*. Delhi: Gian Publishing House, 1986.

Tan Cui 檀萃. *Dian hai yu heng zhi* 滇海虞衡志 (Annals of the groundskeeper of Kunming Lake). Late 18th c. Reprinted—Taibei: Huawen shuju, 1969.

Tan Qixiang 譚其驤, ed. *Zhongguo lishi ditu ji* 中國歷史地圖集 (The historical atlas of China), vol. 8, *Qing shiqi* (The Qing period) 清時期. Beijing: Ditu chubanshe, 1987.

Tian Rukang 田汝康 and Li Huaxing 李華興. "Jinyan yundong de sixiang qianqu: pingjia xin faxian de Zhu Zun Xu Qiu zouzhe" 禁煙運動的思想前驅: 評價新發現的朱嶟許球奏折 (Intellectual precursors of the opium prohibition movement: an evaluation of the newly discovered memorials of Zhu Zun and Xu Qiu). *Fudan xuebao* 1 (1978): 99–107.

Trocki, Carl A. *Opium, Empire and the Global Political Economy: A Study of the Asian Opium Trade, 1750–1950*. London: Routledge, 1999.

Van Dyke, Paul. "Port Canton and the Pearl River Delta, 1690–1845." Ph.D. diss., University of Southern California, 2001.

Veniukof, M. "The Beolors and Their Country." Trans. J. Michell. *Journal of the Royal Geographical Society of London* 36 (1866): 265–79.

Viraphol, Sarasin. *Tribute and Profit: Sino-Siamese Trade, 1652–1853*. Cambridge, Mass.: Harvard University, East Asian Research Center, 1977.

von Glahn, Richard. *Fountain of Fortune: Money and Policy in China, 1000–1700*. Berkeley: University of California Press, 1996.

Wakeman, Frederick, Jr. "The Canton Trade and the Opium War." In *The Cambridge History of China*, vol. 10, *Late Ch'ing, 1800–1911, Part 1*, ed. John K. Fairbank, pp. 163–212. Cambridge, Eng.: Cambridge University Press, 1978.

———. *Strangers at the Gate: Social Disorder in South China, 1839–1861*. Berkeley: University of California Press, 1966.

Waley-Cohen, Joanna. *Exile in Mid-Qing China: Banishment to Xinjiang, 1758–1820*. New Haven: Yale University Press, 1991.

Wang Gesheng 王革生. "Qingdai Dongbei zhong yingsu zhi yapian shulun" 清代東北種罌粟制鴉片述論 (Overview of poppy cultivation and opium production in the northeast during the Qing dynasty). *Beifang wenwu* 43, no. 3 (1995): 124–28.

Wang Hongbin 王宏斌. *Jindu shijian* 禁毒史鑒 (A history of drug prohibition). Beijing: Yuelu shushe, 1997.

Wang Licheng 王立誠. "Yapian zhanzheng qianxi de jinyan juece pingxi" 鴉片戰爭前夕的禁煙決策評析 (An evaluation and analysis of prohibition policy on the eve of the Opium War). *Lanzhou daxue xuebao* 18, no. 4 (1990): 9–15.

Wang, Yeh-chien. "Evolution of the Chinese Monetary System, 1644–1850." In *Modern Chinese Economic History*, ed. Chi-ming Hou and Tzong-shian Yu, pp. 425–56. Academia Sinica, Taibei: Institute of Economics, 1979.

———. *Land Taxation in Imperial China, 1750–1911*. Cambridge, Mass.: Harvard University, East Asian Research Center, 1973.

———. "Secular Trends of Rice Prices in the Yangzi River Delta, 1683–1935." In *Chinese History in Economic Perspective*, ed. Thomas G. Rawski and Lillian M. Li, pp. 35–68. Berkeley: University of California Press, 1992.

Wang Zhichun 王之春. *Qingchao rouyuan ji* 清朝柔遠記 (A record of the Qing's succoring those from afar). 1879. Reprinted—Beijing: Zhonghua Shuju, 1989.

Watt, George. *A Dictionary of the Economic Products of India*, vol. 6, pt. I. Calcutta, 1892.

Waung, W. S. K. "Introduction of Opium Cultivation to China." *Xianggang Zhongwen daxue xuebao* 5, no. 1 (1979): 209–21.

Wei Hsiu-mei 魏秀梅, comp. *Qing ji zhiguan biao* 清季職官表 (Offices and personnel of the late Qing period). 2 vols. Taipei: Zhongyang yanjiuyuan, Jindaishi yanjiusuo, 1977.

Wen Zhuntian 聞鈞天. *Zhongguo baojia zhidu* 中國保甲制度 (China's baojia system). Shanghai, Shangwu yinshuguan, 1935.

Will, Pierre-Etienne, and R. Bin Wong. *Nourish the People: Civilian Grana-ries and Food Redistribution in Qing China, 1650–1850*. Ann Arbor: University of Michigan Press, 1991.

Wilson, E. H. *A Naturalist in Western China*. 2 vols. London: Methuen & Co., 1913. Reprinted—2 vols. in 1. London: Cadogan Books, 1986.

Winichakul, Thongchai. *Siam Mapped: A History of the Geo-body of a Nation*. Honolulu: University of Hawaii Press, 1994.

Winther, Paul. *Anglo-European Science and the Rhetoric of Empire: Malaria, Opium, and British Rule in India*. Lanham, Md.: Lexington Books, 2003.

Wong, J. Y. *Deadly Dreams: Opium, Imperialism and the Arrow War (1856–1860)*. Cambridge, Eng.: Cambridge University Press, 1998.

Wong, R. Bin. *China Transformed: Historical Change and the Limits of European Experience*. Ithaca, N.Y.: Cornell University Press, 1997.

———. "Opium and Modern Chinese State-Making." In *Opium Regimes: China, Britain and Japan, 1839–1952*. Ed. Timothy Brook and Bob Tadashi Wakabayashi, pp. 189–211. Berkeley: University of California Press, 2000.

Woodside, Alexander Barton. *Vietnam and the Chinese Model: A Comparative Study of the Nguyễn and Ch'ing Civil Government in the First Half of the Nineteenth Century*. Cambridge, Mass.: Harvard University Press, 1971.

Wright, H. R. C. "James Augustus Grant and the Gorakhpur Opium, 1789–1796." *Journal of the Royal Asiatic Society*, April 1960, 1–16.

Wu Kangling 吳康零. *Sichuan tongshi* 四川通史 (A complete history of Sichuan), vol. 6. Chengdu: Sichuan daxue chubanshe, 1994.

Wu Xiaogao 伍效高. "Zhengshou yapian teshui de neimu" 征收鴉片特稅的內幕 (The real story behind the special opium tax levy). *Guizhou wenshi ziliao xuanji* 15 (1984): 169–75.

Wu Yixiong 吳義雄. "Guanyu 1838 nian jinyan zhenglun de zai tantao" 關於一八三八年禁煙爭論的再探討 (A re-examination of the prohibition debate of 1838). *Fujian luntai* 6 (1985): 59–64.

Xiao Zhizhi 蕭致治. "Lun 1838–1840 nian de fan yapian douzheng" 論 1838–1840 年的反鴉片斗爭 (The anti-opium struggle, 1838–40). *Wuhan daxue xuebao* 3 (1990): 60–66.

———. *Yapian zhanzheng yu Lin Zexu yanjiu beilan* 鴉片戰爭與林澤徐研究備覽 (A comprehensive reference to research concerning the Opium War and Lin Zexu). Wuhan: Hubei renmin chubanshe, 1995.

Xiao Zhizhi 蕭致治 and Yang Weidong 楊衛東, eds. *Yapian zhanzheng qian Zhong-Xi guanxi jishi* (1517–1840) 鴉片戰爭前中西關系紀事(1517–1840) (Annals of Sino-Western relations before the Opium War, 1517–1840). Wuhan: Hubei renmin chubanshe, 1986.

Xie Jin 謝晉. *Yapian zhanzheng* 鴉片戰爭 (The Opium War). Film, 150 minutes. Chengdu: Emei Film Studio, 1997.

Xinjiang shehuikexueyuan. Lishi yanjiusuo 新疆社會科學院歷史研究所, ed. *Xinjiang jianshi* 新疆簡史 (A concise history of Xinjiang). 3 vols. Urumqi: Xinjiang renmin chubanshe, 1980.

Xinjiang tuzhi 新疆圖志 (Illustrated gazetteer of Xinjiang). 6 vols. Comp. Wang Shunan 王樹枏 et al. 1911. Reprinted—Taibei: Wenhai, 1965.

Xinjiang Weiwuer zizhiqu. Jiaoyu weiyuanhui. Gaojiao lishi jiaocai bianxie zu 新疆維吾爾自治區教育委員會高教歷史教材編寫組, ed. *Xinjiang difang shi* 新疆地方史 (A local history of Xinjiang). Urumqi: Xinjiang daxue chubanshe, 1992.

Xinjiang zhi gao 新疆志稿 (Xinjiang draft gazetteer). 1930. Reprinted—Taibei: Taiwan xuesheng shuju, 1967.

Xu Haiquan 許海泉. "Huang Juezi yu jinyan yundong" 黃爵滋與禁煙運動 (Huang Juezi and the opium prohibition movement). *Jiangxi shifandaxue xuebao* 3 (1990): 40–43.

Xu Jiagan 徐家干. *Miaojiang wen jian lu* 苗疆聞見錄 (A record of things seen and heard in the Miao territory). Ed. Wu Yiwen. 1878. Reprinted—Guiyang: Guizhou renmin chubanshe, 1997.

Xu Ke 徐珂. *Qingbai leichao* 清稗類鈔 (Notes on the Qing compiled by category). 13 vols. 1928. Reprinted—Beijing: Zhonghua shuju, 1996.

Xu Xifa 續西發. "Xinjiang jindu wenti yanjiu" 新疆禁毒問題研究 (A study of the drug prohibition problem in Xinjiang). *Xinjiang daxue xuebao, zhexue shehui kexue ban* 25, no. 2 (1997): 13–16.

Xu Yunnan tongzhi gao 續雲南通志稿 (Draft of the continuation of the gazetteer of Yunnan province). Comp. Wang Wehshou 王文韶 et al. 1900. Reprinted—Taibei: Wenhai chubanshe, 1966.

Yan Deyi 嚴德一. "Pu-Si yanbian:—Yunnan xin ding kenzhi qu" 普思沿邊雲南新定墾殖區 (The Pusi border region: a newly developed area in Yunnan). *Dili xuebao* 6 (1939): 27–40.

Yan Zhongping 嚴中平. *Zhongguo jindai jingji shi tongji ziliao xuanji* 中國近代經濟史統計資料選輯 (Anthology of statistical materials on Chinese modern economic history). Beijing: Kexue chubanshe, 1955.

Yang Kaida 楊開達. "Guanyu 'She jin yapianyan bei'" 關於誓禁鴉片碑 (Concerning the "Stele of the Pledge to Prohibit Opium"). *Yunnan shifandaxue zhexue shehuikexue xuebao* 26, no. 4 (Aug. 1994): 25–26.

Yang Kaiyu 揚開宇. "Jindai Guizhou de yapian liudu" 近代貴州的鴉片流毒 (The venemous course of opium in Guizhou during the Republican period). *Guiyang shiyuan xuebao, sheke ban* 1 (1984): 34–40.

Yang Kaiyu 揚開宇 and Liao Weiyi 廖惟一. *Guizhou zibenzhuyi de chansheng yu fazhan* 貴州資本主義的產生與發展 (The emergence and development of capitalism in Guizhou). Guiyang: Guizhou renmin chu-banshe, 1982.

Yang Xingmao 揚興茂. "Yapian ru Gan ji qi liudu shi shi jilüe" 鴉片入甘及其流毒史實記略 (An outline of opium's entry into Gansu and the historical facts about its venomous course). *Lanzhou xuekan* 4 (1994): 45–48.

Yao Weiyuan 姚薇元. *Yapian zhanzheng shishi kao* 鴉片戰爭史實考 (Verification of historical facts related to the Opium War). 1942. Re-printed—Beijing: Renmin chubanshe, 1984.

Yapian zhanzheng 鴉片戰爭 (The Opium War). 6 vols. Ed. Qi Sihe 齊思和, Lin Shuhui 林樹惠, and Shou Jiyu 壽紀瑜. Shanghai: Shenzhou guoguang she, 1954.

Yongbei fu zhi 永北府志 (Gazetteer of Yongbei prefecture). 2 vols. Comp. Chen Qidian 陳奇典 et. al. 1765. Reprinted—Haikou: Hainan chuban-she, 2001.

Yongchang fu wenzheng 永昌府文徵 (Anthology of writings on Yong-chang prefecture). Comp. Li Genyuan 李根源. Kunming: Teng chong Li shi, 1941.

Yongchang fu zhi 永昌府志 (Gazetteer of Yongchang prefecture). Comp. Liu Yuke 劉毓珂 et al. 1885. Reprinted—Taibei: Chengwen chubanshe, 1967.

Yongzheng chao Hanwen zhupi zouzhe huibian 雍正朝漢文朱批奏摺匯編 (A compilation of the Yongzheng court's vermilion rescripts). Ed. Zhongguo diyi lishi dang'anguan 中國弟一歷史檔案館. Nanjing: Nan-jing guji shudian, 1989–91.

You Zhong 尤中. *Yunnan minzu shi* 雲南民族史 (An ethnic history of Yunnan). Kunming: Yunnan daxue chubanshe, 1994.

———. *Zhongguo xi'nan minzu shi* 中國西南民族史 (A history of China's southwestern ethnic groups). Kunming: Yunnan renmin chubanshe, 1985.

Yu Ende 于恩德. *Zhongguo jinyan faling bianqian shi* 中國禁煙法令變遷史 (A history of changes in China's opium prohibition laws). 1934. Reprinted—Taibei: Wenhai chubanshe, 1973.

Yule, Henry. *A Narrative of the Mission to the Court of Ava in 1855.* 1885. Reprinted—Kuala Lumpur: Oxford University Press, 1968.

Yule, Henry, and A. C. Burnell. *Hobson-Jobson.* 1886. Reprinted—Calcutta: Rupa Press, 1986.

Yunnan tong zhi 雲南通志 (Gazetteer of Yunnan province). Comp. Ortai et al. 1736.

Zelin, Madeline. *The Magistrate's Tael: Rationalizing Fiscal Reforn in Eigh-teenth-Century Ch'ing China.* Berkeley: University of California Press, 1984.

Zeng Wenwu 曾問吾. *Zhongguo jingying xiyu shi* 中國經營西域史 (A history of China's management of its western regions). Shanghai: Shangwu yinshuguan, 1936. Reprinted in Minzu congshu, diyi bian 民族叢書第一編 (Republican period collectanea, first series), no. 81. Shanghai: Shanghai shudian, 1989.

Zhang Pengyuan 張朋園. "Luohou diqu de ziben xingcheng:—Yun Gui de xiexiang yu yapian" 落後地區的資本形成:—雲貴的協餉與鴉片 (Capital formation in an underdeveloped region:—assistance loans and opium in Yunnan and Guizhou). *Guizhou wenshi congkan* 1 (1990): 50-74.

Zhang Weihua 張維華 and Sun Xi 孫西. *Qing qianqi Zhong-E guanxi* 清前期中俄關繫 (Sino-Russian relations in the early Qing period). Ji'nan: Shandong jiaoyu chubanshe, 1997.

Zhang Zuoxi 張左系. "Shae dui Zhongguo de yapian maoyi" 沙俄對中國的鴉片貿易 (Czarist Russia's opium trade in China). *Xuexi yu tansuo* 4 (1979): 140-46.

Zhao Juntong 趙鈞彤. *Xi xing riji* 西行日記 (Diary of a journey west). 1783. Reprinted—Beijing: Zhongyang minzu xueyuan tushuguan, 1983.

Zhao Yuntian 趙雲田. *Qingdai zhili bianchui de shuniu: Lifan yuan* 清代治理邊陲的樞紐: 理藩院 (Axis of Qing frontier rule: the Court of Territorial Affairs). Urumqi: Xinjiang renmin chubanshe, 1995.

Zheng, Yangwen. "The Social Life of Opium in China, 1483-1999." *Modern Asian Studies* 37, no. 1 (2003): 1-39.

Zhongguo diyi lishi dang'an guan 中國弟一歷史檔案館 et al., eds. *Qingdai qianqi Miaomin qiyi dang'an shiliao* 清代前期苗民起義檔案史料 (Archival materials related to the Miao uprisings of the early Qing period). 3 vols. Beijing: Guangming ribao, 1987.

Zhongguo shehuikexueyuan, Jindaishi yanjiusuo 中國社會科學院近代史研究所. *Shae qin Hua shi* 沙俄侵華史 (A history of Czarist Russian aggression against China), vol. 3. Beijing: Renmin chubanshe, 1981.

Zhou Yongming. *Anti-Drug Crusades in Twentieth-Century China: Nationalism, History and State-building*. Lanham, Md.: Rowman & Littlefield, 1999.

Zhu Jinfu 朱金甫. "Yapian zhanzheng qian Daoguang chao yanguan de jinyan lun" 鴉片戰爭前道光朝言官的禁煙論 (The pre-Opium War debate on prohibition among the censors at the Daoguang court). *Jindaishi yanjiu* 2 (1991): 57-66.

Zou Lihong 鄒禮洪. "Jindai Xinjiang jin yapian shulun" 近代新疆禁鴉片述論 (Overview of opium prohibition in Xinjiang during the modern period). *Xinjiang shifandaxue xuebao* 2 (1986): 37-43.

———. "Zuo Zongtang xibei jin yapian shulun" 左宗棠西北禁鴉片述論 (Overview of Zuo Zongtang's opium prohibition in the northwest). *Xinjiang shifandaxue xuebao* 2 (1990): 29-31.

Index

addiction, 30–32, 149–52 *passim*, 157–61, 164–65, 204–5, 304. *See also* codeine; morphine

addictive consumables, 16–26 *passim*, 39, 142, 152–53, 174, 302. *See also* strategic commodities

afurong 阿芙蓉, 125, 142–43, 194, 248–49, 245, 267, 282; in southwest China, 222, 253–55, 260–61, 270, 275–76, 285. *See also xiaotu*

Ai-long-a (n.d.) 愛隆阿, 172*n*

Akbar (r. 1556–1606), 299

akhund 阿渾 (Ch. *a-hun*), 83*n*

Aksu, 195, 196, 201, 209, 210, 212

alcohol, 25*n*, 144*n*, 145–46, 152

Altishahr, 76, 82–86 *passim*, 88, 195*n*

amban 大臣 (Ch. *dachen*), 65

anchashi 按察使, 181, 231*n*

Andijan, 87, 181, 209

Anglo-Maratha War, 56

Anhua district 安化縣, 242

Anhui, 122–23, 140, 174, 195

Annan district 安南縣, 234, 242

Anping district 安平縣, 232, 240

Anshun prefecture 安順府, 104*n*, 232, 240, 255, 256, 264, 274, 275*n*

Ava, 252

Awadh (Oudh), 48–54 *passim*

Badakshan, *see under* merchants, South and Inner Asian; Muslims

Ba district 巴縣, 224

banshi dachen 辦事大臣, 80

Bao Shichen (1774–1855) 包世臣, 9*n*, 132, 168, 249, 263

baojia 保甲, 68–75 *passim*, 83–84, 102–3; and opium, 111–12, 127–28, 145, 184, 187, 226, 229*n*

Baoning district 寶寧縣, 253, 258

Baoshan district 保山縣, 238, 258

baoshe 保社, 70

Bao-xing (1777–1848) 寶興, 235, 244, 245, 247

baozi 包子, *see* opium, varieties of

Barchuk, 196, 201

Barkul, *see* Zhenxi zhili ting

Barluk, 196

Bazhai subprefecture 八寨廳, 232, 240

begs 伯克 (Ch. *bo-ke*), 64, 80–85 *passim*, 90, 179, 187–88, 190, 197, 210, 216; Hakim beg, 189, 208, 209, 211, 215

Beijing, 8, 10, 158, 175*n*, 291*n*; opium offenses in, 119*n*, 120–22, 126, 130, 138, 140, 156*n*, 262, 310–12

Beilu 北路, 76–82 *passim*, 191; opium in, 185–87, 188*n*, 195, 196, 200, 203, 299

Bengal, 23, 45, 47. *See also* opium, varieties of

bian 邊, 105, 107

bian Miao 變苗, 104*n*

biantong 變通, 183

bianwai 邊外, 105

Bihar, 49

Bijie 畢節, 99, 232, 240, 255

Bokhara, 88, 199

Bolor, 200

Bombay, 38, 45, 52*n*, 56, 62, 301

British India, *see* East India Company

bu 部, 80

buben 部本, xxi

bubonic plague, 262

Bu-yan-tai 布彥泰 (1791–1880), 145–46, 277

Burma, *see* Myanmar

Calcutta, 10, 36, 38, 45

Canton system, *see* Guangzhou system

canzan dachen 參贊大臣, 80

Cao Liuxing (n.d.) 曹六興, 249

Cao Xuemin (1718–87) 曹學閔, 119

Ceheng department 冊亨州, 234, 242

Chaghadai Khanate, 81, 85

Chang, Hsin-pao, 10, 58*n*, 134*n*

Chang-qing (d. 1856) 長清, 182–83, 193

Changzhai subprefecture 長寨廳, 241

Chaozhou 潮州, 128

Chen Hongmou (1696–1771) 陳弘謀, 145

Chen Lihe (1761–1825) 陳履和, 155–56

Chen Shen (1641–1722) 陳詵, 97

Chen Xi (n.d.) 陳熺, 244

Cheng Hanzhang (1762–1832) 程含章, 132, 133

Chengde prefecture 承德府, 128*n*, 217

Chengdu prefecture 成都府, 236, 259

Cheng-ge (n.d.) 成格, 182*n*

Chenggong district 呈貢縣, 258

Chengjiang prefecture 澂江府, 250*n*

chengshi fuhao 城市富豪, 158

Chiang Kai-shek, 296

chijin pai 弛禁派, 10

Chongqing prefecture 重慶府, 99, 236, 259, 275

Chung, Tan, 12, 48*n*

Chuxiong district 楚雄縣, 238, 258

Chuxiong prefecture 楚雄府, 238, 250*n*, 256, 258

coca, 19, 20

codeine, 26, 28

Cohen, Paul, 13

consumption, 6, 17–18, 28–29, 49, 54, 63, 143, 299; of medicinal opium, 11–12, 26–27, 30, 138*n*, 142, 158, 272–73. *See also* madak; opuim; prohibition

conversion operations, *see gaitu guiliu*

copper, *see under* Qing dynasty, monetary system

cotton, 25, 35–39 *passim*, 48, 62, 100, 206, 267, 279, 291

Dading prefecture 大定府, 99, 232, 240, 255–56, 259, 264*n*, 265, 274

Daizu 傣族, 2, 6, 97*n*, 106–7, 263, 266, 267, 271

Dali prefecture 大理府, 238, 244–45, 250*n*, 252, 256, 258, 267, 273, 280

Daman, 55

Danjiang subprefecture 丹江廳, 240

Danshui district 淡水縣, *see* Taiwan

Daoguang emperor, 134*n*, 158, 165, 175*n*, 226

Datang village 大塘, 241

Davis, John Francis, 35

Dayao district 大姚縣, 258

deng 燈, 152

Deng Tingzhen (1775–1846) 鄧廷楨, 131, 308

Dengchuan department 鄧川州, 238

dibao 地保, 73, 229*n*

difang guan 地方官, 268

Dihua department 迪化州, *see* Urumqi

Dingfan department 定番州, 233, 241, 255

Dongchuan prefecture 東川府, 99, 107, 250*n*, 252, 254

Donglu 東路, 76, 79, 80, 89, 191; opium in, 193, 195, 200, 201, 203, 205

Du Yanshi (n.d.) 杜彥士, 245, 247

Dujiang subprefecture 都江廳, 232, 240

Dushan department 獨山州, 232, 240

dutong 都統, 80

Dutch, *see under* merchants, Euro-American

Duyun district 都勻縣, 232, 240

Duyun prefecture 都勻府, 232, 240

East India Company, 4, 15, 17, 23, 25, 42–48, 62, 119, 302–3; trade with China, 18, 33–38, 308. *See also* India

East Turkestanis, 76–77, 79–88 *passim*, 191; and opium, 186–89, 196, 215, 264, 291*n*, 299. *See also* Muslims

Eight Trigrams Uprising (1813), 73

E-le-jin-tai (n.d.) 額勒金泰, 185*n*

Elliot, Charles, 173*n*

Elliott, Mark, 13

En-te-heng-e (?–1842) 恩特亨額, 181–82, 186–88, 199, 200, 211–12, 225, 298

E-shan (1770–1838) 鄂山, 251

ethno-geographic diversity, 2–8 *passim*, 13*n*, 14, 20–21, 67, 286, 289–90

Fang Bao (1668–1749) 方苞, 144, 145, 146

Farooqui, Amar, 52

fen 分, xvii

Feng Shaopeng (n.d.) 馮紹彭, 260

Feng Zanxun (fl. 1820) 馮贊勛, 130

Fengtian 奉天, 140, 141, 218

Fletcher, Joseph, 88

free traders, *see under* merchants, Euro-American

Fujian, 64*n*, 116–21 *passim*, 124–30 *passim*, 143, 146, 149, 155–56, 203, 204

Fujian yapian 福建雅片, 119

Fumin district 富民縣, 258

furong, see afurong

Fu-xing-a (n.d.) 富興阿, 211

Fuzhou prefecture 福州府, 120

gaitu guiliu 改土歸流, 91, 95–98 *passim*, 107–10 *passim*

Gansu, 79, 190, 193–94, 196, 253*n*, 291, 295*n*, 296

gao 膏, 150

Gao Zhenwan (n.d.) 高振宛, 169

Gengma native chieftainship 耿馬
土司, 106, 238, 267–70, 301

gengmi 粳米, 123

gentry, 70n, 89–90, 144–45, 158

gezi 格子, *see* opium, varieties of

Gialong emperor (r. 1802–20),
138

Giersch, C. Pat, 104–5

ginseng, 217

Goa, 55

gong 公, 155

gonghang 公行, 34n

Gorakhpur, 50

Grant, James Augustus, 50–51, 53

Great Britain, 17n, 61, 198n, 199–
200, 295. *See also* triangular
trade

Greenburg, Michael, 12–13, 42n

Guangdong, 9, 99, 118–19, 125, 130–
32, 155–56; opium offenses in,
116–17, 120–22, 128, 135–38, 140–
41, 163, 170, 174, 179n; and the
penal exile system, 201–5 *passim*. *See also* Guangzhou;
Guangzhou system

Guangnan prefecture 廣南府, 238,
250n, 256, 258, 281

Guangshun department 廣順州,
233, 241

Guangxi, 99, 128, 152, 174, 231, 250–
51, 260–61, 276, 301

Guangxi department 廣西州, 238,
258

Guangxi prefecture 廣西府, 250n,
256

Guangzhou, 10, 25, 40, 89n, 112,
171, 308. *See also* Guangdong;
Guangzhou system

Guangzhou system, 34–35, 43

Gucheng 古城, 196

Guiding district 貴定縣, 233, 241

Guihua subprefecture 歸化廳, 232,
240

Guiliyang (Gui-liang; 1785–1862)
桂良, 246, 247, 253

Guiyang prefecture 貴陽府, 99,
232, 241, 255, 257, 259, 275n

Guizhou, 91, 96n, 100, 103; opium
in, 174, 251–52, 301; poppies in,
176, 227, 254–56, 260–61, 264–65,
268, 272–79 *passim*, 300n. *See
also* Statistics; *and subprovincial
place-names*

Guizhu district 貴筑縣, 232, 241,
255, 257, 259, 260, 279

Guo Baiyin (d. 1884) 郭伯蔭, 146,
231, 276–80 *passim*, 290, 293

Guo Songtao (1818–91) 郭嵩燾,
296, 304

Guolu 啯嚕, 109, 237, 244

guo yin 過癮, *see* addiction

Guzhou subprefecture 古州廳, 233,
241, 251

hafurong 哈芙蓉, see *afurong*

haiguan jiandu 海關監督, 117, 194

Haitan 海壇, 120

Hakim beg, see under *begs*

Hami, 76, 79n, 90n, 184n, 190n,
191n

Han Sipei (fl. 1824) 罕思沛, 268,
269

Hankou 漢口, 99

Hanmin bian Miao 漢民變苗, 104

Hanzhong prefecture 漢中府, 253

Haoqing department 鶴慶州, 238

Hart, Sir Robert, 135n

Hastings, Warren, 44n, 47

he 和, 155

He Changling (1785–1848) 賀長齡,
235n, 247, 273, 278–79, 290

Heilong jiang, 218

Henan, 146, 190, 262

hezhuang 合椿, 70*n*

Holkar, 57, 61

hong, see yanghang

Hsiao, Kung-ch'uan, 74*n*

huan jue 緩決, 139*n*

Huang Juezi (1793–1853) 黃爵滋, 133, 136, 137, 169, 247

Huang Lezhi (n.d.) 黃樂之, 172, 175*n*

Huang Zhongmo (fl. 1809) 黃中模, 170

Huangping department 黃平州, 234, 242

Huanyang district 緩陽縣, 234, 243

hubao ganjie 互保甘結, 72, 127, 188

Hubei, 99, 120, 251, 301

Huguang, 140

Hūda-i da (Ch. 呼岱達), 199, 208, 212, 213, 216, 220

Hui-feng (d. 1851) 惠豐, 180–83, 189, 193, 207

Hui-ji (d. 1845) 惠吉, 184–85, 196, 200

Huijiang 回疆, 191–92

Huili zhou (district) 會理州, 246–47, 254

Huizu 回族, *see* Muslims

Hunan, 96, 99, 120*n*

huolian cheng gao 火煉成膏, 151

Hu-song-e (d. 1847) 瑚松額, 193

ideology, 10, 153–54, 161–66. *See also gong; he*

Ili, 77, 79, 80, 191; opium in, 182, 187, 203–4, 210, 211*n*, 220, 299*n*

Ili jiangjun 伊梨將軍, 80

Ilibu (Yi-li-bu; d. 1843) 伊里布, 231, 246, 251, 256–57, 267–68, 269

India, 47, 197–99, 298, 299. *See also* East India Company; merchants, South and Inner Asian

indigo, 25, 48

indirect rule, 7, 47, 59, 62, 76, 82–83, 84. *See also* residency systems

Inoue Hiromasa, 8, 132

Jahangir Jihad (1820–28), 82*n*, 83*n*, 84–85

Japan, 41, 44*n*

Jardine, William, 37, 42, 44*n*

jasak 札薩克, 64, 76, 79, 82

Java, 149, 273*n*

Jiang Youxian (1766–1830) 蔣攸銛, 307

Jiangsu, 9, 121, 136*n*, 155–56

Jiangxi, 99, 140–41, 174

Jianshui district 建水縣, 238

Jiaqing emperor, 70, 71, 72, 158, 210*n*

Jiexiu district 介休縣, *see under* Shanxi

jing 境, 105, 107

Jingdong subprefecture 景東廳, 238, 250*n*, 252, 263, 281

Jilin, 218

Ji-qing (d. 1802) 吉慶, 308

junzi 君子, 166

junxian (system) 郡縣, 7, 64–70 *passim*, 79, 111, 113, 128; in southwest China, 91, 95, 100, 102, 105–9 *passim*

Kai department 開州, 232, 241

Kaihua district 開化縣, 281

Kaihua prefecture 開化府, 238, 250*n*, 258

Kaitai district 開泰縣, 233, 241

Kangxi emperor, 97, 144

Kanjut, 200

Karashahr, 178, 188, 189, 195, 196

Kashgar, 77, 209, 210, 211, 213, 299

Kashgaria, 76, 86

Kashmir, *see under* merchants, South and Inner Asian; Muslims

Kazakhs, 77, 88, 191, 207

kemin 客民, 265*n*

Khargalik, 84, 188, 215

Khobdo, 140, 184

Khoja 和卓 (Ch. Hezhuo), 81–86 *passim*

Khotan, 84, 210

Kiakhta, 199, 206

Kokand, 80*n*, 177, 198, 206–11, 213, 214, 220, 302. *See also* Andijan; merchants, South and Inner Asian

kuaixie 快蟹, 135

kuaizi 塊子, *see* opium, varieties of

Kuang Deng (n.d.) 況澄, 162, 164

Kucha, 184*n*, 195, 196

Kulu, 198

Kunming 昆明, 99

Kunming district 昆明縣, 258

Kunyang department 昆陽州, 258

Kur-Kara-Usu, 196

Kürla, 188–89

Langdai subprefecture 朗岱廳, 232, 240

Langqu native chieftainship 滾蕖土司, 238, 270

Lao Chongguang (1802–67) 勞崇光, 300

li 里, xvii

Li Hongbin (d. 1846) 李鴻賓, 130

Li Xingyuan (1797–1851) 李星沅, 246*n*, 252–53, 280

Liang Zhangju (1775–1849) 梁章鉅, 260

Libo district 荔波縣, 232, 241

Lifan yuan 理番院, 65

Lijiang district 麗江縣, 238

Lijiang prefecture 麗江府, 238, 250*n*

Lin, Man-houng, 14–15, 42*n*

Lin Qing (1791–1846) 麟慶, 254, 260–61

Lin Zexu (1785–1850) 林則徐, 89*n*, 135*n*, 136, 165, 173, 174*n*, 209, 212

Lin'an prefecture 臨安府, 238

lingdui dachen 領隊大臣, 185*n*

Lingnan 嶺南, 100, 260, 262

Liping prefecture 黎平府, 233, 241, 251

Liu Guangsan (n.d.) 劉光三, 126, 159, 164

London, 10, 36

Longchuan River 龍川江, 252

Longli district 龍里縣, 233, 241

Longquan district 龍泉縣, 242, 255

lu 路, 76. *See also individual marches by name*

Lu Kun (1772–1835) 盧坤, 131

Lu Yinbo (1760–1839) 盧陰薄, 126

Lu Yinggu (d. 1857) 陸應穀, 237, 252, 270, 281–82

Lufeng district 祿豐縣, 258

Luliang department 陸涼州, 258

Luohu department 羅斛州, 241

Luoping department 羅平州, 258

lupiao 路票, 188

Luquan district 祿勸縣, 258

Luzon, 143, 147

Macao, 39, 56, 121, 122, 149, 171

madak, 116–19 *passim*, 148–51, 155

Madras, 45, 48

Maha department 麻哈州, 232, 241

Malaya, 50

Malwa, 54. *See also* opium, varieties of

Manchuria, 7, 67, 79, 141, 143, 199, 216–19 *passim*, 289

Maolian native chieftainship 茂連
土司, 229, 265–66, 270

mashi 馬屎, *see* opium, varieties
of

Matheson, James, 42–43

Meize district 湄澤縣, 233, 241

Mengding native chieftainship
猛定土司, 271

Menghua subprefecture 蒙化廳,
239, 250*n*, 256, 258, 280, 281

Mengmeng native chieftainship
孟孟土司, 238, 270

Mengzi district 蒙自縣, 281

merchants, 6, 53, 218, 290, 301;
Euro-American, 18, 35–38, 42–
44, 55, 121, 173, 298; South and
Inner Asian, 53, 79, 86–90, 182,
187–88, 197–99, 298; Han maritime, 116, 138, 149, 155–56; Han
Xinjiang, 77, 79, 84, 185, 192,
196, 200–201; Han southwestern, 99–100, 110, 244–45, 256,
260–63, 267. *See also* Muslims,
as foreign traffickers; *yanghang*

Mianning subprefecture 緬寧廳,
238

Miaojiang 苗疆, 103–4

Miao uprising (1794–95), 96*n*

Miaozu 苗族, 6, 70*n*, 96*n*, 97, 98,
103*n*, 104, 108*n*, 263–65

Michie, Alexander, 12–13

Midian 米甸, 244

Ming dynasty, 91, 95, 96, 118, 142–
44, 148, 149, 287

Mingshan (Ming-shan; d. 1834)
明山, 225

Minh-mang emperor (r. 1820–41),
138, 165

Mintz, Sidney, 17, 18*n*

Min-Zhe 閩浙, 126

Mongolia, 64, 71, 77, 79, 81; and
opium, 137, 179, 181, 184, 196–99

passim, 216–18, 289. *See also*
Zunghar Mongols

morphine, 26, 28–31

Morse, H. B., 38, 42*n*, 134*n*, 307,
308, 310

mu 畝, xvii, 296

Muhammad Ali, khan (r. 1822–42),
210*n*, 213

Muslims, 70*n*, 126, 199, 200; in
southwestern China, 110, 264,
265, 281, 300; as foreign traffickers, 178, 181, 183, 205–16 *passim*.
See also East Turkestanis; merchants, South and Inner Asian

Myanmar, 99, 106, 252, 261

Na Zhenxing (n.d.) 那振興, 265–
66

Nandian native chieftainship 南甸
土司, 100–102

Nanlu 南路, 76, 77, 80, 83–85, 112,
182; opium in, 185–91, 196, 200,
201, 208, 211–13, 298, 300*n*

Nanning district 南寧縣, 258

nanyang yapian 南洋鴉片, 311

Naquin, Susan, 289

native chieftainships, 7, 64, 91, 95–
110 *passim*, 222; and opium, 228,
244, 246, 249, 264–71

native states, 47–50 *passim*, 57, 59,
60. *See also individual native
states by name*

neidi 內地, 105, 107, 180, 245, 267,
268

neidi zhi yi 內地之夷, 105

Newman, R. K., 31, 32, 135*n*

New Regulations, *see under* prohibition, important statutes concerning

Nguyễn dynasty (1802–1945),
138

Ningbo 寧波, 125, 172

Ningqiang zhou (district) 寧羌州, 253

Ningyuan prefecture 寧遠府, 237, 245, 254, 266

opium, 1, 8, 11–13, 32–33, 59, 60–63, 67, 109*n*, 113; market systems, 4–5, 16, 122–23, 126–27, 178, 205, 223, 248, 279, 303; varieties of, 28, 29, 38, 44, 48, 122*n*, 199*n*, 301; in Republican China, 109*n*, 196, 290*n*, 291*n*, 295–97, 300*n*; street value of, 122*n*, 123, 195, 244–45, 253, 275; legalization of, 131–35, 139, 160, 171–72, 293. *See also* addiction; addictive consumables; consumption; East India Company; merchants; poppy; prohibition; silver drain; statistics; strategic commodities; *and individual provinces by name*

Opium War (1839–42), 10, 13, 141, 165, 220

Ortai (E-er-tai; 1680–1745) 鄂爾泰, 91*n*, 95*n*, 96*n*, 97, 98, 107

Owen, David Edward, 12–13, 16, 42*n*, 44*n*, 61

pai 牌, 69, 70*n*

palong 爬龍, 135

Panthay Rebellion (1856–73), 110, 285

paozhi cheng gao 炮制成膏, 150

Papaver somniferum, see Poppy

Peng Songyu (fl. 1835) 膨崧毓, 74, 129, 279, 290

pengmin 棚民, 70

Peru, 20

Pingliang prefecture 平涼府, 194

Pingnan Sultanate, 110

Pingyi district 平彝縣, 238

Pingyuan department 平遠州, 232, 240

Pingyue department 平越直隸州, 233, 241

Pizhan 辟展, 79*n*

Polachek, James, 9, 42*n*, 134*n*

poppy, 18–19, 26–28, 74, 124–29, 167–70; cultivation of, 47, 123, 141, 175–76, 292–95, 310; in southwestern China, 222, 225–27, 237, 250–62 *passim*, 272–75 *passim*, 280, 296. *See under afurong*; East India Company; Guo Baiyin; Lu Yinggu; native chieftainships, and opium; prohibition; *xiaotu; and individual provinces and countries by name*

prohibition: comparisons of, 2–5 *passim*, 42, 48–49, 59–62, 67, 113, 179–80, 226–28, 302–3; important statutes concerning, 116–17, 120–21, 125–26, 136–38, 141, 161–62, 183; amnesty, 137, 172–73, 188, 208–9, 211, 235–36; sustainable and absolute forms of, 146–47, 153, 164–65, 174, 178, 205, 216, 219, 284, 292–93. *See also* poppy; *qiangtu*; statistics; *and individual provinces by name*

Puan district 普安縣, 234, 242, 254, 255, 257

Puan subprefecture 普安廳, 241, 255, 274

Puding district 普定縣, 232, 240, 255

Puer prefecture 普洱府, 252

Puning department 普寧州, 258

Qi Gong (n.d.) 祁慎, 131, 134

Qi Junzao (1793–1866) 祁寯藻, 169, 311

Qian Jie (1760–1812) 錢楷, 120, 152, 159

qiangtu 羌土, 190–97 *passim*, 200–201, 219

Qianlong emperor, 70, 83*n*, 144

Qianxi department 黔西州, 232, 240, 255

Qin dynasty, 162

Qin Heping, 11*n*, 152*n*, 231*n*, 281*n*, 282*n*, 296*n*

Qing-bao (n.d.) 慶保, 224*n*

Qing dynasty (1644–1911), 13–14, 171, 191, 201–3, 264, 283–86 *passim*, 301–2; expansionism, 7, 65, 80–81, 112, 289; foreign relations of, 5, 8, 85–89, 206, 213–14, 216, 220; monetary system of, 98, 99, 100, 195*n*, 287–88; military garrisons, 65, 77, 85, 216–17, 237, 254, 294*n*. *See also junxian* (system); prohibition

Qinghai, 77

Qingjiang subprefecture 清江廳, 243

Qingping district 清平縣, 240

Qingzhen district 清鎮縣, 232, 240, 255

Quanzhou prefecture 泉州府, 124, 149

Qujing prefecture 曲靖府, 238, 256, 258

Rawski, Evelyn S., 289

residency systems, 45–46, 48, 65, 80. *See also* indirect rule

Renhuai subprefecture 仁懷廳, 233, 241, 259, 274

Rong Jixiang, *see* merchants, South and Inner Asian

Ruan Yuan (1764–1849) 阮元, 132, 226, 228, 251, 254

Russia, 178, 181, 198–99, 206–8, 220, 298–99

salt, 20*n*, 100, 287

Sarikol, 88

Semipalitinsk, 199, 207

Shaanxi, 141, 146; and inter-provincial trafficking, 190*n*, 193–94, 196, 252–53, 262; poppy in, 295*n*, 296

Shandong, 218

Shanghai, 99, 301

shangmin 商民, 200

Shanxi, 5, 122, 140–41, 146, 155, 156*n*, 190–94 *passim*, 218

Shao Zhenghu (n.d.) 邵正笏, 125, 128, 251, 253

Shaoxing 紹興, 125

Shaybanid Khanate (1500–1599), 85

Shen Peng (n.d.) 沈鵬, 168

Shen Qixian (?–1839) 申啓賢, 161–62, 164

sheng Miao 生苗, *see* Miaozu

Shenhu guan 神護關, 271

shi 石, xvii

Shibing district 施秉縣, 156*n*, 234, 243

Shiping department 石屏州, 238

Shiqian prefecture 石阡府, 233, 242, 255

Shisan hang 十三行, 34*n*

Shizong district 師宗縣, 238, 258

Shuicheng subprefecture 水城廳, 240

shuiyu 水棪, 119

shu Miao 熟苗, *see* Miaozu

Shunning prefecture 順寧府, 105, 109, 238, 250*n*, 256, 258, 264, 267–71 *passim*

Shunqing prefecture 順慶府, 238, 245

Siam, 138

Sichuan, 91*n*, 99–100; and Yunnan border traffic, 109, 237, 244–47, 252, 256, 262, 264–67; opium in, 122, 147, 162, 193, 220, 227, 251, 259, 300; poppy in, 224, 254–55. *See also* statistics; *and sub-provincial place-names*

Sikh empire, 198

silver drain, 40–42, 115, 129–33 *passim*, 292. *See also* Qing dynasty, monetary system

Sinan prefecture 思南府, 233, 242, 274

Sind, 52, 57, 59

Sindia, 48, 57, 61

Sizhou prefecture 思州府, 242

Skinner, G. William, 288

smuggling, *see* merchants

Song Yun (1754–1835) 松筠, 147

Songming department 嵩明州, 258

Song-pu (d. 1846) 嵩溥, 227, 251

Songtao subprefecture 松桃廳, 104, 233, 242

Southeast Asia, 17, 28*n*, 45

Spring Purification Circle, 9, 133

statistics, 38, 124, 135–36, 156*n*, 173, 179; from Xinjiang and north-west China, 194, 209, 211, 253*n*; from southwest China, 228–29, 231, 235–37, 256–60, 269–70, 275. *See also* Opium, street value; Tables 1–10

Staunton, Sir George, 25

strategic commodities, 19, 20, 23–24, 26, 57–58, 62, 145; impact on Qing provincial revenue, 280–81, 285, 289–300 *passim*. *See also* addictive consumables; East India Company

Su Mingliang (n.d.) 蘇明良, 116, 153*n*, 157, 311

Su Yanyu (n.d.) 蘇延玉, 246*n*, 253

sugar, 17, 18, 23, 25, 36, 175*n*

sui 歲, 163, 267

Sun Erzhun (1770–1832) 孫爾準, 126, 127

Sun Jiagan (1683–1753) 孫嘉淦, 146*n*

Suzhou 蘇州, 9

Taigong subprefecture 台拱廳, 234, 243

Taihe district 太和縣, 238

Taiping Rebellion, 142

Taipu si 太僕寺, 119

Taiwan, 64*n*, 68, 116, 117, 149, 151, 166–67, 290

Tai-yong (n.d.) 台湧, 280

Taiyu district 太谷縣, *see* Shanxi

Taizhou prefecture 台州府, 75, 125–26, 167–70, 176

Tan Cui (1725–1801) 檀萃, 249

Tanka (*Dan ren*) 蛋人, 279

Tao Shu (1779–1839) 陶澍, 311–12

Tarbagatai, 79*n*, 80, 185, 191, 195, 196, 200, 207, 208, 210

Tashkent, 207, 212

tea, 12, 17–18, 19, 23–26, 33–38 *passim*

Tengyue subprefecture 騰越廳, 100, 102, 238

Three Feudatories, 98–99, 288

Tiandi hui 天地會, 203

Tianjin, 156*n*, 192, 193, 218

Tianshan 天山, 76

Tiantai district 天台縣, *see* Taizhou

Tianzhu district 天柱縣, 243

Tibet, 216–18, 289

Tixing anchashi si 提刑按察使司, 231*n*

tobacco, 17, 18, 19, 23, 25, 57, 143–47, 153. *See also* madak

tongben 通本, *xxi*

Tongren district 銅仁縣, 233, 242
Tongren prefecture 銅仁府, 233, 242, 251, 274
tongyou 桐油, 212*n*
Tongzi district 桐梓縣, 242
Treaty of Nanjing, 139
triangular trade, 12–13, 35–37
Trocki, Carl A., 16–19, 44*n*
Tuan-duo-bu (n.d.) 湍多布, 197, 207, 208
tubian 土弁, 95*n*
tuguan tusi zhidu 土官土司制度, 95*n*
Tui-yi-bo-te 推依博特, 200
tujia zu 土家族, 96*n*
tuman 土蠻, 96*n*
Tumingga (Tu-ming-a; d. 1847) 圖明阿, 186, 213
tumu 土目, 265*n*
Turfan, 76, 79*n*, 185*n*, 191, 201, 210
tusi 土司, *see* native chieftainships

Uighurs, *see* East Turkestanis
Uliassutai, *see* Mongolia
Urumqi, 77, 79*n*, 182*n*, 184, 185, 191, 195–96, 200, 201, 203*n*, 210
Ush, 195, 196

Vietnam, 99, 138–39, 250, 251, 261, 263

waidi 外地, 105, 106, 107
waidi zhi yi 外地之夷, 106
Wakhan, 200
Wandian native chieftainship 灣甸土司, 238, 270
Wang Hongbin, 150*n*, 308
Wang Zhichun, 307–8
Watt, George, 59–60, 61
Waung, W. S. K., 14, 15, 194*n*, 248*n*
Wei Guangdao (n.d.) 魏光燾, 299*n*
wei junzi 偽君子, 166

Weining department 威寧州, 240, 255, 265
weizhi 違制, 157
Wellesley, Lord, 56
Weng'an district 甕安縣, 233, 241
Wenshan district 文山縣, 238, 258
Wenzhou prefecture 溫州府, *see* Taizhou prefecture
West River, 99
White, Richard, 105
White Lotus rebellions, 71
Winther, Paul, 27, 28*n*, 31, 55*n*
Wong, J. Y., 13, 42*n*, 52*n*
Wu Lanxiu (1789–1837) 吳蘭修, 171–72
Wuchuan district 婺川縣, 233, 242
Wuding department 武定州, 238, 246, 252–58 *passim*, 264, 265, 281
Wu-er-tai-e (d. 1842) 烏爾泰額, 168
Wuhan, 301

Xiajiang subprefecture 下江廳, 233, 241
Xiamen 廈門, 116, 119, 149, 249, 311
Xianfeng emperor, 141
xiangyue 鄉約, 73, 229*n*
xiaotu 小土, 276–77
Xingyi district 興義縣, 234, 242, 255
Xingyi prefecture 興義府, 234, 242, 254–57, 264*n*, 274
Xinjiang, 5–6, 79, 80–85, 177–78, 180, 291, 294*n*; poppy in, 128*n*, 188–89, 218, 224–31, 299; penal exiles in, 203–5. *See also* merchants, South and Inner Asian, Han Xinjiang; *qiangtu*; Statistics; *and subterritorial place-names*
xishi 吸食, 200
Xiuwen district 修文縣, 241, 255

Xu Naiji (fl. 1809) 許乃濟, 131, 134n, 147, 160, 171, 278

Xu Shijie (n.d.) 許士杰, 273

Xu Qiu (fl. 1831) 許球, 133, 134n

Xuehai tang 學海堂, 131, 132

Xundian department 尋甸州, 258

xunsi 巡司, 244n

xuntai yushi 巡台御史, 151

Yakub Beg, 291

yan 煙, *see* tobacco; madak

Yan Botao (d. 1855) 顏伯燾, 231, 244, 245, 246, 270

yanbian zhi yi 沿邊之夷, 106

yancao 煙草, *see* tobacco

Yang Yuchun (1761–1837) 楊遇春, 193

Yang Zhengwen, 11–12

yanghang 洋行, 33n, 37, 43, 135, 308, 310

yangyan 洋煙, *see* tobacco

Yangzi River, 99

yanjin pai 嚴禁派, 10

yansi 煙絲, *see* tobacco

Yao Weiyuan, 309

yaokou 窯口, 135

yapian 鴉片, *see* opium

yapian guan 鴉片館, 117

yapian gui 鴉片鬼, 249

yapian tun 鴉片囤, 135

yapian yan 鴉片煙, *see* madak

yapian yancao 鴉片煙草, 275n

Yarkand, 80, 84, 88; and opium, 185, 188, 195, 196, 200, 201, 210–12, 213, 298

ye 野, *see under* Yunnan, wild zones

yeren 野人, 106

yeren jie 野人界, 271

yeyi 野夷, 101

yidi 夷地, 245, 267, 270

Yidong dao 迤東道, 250n

yifang 夷方, 101

Yiliang district 宜良縣, 258

yin 癮, *see* addiction

Yin Peifen (n.d.) 尹佩棻, 225, 250

yinhuang 銀荒, *see* silver drain

Yinjiang district 印江縣, 242

yinyan 飲煙, 152

Yi-shan (d. 1878) 奕山, 185–87, 200, 204, 205

Yixi dao 迤西道, 250n

Yizu 彝族, 2, 6, 91n, 98, 100–101, 263–66

Yongbei subprefecture 永北廳, 105, 238, 250n, 252, 258, 270

Yongchang prefecture 永昌府, 105, 109, 238, 244–52 *passim*, 256, 258, 261, 270–71, 280

Yongli emperor, 96

Yongning department 永寧州, 240

Yongzheng emperor, 70, 144, 311

Yu Ende, 307–8

Yu Jiao (n.d.) 俞蛟, 151

Yuan dynasty, 95n, 99n

Yuan Wenxiang (n.d.) 袁文祥, 229, 260, 274

Yuan Yulin (n.d.) 袁玉麟, 133, 134n

Yuanmo district 元謀縣, 238, 264, 281

Yubing district 玉屏縣, 233, 242

Yun department, 云州, 238, 258

Yunnan, 220, 221, 280, 282, 294n, 300–301; wild zones, 91, 95, 106–8, 110, 111, 112, 223, 297. *See also afurong*; merchants, poppy, Han southwestern; native chieftainships, and opium; Sichuan, Yunnan border traffic; silver drain; statistics; *and subprovincial place-names*

Yunnan district 雲南縣, 258, 267

Yunnan prefecture 雲南府, 238, 256, 258, 267, 280

Yu-tai (1788–1851) 裕泰, 227, 230, 278

Yuqing district 余慶縣, 233, 241

Zelin, Madeline, 287n, 288n

Zhang Bingde (fl. 1820) 張秉德, 190–92

Zhangzhou 漳州, 118, 149

Zhanxi district 盞西縣, 100

Zhanyi department 沾益州, 239, 258

Zhao department 趙州, 238, 258, 273, 281

Zhaotong prefecture 昭通府, 91n, 99, 107, 238, 250n, 252, 280

Zhejiang, 75, 119n, 124, 128, 130, 152, 155–56

Zhenfeng department 貞豐州, 234, 242

Zheng'an department 正安州, 234, 242

zhengjiao 政教, 104

Zhenkang native chieftainship 鎮康土司, 238, 270

Zhennan department 鎮南州, 258

Zhenning department 鎮寧州, 232, 240

Zhenxi zhili ting 鎮西直隸廳, 79n

Zhenyuan district 鎮遠縣, 234, 243

Zhenyuan prefecture 鎮遠府, 234, 242, 255

zhenzong bing 鎮總兵, 116

Zhili, 138, 140–41, 217

zhisi 識司, 231n

Zhou Shu (n.d.) 周澍, 101

Zhou Xuejian (d. 1748) 周學健, 146

Zhu Zun (d. 1862) 朱嶟, 133, 134n, 147, 278

zhucheng yapian ban yan 煮成鴉片拌煙, 151

zongjia 總家, 71n

Zungharia, 76, 82

Zunghar Mongols, 76, 82–83, 288

Zunyi district 遵義縣, 243

Zunyi prefecture 遵義府, 234, 243, 256, 264n, 274

Zuo Zongtang (1812–85) 左宗堂, 291, 298

Harvard East Asian Monographs
(* out-of-print)

*1.   Liang Fang-chung, *The Single-Whip Method of Taxation in China*

*2.   Harold C. Hinton, *The Grain Tribute System of China, 1845–1911*

3.   Ellsworth C. Carlson, *The Kaiping Mines, 1877–1912*

*4.   Chao Kuo-chün, *Agrarian Policies of Mainland China: A Documentary Study, 1949–1956*

*5.   Edgar Snow, *Random Notes on Red China, 1936–1945*

*6.   Edwin George Beal, Jr., *The Origin of Likin, 1835–1864*

7.   Chao Kuo-chün, *Economic Planning and Organization in Mainland China: A Documentary Study, 1949–1957*

*8.   John K. Fairbank, *Ching Documents: An Introductory Syllabus*

*9.   Helen Yin and Yi-chang Yin, *Economic Statistics of Mainland China, 1949–1957*

*10. Wolfgang Franke, *The Reform and Abolition of the Traditional Chinese Examination System*

11. Albert Feuerwerker and S. Cheng, *Chinese Communist Studies of Modern Chinese History*

12. C. John Stanley, *Late Ching Finance: Hu Kuang-yung as an Innovator*

13. S. M. Meng, *The Tsungli Yamen: Its Organization and Functions*

*14. Ssu-yü Teng, *Historiography of the Taiping Rebellion*

15. Chun-Jo Liu, *Controversies in Modern Chinese Intellectual History: An Analytic Bibliography of Periodical Articles, Mainly of the May Fourth and Post-May Fourth Era*

*16. Edward J. M. Rhoads, *The Chinese Red Army, 1927–1963: An Annotated Bibliography*

17. Andrew J. Nathan, *A History of the China International Famine Relief Commission*

*18. Frank H. H. King (ed.) and Prescott Clarke, *A Research Guide to China-Coast Newspapers, 1822–1911*

Harvard East Asian Monographs

19. Ellis Joffe, *Party and Army: Professionalism and Political Control in the Chinese Officer Corps, 1949–1964*

*20. Toshio G. Tsukahira, *Feudal Control in Tokugawa Japan: The Sankin Kōtai System*

21. Kwang-Ching Liu, ed., *American Missionaries in China: Papers from Harvard Seminars*

22. George Moseley, *A Sino-Soviet Cultural Frontier: The Ili Kazakh Autonomous Chou*

23. Carl F. Nathan, *Plague Prevention and Politics in Manchuria, 1910–1931*

*24. Adrian Arthur Bennett, *John Fryer: The Introduction of Western Science and Technology into Nineteenth-Century China*

25. Donald J. Friedman, *The Road from Isolation: The Campaign of the American Committee for Non-Participation in Japanese Aggression, 1938–1941*

*26. Edward LeFevour, *Western Enterprise in Late Ching China: A Selective Survey of Jardine, Matheson and Company's Operations, 1842–1895*

27. Charles Neuhauser, *Third World Politics: China and the Afro-Asian People's Solidarity Organization, 1957–1967*

28. Kungtu C. Sun, assisted by Ralph W. Huenemann, *The Economic Development of Manchuria in the First Half of the Twentieth Century*

*29. Shahid Javed Burki, *A Study of Chinese Communes, 1965*

30. John Carter Vincent, *The Extraterritorial System in China: Final Phase*

31. Madeleine Chi, *China Diplomacy, 1914–1918*

*32. Clifton Jackson Phillips, *Protestant America and the Pagan World: The First Half Century of the American Board of Commissioners for Foreign Missions, 1810–1860*

33. James Pusey, *Wu Han: Attacking the Present Through the Past*

34. Ying-wan Cheng, *Postal Communication in China and Its Modernization, 1860–1896*

35. Tuvia Blumenthal, *Saving in Postwar Japan*

36. Peter Frost, *The Bakumatsu Currency Crisis*

37. Stephen C. Lockwood, *Augustine Heard and Company, 1858–1862*

38. Robert R. Campbell, *James Duncan Campbell: A Memoir by His Son*

39. Jerome Alan Cohen, ed., *The Dynamics of China's Foreign Relations*

40. V. V. Vishnyakova-Akimova, *Two Years in Revolutionary China, 1925–1927,* trans. Steven L. Levine

*41. Meron Medzini, *French Policy in Japan During the Closing Years of the Tokugawa Regime*

42. Ezra Vogel, Margie Sargent, Vivienne B. Shue, Thomas Jay Mathews, and Deborah S. Davis, *The Cultural Revolution in the Provinces*

*43. Sidney A. Forsythe, *An American Missionary Community in China, 1895–1905*

Harvard East Asian Monographs

*44. Benjamin I. Schwartz, ed., *Reflections on the May Fourth Movement.: A Symposium*

*45. Ching Young Choe, *The Rule of the Taewŏngun, 1864–1873: Restoration in Yi Korea*

46. W. P. J. Hall, *A Bibliographical Guide to Japanese Research on the Chinese Economy, 1958–1970*

47. Jack J. Gerson, *Horatio Nelson Lay and Sino-British Relations, 1854–1864*

48. Paul Richard Bohr, *Famine and the Missionary: Timothy Richard as Relief Administrator and Advocate of National Reform*

49. Endymion Wilkinson, *The History of Imperial China: A Research Guide*

50. Britten Dean, *China and Great Britain: The Diplomacy of Commercial Relations, 1860–1864*

51. Ellsworth C. Carlson, *The Foochow Missionaries, 1847–1880*

52. Yeh-chien Wang, *An Estimate of the Land-Tax Collection in China, 1753 and 1908*

53. Richard M. Pfeffer, *Understanding Business Contracts in China, 1949–1963*

54. Han-sheng Chuan and Richard Kraus, *Mid-Ching Rice Markets and Trade: An Essay in Price History*

55. Ranbir Vohra, *Lao She and the Chinese Revolution*

56. Liang-lin Hsiao, *China's Foreign Trade Statistics, 1864–1949*

*57. Lee-hsia Hsu Ting, *Government Control of the Press in Modern China, 1900–1949*

58. Edward W. Wagner, *The Literati Purges: Political Conflict in Early Yi Korea*

*59. Joungwon A. Kim, *Divided Korea: The Politics of Development, 1945–1972*

*60. Noriko Kamachi, John K. Fairbank, and Chūzō Ichiko, *Japanese Studies of Modern China Since 1953: A Bibliographical Guide to Historical and Social-Science Research on the Nineteenth and Twentieth Centuries, Supplementary Volume for 1953–1969*

61. Donald A. Gibbs and Yun-chen Li, *A Bibliography of Studies and Translations of Modern Chinese Literature, 1918–1942*

62. Robert H. Silin, *Leadership and Values: The Organization of Large-Scale Taiwanese Enterprises*

63. David Pong, *A Critical Guide to the Kwangtung Provincial Archives Deposited at the Public Record Office of London*

*64. Fred W. Drake, *China Charts the World: Hsu Chi-yü and His Geography of 1848*

*65. William A. Brown and Urgrunge Onon, trans. and annots., *History of the Mongolian People's Republic*

66. Edward L. Farmer, *Early Ming Government: The Evolution of Dual Capitals*

Harvard East Asian Monographs

*67. Ralph C. Croizier, *Koxinga and Chinese Nationalism: History, Myth, and the Hero*

*68. William J. Tyler, trans., *The Psychological World of Natsume Sōseki*, by Doi Takeo

69. Eric Widmer, *The Russian Ecclesiastical Mission in Peking During the Eighteenth Century*

*70. Charlton M. Lewis, *Prologue to the Chinese Revolution: The Transformation of Ideas and Institutions in Hunan Province, 1891–1907*

71. Preston Torbert, *The Ching Imperial Household Department: A Study of Its Organization and Principal Functions, 1662–1796*

72. Paul A. Cohen and John E. Schrecker, eds., *Reform in Nineteenth-Century China*

73. Jon Sigurdson, *Rural Industrialism in China*

74. Kang Chao, *The Development of Cotton Textile Production in China*

75. Valentin Rabe, *The Home Base of American China Missions, 1880–1920*

*76. Sarasin Viraphol, *Tribute and Profit: Sino-Siamese Trade, 1652–1853*

77. Ch'i-ch'ing Hsiao, *The Military Establishment of the Yuan Dynasty*

78. Meishi Tsai, *Contemporary Chinese Novels and Short Stories, 1949–1974: An Annotated Bibliography*

*79. Wellington K. K. Chan, *Merchants, Mandarins and Modern Enterprise in Late Ching China*

80. Endymion Wilkinson, *Landlord and Labor in Late Imperial China: Case Studies from Shandong by Jing Su and Luo Lun*

*81. Barry Keenan, *The Dewey Experiment in China: Educational Reform and Political Power in the Early Republic*

*82. George A. Hayden, *Crime and Punishment in Medieval Chinese Drama: Three Judge Pao Plays*

*83. Sang-Chul Suh, *Growth and Structural Changes in the Korean Economy, 1910–1940*

84. J. W. Dower, *Empire and Aftermath: Yoshida Shigeru and the Japanese Experience, 1878–1954*

85. Martin Collcutt, *Five Mountains: The Rinzai Zen Monastic Institution in Medieval Japan*

86. Kwang Suk Kim and Michael Roemer, *Growth and Structural Transformation*

87. Anne O. Krueger, *The Developmental Role of the Foreign Sector and Aid*

*88. Edwin S. Mills and Byung-Nak Song, *Urbanization and Urban Problems*

89. Sung Hwan Ban, Pal Yong Moon, and Dwight H. Perkins, *Rural Development*

*90. Noel F. McGinn, Donald R. Snodgrass, Yung Bong Kim, Shin-Bok Kim, and Quee-Young Kim, *Education and Development in Korea*

Harvard East Asian Monographs

91. Leroy P. Jones and Il SaKong, *Government, Business, and Entrepreneurship in Economic Development: The Korean Case*

92. Edward S. Mason, Dwight H. Perkins, Kwang Suk Kim, David C. Cole, Mahn Je Kim et al., *The Economic and Social Modernization of the Republic of Korea*

93. Robert Repetto, Tai Hwan Kwon, Son-Ung Kim, Dae Young Kim, John E. Sloboda, and Peter J. Donaldson, *Economic Development, Population Policy, and Demographic Transition in the Republic of Korea*

94. Parks M. Coble, Jr., *The Shanghai Capitalists and the Nationalist Government, 1927–1937*

95. Noriko Kamachi, *Reform in China: Huang Tsun-hsien and the Japanese Model*

96. Richard Wich, *Sino-Soviet Crisis Politics: A Study of Political Change and Communication*

97. Lillian M. Li, *China's Silk Trade: Traditional Industry in the Modern World, 1842–1937*

98. R. David Arkush, *Fei Xiaotong and Sociology in Revolutionary China*

*99. Kenneth Alan Grossberg, *Japan's Renaissance: The Politics of the Muromachi Bakufu*

100. James Reeve Pusey, *China and Charles Darwin*

101. Hoyt Cleveland Tillman, *Utilitarian Confucianism: Chen Liang's Challenge to Chu Hsi*

102. Thomas A. Stanley, *Ōsugi Sakae, Anarchist in Taishō Japan: The Creativity of the Ego*

103. Jonathan K. Ocko, *Bureaucratic Reform in Provincial China: Ting Jih-ch'ang in Restoration Kiangsu, 1867–1870*

104. James Reed, *The Missionary Mind and American East Asia Policy, 1911–1915*

105. Neil L. Waters, *Japan's Local Pragmatists: The Transition from Bakumatsu to Meiji in the Kawasaki Region*

106. David C. Cole and Yung Chul Park, *Financial Development in Korea, 1945–1978*

107. Roy Bahl, Chuk Kyo Kim, and Chong Kee Park, *Public Finances During the Korean Modernization Process*

108. William D. Wray, *Mitsubishi and the N.Y.K, 1870–1914: Business Strategy in the Japanese Shipping Industry*

109. Ralph William Huenemann, *The Dragon and the Iron Horse: The Economics of Railroads in China, 1876–1937*

110. Benjamin A. Elman, *From Philosophy to Philology: Intellectual and Social Aspects of Change in Late Imperial China*

111. Jane Kate Leonard, *Wei Yüan and China's Rediscovery of the Maritime World*

Harvard East Asian Monographs

112. Luke S. K. Kwong, *A Mosaic of the Hundred Days:. Personalities, Politics, and Ideas of 1898*

113. John E. Wills, Jr., *Embassies and Illusions: Dutch and Portuguese Envoys to K'ang-hsi, 1666–1687*

114. Joshua A. Fogel, *Politics and Sinology: The Case of Naitō Konan (1866–1934)*

*115. Jeffrey C. Kinkley, ed., *After Mao: Chinese Literature and Society, 1978–1981*

116. C. Andrew Gerstle, *Circles of Fantasy: Convention in the Plays of Chikamatsu*

117. Andrew Gordon, *The Evolution of Labor Relations in Japan: Heavy Industry, 1853–1955*

*118. Daniel K. Gardner, *Chu Hsi and the "Ta Hsueh": Neo-Confucian Reflection on the Confucian Canon*

119. Christine Guth Kanda, *Shinzō: Hachiman Imagery and Its Development*

*120. Robert Borgen, *Sugawara no Michizane and the Early Heian Court*

121. Chang-tai Hung, *Going to the People: Chinese Intellectual and Folk Literature, 1918–1937*

*122. Michael A. Cusumano, *The Japanese Automobile Industry: Technology and Management at Nissan and Toyota*

123. Richard von Glahn, *The Country of Streams and Grottoes: Expansion, Settlement, and the Civilizing of the Sichuan Frontier in Song Times*

124. Steven D. Carter, *The Road to Komatsubara: A Classical Reading of the Renga Hyakuin*

125. Katherine F. Bruner, John K. Fairbank, and Richard T. Smith, *Entering China's Service: Robert Hart's Journals, 1854–1863*

126. Bob Tadashi Wakabayashi, *Anti-Foreignism and Western Learning in Early-Modern Japan: The "New Theses" of 1825*

127. Atsuko Hirai, *Individualism and Socialism: The Life and Thought of Kawai Eijirō (1891–1944)*

128. Ellen Widmer, *The Margins of Utopia: "Shui-hu hou-chuan" and the Literature of Ming Loyalism*

129. R. Kent Guy, *The Emperor's Four Treasuries: Scholars and the State in the Late Chien-lung Era*

130. Peter C. Perdue, *Exhausting the Earth: State and Peasant in Hunan, 1500–1850*

131. Susan Chan Egan, *A Latterday Confucian: Reminiscences of William Hung (1893–1980)*

132. James T. C. Liu, *China Turning Inward: Intellectual-Political Changes in the Early Twelfth Century*

133. Paul A. Cohen, *Between Tradition and Modernity: Wang T'ao and Reform in Late Ching China*

Harvard East Asian Monographs

134. Kate Wildman Nakai, *Shogunal Politics: Arai Hakuseki and the Premises of Tokugawa Rule*

135. Parks M. Coble, *Facing Japan: Chinese Politics and Japanese Imperialism, 1931–1937*

136. Jon L. Saari, *Legacies of Childhood: Growing Up Chinese in a Time of Crisis, 1890–1920*

137. Susan Downing Videen, *Tales of Heichū*

138. Heinz Morioka and Miyoko Sasaki, *Rakugo: The Popular Narrative Art of Japan*

139. Joshua A. Fogel, *Nakae Ushikichi in China: The Mourning of Spirit*

140. Alexander Barton Woodside, *Vietnam and the Chinese Model.: A Comparative Study of Vietnamese and Chinese Government in the First Half of the Nineteenth Century*

141. George Elision, *Deus Destroyed: The Image of Christianity in Early Modern Japan*

142. William D. Wray, ed., *Managing Industrial Enterprise: Cases from Japan's Prewar Experience*

143. T'ung-tsu Ch'ü, *Local Government in China Under the Ching*

144. Marie Anchordoguy, *Computers, Inc.: Japan's Challenge to IBM*

145. Barbara Molony, *Technology and Investment: The Prewar Japanese Chemical Industry*

146. Mary Elizabeth Berry, *Hideyoshi*

147. Laura E. Hein, *Fueling Growth: The Energy Revolution and Economic Policy in Postwar Japan*

148. Wen-hsin Yeh, *The Alienated Academy: Culture and Politics in Republican China, 1919–1937*

149. Dru C. Gladney, *Muslim Chinese: Ethnic Nationalism in the People's Republic*

150. Merle Goldman and Paul A. Cohen, eds., *Ideas Across Cultures: Essays on Chinese Thought in Honor of Benjamin L Schwartz*

151. James M. Polachek, *The Inner Opium War*

152. Gail Lee Bernstein, *Japanese Marxist: A Portrait of Kawakami Hajime, 1879–1946*

153. Lloyd E. Eastman, *The Abortive Revolution: China Under Nationalist Rule, 1927–1937*

154. Mark Mason, *American Multinationals and Japan: The Political Economy of Japanese Capital Controls, 1899–1980*

155. Richard J. Smith, John K. Fairbank, and Katherine F. Bruner, *Robert Hart and China's Early Modernization: His Journals, 1863–1866*

156. George J. Tanabe, Jr., *Myōe the Dreamkeeper: Fantasy and Knowledge in Kamakura Buddhism*

157. William Wayne Farris, *Heavenly Warriors: The Evolution of Japan's Military, 500–1300*

158. Yu-ming Shaw, *An American Missionary in China: John Leighton Stuart and Chinese-American Relations*

159. James B. Palais, *Politics and Policy in Traditional Korea*

160. Douglas Reynolds, *China, 1898–1912: The Xinzheng Revolution and Japan*

161. Roger R. Thompson, *China's Local Councils in the Age of Constitutional Reform, 1898–1911*

162. William Johnston, *The Modern Epidemic: History of Tuberculosis in Japan*

163. Constantine Nomikos Vaporis, *Breaking Barriers: Travel and the State in Early Modern Japan*

164. Irmela Hijiya-Kirschnereit, *Rituals of Self-Revelation: Shishōsetsu as Literary Genre and Socio-Cultural Phenomenon*

165. James C. Baxter, *The Meiji Unification Through the Lens of Ishikawa Prefecture*

166. Thomas R. H. Havens, *Architects of Affluence: The Tsutsumi Family and the Seibu-Saison Enterprises in Twentieth-Century Japan*

167. Anthony Hood Chambers, *The Secret Window: Ideal Worlds in Tanizaki's Fiction*

168. Steven J. Ericson, *The Sound of the Whistle: Railroads and the State in Meiji Japan*

169. Andrew Edmund Goble, *Kenmu: Go-Daigo's Revolution*

170. Denise Potrzeba Lett, *In Pursuit of Status: The Making of South Korea's "New" Urban Middle Class*

171. Mimi Hall Yiengpruksawan, *Hiraizumi: Buddhist Art and Regional Politics in Twelfth-Century Japan*

172. Charles Shirō Inouye, *The Similitude of Blossoms: A Critical Biography of Izumi Kyōka (1873–1939), Japanese Novelist and Playwright*

173. Aviad E. Raz, *Riding the Black Ship: Japan and Tokyo Disneyland*

174. Deborah J. Milly, *Poverty, Equality, and Growth: The Politics of Economic Need in Postwar Japan*

175. See Heng Teow, *Japan's Cultural Policy Toward China, 1918–1931: A Comparative Perspective*

176. Michael A. Fuller, *An Introduction to Literary Chinese*

177. Frederick R. Dickinson, *War and National Reinvention: Japan in the Great War, 1914–1919*

178. John Solt, *Shredding the Tapestry of Meaning: The Poetry and Poetics of Kitasono Katue (1902–1978)*

179. Edward Pratt, *Japan's Protoindustrial Elite: The Economic Foundations of the Gōnō*

180. Atsuko Sakaki, *Recontextualizing Texts: Narrative Performance in Modern Japanese Fiction*

181. Soon-Won Park, *Colonial Industrialization and Labor in Korea: The Onoda Cement Factory*

Harvard East Asian Monographs

182. JaHyun Kim Haboush and Martina Deuchler, *Culture and the State in Late Chosŏn Korea*

183. John W. Chaffee, *Branches of Heaven: A History of the Imperial Clan of Sung China*

184. Gi-Wook Shin and Michael Robinson, eds., *Colonial Modernity in Korea*

185. Nam-lin Hur, *Prayer and Play in Late Tokugawa Japan: Asakusa Sensōji and Edo Society*

186. Kristin Stapleton, *Civilizing Chengdu: Chinese Urban Reform, 1895–1937*

187. Hyung Il Pai, *Constructing "Korean" Origins: A Critical Review of Archaeology, Historiography, and Racial Myth in Korean State-Formation Theories*

188. Brian D. Ruppert, *Jewel in the Ashes: Buddha Relics and Power in Early Medieval Japan*

189. Susan Daruvala, *Zhou Zuoren and an Alternative Chinese Response to Modernity*

190. James Z. Lee, *The Political Economy of a Frontier: Southwest China, 1250–1850*

191. Kerry Smith, *A Time of Crisis: Japan, the Great Depression, and Rural Revitalization*

192. Michael Lewis, *Becoming Apart: National Power and Local Politics in Toyama, 1868–1945*

193. William C. Kirby, Man-houng Lin, James Chin Shih, and David A. Pietz, eds., *State and Economy in Republican China: A Handbook for Scholars*

194. Timothy S. George, *Minamata: Pollution and the Struggle for Democracy in Postwar Japan*

195. Billy K. L. So, *Prosperity, Region, and Institutions in Maritime China: The South Fukien Pattern, 946–1368*

196. Yoshihisa Tak Matsusaka, *The Making of Japanese Manchuria, 1904–1932*

197. Maram Epstein, *Competing Discourses: Orthodoxy, Authenticity, and Engendered Meanings in Late Imperial Chinese Fiction*

198. Curtis J. Milhaupt, J. Mark Ramseyer, and Michael K. Young, eds. and comps., *Japanese Law in Context: Readings in Society, the Economy, and Politics*

199. Haruo Iguchi, *Unfinished Business: Ayukawa Yoshisuke and U.S.-Japan Relations, 1937–1952*

200. Scott Pearce, Audrey Spiro, and Patricia Ebrey, *Culture and Power in the Reconstitution of the Chinese Realm, 200–600*

201. Terry Kawashima, *Writing Margins: The Textual Construction of Gender in Heian and Kamakura Japan*

202. Martin W. Huang, *Desire and Fictional Narrative in Late Imperial China*

203. Robert S. Ross and Jiang Changbin, eds., *Re-examining the Cold War: U.S.-China Diplomacy, 1954–1973*

Harvard East Asian Monographs

204. Guanhua Wang, *In Search of Justice: The 1905–1906 Chinese Anti-American Boycott*

205. David Schaberg, *A Patterned Past: Form and Thought in Early Chinese Historiography*

206. Christine Yano, *Tears of Longing: Nostalgia and the Nation in Japanese Popular Song*

207. Milena Doleželová-Velingerová and Oldřich Král, with Graham Sanders, eds., *The Appropriation of Cultural Capital: China's May Fourth Project*

208. Robert N. Huey, *The Making of 'Shinkokinshū'*

209. Lee Butler, *Emperor and Aristocracy in Japan, 1467–1680: Resilience and Renewal*

210. Suzanne Ogden, *Inklings of Democracy in China*

211. Kenneth J. Ruoff, *The People's Emperor: Democracy and the Japanese Monarchy, 1945–1995*

212. Haun Saussy, *Great Walls of Discourse and Other Adventures in Cultural China*

213. Aviad E. Raz, *Emotions at Work: Normative Control, Organizations, and Culture in Japan and America*

214. Rebecca E. Karl and Peter Zarrow, eds., *Rethinking the 1898 Reform Period: Political and Cultural Change in Late Qing China*

215. Kevin O'Rourke, *The Book of Korean Shijo*

216. Ezra F. Vogel, ed., *The Golden Age of the U.S.-China-Japan Triangle, 1972–1989*

217. Thomas A Wilson, ed., *On Sacred Grounds: Culture, Society, Politics, and the Formation of the Cult of Confucius*

218. Donald S. Sutton, *Steps of Perfection: Exorcistic Performers and Chinese Religion in Twentieth-Century Taiwan*

219. Daqing Yang, *Technology of Empire: Telecommunications and Japanese Imperialism, 1930–1945*

220. Qianshen Bai, *Fu Shan's World: The Transformation of Chinese Calligraphy in the Seventeenth Century*

221. Paul Jakov Smith and Richard von Glahn, eds., *The Song-Yuan-Ming Transition in Chinese History*

222. Rania Huntington, *Alien Kind: Foxes and Late Imperial Chinese Narrative*

223. Jordan Sand, *House and Home in Modern Japan: Architecture, Domestic Space, and Bourgeois Culture, 1880–1930*

224. Karl Gerth, *China Made: Consumer Culture and the Creation of the Nation*

225. Xiaoshan Yang, *Metamorphosis of the Private Sphere: Gardens and Objects in Tang-Song Poetry*

226. Barbara Mittler, *A Newspaper for China? Power, Identity, and Change in Shanghai's News Media, 1872–1912*

Harvard East Asian Monographs

227.   Joyce A. Madancy, *The Troublesome Legacy of Commissioner Lin: The Opium Trade and Opium Suppression in Fujian Province, 1820s to 1920s*

228.   John Makeham, *Transmitters and Creators: Chinese Commentators and Commentaries on the Analects*

229.   Elisabeth Köll, *From Cotton Mill to Business Empire: The Emergence of Regional Enterprises in Modern China*

230.   Emma Teng, *Taiwan's Imagined Geography: Chinese Colonial Travel Writing and Pictures, 1683–1895*

231.   Wilt Idema and Beata Grant, *The Red Brush: Writing Women of Imperial China*

232.   Eric C. Rath, *The Ethos of Noh: Actors and Their Art*

233.   Elizabeth J. Remick, *Building Local States: China During the Republican and Post-Mao Eras*

234.   Lynn Struve, ed., *The Qing Formation in World-Historical Time*

235.   D. Max Moerman, *Localizing Paradise: Kumano Pilgrimage and the Religious Landscape of Premodern Japan*

236.   Antonia Finnane, *Speaking of Yangzhou: A Chinese City, 1550–1850*

237.   Brian Platt, *Burning and Building: Schooling and State Formation in Japan, 1750–1890*

238.   Gail Bernstein, Andrew Gordon, and Kate Wildman Nakai, eds., *Public Spheres, Private Lives in Modern Japan, 1600–1950: Essays in Honor of Albert Craig*

239.   Wu Hung and Katherine R. Tsiang, *Body and Face in Chinese Visual Culture*

240.   Stephen Dodd, *Writing Home: Representations of the Native Place in Modern Japanese Literature*

241.   David Anthony Bello, *Opium and the Limits of Empire: Drug Prohibition in the Chinese Interior, 1729–1850*